N THE TIP OF MY TONGUE

012

D0542420

ON THE TIP OF MY TONGUE

*Questions, Facts, Curiosities
and Games of a Quizzical Nature*

DAVID GENTLE

BLOOMSBURY

LONDON · BERLIN · NEW YORK

First published in Great Britain 2007

This paperback edition published 2009

Copyright © 2007 by David Gentle

The moral right of the author has been asserted

Bloomsbury Publishing Plc
36 Soho Square
London W1D 3QY

A CIP catalogue record for this book is available from the British Library

ISBN 978 1 4088 0217 5

10 9 8 7 6 5 4 3 2 1

Typeset by Hewer Text UK Ltd, Edinburgh
Printed by Clays Ltd, St Ives plc

Bloomsbury Publishing, London, New York and Berlin

FSC
Mixed Sources
Product group from well-managed
forests and other controlled sources
www.fsc.org
Cert no. SGS - COC - 2061
www.fsc.org
© 1996 Forest Stewardship Council

www.bloomsbury.com/davidgentle
www.onthetipofmytongue.co.uk

Dear Reader

Welcome to *On the Tip of My Tongue*, a user-friendly, interactive and indispensable quiz book. It contains numerous quizzes* and games† for you to play as you navigate through a world of curiosity‡ and trivia. Use this book exactly as you wish: read and play it by yourself, or lock horns with friends and family in gentle, or perhaps zealous, competition. Play the games as suggested or create new ones of your own; dive straight in to the solutions§ or resist their allure and give your brain a workout instead. Whatever you do, have fun with this book – even if you find the answer¶ is, as you will no doubt say, 'On the Tip of My Tongue'.

---

* Quizzes start on page 1. The objective of some quizzes is to name items from a list, others to answer questions related to a particular topic. The target figures provided may be used as a yardstick, a goal or an indication of difficulty.

† Games start on page 355.

‡ Footnotes are provided throughout this book to supply additional information, to help clarify a question or solution, or to illuminate disputes or ambiguities that may exist in the content.

§ The solutions start on page 209.

¶ While great care has been taken in assembling the content of this book, it is possible that factual inaccuracies may have crept in either through the passage of time (England fans will surely see Steven Gerrard score again?), through disputed or debatable subject material (is the Nile really longer than the Amazon?) or through simple . . . ahem. Please send any comments or ideas you have to comments@onthetipofmytongue.co.uk

This book is dedicated to Kate, Zac and Alex with love

I would like to thank the following people for their advice, efforts or enthusiasm:

Andrew Walsh, Charles Beach, Emily Walton, Gordon Wise, Heather Goldstein, Helen Miller, Holly MacDonald, Holly Roberts, Jackie Bishop, James Hollands, James Miller, Jenny Parrott, Jon Hampson, Jonathan Derwent, Jules Kirby, Kate Derwent, Mark Littlewood, Mary Instone, Mike Jones, Neil Peplow, Nick Humphrey, Pam Gentle, Peter Gentle, Richard Atkinson, Sarah Morris, Sophie White, Sarah Hall and especially Kate Gentle.

CONTENTS

QUIZZES

'Go to your bosom, knock there,
and ask your heart what it doth know.'

William Shakespeare

FIRST LINES OF POPULAR NOVELS I Identify the novels or works of literature* that have these opening lines. If you wish, name the authors as well. The solutions are on page 333. [**Target: 12 correct answers**]

1. 'In a hole in the ground there lived a hobbit.'
2. 'One day when Pooh Bear had nothing else to do, he thought he would do something, so he went round to Piglet's house to see what Piglet was doing.'
3. 'It is a truth universally acknowledged, that a single man in possession of a good fortune, must be in want of a wife.'
4. 'It was the best of times, it was the worst of times, it was the age of wisdom, it was the age of foolishness, it was the epoch of belief, it was the epoch of incredulity, it was the season of Light, it was the season of Darkness, it was the spring of hope, it was the winter of despair . . .'
5. 'Once there were four children whose names were Peter, Susan, Edmund and Lucy.'
6. 'The Mole had been working very hard all the morning, spring-cleaning his little home.'
7. 'Whan that Aprill with his shoures soote / The droghte of March hath perced to the roote.'
8. 'It was a bright cold day in April, and the clocks were striking thirteen.'
9. 'A wide plain, where the broadening Floss hurries on between its green banks to the sea and the loving tide, rushing to meet it, checks its passage with an impetuous embrace.'
10. 'Last night I dreamt I went to Manderley again.'
11. 'At the age of fifteen my grandmother became the concubine of a warlord general.'
12. ' "Christmas won't be Christmas without any presents," grumbled Jo, lying on the rug.'
13. 'Dr Iannis had enjoyed a satisfactory day in which none of his patients had died or got any worse.'

---

* A candidate for the first recorded novel is *The Education of Cyrus*, written in the fourth century BC by Xenophon, a Greek soldier and philosopher. It is a fictional account of the education of King Cyrus II of Persia (who effectively founded the Persian Empire after becoming King in 559BC).

---

14. 'Emma Woodhouse, handsome, clever, and rich, with a comfortable home and happy disposition, seemed to unite some of the best blessings of existence; and had lived nearly twenty-one years in the world with very little to distress or vex her.'

15. 'I fell in love with football as I was later to fall in love with women: suddenly, inexplicably, uncritically, giving no thought to the pain or disruption it would bring with it.'

16. '1801 – I have just returned from a visit to my landlord – the solitary neighbour that I shall be troubled with.'

17. 'Like the brief doomed flare of exploding suns that registers dimly on blind men's eyes, the beginning of the horror passed almost unnoticed; in the shriek of what followed, in fact, was forgotten and perhaps not connected to the horror at all.'

18. 'The Time Traveller (for so it will be convenient to speak of him) was expounding a recondite matter to us.'

19. 'The boy with fair hair lowered himself down the last few feet of rock and began to pick his way toward the lagoon.'

20. 'The drought had lasted now for ten million years, and the reign of the terrible lizards had long since ended.'

21. 'Renowned curator Jacques Saunière staggered through the vaulted archway of the museum's Grand Gallery.'

22. 'Samuel Spade's jaw was long and bony, his chin a jutting v under the more flexible v of his mouth.'

23. 'On an evening in the latter part of May a middle-aged man was walking homeward from Shaston to the village of Marlott, in the adjoining Vale of Blakemore or Blackmoor.'

24. 'Early in the morning, late in the century, Cricklewood Broadway.'

ORIGINAL MEMBERS OF LEAGUE AND PREMIERSHIP List the only *three* teams to be founding members of the Football League in 1888 and also of the Premiership in 1992. The solution is on page 231. [Target: 2]

BRONTË SISTERS Name the *three* Brontë sisters. Turn to page 211 for the solution. [Target: 3]

FILMS AND THEIR STARS I Identify the films from these selected cast members and the date of release. Find the solutions on page 333. [**Target: 15**]

1. Leonardo DiCaprio, Kate Winslet (1997)
2. Harrison Ford, Carrie Fisher, Alec Guinness, Peter Cushing (1977)
3. Sean Connery, Ursula Andress, Joseph Wiseman (1962)
4. Marilyn Monroe, Jack Lemmon, Tony Curtis (1959)
5. Janet Leigh, Anthony Perkins (1960)
6. Katharine Ross, Robert Redford, Paul Newman (1969)
7. Helen Hunt, Jack Nicholson (1997)
8. Debra Winger, Richard Gere (1982)
9. Audrey Hepburn, George Peppard (1961)
10. Alastair Sim, Joyce Grenfell, Beryl Reid, George Cole (1954)
11. Thandie Newton, Matt Dillon, Sandra Bullock (2006)
12. Charlton Heston, Roddy McDowall (1968)
13. Geoffrey Rush, John Gielgud (1996)
14. Stanley Baker, Jack Hawkins, Michael Caine (1964)
15. Frances McDormand, William H. Macy, Steve Buscemi (1996)
16. Steve Guttenberg, Mickey Rourke, Kevin Bacon* (1982)
17. Spencer Tracy, Sidney Poitier, Katharine Hepburn (1967)
18. Sigourney Weaver, Gérard Depardieu (1992)
19. Amy Madigan, Ray Liotta, Burt Lancaster, Kevin Costner (1989)
20. Danny DeVito, Annette Bening, Michael J. Fox, Pierce Brosnan, Glenn Close, Jack Nicholson (1996)
21. Dustin Hoffman, Steve McQueen (1973)

---

* Kevin Bacon is the subject of a game called 'Six Degrees of Kevin Bacon', the aim of which is to link another actor to Bacon by common film appearances with other actors in the fewest number of steps. Taking Sylvester Stallone for example, Stallone appeared in *Cliffhanger* with John Lithgow; Lithgow was in *Footloose* with Bacon, giving two steps. The name derives from the fact that it is always seems possible to link Kevin Bacon with any other actor in six steps or fewer. In fact, for any well-known actor it is possible to get to Bacon in no more than two steps. Computer scientists at the University of Virginia have allocated Bacon Numbers to all credited actors and actresses. Kevin Bacon has a Bacon Number of 0; 1,806 actors have a Bacon Number of 1 (Bacon's various co-stars) and 145,024 actors have a Bacon Number of 2.

22. George C. Scott, Peter Sellers (1963)
23. David Bowie, Barbara Hershey, Harvey Keitel, Willem Dafoe (1988)
24. Elizabeth Taylor, Richard Burton, George Segal (1966)

PRIMARY COLOURS Name the *three* traditional primary colours. Turn to page 273 for the solution. [**Target: 3**]

NEWTON'S LAWS OF MOTION List Newton's *three* laws of motion. You will find the solution on page 293. [**Target: 1**]

NOTORIOUS SHIPS I Identify the renowned vessels* from the descriptions that follow. Turn to page 313 for the solutions. [**Target: 14**]

1. White Star liner sunk by an iceberg on her maiden voyage in 1912 with the loss of 1,500 lives.
2. Greenpeace ship sunk by French agents in Auckland harbour in 1985.
3. Subject to a mutiny in 1789 when Fletcher Christian set Captain William Bligh and eighteen crew adrift in the Pacific.
4. Nelson's flagship at the Battle of Trafalgar.
5. Found adrift and deserted in the Atlantic between Portugal and the Azores in 1872.
6. Pleasure steamer sunk by a collision with the dredger Bowbelle on the Thames in 1989.
7. The large transatlantic passenger liner built by Cunard in 1968.
8. Ship on which Drake circumnavigated the world in 1580.
9. First iron-hulled propeller-driven vessel; built by Isambard Kingdom Brunel in 1843.
10. Passenger liner sunk by a German torpedo in 1915 with the loss of 1,200 lives.

---

* In the eighteenth century it was common practice for cargo ships to be overloaded by their owners, ever hopeful of collecting insurance payouts should they sink. To lessen the prevalence of these 'coffin ships', Samuel Plimsoll's successful campaign brought about the Merchant Shipping Act in 1875; a piece of legislation which ensured all ships were marked with a line on the hull to indicate the limit of the waterline under full load.

11. Vessel on which James Cook explored the Southern Hemisphere between 1768 and 1771.
12. Legendary phantom ship, the subject of Richard Wagner's 1843 opera.
13. Vessel captained by Robert Fitzroy, from which Charles Darwin collected evidence for *The Origin of Species*.
14. Supertanker that ran aground off the coast of Brittany in 1978.
15. P&O cruiser converted to a hospital ship to serve during the Falklands Conflict.
16. German battleship of the Second World War, and sister ship of the Bismarck; sunk off the Norwegian coast in 1944.
17. Wooden raft on which Thor Heyerdahl crossed the pacific in 1947.
18. Submarine featuring in *Twenty Thousand Leagues Under the Sea* by Jules Verne.
19. The first propeller-driven ocean-going steamship.
20. Jacques Cousteau's exploration vessel.
21. British submarine that sank the *General Belgrano* during the Falklands Conflict.
22. Japanese warship commissioned in 1941 and the largest battleship ever constructed.
23. Quint's fishing boat in *Jaws*.
24. Sister ship of the *Titanic*; sunk in the Mediterranean in 1916 while serving as a hospital ship.

MUSKETEERS List the *three* title characters from *The Three Musketeers*. The solution is on page 333. [**Target: 3**]

CREAM Name the *three* members of Cream. Find the solution on page 211. [**Target: 2**]

LINKED MISCELLANY I In this quiz, the solutions are linked by a connecting theme. Evaluate the clues and deduce the connection. The solutions are on page 231. [**Target: 6**]

1. What name is given to the rocky island off the south coast of Cornwall, home to a Benedictine priory connected to the mainland via a tidal causeway?
2. How was the Young Pretender more commonly known to his Jacobite supporters?

3. Which character was played by Richard Wilson in *One Foot in the Grave*?
4. During which month does St Andrew's day fall?
5. What name, meaning 'snowy range', is given to the mountains found in the Andalusia region of Spain?
6. Which Asian country is the seventh largest country in the world by area?
7. With which song did Martha and the Muffins have their only UK hit?
8. Which word describes both a radioactive particle consisting of two protons and two neutrons, and a dominant male?
9. In which battle were French forces defeated by General James Wolfe in 1759?
10. What was discovered by Wilhelm Röntgen in 1895?

MAGI List the names traditionally given to the *three* Wise Men. Turn to page 250 for the solution. [**Target: 1**]

TRIANGLES Name the *three* types of triangle (as classified by the length of their sides)*. You can find the solution on page 273. [**Target: 2**]

CAPITAL CITIES I Identify the countries that have these capital cities. The solutions are on page 293. [**Target: 16**]

1.	Bangkok	2.	Seoul
3.	Helsinki	4.	Prague
5.	Sofia	6.	Addis Ababa
7.	Nairobi	8.	Tripoli
9.	Sarajevo	10.	Harare
11.	Colombo	12.	Rangoon
13.	Baku	14.	Kiev
15.	Pyongyang	16.	Abu Dhabi
17.	Nassau	18.	Dhaka†

---

* Triangles may also be defined by their internal angles. These are known as the right-angle triangle (with one 90° angle), the obtuse-angle triangle (one angle that is greater than 90°) and the acute-angle triangle (all three angles less than 90°).
† Note the spelling differs from Dakar in Senegal.

19.	Yerevan	20.	Kinshasa
21.	San José	22.	Astana
23.	Podgorica	24.	Ouagadougou

STOOGES List the *three* Stooges. The solution can be found on page 313. [**Target: 2**]

SONS OF ADAM AND EVE Name the *three** sons of Adam and Eve. Turn to page 333 for the solution. [**Target: 2**]

WIT AND WISDOM I The following quotations are attributed to either Winston Churchill or Oscar Wilde† or Mark Twain. Identify the correct author of each quotation. The solutions are on page 211. [**Target: 18**]

1. 'I have nothing to declare but my genius.'
2. '. . . and you, madam, are ugly. But in the morning I shall be sober.'
3. 'I can resist anything but temptation.'
4. 'The report of my death was an exaggeration.'
5. 'It is better to keep your mouth closed and let people think you are a fool than to open it and remove all doubt.'
6. 'There is only one thing in the world worse than being talked about, and that is not being talked about.'
7. 'I have taken more out of alcohol than alcohol has taken out of me.'
8. 'A classic is something that everybody wants to have read and nobody wants to read.'
9. 'This is the sort of English up with which I will not put.'
10. 'Work is the curse of the drinking classes.'
11. 'He hadn't a single redeeming vice.'
12. 'I am ready to meet my Maker. Whether my Maker is prepared for the great ordeal of meeting me is another matter.'
13. 'Truth is more of a stranger than fiction.'

---

* Only three sons are named in Genesis although the text states there were many more sons and daughters. According to the Bible Adam lived to the age of 930.
† It is apocryphal that Oscar Wilde's dying words were, 'Either that wallpaper goes – or I do.'

14. 'He has all the virtues I dislike and none of the vices I admire.'
15. 'I must decline your invitation owing to a subsequent engagement.'
16. 'Man is the only animal that blushes. Or needs to.'
17. 'A modest man, who has much to be modest about.'
18. 'If you tell the truth you don't have to remember anything.'
19. 'I am not young enough to know everything.'
20. 'I am always ready to learn although I do not always like being taught.'
21. 'Familiarity breeds contempt – and children.'
22. 'It has been said that democracy is the worst form of government except all the others that have been tried.'
23. 'America is the only country to go from barbarism to decadence without civilisation in between.'
24. 'Men stumble over the truth from time to time, but most pick themselves up and hurry off as if nothing happened.'

THE POLICE List the *three* members of The Police. Find the solution on page 231. [**Target: 2**]

BONES OF THE EAR Name the *three* bones* of the middle ear. Turn to page 251 for the solution. [**Target: 2**]

MISCELLANY I These questions are of a miscellaneous nature. The solutions can be found on page 273. [**Target: 15**]

1. What was invented by Kenneth Wood in 1947?
2. How is the Jewish Day of Atonement better known?
3. How many times does the letter 'p' occur in the first line of the tongue-twister about Peter Piper?
4. Which English county apparently changed its name from 'Scrobbesbyrigscir' because Norman invaders could not pronounce it?
5. Which country's name means 'The Saviour'?
6. How many of Snow White's seven dwarfs had beards?
7. Which two elements are liquid at room temperature?

---

* The bones of the middle ear are collectively known as ossicles.

8. Which amendment to the American constitution protects witnesses from self-incrimination?
9. Who wrote *Tosca*?
10. In the northern hemisphere, does water drain down a plughole clockwise or anti-clockwise?
11. What morbid coincidence links Mama Cass and Keith Moon?
12. What is known in France as 'mercredi des Cendres'?
13. In which film did the song 'Moon River' originally appear?
14. Which best-selling book was first published in 1936 by Phyllis Pearson after she had walked an estimated 3,000 miles?
15. In which sport do competing teams try to travel backwards and in opposite directions?
16. What is the name of the Manchester Orbital Motorway?
17. Where is the official residence of the First Lord of the Treasury?
18. Who sang the opening line of the original Band Aid single 'Do They Know It's Christmas'?
19. A mother and father have five sons. Each son has one sister. How many people are there in this family?
20. Which 1949 novel was originally titled *The Last Man in Europe*?
21. Which Thames bridge is the first that the University Boat Race passes under?
22. Which note does an orchestra tune up to?
23. What type of fruit is a cantaloupe?
24. A man jumps from a bridge into a river and swims for a kilometre upstream. At exactly one kilometre, he passes a bottle floating in the river. He continues swimming in the same direction for half an hour and then turns around and swims back towards the bridge. The man and the bottle arrive at the bridge at the same time. If the man has been swimming at a constant speed, how fast is the river flowing?

GHOSTS VISITING EBENEZER SCROOGE Name the *four* ghosts who visited Ebenezer Scrooge in *A Christmas Carol*. Turn to page 294 for the solution. [**Target: 4**]

GOLF MAJORS List the *four* major golf* tournaments. The solution is on page 313. [**Target: 4**]

CELEBRITY BABY NAMES Name the celebrity parent(s) of these children. Note that the same celebrity parents may feature in the solutions to more than one of these questions. Look for the solutions on page 250. [**Target: 10**]

1.	Brooklyn	2.	Fifi Trixibelle
3.	Zowie	4.	Heavenly Hiraani Tiger Lily
5.	Prince Michael	6.	Lourdes
7.	Apple	8.	Moon Unit
9.	Lennon	10.	Rocco
11.	Sean Preston	12.	Little Pixie
13.	Bluebell Madonna	14.	Shiloh Nouvel
15.	Daisy Boo	16.	Dweezil
17.	Rafferty	18.	Tallulah Pine
19.	Scout LaRue	20.	Pilot Inspektor
21.	Misty Kyd	22.	Elijah Bob Patricius Guggi Q
23.	Sage Moonblood	24.	Betty Kitten

CROQUET COLOURS Identify the *four* colours used in the game of croquet. Turn to page 211 for the solution. [**Target: 4**]

---

* Golf originated in Scotland in the fifteenth century. It is thought to have descended from the games of Kolven (from Holland) and Chole (from Belgium), which involved players chasing a pebble around a course with a stick. The Scots gave the game its defining characteristic by adding a hole and making this the objective of the game. Golf became so popular in Scotland that King James II (of Scotland) banned the sport in 1457 to prevent military training being neglected. Many of his subjects defied the ban, continuing to play the sport on dunes and beaches around the coastline on courses they called 'links'. The game was adopted in the rest of Britain under the patronage of James I (formerly James VI of Scotland) from where it was exported to North America and then the rest of the world. There are now many thousands of courses worldwide with their own unique characteristics. The longest hole in the world, at 909 yards, is the (par 7) 7th hole of the Sano Course at the Satsuki Golf Club in Japan; the world's largest bunker is Hell's Half Acre on the 585-yard 7th hole of the Pine Valley Course in New Jersey.

THE MONKEES Name the *four* members of The Monkees. The solution is on page 231. [**Target: 3**]

FIRST LINES OF POP SONGS I Deduce the titles of these songs from the first lines presented. (The year each song was a hit is supplied to assist you.) For advanced play, also name the performers. Turn to page 251 for the solutions. [**Target: 16**]

1. 'Sometimes it's hard to be a woman.' (1975)
2. 'And now, the end is near.' (1969)
3. 'A few questions that I need to know, how you could ever treat me so.' (1997)
4. 'There's nothing you can do that can't be done.' (1967)
5. 'There's dancing behind movie scenes.' (1998)
6. 'I bet you're wondering how I knew.' (1969)
7. 'I used to think maybe you loved me, now baby I'm sure.' (1985)
8. 'Today is gonna be the day that they're gonna throw it back to you.' (1995)
9. 'When I'm feeling blue, all I have to do is take a look at you.' (1988)
10. 'I wonder if one day that you'll say that you care.' (1967)
11. 'Fire in the disco.' (2003)
12. 'The silicon chip inside her head.' (1979)
13. 'Almost heaven, West Virginia, Blue Ridge Mountains, Shenandoah River.' (1972)
14. 'You keep saying you've got something for me.' (1966)
15. 'When I am down and, oh, my soul, so weary.' (2005)
16. 'I know I stand in line until you think you have the time to spend an evening with me.' (1967)
17. 'Some people might say my life is in a rut.' (1980)
18. 'I get knocked down.' (1997)
19. 'I got my head checked by a jumbo jet.' (1997)
20. 'The Mississippi Delta was shining like a national guitar.' (1986)
21. 'Sometimes you're better off dead, there's a gun in your hand, it's pointing at your head.' (1986)
22. 'Look into my eyes, you will see what you mean to me.' (1991)
23. 'When I was young, it seemed that life was so wonderful, a miracle.' (1970)
24. 'I'm here just like I said, though it's breaking every rule I've ever made.' (2003)

TEA-PARTY IN WONDERLAND Name the *four* attendees at the Mad Tea-party in *Alice's Adventures in Wonderland*. Find the solution on page 274. [**Target: 4**]

U2 List the *four* members of U2. Turn to page 294 for the solution. [**Target: 3**]

CHARACTERS IN LITERATURE I Identify the works of literature in which these characters appear. For advanced play, also name the authors. The solutions are on page 313. [**Target: 10**]

1.	Bilbo Baggins	2.	Rhett Butler
3.	Elizabeth Bennet	4.	Captain Nemo
5.	Jim Hawkins	6.	John Clayton, Lord Greystoke
7.	Captain Yossarian	8.	Daniel Cleaver
9.	Edmond Dantès	10.	Sancho Panza
11.	Blanche DuBois	12.	Benjamin Braddock
13.	Mr Willoughby	14.	John the Savage
15.	Anne Elliot	16.	Dorothea Brooke
17.	William of Baskerville	18.	Nick Carraway
19.	Abel Magwitch	20.	Agatha Trunchbull
21.	Becky Sharp	22.	The Mock Turtle
23.	Ignatius J. Reilly	24.	John Blackthorne

GRAND SLAM TENNIS TOURNAMENTS Name the *four* Grand Slam tennis* tournaments. The solution is on page 333. [**Target: 4**]

---

* The game of tennis owes its existence to two quite different nineteenth-century inventions. In 1839, Charles Goodyear discovered the process for creating vulcanised rubber, enabling the material to be commercially usable for the first time (before Goodyear's invention, rubber would get too soft when warm and be too brittle in the cold). Nineteen years earlier, Gloucester engineer Edward Beard Budding had the notion that the cloth-trimming machines he had designed could be adapted to cut grass, a hugely labour-intensive process at the time, giving rise to the lawnmower. When in 1874 Major Walter Wingfield invented the game of lawn tennis (which he originally named 'Sphairistikè'), it featured rubber balls that would bounce on the neatly mowed lawns of England's wealthy classes and became an immediate success.

MONOPOLY STATIONS List the *four* London stations that are found on the standard Monopoly board. Find the solution on page 211. [**Target: 4**]

ADVERTISING SLOGANS I* Name the products that were being marketed with these slogans. Turn to page 231 for the solutions. [**Target: 16**]

1. '1,000 songs in your pocket'
2. 'Full of Eastern promise'
3. 'The best a man can get'
4. 'And all because the lady loves _____'
5. 'I'm a secret lemonade drinker'
6. 'Vorsprung durch Technik'
7. 'Connecting people'
8. 'Made to make your mouth water'
9. 'Your flexible friend'
10. 'Forward with Britain'
11. 'Liquid engineering'
12. 'The power of dreams'
13. 'Because mums are heroes'
14. 'It comes from paradise and tastes like heaven'
15. 'Solutions for a small planet'
16. 'Ahh! _____'
17. 'If you like a lot of chocolate on your biscuit'
18. 'The appliance of science'
19. 'Apples hazelnuts bananas, raisins coconuts sultanas'
20. 'The biggest snack pennies can buy'
21. 'A major contribution to road safety'
22. 'The all-over body programme'
23. 'We keep your promises'
24. 'One instinctively knows when something is right'

---

* Adverts date back to Roman times and have even been found in the ruins of Pompeii; advertising as we would recognise it first emerged with the rise of popular media, and particularly as the newspapers of the seventeenth and eighteenth centuries began to enjoy wide circulation. A candidate for the first truly memorable slogan to appear was Lord Kitchener's 'Your Country Needs You' on the Army recruitment poster campaign at the onset of the First World War.

BLOOD GROUPS Name the *four* blood groups. Find the solution on page 251. [**Target: 4**]

RAF FIGHTER AIRCRAFT List the *three* types of fighter aircraft currently in active service in the RAF. The solution is on page 274. [**Target: 3**]

RECENT HISTORY I Identify each of these years by the clues provided. Turn to page 294 for the solutions. [**Target: 10**]

1. An international group of volunteers travel to Iraq to act as human shields in an attempt to avert an invasion; the space shuttle Columbia disintegrates during re-entry, killing all seven crew members; Iraq is invaded by coalition forces and Saddam Hussein is overthrown; David Kelly is found dead after appearing before a parliamentary committee investigating Weapons of Mass Destruction; Arnold Schwarzenegger is elected as Governor of California; Concorde makes its last commercial flight; Michael Jackson is arrested on charges of child molestation; England win the Rugby World Cup.

2. Charles Kennedy steps down as leader of the Liberal Democrats after admitting a drink problem; US Vice President Dick Cheney accidentally shoots his friend Harry Whittington; Slobodan Milosevic commits suicide in his cell during his trial for war crimes; Pluto is demoted in status to a 'Dwarf Planet'; North Korea claims to have conducted a nuclear test; Saddam Hussein is executed in Baghdad.

3. Hong Kong is handed back to China; Tony Blair becomes Prime Minister for the first time; Princess Diana is killed in a car crash in Paris, her funeral is watched by one billion people worldwide; Mother Theresa dies in Calcutta; O.J. Simpson is found liable for murder in a civil case and ordered to pay $35m in damages; comet Hale-Bopp passes close to Earth; Radiohead release *OK Computer*; Michael Hutchence is found hanged in an Australian hotel room; *Harry Potter and the Philosopher's Stone* is published.

4. Atomic bombs are detonated on Hiroshima and Nagasaki; the Allied leadership meets at the Potsdam conference in Germany; Auschwitz is liberated; the Japanese surrender is taken on

board the USS Missouri, ending the Second World War; Clement Attlee defeats Winston Churchill in the general election with a landslide victory; the United Nations and the Arab League are formed.

5. The world's population exceeds six billion for the first time; Jill Dando is shot dead on the doorstep of her London home; Manchester United win the Champions League to complete the Treble; a solar eclipse falls over south-west England; *Star Wars Episode I The Phantom Menace* is released; *Shakespeare in Love* wins the Oscar for best film; thirty-one people lose their lives in the Ladbroke Grove rail crash.

6. Gas escapes from the Union Carbide plant in Bhopal killing 2,000 and poisoning 200,000 people; Indira Gandhi is assassinated by Sikh extremists angered by the storming of the Golden Temple; the Soviet Union boycotts the Los Angeles Olympics; Liverpool beat Roma to win the European Cup; *Miami Vice* airs for the first time; Band Aid record 'Do They Know It's Christmas'.

7. Republican forces surrender, ending the Spanish Civil War; Germany occupies Czechoslovakia and Poland; Britain and France declare war on Germany; Russia invades Finland and the Baltic States; the *Graf Spee* is scuttled after the Battle of the River Plate; *The Grapes of Wrath* is published by John Steinbeck; *The Wizard of Oz* premieres.

8. Spain and Portugal join the EEC; the space shuttle *Challenger* explodes shortly after take-off; the Chernobyl nuclear power plant melts down; America bombs Libya in response to terrorist attacks; Mikhail Gorbachev campaigns for 'glasnost' and 'perestroika'; Prince Andrew marries Sarah Ferguson; the 'Big Bang' in the London Stock Exchange paves the way for electronic trading.

9. The Maastricht Treaty takes effect, creating the European Union; the Waco siege ends with a fire that kills seventy-six people; Manchester United become the first winners of the Premiership; Bobby Moore dies; six people are killed in a bomb attack on the World Trade Center; a tribute concert to Freddie Mercury takes place at Wembley Stadium; *Jurassic Park* is released; Prince changes his name to an unpronounceable symbol.

10. Concorde enters regular passenger service; Israeli commandos storm a hijacked plane at Entebbe in Uganda and rescue the hostages; the Apple II personal computer is introduced; Mao Tse-tung dies; Harold Wilson resigns as Prime Minister; The Brotherhood of Man win the Eurovision Song Contest; the UK experiences a heatwave and drought, America celebrates its Bicentennial.

11. Idi Amin seizes power in Uganda; decimal currency is introduced in Britain; sixty-six football supporters lose their lives after a stairway collapses at Ibrox; Jim Morrison dies in Paris; Apollo 15 astronauts ride in the Lunar Rover on the moon; Stanley Kubrick directs *A Clockwork Orange*.

12. Kim Philby defects to the Soviet Union; the Profumo Crisis leads to the resignation of Harold Macmillan; Martin Luther King makes his 'I have a dream' speech; John F. Kennedy is assassinated in Dallas; the Beatles top the charts for the first time with 'From Me To You'.

13. Bolsheviks murder Tsar Nicholas II and his family; Russia withdraws from the First World War; the Allies are victorious at the Battle of Amiens, which has a decisive impact on the outcome of war; the First World War ends with the signing of the Armistice on 11 November; the Representation of the People Act in Britain gives men over twenty-one and women over thirty the right to vote; an influenza pandemic kills twenty-six million people worldwide.

14. Operation Desert Storm liberates Kuwait; Communist hard-liners stage a failed coup in the USSR; Mikhail Gorbachev resigns, Boris Yeltsin becomes the Russian President; the USSR dissolves; the IRA launch a mortar attack on 10 Downing Street; Mike Tyson is arrested for rape; England lose to Australia at Twickenham in the final of the Rugby World Cup; Robert Maxwell drowns; Terry Waite is released; Freddy Mercury dies of AIDS; Nirvana release *Nevermind*.

15. Mohammed Al Fayed buys Harrods; Mikhail Gorbachev becomes leader of the Soviet Union; thirty-eight people are killed in the Heysel stadium by rioting Liverpool fans; Live Aid concerts take place in London and Philadelphia; the Greenpeace vessel the *Rainbow Warrior* is sunk by French agents in Auckland harbour.

16. British and Commonwealth forces are repelled by the Turks at Gallipoli; the *Lusitania* is torpedoed and sunk by a German U-boat; the German Army uses chlorine gas at the Second Battle of Ypres.

17. The Six Day War takes place in the Middle East; colour television begins in Britain; Che Guevara is captured and shot; Sandy Shaw wins the Eurovision Song Contest for Britain with 'Puppet on a String'; San Francisco experiences the summer of love; the *Torrey Canyon* runs aground off Land's End; Donald Campbell is killed on Coniston Water in *Bluebird*; the Beatles release *Sgt. Pepper's Lonely Hearts Club Band*.

18. The PLO is founded; the Civil Rights Act is signed in the US outlawing discrimination on grounds of race, religion, sex or nationality; the Beatles top the US Charts with 'I Want to Hold Your Hand'; The Warren Commission delivers its report on the Kennedy assassination and concludes that Lee Harvey Oswald had acted alone; Martin Luther King receives the Nobel Peace Prize.

19. Willy Brandt is forced to resign as German Chancellor; Nixon resigns after the Watergate scandal; Haile Selassie is deposed in Ethiopia, Abba win the Eurovision Song Contest with 'Waterloo'; Labour wins two general elections under Harold Wilson; Muhammad Ali and George Foreman fight the 'Rumble in the Jungle' in Kinshasa in Zaire, Ali wins in eight rounds.

20. Albert Einstein publishes the General Theory of Relativity; German and British fleets engage in the Battle of Jutland; the Battle of the Somme takes place with unprecedented loss of life; Rasputin* is assassinated in Moscow; the Easter Rising occurs in Dublin; tanks are used on a large scale for the first

---

* Grigori Rasputin was a faith healer who played a role in the downfall of the Romanov dynasty. Tsarina Alexandra (the wife of Tsar Nicholas II) invited Rasputin to help her haemophiliac son, the Tsarevich Alexei. Under Rasputin's treatments Alexei's condition seemed to improve and consequently so did the healer's standing in the court. As his reputation increased, so Rasputin indulged himself in an ever more scandalous personal life which revolved around St Petersburg society ladies, prostitutes and heavy drinking. During the First World War, the (German) Tsarina's relationship with Rasputin was a cause of much suspicion, with many Russians believing Rasputin to be a spy, and this heaped yet more pressure on the already unpopular Romanovs. In an attempt to rectify the situation, Prince Felix Yusupov and the Tsar's cousin, Grand Duke Dmitri Pavlovitch Romanov, murdered Rasputin.

time in the Battle of Cambrai; David Lloyd George becomes British Prime Minister.

21. The Warsaw Pact is established; Juan Perón is ousted by a military coup in Argentina; the first McDonald's restaurant opens, in Des Plains, Illinois; Winston Churchill resigns and Anthony Eden becomes British Prime Minister.

22. Anthony Eden resigns over the Suez crisis and is succeeded by Harold Macmillan; the EEC is created by the Treaty of Rome; *Sputnik I* is launched; civil rights violence takes place in Little Rock, Arkansas, as black students are prevented from enrolling in high school; the US and USSR both successfully test ICBMs.

23. The Treaty of Versailles is signed placing harsh post-war terms on Germany; the League of Nations is founded; the Eighteenth Amendment is passed establishing Prohibition in America; Alcock and Brown fly the Atlantic; British forces massacre 379 demonstrators in Amritsar.

24. Japan annexes Korea; Edward VII dies and is succeeded by George V; the Union of South Africa is founded; Tories and Liberals are tied after the election causing Herbert Asquith to rely on Labour and Irish Nationalist votes; Halley's Comet is photographed for the first time.

FOOTBALL TEAMS STARTING AND ENDING WITH THE SAME LETTER
Identify the *four* teams in the English Football League that start and end with the same letter. Find the solution on page 314. [**Target: 3**]

CLASSICAL COLUMNS
Name the *four* types of column of classical architecture. The solution is on page 333. [**Target: 3**]

MISCELLANY II
These questions are of a miscellaneous nature. Turn to page 212 for the solutions. [**Target: 12**]

1. What is the freezing point of water in degrees Kelvin?
2. New York stands on which river?
3. Which historical event is celebrated in England on Oak Apple Day, 29 June?
4. Armand Zildjian is associated with which type of musical instrument?

5. A man says 'Everything I say is false.' Is he telling the truth?
6. Who was the first person to appear on Channel 4?
7. With which country is the anthem 'Land of My Fathers' associated?
8. What are the first three words in the Bible?
9. What type of gemstone was in Diana Spencer's engagement ring?
10. Who was the victim of the world's first live televised murder?
11. Who, upon splitting with her partner, famously said, 'At least I can wear high heels now'?
12. Which two letters are worth the most in a game of Scrabble?
13. On a standard dartboard, what is the lowest number that cannot be scored with a single dart?
14. Which playwright was killed during a brawl in a Deptford tavern in 1593?
15. What links Cheriton and Sangatte?
16. Which is the only muscle in the human body anchored only at one end?
17. Which Sanskrit phrase may be translated literally as 'love discourse'?
18. From which wood are longbows traditionally made?
19. How many times would a football rotate if it was rolled around the circumference of another football of the same size?
20. Which American state flag features the Pole Star and the Great Bear on a blue background?
21. In Greek mythology, who solved the riddle of the Sphinx?
22. What links the words 'scissors', 'shorts' and 'doldrums'?
23. The name of which liqueur means literally 'Aunt Mary'?
24. The power ballad 'All By Myself', written in 1976 by Eric Carmen and popularised by Céline Dion in 1996, is based on a classical piece by which composer?

ASSASSINATED US PRESIDENTS Name the *four* Presidents of the United States who have died in office as a result of assassinations. Find the solution on page 231. [**Target: 3**]

BOY BANDS Identify the Boy Bands from these clues. Turn to page 274 for the solutions. [**Target: 10**]

1. Gary, Mark, Robbie, Jason, Howard
2. Jackie, Tito, Jermaine, Marlon, Michael
3. Ronan, Stephen, Mikey, Shane, Keith

4. Nick, John, Roger, Andy, Simon
5. Micky, Davy, Michael, Peter
6. Alan, Donny, Merrill, Jay, Wayne
7. Les, Eric, Woody, Alan, Derek
8. Luke, Matt, Craig
9. George, Andrew
10. Bryan, Shane, Mark, Nicky, Kian
11. Antony, Duncan, Lee, Simon
12. Charlie, Matt, James
13. Donnie, Jordan, Jon, Danny, Joe
14. JC, Justin, Chris, Joey, James
15. J, Ritchie, Scott, Richard, Sean
16. Tom, Danny, Harry, Dougie
17. Nick, Howie, Brian, AJ, Kevin
18. Tony, Brian, John, Terry
19. Bobby, Ralph, Michael, Ricky, Ronnie
20. Wanya, Michael, Shawn, Nathan
21. Joe, Ron, Terry, Otis, G.C.
22. Jeff, Eric, Ray, Felipe, Alex, David
23. Phil, Mark, Jason
24. Ben, Christian, Paul, Mark

THE GOOD LIFE Name the *four* main characters in *The Good Life*. Turn to page 314 for the solution. [**Target: 4**]

HOBBIES AND PROFESSIONS I Describe these hobbies and professions.* Find the solutions on page 333. [**Target: 8**]

1. Origamist
2. Chandler
3. Philatelist
4. Wainwright
5. Apiarist
6. Broderer
7. Roughneck
8. Sommelier

---

* The word 'hobby' derives from 'hobby horse', a term appearing in the sixteenth century to describe a child's toy riding horse. In the seventeenth century this took on the meaning of a pastime, with the connecting notion of it being an activity that led to nothing. 'Profession' is an older word, appearing around the thirteenth century to refer to the declaration of vows on entering a religious order. By the sixteenth century, the meaning had expanded closer to its current sense of an occupation that 'one professes' to be skilled in.

9.	Mercer	10.	Founder
11.	Charcutier	12.	Jobber
13.	Tanner	14.	Bowyer
15.	Stringer	16.	Campanologist
17.	Cooper	18.	Lepidopterist
19.	Arborist	20.	Numismatist
21.	Assayer	22.	Cartophilist
23.	Chapman	24.	Almoner

TELETUBBIES List the *four* Teletubbies. The solution is on page 212. [Target: 4]

AMERICAN STATES BEGINNING WITH 'I' Name the *four* US states that begin with the letter 'I'. Turn to page 231 for the solution. [Target: 4]

LINKED MISCELLANY II The solutions to these questions are linked by a connecting theme. Evaluate the clues and deduce the connection. The solution is on page 252. [Target: 5]

1. How is 28 October 1929, the day of the Wall Street Crash, better known?
2. Who had hits with 'I Can't Go for That' and 'Maneater'?
3. Which toxic, metallic element has an atomic number of 82?
4. What is the nickname of the US Special Forces?
5. How is albumen better known?
6. Which public building, opened by the Queen in 1998, is located at 96 Euston Road, London?
7. Where do the San Francisco 49ers play their home games?
8. What is the name of the chemical agent used by the Germans at the Battle of Ypres in 1917 and by Saddam Hussein in 1988?
9. Which Beatles album contains the songs 'Eleanor Rigby', 'Yellow Submarine' and 'Taxman'?
10. Who starred in *Lost in Translation* and *Girl with a Pearl Earring*?

PAC-MAN GHOSTS List the *four* ghosts in the game of Pac-Man. Turn to page 274 for the solution. [**Target: 1**]

BIG FOUR RAILWAY COMPANIES Name the *four* railway companies that operated the rail network in Britain between 1923 and the creation of British Rail in 1947*. The solution is on page 294. [**Target: 3**]

NICKNAMES OF PEOPLE I Identify the people who have been given these nicknames. The solutions can be found on page 314. [**Target: 12**]

1.	Turnip	2.	Hanoi Jane
3.	The Maid of Orleans	4.	The Body
5.	The Hairy Cornflake	6.	Beefy
7.	Mahatma	8.	Fluff
9.	The Governator	10.	Interesting
11.	Baby Spice	12.	Superbrat
13.	The Crafty Cockney	14.	Marky Mark
15.	Mr Mojo Risin'	16.	Bird
17.	The Louisville Lip	18.	Duke
19.	Marvellous	20.	The Galloping Gourmet
21.	Calamity Jane	22.	The Divine Miss M
23.	The Refrigerator	24.	Lady Day

ENGLISH QUARTER DAYS Name the *four* English Quarter Days. Turn to page 334 for the solution. [**Target: 2**]

BONES OF THE LEG List the *four* bones found in the human leg (exclude bones found in the foot from your response). The solution is on page 212. [**Target: 3**]

---

* By the time of nationalisation, demand for rail was declining as other forms of transport began to challenge it. Dr Richard Beeching was appointed as chairman of British Rail in 1960 with a brief to stem its spiralling losses and the 'Beeching Axe' fell in 1963 on many of the country's branch lines in the first major reduction in the size of the network. Operations were again privatised in the 1990s with the creation of Railtrack in 1994 (becoming Network Rail in 2002) and passenger numbers are now rising.

INFORMATION SUPPLIED BY PRISONERS OF WAR Identify the *four* pieces of information that, under provision of the Third Geneva Convention, a prisoner of war can only be required to supply. Turn to page 252 for the solution. [**Target: 4**]

HOUSES AT HOGWARTS Name the *four* houses at Hogwarts (from the *Harry Potter* stories). Find the solution on page 274. [**Target: 3**]

MISCELLANY III These questions are of a miscellaneous nature. The solutions are on page 295. [**Target: 10**]

1. What colour is Mr Nosey?
2. How is Shropshire normally abbreviated?
3. The opera *Die Zauberflöte* is better known as what?
4. In which part of a living cell is DNA found?
5. Logically, which body feature was not possessed by either Adam or Eve?
6. In a street of 100 numbered houses, how many number nines are there?
7. In which sport is the Vince Lombardi Trophy awarded?
8. Which well-known film features Carnforth station in Lancashire?
9. The name for which animal comes from Malay and means 'man of the woods'?
10. What flag does a ship traditionally fly to indicate it is about to set sail?
11. What links Wallsend and Bowness?
12. In medicine, how is the laryngeal prominence more commonly known?
13. In which country is the European Court of Justice?
14. What was the title of the hit duet between Roberta Flack and Peabo Bryson?
15. In which river was Jesus baptised?
16. What colour was Moby-Dick?
17. In Beatrix Potter, what type of animal was Mr Jeremy Fisher?
18. What is a perfect score in a game of tenpin bowling?
19. What was commissioned by Sir Benjamin Hall in London in 1838?

20. What are 'First', 'Middle', 'Morning', 'Forenoon', 'Afternoon', 'First Dog' and 'Last Dog'?
21. Who wrote 'You'll Never Walk Alone'?
22. Which twelve-letter word contains six alternate letter 'a's?
23. What is the Queen's official residence in Northern Ireland?
24. Some apes are playing a tug of war. When three baboons played two chimpanzees, the game was a draw. When three gorillas played against four chimpanzees, the game also ended in a draw. If two gorillas played five baboons, which side, if any, would win?

AUTOMATIC EUROVISION QUALIFIERS List the *four* countries that automatically qualify for the finals of the Eurovision Song Contest. Turn to page 314 for the solution. [**Target: 4**]

GOONS Name the *four* members of the Goons. Look for the solution on page 334. [**Target: 4**]

EVENTS IN HISTORY I Identify the century in which each of these events in history* took place (be even more precise and attempt the year if you wish). Find the solutions on page 212. [**Target: 12**]

1. Great Fire of London.
2. Florence Nightingale founds her nursing school at St Thomas' Hospital, London.
3. Completion of the Domesday Book.
4. American Declaration of Independence.
5. Defeat of Napoleon Bonaparte at Waterloo.
6. Publication of the Communist Manifesto.
7. Defeat of George Custer at the Battle of Little Big Horn.
8. The Black Death first arrives in Europe.

---

* Although there had been chroniclers before him, Herodotus is known as the 'father of history' for being the first person to record events with the objective of trying to understand human behaviour and learn from it. In the fifth century BC Herodotus wrote about the Persian invasion of Greece and described his work as a 'historia' – a Greek word meaning 'learning by enquiry', from which the modern connotation is derived.

9. Beginning of the English Civil War.
10. Henry VIII breaks with Rome.
11. English defeat the French at Agincourt.
12. Declaration of Papal infallibility.
13. Accession of William of Orange in the Glorious Revolution.
14. Magna Carta signed at Runnymede.
15. Pilgrims reach New England on the Mayflower.
16. Scots defeat the English at Bannockburn.
17. King Harold victorious at the Battle of Stamford Bridge.
18. Act of Union unites England and Scotland.
19. Fall of Constantinople to the Turks.
20. St Augustine lands in Britain.
21. Arrival of Arab arithmetical notation in Europe.
22. Genghis Khan begins Mongol conquest of Asia.
23. Muhammad begins dictation of the Koran.
24. Beginning of the Hundred Years' War between England and France.

BALEARIC ISLANDS Name the *four* major Balearic Islands. The solution is on page 232. [**Target: 3**]

LITTLE WOMEN List the *four* eponymous characters of Louisa May Alcott's novel. Turn to page 252 for the solution. [**Target: 3**]

ASTRONOMERS, MATHEMATICIANS AND PHYSICISTS

Identify the scientists* from the clues presented. Find the solutions on page 275. [**Target: 10**]

1. German theoretical physicist whose General Theory of Relativity defined the relationship between energy, matter, time, space and gravity.

---

* In antiquity, classical scholars would study and master a variety of subjects (and often all of the known subjects). To them, the fields that we now call theology, philosophy and astrology were no less 'scientific' than the disciplines that we term natural sciences. A feature of the classical scientific method was its reliance on intuition; sometimes this led to brilliant insights but classical scholars were also guilty of turning out errors which could last for centuries (famously Ptolemy's model of the solar system). The modern scientific method of deduction from observation was first proposed by the philosopher Francis Bacon *cont'd over/*

2. Lucasian professor at Cambridge University who revolutionised the sciences of maths and physics by defining gravitation and the laws of motion which he published in his work *Philosophiae Naturalis Principia Mathematica* in 1687.

3. Greek mathematician who famously discovered the principles of density and buoyancy while taking a bath (proclaiming, 'Eureka!' meaning, 'I have it!').

4. Polish astronomer who challenged Ptolemy's view of the universe and proposed a heliocentric model of the solar system, published in 1543 as *De Revolutionibus Orbium Coelestium* ('On the Revolution of Celestial Spheres'), thereby upsetting the establishment and particularly the Catholic Church.

5. Italian astronomer who was the first person to use a telescope to observe the night sky and discover, among other things, the moons of Jupiter and the rings of Saturn.

6. American astronomer who was the first to observe galaxies beyond the Milky Way; who discovered the expansion of the universe and derived a law to describe it and gave his name to the space telescope launched by NASA in 1990.

7. British astronomer who discovered the comet that now bears his name, correctly observing its seventy-six-year orbit and predicting its reappearance in 1758 (after his death).

---

cont'd   in his *Novum Organum* (meaning 'True Suggestions for the Interpretation of Nature') of 1620. The title page of this work contained a picture of a ship passing the Pillars of Hercules; in Greek mythology this marked the edge of the world. Carefully chosen to upset the establishment, the image made the emphatic point that ancient learning had now become a limiting factor from which man had to break free for his quest for knowledge and betterment to continue. The seventeenth century marked a real turning point in the history of scientific investigation with the subjective fields of philosophy and astrology departing for ever to be replaced by the specialised disciplines of astronomy, physics, medicine and the multitude of other subjects that are studied today. When, in 1663, Henry Lucas created the Lucasian Chair of Mathematics at Cambridge University, he insisted that the professorship should not be held by anyone who was active in the church. Charles II was even persuaded to pass legislation excusing holders of the post from taking holy orders (a requirement for all Cambridge professors at the time). These events, which presumably horrified churchmen of the time, seem to have been foreseen centuries earlier by St Augustine when he wrote: 'The good Christian should beware of mathematicians, and all those who make empty prophecies. The danger already exists that the mathematicians have made a covenant with the devil to darken the spirit and to confine man in the bonds of Hell.'

8.   Greek mathematician who deduced that the sum of the squares of the sides of a right-angled triangle is equal to the square of the hypotenuse.

9.   Austrian physicist who discovered the apparent shift in frequency and wavelength that occurs as the source of a wave moves nearer or further from the observer, accounting for example for the change in pitch of a fire engine siren as it passes or the red shift in light emitted from stars that are travelling away from the earth.

10.   French mathematician and philosopher who invented the system of coordinates influential in the development of modern calculus and who famously wrote, 'I think, therefore I am.'

11.   British mathematician and Second World War cryptologist who made a large contribution towards the modern concept of electronic computing and whose insights led to the development of Colossus (in 1945), the first programmable digital electronic computer.

12.   Austrian physicist who made significant contributions to quantum theory and famously illustrated its counter-intuitive nature with a thought experiment featuring a cat.

13.   British nurse whose work with public health data led to advancements in the field of statistics; she was the first person to illustrate data using a pie chart.

14.   British physicist who discovered the concept of electromagnetic induction and built the first dynamo; he founded the Christmas lectures for young people at the Royal Institution which bear his name.

15.   Greek mathematician and 'father of geometry' whose work *Elements* (*c.*300BC) defined the rudiments of geometry and the properties of numbers.

16.   German physicist whose work on thermodynamics (black body radiation) led to the development of quantum theory.

17.   British mathematician and Lucasian Professor who designed the first programmable computer, a mechanical device called a difference engine, that was never completed.

18.   German physicist who worked on quantum theory and in 1927 originated the 'uncertainty principle': that at any given instant it is possible either to know the direction an electron is

travelling in or the position of the electron, but never both at the same time.

19. French physicist and mathematician who clarified the concepts of pressure and vacuum and gave his name to a unit of pressure.

20. German-born astronomer who discovered Uranus and was given the title King's Astronomer by George III.

21. Greek astronomer who formulated the geocentric model of the universe in the second century (in a work called *Almagest*, meaning 'The Great Treatise') which was accepted until the sixteenth century.

22. British physicist (born in New Zealand) who discovered alpha and beta radiation and in 1911 deduced that atomic structure must include a dense nucleus at its centre.

23. Danish physicist who combined quantum theory with the concept of atomic structure and proposed in 1913 the modern model of atomic structure with electrons orbiting a nucleus.

24. British physicist and contemporary of Isaac Newton and Christopher Wren who discovered the law of elasticity describing the relationship between tension and elasticity in a spring.

AMERICAN STATES BEGINNING WITH 'A' List the *four* American states whose names begin with the letter 'A'. The solution is on page 295. [**Target: 4**]

CLASSICAL ELEMENTS Name the *four* classical elements. Find the solution on page 314. [**Target: 4**]

SPORTS GOVERNING BODIES I Identify the sports represented by these sporting governing bodies. Go to page 334 for the solutions. [**Target: 12**]

1.	MCC	2.	FIFA
3.	PGA	4.	WBO
5.	NHL	6.	TCCB
7.	FIA	8.	IAAF
9.	WBA	10.	CONCACAF
11.	BAGA	12.	AELTC
13.	NBA	14.	IIHF
15.	FIS	16.	ITF

17.	FIM	18.	BDO
19.	FIBA	20.	ITTF
21.	WPBSA	22.	WWSU
23.	FIG	24.	WKF

CHARACTERISTICS OF DIAMONDS List the *four* 'c's used to describe the characteristics of diamonds. Find the solution on page 212. [**Target: 3**]

HORSEMEN OF THE APOCALYPSE Name the *Four* Horsemen of the Apocalypse. You can find the solution on page 232. [**Target: 4**]

ADVERTISING SLOGANS II Identify the products that were promoted using these advertising slogans*. Look for the solutions on page 252. [**Target: 12**]

1. 'All over the body'
2. 'If you see Sid, tell him'
3. 'Top breeders recommend it'
4. 'Central heating for kids'
5. 'It's good to talk'
6. 'You can be sure of _____'
7. 'Follow the bear'
8. 'Tell them about the honey, mummy'

---

* The cigarette manufacturer Philip Morris introduced the Marlboro brand of cigarette in 1924. The brand was one of the first to have a filter and as such was deliberately targeted at female smokers; it was launched with the slogan 'Mild as May'. The brand did poorly until the 1950s when reports linking smoking with health problems first began to appear. Many smokers switched to filtered cigarettes, perceived to be lower risk, but Marlboro with their feminine image had a problem in attracting new consumers. The company rectified this by launching a series of adverts featuring a range of masculine characters, one of which, a cattle rancher, would endure as the Marlboro Man; the most recognisable advert in history. In the eight months after the advert was first introduced, sales of Marlboro increased by 5,000 per cent. In 1990, Wayne McLaren, one of the models who had portrayed the Marlboro Man, was diagnosed with lung cancer. McLaren, a lifelong smoker, devoted the last years of his life to anti-smoking campaigns, even lobbying Philip Morris at a shareholders meeting to voluntarily restrict their advertising. Wayne McLaren died in 1992 at the age of fifty-one. The same year Marlboro became the number one cigarette brand in the world with a market value of $32bn; the ultimate example of the effectiveness of advertising.

9. 'A diamond is for ever'
10. 'How are you?'
11. 'Plink plink fizz'
12. 'Switch to _____'
13. 'Everything we do is driven by you'
14. 'Kills all known germs. Dead.'
15. 'The car in front is a _____'
16. 'Do it right'
17. 'It's a _____. Honest.'
18. 'The listening bank'
19. 'Washing machines live longer with _____'
20. 'I never knew it had so much in it'
21. 'They're tasty tasty, very very tasty, they're very tasty'
22. 'Better by design'
23. 'The drive of your life'
24. 'And on and on and on . . .'

GANG OF FOUR Recall the *four* members of the Gang of Four (of British politics*). The solution is on page 275. [**Target: 3**]

FAMILY HOMINIDAE Name the *four* members of the family Hominidae (apes). Find the solution on page 295. [**Target: 4**]

ENTREPRENEURS I Identify the companies most associated with these entrepreneurs†. Turn to page 315 for the solutions. [**Target: 12**]

1. Victor Kiam
2. Alan Sugar
3. Anita Roddick

---

* In China, the Gang of Four were a group of prominent Communist Party leaders arrested following the death of Mao Tse-tung for their actions during the Cultural Revolution. The group consisted of Zhang Chunqiao, Yao Wenyuan, Wang Hongwen and Mao's widow, Jiang Qing.
† To qualify to be called a true entrepreneur usually requires the achievement of something above and beyond simple commercial success. Businessmen and businesswomen stand out as entrepreneurs largely because of: (i) their creation of a large amount of wealth; (ii) their rapid accumulation of wealth, usually in less than five years; (iii) their acceptance of ventures with a very high level of risk; and (iv) their ability to innovate, either in their products or their business processes.

4.   Steve Jobs and Steve Wozniak
5.   Ben Cohen and Jerry Greenfield
6.   Louis Mayer
7.   Paul Allen
8.   Jerry Yang and David Filo
9.   Robert Woodruff
10. Jeff Bezos
11. Akio Morita
12. Ingvar Kamprad
13. Howard Schultz
14. Scott McNealy
15. Allen Lane
16. George Eastman
17. Jorma Jaakko Ollila
18. Ray Kroc
19. Phil Knight
20. Sergey Brin and Larry Page
21. Pierre Omidyar
22. William Durant
23. Samuel Walton
24. Larry Ellison

FACES OF MOUNT RUSHMORE List the *four* American
Presidents honoured at the Mount Rushmore National Memorial.
Find the solution on page 334. [**Target: 3**]

EVANGELISTS Name the *four* biblical evangelists (Gospel writers).
The solution is on page 212. [**Target: 4**]

MISCELLANY IV These questions are of a miscellaneous nature.
Go to page 232 for the solutions. [**Target: 10**]

1.   What new technique was pioneered by Dick Fosbury at the
     Mexico City Olympics in 1968?
2.   Who wrote *The Strange Case of Dr Jekyll and Mr Hyde*?
3.   Which two countries fought the Pastry War ('La Guerra de los
     Pasteles') of 1838?
4.   Which computing related word is derived from the words
     'picture element'?

5. Which fabric is most closely associated with athletes, super-heroes and glam rock bands?

6. Who preceded Gordon Brown as Chancellor of the Exchequer?

7. How many stars are on the New Zealand flag?

8. Which letters of the alphabet have a 'tittle'?

9. After the British mainland and Ireland, which is the largest island in the British Isles?

10. After a successful libel action against a British newspaper, which entertainer famously said he 'cried all the way to the bank'?

11. Which element has an atomic number of one?

12. What cost 37p when it was abolished in 1988?

13. Which city is served by Waverley and Haymarket railway stations?

14. Who was the first poet to be buried in Poets' Corner in Westminster Abbey?

15. Within a standard domino set, how many unique blocks are there (given that each block is unique)?

16. Who was the first President of the French Fifth Republic?

17. Which car manufacturer features a Viking ship as its logo?

18. Ted Bovis and Spike Dixon are characters in which TV programme?

19. What did football referees get for the first time in 1970?

20. Which author's given names were John Ronald Reuel?

21. What is the angle in degrees between the hands of a clock when the time is ten minutes to one?

22. Which sea does the Danube flow into?

23. Which 1950 film was the first non-animated Disney film?

24. In a group of men and horses there are twenty-two heads and seventy-two feet. How many of the group are horses and how many are men?

BATMEN Recall the *five* actors to have played the role of Batman in feature films. Look for the solution on page 252. [**Target:** 4]

NORDIC COUNCIL Name the *five* members of the Nordic Council. The solution is on page 275. [**Target:** 5]

MEANINGS OF PLACE NAMES Identify the places from the clues provided. Turn to page 295 for the solutions. [Target: 18]

1. South American city meaning 'river of January'
2. English county, formerly 'East Saxony'
3. Country meaning 'land of silver'
4. Canadian province meaning 'New Scotland'
5. North American city meaning 'red stick'
6. African city, name derives from 'South Western Townships'
7. Country meaning 'rich coast'
8. African city meaning 'white house'
9. Caribbean town meaning 'rich harbour'
10. New York district, deriving its name from 'south of Houston Street'
11. Country meaning 'black mountain'
12. Irish city meaning 'monastery'
13. African city meaning 'three towns'
14. Mountain range meaning 'snowy range'
15. Country meaning 'white Russia'
16. Country meaning 'lion mountains'
17. African city, meaning 'fountain of flowers'
18. Indian state meaning 'land of kings'
19. London district, named from a hunting cry
20. US state meaning 'place of the gods'
21. North American city meaning 'the fertile valleys'
22. African city meaning 'lakes'
23. North American city meaning 'royal mountain'
24. Caribbean island meaning 'bearded'

TRAVELING WILBURYS Name the *five* Traveling Wilburys. Find the solution on page 315. [Target: 5]

THE YOUNG ONES Name the *five* main characters in the BBC comedy *The Young Ones*. The solution is on page 334. [Target: 4]

FILMS AND THEIR STARS II Identify the films from these selected cast members and the date of release. Look for the solutions on page 212. [**Target: 14**]

1. Uma Thurman, John Travolta, Samuel L. Jackson (1995)
2. Dustin Hoffman, Meryl Streep (1979)
3. Tom Hanks, Audrey Tautou, Ian McKellen, Jean Reno (2006)
4. Martin Sheen, Charlie Sheen, Michael Douglas (1987)
5. Sean Young, Rutger Hauer, Harrison Ford (1982)
6. Kevin Bacon, Ed Harris, Tom Hanks (1995)
7. Ralph Fiennes, Rachel Weisz, Bill Nighy (2005)
8. Matt Damon, Brian Cox, Clive Owen (2002)
9. Dennis Hopper, Natalie Wood, James Dean (1955)
10. Edward Norton, Brad Pitt, Helena Bonham Carter (1999)
11. Lily Tomlin, Dolly Parton, Jane Fonda (1980)
12. Lori Singer, John Lithgow, Kevin Bacon (1984)
13. Jack Nicholson, Faye Dunaway, Roman Polanski (1974)
14. Dirk Bogarde, James Caan, Michael Caine, Sean Connery, Denholm Elliott, Elliott Gould, Edward Fox, Gene Hackman, Anthony Hopkins, Laurence Olivier, Robert Redford, Hardy Krüger, Ryan O'Neal (1977)
15. Nicole Kidman, Julianne Moore, Meryl Streep (2002)
16. Peter Ustinov, Farrah Fawcett, Jenny Agutter, Michael York (1976)
17. Adrien Brody, Thomas Kretschmann, Maureen Lipman (2002)
18. Angela Lansbury, Mickey Rooney, Elizabeth Taylor (1945)
19. Humphrey Bogart, Katharine Hepburn, Robert Morley (1951)
20. Henry Travers, Donna Reed, James Stewart (1946)
21. Roy Scheider, Donald Sutherland, Jane Fonda (1971)
22. Kenneth Branagh, Emma Thompson, Andy Garcia (1991)
23. Charlize Theron, Woody Harrelson, Frances McDormand (2006)
24. Jim Carrey, Kate Winslet, Elijah Wood (2004)

UNITED NATIONS SECURITY COUNCIL Name the *five* permanent* members of the United Nations Security Council. The solution is on page 232. [**Target: 5**]

---

* The Security Council has five permanent members and ten temporary members. The ten temporary seats are voted on by the United Nations General Assembly and held for two years.

EVENTS OF THE MODERN PENTATHLON List the *five* events of the modern pentathlon. Find the solution on page 252. [Target: 5]

LINKED MISCELLANY III The solutions to these questions are linked by a connecting theme. Evaluate the clues and deduce the connection. The solution is on page 276. [Target: 6]

1. Who had a number three hit in 1979 with 'I'm in the Mood for Dancing'?
2. Which 1984 film starred Harrison Ford and Kate Capshaw?
3. Which rank of the peerage is below a Marquess and above a Viscount?
4. Which antiquity was brought to Britain in 1806 by Thomas Bruce and has been a source of controversy ever since?
5. Who was responsible for security at the 1969 Rolling Stones concert in Altamont, California, in which a fan was stabbed to death?
6. Which 1948 Ealing comedy contains the line: 'Blimey! I'm a foreigner!'?
7. What other name has historically been used in Britain for members of the Dominican Order?
8. What nationality are Sepp Blatter, Ursula Andress and Roger Federer?
9. Which animal family belongs to the order Proboscidea?
10. Which Robert Louis Stevenson novel portrayed what would now be called dissociative identity disorder?

NEW YORK BOROUGHS List the *five* boroughs of New York. Turn to page 295 for the solution. [Target: 4]

SPICE GIRLS Name the *five* Spice Girls (real names rather than nicknames). Go to page 315 for the solution. [Target: 4]

HOLY PLACES Identify the religion associated with each of these Holy Places*. The solutions are on page 335. [**Target: 14**]

1. Church of the Nativity (Bethlehem)
2. The Vatican
3. Mecca (Saudi Arabia)
4. Nazareth (Israel)
5. Canterbury (UK)
6. Lourdes (France)
7. Medina (Saudi Arabia)
8. Salt Lake City (USA)
9. Amritsar (India)
10. Mount Sinai (Egypt)
11. Mount Fuji (Japan)
12. The Western Wall (Jerusalem)
13. The Dome of the Rock (Jerusalem)
14. River Ganges (India)
15. Istanbul (Turkey)
16. Bodh Gaya (India)
17. Varanasi (India)
18. Potala Palace (Tibet)
19. The Holy Sepulchre (Jerusalem)
20. Mount Athos (Greece)
21. Mount Tai Shan (China)
22. Church of St Mary of Zion (Ethiopia)
23. Palitana (India)
24. Kusinara (India)

JACKSON 5 Name the *five* members of the Jackson 5. Turn to page 213 for the solution. [**Target: 3**]

---

* The world's most popular religion is Christianity with around 2 billion adherents. Christianity and Islam (the second most popular religion with around 1.2 billion followers) are both derivations of Judaism; all three share beliefs in the biblical patriarch Abraham and are sometimes described as 'desert monotheism'. Judaism dates from around 2000BC, Christianity from around AD100 and Islam first appeared in the Arabian Peninsula at the beginning of the seventh century. The oldest religion in the world however is Hinduism, which has been practised for nearly 5,000 years. Most religions have geographical sites associated with them that are held to be sacred, often at locations where important events in the evolution of the religion took place.

HOUSE OF TUDOR Identify the *five* Tudor monarchs. Go to page 232 for the solution. [**Target:** 4]

AIRPORT CODES I Name the cities that are served by these airports, from their three-letter IATA codes*. The solutions are on page 252. [**Target:** 14]

1.	LGW	2.	JFK
3.	LAX	4.	HKG
5.	MEX	6.	BRU
7.	GLA	8.	BCN
9.	CDG	10.	BKK
11.	EDI	12.	AMS
13.	LPL	14.	BOM
15.	SFO	16.	AKL
17.	LAS	18.	SEA
19.	ORD	20.	JNB
21.	SVO	22.	SXF
23.	DBX	24.	NRT

MARX BROTHERS List the *five* Marx brothers. Find the solution on page 276. [**Target:** 4]

CHILDREN IN CHARLIE AND THE CHOCOLATE FACTORY Name the *five* children in *Charlie and the Chocolate Factory*. The solution is on page 296. [**Target:** 4]

MISCELLANY V Supply the correct answers to the miscellaneous questions presented. Go to page 315 for the solutions. [**Target:** 12]

1. Which monument stands 20m tall and has a wingspan of 54m?
2. The name of which film star is an anagram of 'Old West Action'?
3. By what name are the Yeomen of the Guard better known?

---

* The International Air Transport Association (IATA) is responsible for defining and allocating three-letter codes to airports that are used for flight reservations, flight information and baggage handling.

4. Who was leader of the Labour Party before Tony Blair?
5. What colour is the maple leaf on the Canadian flag?
6. Who wrote the *Just So Stories*?
7. Which film star has a statue in Leicester Square?
8. Which is the only marsupial native to North America?
9. Which literary work features a pig and a turkey as well as the eponymous animal and bird?
10. What was Tom Jones's first UK number one single?
11. Who built the first steam locomotive?
12. Which country has its map on its national flag?
13. Which three horse races form the English Triple Crown?
14. A man spends a fifth of the money in his wallet. He then spends a fifth of the money remaining. He spends £36 in total. How much money was in his wallet to begin with?
15. What did Ismail Pasha, the Viceroy of Egypt, sell to the United Kingdom for £400,000 in 1885?
16. Which vitamin does the body get from sunshine?
17. What were 'Little Boy' and 'Fat Man'?
18. What is the only anagram of the word 'Monday'?
19. Who was the Captain of the *Pequod*?
20. What colour is the number ten on the door of 10 Downing Street?
21. The winner of the Louis Vuitton Cup is eligible to compete in which sporting contest?
22. Who sang 'Two Pints of Lager and a Packet of Crisps'?
23. A paragon is a unit used to measure what?
24. A wooden block measures 4cm x 7cm x 11cm and is painted orange on the outside. The block is cut into 308 cubes measuring 1cm x 1 cm x 1cm. How many of these cubes have orange paint on them?

NOVELS BY F. SCOTT FITZGERALD Name the *five* novels written by F. Scott Fitzgerald. Turn to page 335 for the solution. [Target: 2]

RAT PACK Recall the *five* members of the Rat Pack. The solution is on page 213. [Target: 4]

CATCHPHRASES I Identify the people or characters associated with these catchphrases*. Go to page 232 for the solutions. [**Target: 12**]

1. 'I don't believe it!'
2. 'Stupid boy'
3. 'A-ha!'
4. 'It's the way I tell 'em'
5. 'Ding dong!'
6. 'I love it when a plan comes together'
7. 'Stop messin' abaht!'
8. 'How you doin'?'
9. 'Not 'arf'
10. 'There's just one more thing'
11. ''Er indoors'
12. 'Sit on it!'
13. 'I wanna tell you a story'
14. 'It's turned out nice again'
15. 'She who must be obeyed'
16. 'Go on, go on, go on, go on, go on!'
17. 'Ooh, you are awful!'
18. 'Yeah I know'
19. 'Book 'em, Danno'
20. 'Get yer trousers on, you're nicked!'
21. 'Respect my authority!'
22. 'Flippin' kids'
23. 'Just the facts, ma'am . . .'
24. 'You lucky people'

BONES OF THE SHOULDER AND ARM List the *five* bones of the arm (excluding the bones of the wrist and the hand). The solution is on page 253. [**Target: 3**]

PLATONIC SOLIDS Identify the *five* Platonic Solids. Turn to page 276 for the solution. [**Target: 2**]

---

* A phrase that becomes associated with a particular person or fictional character, usually through its repetition. Catchphrases are particularly loved by comedy writers as they give their characters a trademark by which they can easily be identified. It is a device that has been found to greatly increase the popularity of comedy shows when used effectively.

EVENTS IN HISTORY II Identify the century in which each of these historical events took place (be even more precise and attempt the year if you wish). Find the solutions on page 296. [**Target: 14**]

1. George Washington becomes the first American President.
2. The Gunpowder Plot is foiled.
3. Napoleon Bonaparte invades Russia.
4. The Battle of Trafalgar.
5. The Roman Conquest of Britain.
6. Mutiny on the *Bounty*.
7. The Boston Tea Party.
8. Abolition of slavery in the British Empire.
9. Isaac Newton publishes *Principia*.
10. Leonardo da Vinci paints the *Mona Lisa*.
11. Mary Queen of Scots is executed.
12. The British East India Company is founded.
13. The last Western Roman Emperor is deposed.
14. Charles I is executed.
15. Oliver Cromwell becomes Lord Protector of England.
16. The storming of the Bastille.
17. Cortes begins conquest of the Aztecs.
18. Pompeii is destroyed by the eruption of Mount Vesuvius.
19. Building of Hadrian's Wall commences.
20. Joan of Arc burned at Rouen.
21. Alfred the Great defeats the Danes at Edington.
22. Defeat of British revolt under Boadicea.
23. Westminster Abbey is consecrated.
24. Constantine unites the Roman Empire.

DISNEY THEME PARKS Name the *five* Disney theme parks in the world. Look for the solution on page 315. [**Target: 4**]

OLYMPIC RINGS Identify the *five* colours of the rings* of the Olympic flag. You can find the solution on page 335. [**Target: 5**]

---

* The Olympic flag was introduced at the 1920 Olympics in Antwerp. The five rings represent the five (populated) continents of the world. At the end of the closing ceremony of each Olympics, the Olympic flag is handed from the mayor of the host city to the President of the IOC who then presents it to the mayor of the next host city. This is known as the Antwerp Ceremony.

CAPITAL CITIES II Name the capital cities of each of these countries. The solutions are on page 213. [**Target: 12**]

1.	Sweden	2.	India
3.	Brazil	4.	Sudan
5.	Cambodia	6.	Vietnam
7.	Iceland	8.	Venezuela
9.	Algeria	10.	Saudi Arabia
11.	Romania	12.	Peru
13.	Canada	14.	Uzbekistan
15.	Nigeria	16.	Malaysia
17.	Belarus	18.	Cyprus
19.	Indonesia	20.	Liberia
21.	Jordan	22.	Turkmenistan
23.	Malawi	24.	Lesotho

FAMOUS FIVE Name the *five* members of the Famous Five. Go to page 233 for the solution. [**Target: 3**]

HOLLYWOOD FILM STUDIOS List the *five* prominent studios of the Golden Age of Hollywood. You will find the solution on page 253. [**Target: 4**]

OLOGIES I Describe the objectives of these fields of study. Turn to page 276 for the solutions. [**Target: 12**]

1.	Ornithology	2.	Genealogy
3.	Meteorology	4.	Neurology
5.	Apiology	6.	Dermatology
7.	Cosmology	8.	Campanology
9.	Gerontology	10.	Phonology
11.	Rhinology	12.	Chronology
13.	Pathology	14.	Cardiology
15.	Haematology	16.	Lithology
17.	Entomology	18.	Cytology
19.	Dendrology	20.	Cetology
21.	Oology	22.	Formicology
23.	Dactylology	24.	Exobiology

PILLARS OF ISLAM Name (or describe) the *five* Pillars of Islam. The solution is on page 296. [**Target: 3**]

THE LADYKILLERS Name the *five* actors who played the eponymous characters in the 1955 film. Turn to page 316 to find the solution. [**Target: 3**]

BATTLES I Identify the wars in which each of these battles* were fought. Note that some may share the same answer. Look for the solutions on page 335. [**Target: 10**]

1.	Hastings	2.	Marston Moor
3.	Balaclava	4.	Midway
5.	Jutland	6.	Gettysburg
7.	Somme	8.	Iwo Jima
9.	Bunker Hill	10.	Salamis
11.	Orleans	12.	Hamburger Hill
13.	Shiloh	14.	Leningrad
15.	Yorktown	16.	Agincourt
17.	Alamo	18.	Quebec
19.	Issus	20.	Plassey
21.	Crecy	22.	Poitiers
23.	Edgehill	24.	Princeton

BOOKS OF MOSES Name the *five* Books of Moses†; that is, the first five books of the Hebrew Bible or the Christian Old Testament. The solution is on page 213. [**Target: 3**]

---

* Pyrrhus (318BC–272BC) was the King of Epirus, an area of north-western Greece, and was revered as the greatest military commander of his day. History remembers him for the Battle of Asculum (279BC); a massive battle for its time, fought in south-east Italy against the Romans led by Publius Decius Mus. Roman tactics and the terrain of the battlefield, spread as it was across hills and woods, prevented Pyrrhus from using his elephant cavalry effectively (which was usually decisive) and although he ended the battle in the ascendancy it was after the loss of 3,500 of his own men and 6,000 Romans. He gave his name to the term 'pyrrhic victory' – a victory that is won at a high cost – from a quote attributed to him on the battlefield. When congratulated on the result Pyrrhus replied: 'One more such victory and I will be undone.'

† The Five Books of Moses are known as the 'Pentateuch'. It is traditionally believed that these five books were written by Moses.

HALOGENS List the *five* halogens; that is, the elements found in Group VII of the Periodic Table. You can find the solution on page 233. [**Target:** 4]

MISCELLANY VI These questions are of a miscellaneous nature. The solutions can be found on page 253. [**Target:** 14]

1. Which famous harbour city does Sugarloaf Mountain overlook?
2. Adrenaline is produced by the adrenal glands, located where in the body?
3. Which landmark stands on the Champ de Mars in Paris?
4. Which three English footballers were named European Footballer of the Year in the twentieth century?
5. Who was the last person to simultaneously hold both the water and land speed records?
6. Which Hollywood actress is an anagram of the word 'Germany'?
7. What type of car is associated with Lady Creighton-Ward?
8. In which country is the Masai Mara game reserve?
9. What is the cube root of 1,728?
10. What breed of dog was Snoopy?
11. What are the three possible verdicts in Scottish law?
12. How is Severe Acute Respiratory Syndrome better known?
13. Whose autobiography is entitled *Take It Like a Man*?
14. Which famous ship has a name meaning 'short skirt' and was a character in 'Tam O'Shanter' by Robert Burns?
15. King Charles I was the last British monarch to be admitted into which building (in 1642)?
16. In what sport do participants compete for the 'Tourist Trophy'?
17. Who wrote *Crime and Punishment*?
18. Which three South American countries does the Equator cross?
19. The eruption of Vesuvius in AD79 destroyed which two cities?
20. What links the Mediterranean Sea and *The Hobbit*?
21. Which model of car became in 1997, and remains today, the best-selling design in history?
22. What links Thomas 'Boston' Corbett and Jack Ruby?
23. Which distinctive drink is flavoured with the bergamot orange?

24. It takes two farm labourers eight days to plough a field. One is lazy and one is hard-working. The hard-working labourer would take twelve days to plough it on his own. How many days would the lazy farm labourer take to plough the field if he were to work on his own?

TASTES Name the *five* tastes to which the human tongue is responsive. Turn to page 276 for the solution. [**Target: 4**]

SQUASH BALLS Recall the *five* types of squash ball (as indicated by the coloured dot). The solution may be found on page 296. [**Target: 5**]

PSEUDONYMS I Identify the pseudonyms* by which these people are famously known. Find the solutions on page 316. [**Target: 14**]

1. Katie Price
2. Andrés Arturo García Menéndez
3. Marshall Bruce Mathers III
4. Eric Clapp
5. Norman Cook
6. Jean-Claude van Varenberg
7. Norma Jean Baker

---

* A pseudonym is a fabricated name adopted by an individual and used instead of their given name. The word pseudonym itself can go under many different assumed names: moniker, nickname, sobriquet, epithet, appellation, alias, nom de plume and alter ego, to name a few. The suffix '-onym' comes from Greek meaning 'name' and crops up in words that are used to describe other words. Heteronyms are words that are spelt the same but have different meanings with different pronunciations. For example, pasty (meaning either pale looking or a meat pie), record (a list or to write down), desert (a dry place or to abandon), intermediate (in-between or to intervene). Conversely, homonyms are words that have different spellings and meanings but are pronounced the same way. For example, berth and birth, gorilla and guerrilla, mints and mince, tacks and tax, yoke and yolk, cited, sited and sighted. More unusually, contronyms are words that have contradictory meanings. Examples of these are cleave (meaning to split apart or to cling to), sanction (to approve or to penalise), transparent (easily seen or invisible). Rarer still are capitonyms, words that change their pronunciation when capitalised; for example, polish / Polish, job / Job, nice / Nice, reading / Reading and tangier / Tangier.

8. Edson Arantes do Nascimento
9. Eldrick Woods
10. George O'Dowd
11. David Williams
12. Florian Cloud de Bounevialle Armstrong
13. Frederick Austerlitz
14. Georgios Panaylotou
15. Marion Morrison
16. Sealhenry Samuel
17. Annie Mae Bullock
18. George Ivan Morrison
19. Shirley Crabtree
20. Robert Zimmerman
21. William Cody
22. Archibald Leach
23. Derek van den Bogaerde
24. Pablo Ruiz

THE A-TEAM Name the *five* original characters in *The A-Team**. The solution is on page 336. [**Target: 4**]

ENGLISH CLASSIC HORSE RACES Name the *five* English classics. Look for the solution on page 213. [**Target: 5**]

FILMS AND THEIR STARS III Identify these films according to the selected cast members and the date of release provided. Find the solutions on page 233. [**Target: 14**]

1. Marlon Brando, Al Pacino, James Caan, Robert Duvall (1972)
2. Ian Holm, Sean Bean, Orlando Bloom, Ian McKellen (2001)
3. Liam Neeson, Ben Kingsley, Ralph Fiennes (1993)

---

* Each episode began with the following voiceover: 'Ten years ago, a crack commando unit was sent to prison by a military court for a crime they didn't commit. These men promptly escaped from a maximum security stockade to the Los Angeles underground. Today, still wanted by the government, they survive as soldiers of fortune. If you have a problem, if no one else can help, and if you can find them, maybe you can hire . . . The A-Team.'

4. Denholm Elliot, Jamie Lee Curtis, Dan Aykroyd, Eddie Murphy (1983)
5. Ingrid Bergman, Peter Lorre, Sidney Greenstreet, Humphrey Bogart (1942)
6. Kim Basinger, Kevin Spacey, Russell Crowe, Guy Pearce (1997)
7. Morgan Freeman, Jessica Tandy (1989)
8. Jodie Foster, Kelly McGillis (1988)
9. Bruce Cabot, Robert Armstrong, Fay Wray (1933)
10. Jack Hawkins, Alec Guinness, Omar Sharif, Peter O'Toole (1962)
11. Sean Connery, Christian Slater (1986)
12. Albert Finney, Julia Roberts (1999)
13. Cate Blanchett, Gwyneth Paltrow, Matt Damon, Jude Law (1999)
14. Clint Eastwood, Hilary Swank, Morgan Freeman (2004)
15. Steve McQueen, Faye Dunaway (1968)
16. Tim Robbins, Sean Penn, Kevin Bacon, Laurence Fishburne (2003)
17. Suzanna Hamilton, Richard Burton, John Hurt (1984)
18. Edward Norton, Courtney Love, Woody Harrelson (1996)
19. Alan Rickman, Hugh Grant, Emma Thompson, Kate Winslet (1995)
20. Raymond Burr, Grace Kelly, James Stewart (1954)
21. Joaquin Phoenix, Reese Witherspoon (2005)
22. Jessica Tandy, Kathy Bates (1991)
23. Bob Hoskins, Michael Palin, Jonathan Pryce, Robert De Niro (1985)
24. Don Cheadle, Sophie Okonedo, Nick Nolte, Joaquin Phoenix (2004)

ELEMENTS WITH FOUR-LETTER NAMES List the *five* elements that have four-letter names. Turn to page 276 for the solution. [**Target: 3**]

CINQUE PORTS Name the *five* Cinque* Ports. The solution is on page 253. [**Target: 3**]

---

* Pronounced 'sink'.

LINKED MISCELLANY IV Answer these questions and deduce the connection that links them. Look for the solutions on page 296. [**Target: 7**]

1. How is the United States Military Academy better known?
2. Which comic features Desperate Dan and Korky the Cat?
3. Which 1995 film starring Kevin Spacey takes its title from a line of dialogue in *Casablanca*?
4. What song did Dave Stewart and Barbara Gaskin take to number one in 1981?
5. Which language does the word 'kiwi' come from?
6. What is the largest solid body in the solar system?
7. How would the word 'snail' appear on a French menu?
8. Which 1973 film was based on the novel by Henri Charrière and starred Steve McQueen and Dustin Hoffman?
9. What is the tallest mountain in the UK?
10. What is the main alcoholic ingredient of a mojito?

GREAT LAKES List the *five* Great Lakes (of North America). Turn to page 316 for the solution. [**Target: 4**]

BRITISH WINNERS OF THE BALLON D'OR Name the *six* players from the UK to be awarded the title of European Footballer of the Year. The answer is on page 336. [**Target: 5**]

SINGERS AND BACKERS I Complete the names of these groups by naming the singer (most closely associated with the backing band). Find the solutions on page 213. [**Target: 16**]

1. _____ and the Pacemakers
2. _____ and the Shadows
3. _____ and the Blockheads
4. _____ and the Banshees
5. _____ and Wings
6. _____ and the Range
7. _____ and the Medics
8. _____ and Cockney Rebel
9. _____ and the Vandellas

10. _____ and the Attractions
11. _____ and the Blackhearts
12. _____ and the Revolution
13. _____ and the Waves
14. _____ and the Four Seasons
15. _____ and Crazy Horse
16. _____ and the G.B. Experience
17. _____ and His Skiffle Group
18. _____ and the Paramount Jazz Band
19. _____ with The Jordanaires
20. _____ and the Bluenotes
21. _____ and the Medicine Show
22. _____ and the Hurricanes
23. _____ and the Dinosaurs
24. _____ and the Hotrods

COLOURS OF THE RUBIK'S CUBE Recall the *six* colours of the sides of the original Rubik's Cube*. You can find the solution on page 233. [**Target: 6**]

MENTAL DISORDERS Identify the mental disorders† from the clues provided. Find the solutions on page 276. [**Target: 16**]

1. An inability to sleep.
2. A compulsion to steal.
3. An eating disorder characterised by voluntary starvation.

---

* The puzzle was invented by Erno Rubik, a Hungarian maths professor with a fascination with three-dimensional geometry, in 1974. It became popular with Rubik's students and friends, and slowly grew in popularity in Hungary. In 1980, the cube crossed the Iron Curtain and arrived in West Germany from where it exploded into a worldwide craze. An estimated 100 million cubes were sold in 1982, many of them pirate copies.

† The Diagnostic and Statistical Manual of Mental Disorders (DSM-IV) categorises mental illnesses into thirteen groups according to their common symptoms. These include psychotic disorders (where perception of reality is distorted), cognitive disorders (where the normal cognitive function of the brain becomes limited), mood disorders (affecting the emotional state of the sufferer), anxiety disorders (such as phobias), impulse control disorders (where sufferers are unable to suppress strong compulsions) and personality disorders (categorised by serious behavioural changes).

4. An inability to remember.
5. An eating disorder characterised alternately by binge eating and vomiting.
6. An experience of overwhelming sadness or complete lack of emotion or energy.
7. A tendency towards extravagant behaviour and a need to capture the attention of others, often by exposing oneself.
8. An abnormal and excessive need or desire in women for sexual intercourse.
9. An anxiety disorder caused by exposure to extreme mental or physical stress in which symptoms will not typically appear until three months or more after the event.
10. A compulsion to light fires.
11. An inability to separate real from unreal experiences with sufferers typically experiencing both 'positive' symptoms (additional to normal behaviour such as delusions and hallucinations) and 'negative' symptoms (a lack or decline in normal behaviour such as attention deficit or lacking energy); historically regarded as a 'split personality'.
12. A progressive decline in cognitive function, normally as a result of ageing.
13. A disorder in which sufferers experience involuntary, sudden, rapid, recurrent vocalisations.
14. A fear caused by a specific object or situation, exposure to which provokes an anxiety response.
15. A fear of disease and a conviction that one is suffering from an illness.
16. An experience of grandiose delusions of power, wealth, or fame.
17. An excessive feeling of sleepiness and need for daytime sleep even after adequate sleep at night.
18. A psychological response often seen in hostage situations where the hostage shows loyalty towards their captor.
19. A personality disorder characterised by passive resistance (such as forgetfulness, procrastination, inefficiency and negative attitude) to acceptable social or occupational performance.
20. An anxiety disorder in which sufferers experience obsessions and/or compulsions that are time consuming and interfere with their normal routine.

21. A disorder in which sufferers experience delusions such as inflated self-power or of persecution by others.
22. A mood disorder in which sufferers are given to inflated self-esteem, hyperactivity, elation, decreased need for sleep and accelerated thought and speech.
23. A disorder in which sufferers fabricate medical symptoms in order to be subjected to medical tests and procedures.
24. A disorder in which parents fabricate symptoms in their children thereby subjecting them to unnecessary medical tests and procedures.

NOBLE GASES Name the *six* noble (or inert) gases. Find the solution on page 296. [**Target: 5**]

VOCAL RANGES Name the *six* standard classifications of vocal range. Turn to page 316 for the solution. [**Target: 5**]

MISCELLANY VII Answer the miscellaneous questions posed below. Go to page 336 for the solutions. [**Target: 12**]

1. According to the sea shanty in *Treasure Island*, how many men are 'on a dead man's chest'?
2. Traditionally, on which playing card in a deck is the card maker's trademark?
3. Which character was played by John Inman in *Are You Being Served*?
4. What name is given to the bending of light as it passes from one medium to another?
5. Who plays Grace in *Will and Grace*?
6. The performance of which Olympian in 1988 led to the IOC instituting a rule that Olympic hopefuls must have placed in either the top 30% or the top fifty competitors of an international event?
7. What is a pangram?
8. What word links magnesium sulphate with horse racing?
9. Which is the only letter of the alphabet that does not appear in any of the names of the fifty American states?
10. The *Britannia*, decommissioned in 1997, was prefixed by which three-letter title?

11. Which Second World War assault was led by Guy Gibson?
12. Since Roman times, which year has so far been the longest to write out in Roman numerals?
13. At which course did Frankie Dettori win all seven races on the card in 1996?
14. How is the practice of chiromancy better known?
15. What links the words 'almost' and 'biopsy'?
16. Which British lake contains the largest volume of water?
17. Hibernia was the Roman name for which modern-day country?
18. Which chemical caused hatters to go mad?
19. Where were the Pillars of Hercules?
20. Which South American country is named after an Italian city?
21. Which Hollywood actress made her first film appearance playing a little girl called Gertie?
22. Which German line lay opposite the French Maginot Line?
23. Which company is associated with a character called Bibendum?
24. A man is walking home with his dog at a steady four miles per hour. With six miles to go the dog is let off the lead and runs all the way home at six miles per hour. The dog immediately turns and runs back to the man at the same speed, and upon meeting him it turns and runs home again. It continues to run back and forth at the same speed until the man reaches home. What distance has the dog run since being let off the lead?

NEW ENGLAND STATES List the *six* American states that constitute New England. The solution is on page 213. [**Target: 5**]

NUTRIENTS List the *six* nutrients required to sustain a healthy life*. Find the solution on page 233. [**Target: 6**]

FIRST LINES OF POPULAR NOVELS II Identify the novels that have these opening lines. For advanced play, name the authors as well. Go to page 254 for the solutions. [**Target: 10**]

1. '9 st 3 (but post-Christmas), alcohol units 14 (but effectively covers 2 days as 4 hours of party was on New Year's Day), cigarettes 22, calories 5424.'

---

* Sometimes water is also included in this list, being an essential part of diet.

---

2. 'Call me Ishmael.'
3. 'Far out in the uncharted backwaters of the unfashionable end of the Western Spiral Arm of the Galaxy lies a small unregarded yellow sun.'
4. 'Mr and Mrs Dursley, of number four, Privet Drive, were proud to say that they were perfectly normal, thank you very much.'
5. 'Mr Sherlock Holmes, who was usually very late in the mornings, save upon those not infrequent occasions when he stayed up all night, was seated at the breakfast table.'
6. 'Marley was dead: to begin with. There is no doubt whatever about that.'
7. 'At a village of La Mancha, whose name I do not wish to remember, there lived a little while ago one of those gentlemen who are wont to keep a lance in the rack, an old buckler, a lean horse and a swift greyhound.'
8. 'Happy families are all alike; every unhappy family is unhappy in its own way.'
9. 'James Bond, with two double bourbons inside him, sat in the final departure lounge of Miami Airport and thought about life and death.'
10. 'Most motor-cars are conglomerations (this is a long word for bundles) of steel and wire and rubber and plastic, and electricity and oil and gasoline and water, and the toffee papers you pushed down the crack in the back seat last Sunday.'
11. 'No one would have believed, in the last years of the nineteenth century, that this world was being watched keenly and closely by intelligences greater than man's and yet as mortal as his own; that as men busied themselves about their various concerns they were scrutinized and studied, perhaps almost as narrowly as a man with a microscope might scrutinize the transient creatures that swarm and multiply in a drop of water.'
12. 'The primroses were over.'
13. 'There was no possibility of taking a walk that day.'
14. 'Tom!'
15. 'You will rejoice to hear that no disaster has accompanied the commencement of an enterprise which you have regarded with such evil forebodings.'
16. 'The past is a foreign country; they do things differently there.'

17.   'It was 7 minutes after midnight. The dog was lying on the grass in the middle of the lawn in front of Mrs Shears' house. Its eyes were closed.'

18.   '3 May. Bistritz. – Left Munich at 8:35 P.M., on 1st May, arriving at Vienna early next morning; should have arrived at 6:46, but the train was an hour late. Buda-Pesth seems a wonderful place, from the glimpse which I got of it from the train and the little I could walk through the streets.'

19.   'It was a pleasure to burn.'

20.   'When Mary Lennox was sent to Misselthwaite Manor to live with her uncle, everybody said she was the most disagreeable-looking child ever seen.'

21.   'In my younger and more vulnerable years my father gave me some advice that I've been turning over in my mind ever since.'

22.   'He was an old man who fished alone in a skiff in the Gulf Stream and he had gone eighty-four days now without taking a fish.'

23.   'The schoolmaster was leaving the village, and everybody seemed sorry.'

24.   'It was love at first sight.'

FIGHTERS OF THE BATTLE OF BRITAIN Name the *six* fighter aircraft the RAF deployed in the Battle of Britain. Turn to page 277 for the solution. [**Target: 3**]

MOON LANDINGS List the *six* Apollo missions that landed men on the moon. Look for the solution on page 297. [**Target: 5**]

CURRENCIES Identify the countries where you might spend these currencies*. The solutions are on page 316. [**Target: 10**]

1.	Rouble	2.	Yen
3.	Rupee	4.	Baht

---

* The most popular currency in the world is the US dollar, with an estimated $700bn in circulation, two-thirds of which are thought to be held outside of the United States. Countries that produce their own dollar currencies include Australia, Barbados, the Bahamas, Belize, Bermuda, Brunei, Canada, the Cayman Islands, Fiji, Guyana, Hong Kong, Jamaica, Liberia, Namibia, New Zealand, Singapore, the Solomon Islands, Suriname, Taiwan, Trinidad and Tobago, and Zimbabwe.

5.	Shekel	6.	Rand
7.	Boliviano	8.	Zloty
9.	Lira	10.	Real
11.	Rupiah	12.	Krona
13.	Krone	14.	Yuan
15.	Bolivar	16.	Quetzal
17.	Won	18.	Lek
19.	Sucre	20.	Lat
21.	Dirham	22.	Colon
23.	Nuevo Sol	24.	Todrog

VILLAGE PEOPLE List the characters played by the *six* members of Village People. Find the solution on page 336. [**Target: 6**]

ENGLISH ROMANTIC POETS Name the *six* poets central to the English Romantic movement, sometimes known as the 'Big Six'. The solution is on page 213. [**Target: 4**]

DANCES Identify the dances* according to the clues provided. You can find the solutions on page 233. [**Target: 20**]

1. Caribbean dance in which dancers pass under a low bar.
2. Rock-and-roll dance of the 1960s popularised by Chubby Checker.
3. Solo dance of Arabic origin performed by a woman and featuring improvisational gyration of the whole body and especially the stomach.
4. Spanish dance performed usually by a solo woman involving fast hand-clapping and stamping and accompanied by guitar and castanets.
5. Boisterous music-hall dance performed by a chorus line, originating in Algeria in the 1830s and popularised in Parisian clubs such as the Moulin Rouge.

---

* In 1928, a Hungarian named Rudolf von Laban came up with an unwieldy system of notation that enabled dance movements to be written down for the first time. He called it Labanotation. His system has a staff, similar to musical notation, on to which symbols are placed relating to body parts, and an indication of the length of duration of movement, the direction of movement and the intensity of the movement.

6. Erotic dance, usually a striptease, performed in private to a seated patron.

7. Latin American dance consisting of three steps and a kick in repetition usually performed by a long line of people.

8. Quadruple-time ballroom dance combining long and short steps in the tempo 'slow-quick-quick-slow'; named after a New York vaudeville performer called Harry Fox.

9. Emotionally charged Argentinian ballroom dance characterised by long gliding steps and sudden staccato movements.

10. Spanish ballroom dance in which double steps are taken in fast 2/4 time; the name means 'two step' in Spanish and the actions mimic a bull fight.

11. Popular Latin American dance combining Latin rhythms with rock; the name means 'sauce' in Spanish.

12. Moderately slow Spanish dance set in triple time and performed solo or by a couple; popularised by the composer Maurice Ravel in 1928.

13. A lively and energetic Brazilian dance in 2/4 time; the popular dance at the Rio carnival.

14. Brazilian musical and dance style with jazz roots popularised in Rio de Janeiro in the 1950s; its name translates as 'new beat'.

15. Folk dance usually in 6/8 time and particularly associated with Ireland.

16. Traditional Mexican dance in which sombreros feature prominently.

17. Fast foxtrot named after a town in South Carolina which became popular in New York in the 1920s.

18. Ritualised traditional dance performed in the Hawaiian islands.

19. European ballroom dance in 3/4 time that emerged in Vienna in the 1780s.

20. Punjabi dance, performed by Indian men often at social occasions to rhythmic accompaniment by a dohl (drum) and chimta (percussion); the term is now more associated with a type of contemporary dance music played in night clubs.

21. Latin American ballroom dance in which steps are made on the beat with one leg slightly dragging as if to give the appearance of having a limp.

22. Slow and romantic Cuban dance performed in 8/8 time. Similar to salsa, it first appeared in the 1920s and is now a popular ballroom dance.
23. Fast, rhythmic and erotic Brazilian dance popularised in the 1980s, in which couples dance with touching hips.
24. Bohemian dance, popular in the nineteenth century, comprising three steps and a hop to fast 2/4 time.

MONOPOLY TOKENS List the *six* tokens used in the original Monopoly set. Go to page 254 for the solution. [**Target: 6**]

NOBEL PRIZES Identify the *six* fields of accomplishment for which Nobel Prizes are awarded. The solution is on page 277. [**Target: 6**]

CAPITAL CITIES III Identify the capital city of each country. Find the solutions on page 297. [**Target: 12**]

1.	Australia	2.	Norway
3.	Poland	4.	Egypt
5.	Portugal	6.	Argentina
7.	Chile	8.	Turkey
9.	Colombia	10.	Cuba
11.	Ecuador	12.	Tunisia
13.	Taiwan	14.	El Salvador
15.	Albania	16.	Serbia
17.	Uruguay	18.	Slovakia
19.	Latvia	20.	Senegal
21.	Georgia	22.	Tajikistan
23.	Madagascar	24.	Liechtenstein

ROYAL RESIDENCES Name the *six* residences of the Queen and the Duke of Edinburgh in the United Kingdom. The solution is on page 316. [**Target: 5**]

MONTY PYTHON Identify the *six* members of *Monty Python's Flying Circus*. Go to page 336 for the solution. [**Target: 6**]

COOKING TERMS I Identify each cooking* term from the clues provided. The solutions can be found on page 213. [**Target: 12**]

1. From Mexico, minced beef with tomato, beans and chilli.
2. Flat, wide sheets of pasta and an Italian dish in which they are commonly used.
3. Greek dish of minced lamb and layers of potato and aubergine baked with white sauce and cheese.
4. Traditional Spanish dish of rice, chicken and seafood, flavoured with saffron.
5. Mexican relish made from tomatoes, onions, chillies and coriander.
6. From Russia, a small pancake often served with caviar and sour cream.
7. Italian term for small pasta-like dumplings made from potato.
8. North African wheat and semolina mixture formed into tiny pellets.
9. A stuffed pizza folded over and baked.
10. A slice of meat (usually veal) that has been beaten thin and fried in breadcrumbs.
11. French term for 'juice', usually applied to the juices from a roast meat.
12. Italian term for an appetiser (literally 'before the meal').
13. Dried fish from India or Bangladesh that is crumbled and sprinkled over curry dishes.
14. French term for a small young chicken, sometimes called a 'spring chicken'.
15. Pasta tubes with diagonally cut ends.
16. Italian term for thin strips of ham such as Parma ham.

---

* The Anglo-Saxons were not renowned for their culinary flair, a fact possibly reflected in their language. In Old English there was no distinction between an animal and the food that comes from it. (This is also true of modern German, where words like 'rindfleisch' [literally 'cow flesh'] and 'schweinefleisch' ['pig flesh'] are used for beef and pork.) We left it to the French, a country more passionate about their food, to give us our words for beef, pork, veal, mutton and so on, words which arrived with the Normans in 1066 (it is also notable that in medieval times, although many people worked with animals, few could afford to eat meat; those who could were in the main the French-speaking ruling classes). It is indicative of the culinary sophistication of the French that so many cooking terms have come to us from France; while the English boiled and roasted the French blanched and sautéed.

---

17. North African stew which takes its name from the earthenware pot with a distinctive conical lid in which it is cooked.
18. Prunes wrapped in bacon.
19. French term for fruit cooked in a light sugary syrup (more liquid in consistency than jam), which may be served hot or cold.
20. French term meaning 'in pastry'.
21. A cooked mixture of flour and butter used as a basis for any sauce.
22. French term usually applied to preparation of shellfish (especially mussels) meaning 'cooked in white wine and shallots'.
23. Italian cold dessert similar to crème caramel, meaning 'cooked cream'.
24. Provençal mayonnaise made with plenty of garlic.

COURTS OF ENGLAND AND WALES Name the *six* levels of court which make up the court hierarchy of England and Wales*. Turn to page 234 for the solution. [Target: 4]

WOODWIND INSTRUMENTS Name the *six* instruments commonly found in the woodwind section of an orchestra. Turn to page 254 for the solution. [Target: 6]

MISCELLANY VIII Answer these miscellaneous questions. Go to page 277 for the solutions. [Target: 14]

1. Who in Greek mythology fell in love with his own reflection?
2. The name for which English county is derived from a phrase meaning 'northern people'?
3. The *Encyclopaedia Galactica* is the chief rival to which other book?
4. Who founded the Church of England?
5. Which private eye operated out of a caravan on Malibu Beach?
6. What links Chiswick in London with Pontarddulais in Wales?

---

* Scotland and Northern Ireland have separate judicial systems.

7. If Air Force One is the US President's plane, what is Marine One?

8. What material is named after a French phrase meaning 'cloth of the king'?

9. What was originally known as 'battledore and shuttlecock'?

10. In medicine, what does the term 'vascular' refer to?

11. How many square inches are there in a square foot?

12. On which island were American marines famously photographed raising the US flag over Mount Suribachi in February 1945?

13. What are the surnames of Romeo and Juliet?

14. What line from 'Bohemian Rhapsody' was also a title of a number one in the same year?

15. How is *La Giaconda* better known?

16. What is the name of a female cat?

17. Which lost city was discovered by Hiram Bingham III in 1911?

18. Which member of England's 2003 Rugby World Cup-winning team has an uncle who was a member of the 1966 Football World Cup-winning team?

19. What links Bernard Cribbins with Richard Fairbrass?

20. Which Scottish clan, often accused of collusion with the English, murdered members of the MacDonald clan in the Massacre of Glencoe?

21. At the outbreak of the First World War who was the British Prime Minister?

22. Which drink did Michael Portillo advertise as a child?

23. Which world city has the highest number of residents born outside its parent country?

24. I had ten pence and a pound and I bought a horse and a hound; the horse cost a pound more than the hound, how much did I pay for the hound?

PINK PANTHER FILMS Identify the *six Pink Panther* films which featured Peter Sellers as Inspector Clouseau. The solution is on page 297. [**Target:** 4]

NOVELS BY JANE AUSTEN Name the *six* novels written by Jane Austen. Go to page 317 for the solution. [**Target:** 5]

FOREIGN WORDS AND PHRASES I Identify the foreign word or phrase from the description provided. Each word or phrase is in common use in English but has been loaned from another language*. Find the solutions on page 337. [**Target: 16**]

1. Already seen (French)
2. A school for the very young (German)
3. Nothing (Arabic)
4. A human-like machine (Czech)
5. An important person, especially in the media (Hindi)
6. The intellectual social class (Russian)
7. A duty levied on goods (Arabic)
8. Dread and anxiety (German)
9. An annually published book of information (Arabic)
10. The good life (Italian)
11. A low house, literally 'house in the Bengal style' (Hindi)
12. A rich and powerful businessman (Japanese)
13. A priest, teacher, mentor or expert (Hindi)
14. In relation to, literally 'face to face' (French)
15. Forbidden (German)
16. To behave in a servile manner; to go along with the wishes of another (Chinese)
17. A great yield of riches (Spanish)
18. A lookalike (German)

---

* English has a vocabulary much larger than any other language. It is estimated that the English language has in the region of 600,000 words (in comparison, German has around 180,000 and French has around 100,000). Most English speakers know a fraction of these; a well-educated person will have on average a vocabulary of around 25,000 words, less than 5% of the total. English has a propensity to borrow words from other languages and has done so with an enthusiasm unmatched by any other language. The language derives from three main sources. Shorter, commonplace words tend to come from Old English, introduced by the Anglo-Saxons and used by the common people. Literary words tend to come from French, arriving with the Normans and being used initially by the wealthy and the ruling classes. Intellectual words typically come from classical Latin and Greek and started arriving during the Renaissance, driven by the acceleration in learning which has continued since. In selecting a word, an English speaker is therefore unique in that a choice of at least three words is usually available. For example, one may think (Anglo-Saxon), ponder (French) or cogitate (Latin); a monarch may be kingly (Anglo-Saxon), royal (French) or regal (Latin); one may seek freedom (Anglo-Saxon), liberty (French) or autonomy (Greek).

19. An enthusiastic amateur (Spanish)
20. A platform from which a candidate speaks prior to an election (Norwegian)
21. Vulgarity, tastelessness or ostentation, literally 'worthless art' (German)
22. A potential danger (Arabic)
23. Elevated wasteland (Russian)
24. Literally, 'the king has died.' (Arabic)

WEAPONS IN CLUEDO

Recall the *six* murder weapons featured in the game of Cluedo*. The solution is on page 214. [**Target: 6**]

WIVES OF HENRY VIII

Recall the *six* wives of Henry VIII. Turn to page 234 for the solution. [**Target: 6**]

TAGLINES OF POPULAR FILMS I

Identify the films† from the clues provided. The solutions are on page 254. [**Target: 14**]

1. 'A long time ago in a galaxy far, far away . . .'(1977)
2. 'Life is like a box of chocolates – you never know what you're gonna get.' (1994)

---

* Anthony E. Pratt, a solicitor's clerk from Birmingham, invented Cluedo as a means of escaping boredom during air raids in the war. Pratt and his wife, Elva (who designed the board), presented the game in 1946 to Waddingtons who liked what they saw and released the game in 1949. Pratt had originally called the game 'Murder' but Waddingtons decided on Cluedo, being a play on the name Ludo, a popular game at the time. (Ludo means 'I play' in Latin.)

† Two French brothers, Auguste and Louis Lumière, are credited with the invention of cinema. They introduced their new device, the cinematograph at a screening on 28 December 1895 in the basement lounge of the Grand Café on the Boulevard des Capucines in Paris. The brothers showed ten short films, lasting only twenty minutes in total, of subjects ranging from people walking along a boulevard to a train pulling into a station. Although their subject matter was a touch mundane, the effect on their audience was striking; the train sequence in particular caused panic among a section of the audience who believed the train was about to crash through the screen. Ironically, the two French inventors never thought their idea would take off. Perhaps feeling that people would tire of watching everyday scenes, the brothers couldn't anticipate the application of their technology to creative storytelling and the multi-billion-pound film industry that the cinematograph would spawn. 'The cinema is an invention without a future,' Louis Lumière once said.

3. 'Seven deadly sins. Seven ways to die.' (1995)
4. 'If he were any cooler, he'd still be frozen, baby!' (1997)
5. 'A romantic comedy. With zombies.' (2004)
6. 'She brought a small town to its feet and a huge corporation to its knees.' (2000)
7. 'The greatest picture in the history of entertainment.' (1939)
8. 'They were seven – and they fought like seven hundred!' (1960)
9. 'Expect the Impossible.' (1996)
10. 'An adventure 65 million years in the making.' (1993)
11. 'They changed her diapers. She changed their lives.' (1987)
12. 'Feel its fury.' (2000)
13. 'First comes love. Then comes the interrogation.' (2000)
14. 'Not every gift is a blessing.' (1999)
15. 'The mission is a man.' (1998)
16. 'Make your last breath count.' (1996)
17. 'Fear can hold you prisoner. Hope can set you free.' (1994)
18. 'Paul Sheldon used to write for a living. Now, he's writing to stay alive.' (1990)
19. 'Music was his passion. Survival was his masterpiece.' (2002)
20. 'Reality is a thing of the past.' (1999)
21. 'Get ready for rush hour.' (1994)
22. 'She's a blessing . . . in disguise.' (1993)
23. 'Love is a force of nature.' (2005)
24. 'Catch it.' (1977)

HOUSE OF STUART List the *seven* monarchs of the House of Stuart* who ruled Britain from 1603 to 1714. The solution is on page 277. [**Target: 5**]

SEVEN SUMMITS Name the highest peaks in each of the *seven* continents and which make up the Seven Summits† mountaineering challenge. The solution is on page 251. [**Target: 3**]

---

* Originally 'Stewart', the current spelling was adopted by Mary Queen of Scots while she was in France to ensure that it was pronounced correctly in the French court. The name originates from the title of High Steward of Scotland.
† As postulated by Rheinhold Messner.

NOVELS BY GEORGE ELIOT List the *seven* novels penned by George Eliot. The solution is on page 253. [**Target: 4**]

POSITIONS IN A NETBALL TEAM Name the *seven* positions in a netball team. Turn to page 297 for the solution. [**Target: 6**]

LINKED MISCELLANY V In the course of answering these questions, deduce the connection that links them. Look for the solutions on page 317. [**Target: 5**]

1. How is the Central Criminal Court better known?
2. With which song did Status Quo open Live Aid?
3. How long is the period of Lent?
4. When does Independence Day fall in the US?
5. Who captained Scotland to a Grand Slam-winning victory against England at Murrayfield in 1990?
6. Which Hollywood star wrote the semi-autobiographical novel *Postcards from the Edge*?
7. What was the name of the first unmanned NASA mission to Mars?
8. Which 1980s animated children's programme featured an eponymous lighthouse-keeper?
9. Where was the sculpture *Alison Lapper Pregnant* unveiled in September 2005?
10. How is *Fingal's Cave*, Opus 26, by Mendelssohn alternatively known?

HARRY POTTER NOVELS Name the *seven Harry Potter* novels in the series by J.K. Rowling. Find the solution on page 337. [**Target: 6**]

SYMBOLS IN ROMAN NUMERALS List the *seven* letters that are used to represent figures in Roman numerals. The solution is on page 214. [**Target: 7**]

FRUIT AND VEGETABLES Name the fruit or vegetable from the varieties listed. Go to page 234 for the solutions. [**Target: 14**]

1. Admiral, Golden Wonder, Jersey Royal, King Edward, Maris Piper
2. Parson Brown, Washington Navel, Seville, Jaffa

3. Laxton's Superb, Rome Beauty, York Imperial, Cox's Orange Pippin, Bramley
4. Riesling, Almeria, Syrah, Zinfandel, Muscat
5. Bird's Eye, Scotch Bonnet, Hungarian Hot Wax, Jalapeño, Ring of Fire
6. Blewits, Chestnut, Oyster, Shitake, White Cap
7. Green Zebra, Liberty Belle, Plum, Red Alert, Cherry
8. Bordeaux, Claret, Purple Sprouting, White Sprouting, Wok Brocc
9. Buttercrunch, Little Gem, Lizzie, Saladin, Cos
10. Laxton's Cropper, Victoria, Warwickshire Drooper, Damson, Green Gage
11. Derby Day, Spring Hero, Wong Bok, Tatsoi, Savoy
12. Black Beauty, Long Purple, Mini Finger, Tres Hative de Barbentane, Violetta di Firenza
13. Bolthardy, Carillon, Crimson Globe, Egyptian Turnip Rooted, Red Ace
14. Burpless Tasty Green, Long Maraicher, Muncher, Slice King, Tokyo Slicer
15. Dobies All Rounder, Marshall's Giant Fenglobe, Pearl Pickler, Spring, Red Baron
16. Feltham First, Histon Mini, Kelvedon Wonder, Little Marvel, Meteor
17. Amsterdam Forcing, Autumn King, Figaro, Long Red Surrey, Regulus Imperial
18. Bedford-Fillbasket, Brilliant, Cambridge No. 5, Half Tall, Noisette
19. Black Republic, Black Tartarian, Maraschino, Morello, Napoleon
20. Avonresister, Gladiator, Half Long Guernsey, Tender and True, White Gem
21. Baboon, Escondido, Lisbon, Meyer, Sicilian
22. Cavendish, Green, Red, Lady Finger, Golden Beauty
23. Burgundy, Duncan, Marsh, Ruby Red, Star Ruby
24. Anjou, Bartlett, Conference, Josephine de Malines, Louise Bonne de Jersey

SPACE SHUTTLES Name the *seven* NASA space shuttles. The solution is on page 254. [Target: 5]

WORLD CUP WINNERS Recall the *seven* countries to have won the Football World Cup*. Find the solution on page 277. [**Target: 7**]

QUOTATIONS FROM SHAKESPEARE I Name the plays of Shakespeare† from which these quotations are taken. (Note that the same play may be the solution to more than one quotation.) If you wish, also name the charcter who is quoted. Go to page 297 for the solutions. [**Target: 12**]

1. 'To be, or not to be; that is the question'
2. 'Double, double, toil and trouble / Fire burn, and cauldron bubble'
3. 'A horse! a horse! my kingdom for a horse!'
4. 'Something is rotten in the state of Denmark'
5. 'If music be the food of love, play on'
6. 'Beware the Ides of March'

---

* The Football World Cup was the brainchild of Jules Rimet who was President of the World Football Federation from 1921 to 1954. Rimet organised the first World Cup tournament in 1930, and on 13 July it kicked off with France beating Mexico 4–1.

† Shakespeare's literary output was extraordinary, both in terms of quantity and quality and few would doubt his status as the greatest English-language writer. But he has perhaps made an even greater contribution to the English language itself, inventing around 2,000 new English words, many of which are in everyday use. Words attributed to Shakespeare include: alligator, bandit, barefaced, bedroom, besmirch, bloodstained, bump, castigate, cold-blooded, courtship, critical, dwindle, employer, equivocal, elbow, excitement, excellent, eyesore, football, frugal, gloomy, glow, gossip, hoodwinked, lacklustre, leapfrog, lonely, luggage, majestic, manager, mimic, moonbeam, monumental, negotiate, obscene, outbreak, radiance, shooting star, shudder, submerged, tranquil, undress, watchdog, and zany. Shakespeare coined an equally large number of phrases. For example: a sorry sight, all that glitters is not gold, as good luck would have it, bated breath, the be-all and the end-all, brave new world, break the ice, budge an inch, cold comfort, dead as a doornail, devil incarnate, eaten me out of house and home, elbow room, faint-hearted, fair play, fancy-free, fool's paradise, foregone conclusion, foul play, full circle, good riddance, heart of gold, high time, improbable fiction, in a pickle, in my mind's eye, into thin air, laughing stock, give short shrift, milk of human kindness, more in sorrow than in anger, naked truth, neither a borrower nor a lender be, not slept one wink, one fell swoop, own flesh and blood, pitched battle, play fast and loose, pound of flesh, rhyme and reason, sea change, seen better days, send packing, set my teeth on edge, shuffle off this mortal coil, spotless reputation, too much of a good thing, tower of strength, wear my heart upon my sleeve, wild goose chase.

7. 'And gentlemen in England now abed / Shall think themselves accursed they were not here, / And hold their manhoods cheap whiles any speaks / That fought with us upon Saint Crispin's day'
8. 'Lord, what fools these mortals be!'
9. 'When we have shuffled off this mortal coil'
10. 'Where's my serpent of old Nile?'
11. 'Is this a dagger which I see before me?
12. 'Goodnight, sweet prince, / And a flight of angels sing thee to thy rest'
13. 'We few, we happy few, we band of brothers'
14. 'Parting is such sweet sorrow'
15. 'How sharper than a serpent's tooth it is / To have a thankless child?'
16. 'We are such stuff / As dreams are made on'
17. 'Some are born great . . . / Some achieve greatness . . . / And some have greatness thrust upon them'
18. 'Thus with a kiss I die'
19. 'I am a man / More sinned against than sinning'
20. 'If you prick us do we not bleed? If you tickle us do we not laugh? If you poison us do we not die? And if you wrong us shall we not revenge?'
21. 'I must be cruel only to be kind'
22. 'Things that love night, love not such nights as this'
23. 'Many a good hanging prevents a bad marriage'
24. 'All the world's a stage / And all the men and women merely players'

AFRICAN COUNTRIES BEGINNING WITH 'M' Name the *seven* African countries that begin with the letter 'M'. The solution is on page 317. [**Target: 5**]

DWARFS List the *Seven* Dwarfs. Turn to page 337 for the solution. [**Target: 6**]

MISCELLANY IX These questions are of a miscellaneous nature. Find the solutions on page 214. [**Target: 16**]

1. Which drug is named after the Greek god of dreams?
2. The *1812 Overture* contains passages of the national anthems of which two countries?

3. Which abbreviation for an imperial unit comes from a sign of the zodiac?
4. Who was the first person to reach the South Pole?
5. What links Tunbridge Wells and Leamington Spa?
6. From which animal does cashmere wool come from?
7. Which well-known film title is an anagram of 'Con Bites the Male Flesh'?
8. Which institution is sometimes called the 'Old Lady of Threadneedle Street'?
9. After Paris, which is the next largest French-speaking city?
10. Which play by Shakespeare has a title that is also a proverb?
11. The cortex and medulla are parts of which human organ?
12. Which artist wore a diving suit to the opening of an exhibition at London's New Burlington Gallery in 1936?
13. What were the first names of the characters played by John Travolta and Olivia Newton-John in *Grease*?
14. What word is used in fencing to acknowledge a valid hit?
15. Which was the first UN member country in history to invade another UN member country?
16. Who played Jessica Fletcher in a long-running TV series?
17. Which country has the world's largest Muslim population?
18. A woman is twelve years old plus half her age. How old is she?
19. Which musical instrument takes its name from the Greek meaning 'wooden sound'?
20. What was the name of the butler in *To the Manor Born*?
21. Followers of which religion assemble at what is the largest gathering of people anywhere in the world?
22. In children's television, what does TISWAS stand for?
23. Canaletto was best known for his paintings of Venice and which other city?
24. Which number is equal to six times the sum of its digits?

SOVIET COMMUNIST PARTY LEADERS Name the *seven* people to have led the Soviet Communist Party. The solution is on page 234. [**Target: 6**]

VON TRAPP CHILDREN List the *seven* von Trapp children from *The Sound of Music*. Look for the solution on page 255. [**Target: 4**]

ANIMAL ADJECTIVES Identify the animal that is described by each adjective. Turn to page 278 for the solutions. [**Target: 10**]

1.	Equine	2.	Leonine
3.	Avian	4.	Zebrine
5.	Simian	6.	Bovine
7.	Piscine	8.	Porcine
9.	Taurine	10.	Delphine
11.	Ostracine	12.	Ursine
13.	Apian	14.	Caprine
15.	Cervine	16.	Hircine
17.	Lupine	18.	Murine
19.	Ovine	20.	Vespine
21.	Leporine	22.	Vulpine
23.	Anserine	24.	Columbine

CATHOLIC SACRAMENTS Name the *seven* Catholic Sacraments. Find the solution on page 298. [**Target: 4**]

WONDERS OF THE ANCIENT WORLD Name the *Seven* Wonders of the Ancient World. The solution is on page 317. [**Target: 5**]

HOBBIES AND PROFESSIONS II Describe these hobbies and professions. Find the solutions on page 337. [**Target: 10**]

1.	Topiarist	2.	Haberdasher
3.	Vintner	4.	Hosier
5.	Barista	6.	Ham
7.	Draper	8.	Equerry
9.	Milliner	10.	Artificer
11.	Pedagogue	12.	Bibliopole
13.	Subaltern	14.	Fletcher
15.	Farrier	16.	Stenographer
17.	Wrangler	18.	Horologist
19.	Cartomancer	20.	Funambulist
21.	Phillumenist	22.	Ecdysiast
23.	Costermonger	24.	Prestidigator

DEADLY SINS Name the *Seven* Deadly Sins*. Turn to page 214 for the solution. [Target: 6]

MOST OSCAR-NOMINATED ACTRESSES Name the *seven* actresses who have received seven or more Oscar† nominations in their careers. You can find the solution on page 235. [Target: 3]

EPONYMOUS AIRPORTS Identify the cities that are served by airports named after these people. Go to page 255 for the solutions. [Target: 14]

1.	John F. Kennedy	2.	Charles de Gaulle
3.	Leonardo da Vinci	4.	John Lennon
5.	Ayatollah Khomeini	6.	Indira Gandhi
7.	Louis Armstrong	8.	Marco Polo
9.	Mustafa Kemal Ataturk	10.	David Ben-Gurion
11.	Galileo Galilei	12.	Wolfgang Amadeus Mozart
13.	Edward O'Hare	14.	Pierre Trudeau
15.	Ronald Reagan	16.	George H.W. Bush
17.	Benito Juárez	18.	Lech Walesa
19.	Pope John Paul II	20.	Edward Lawrence Logan
21.	Frédéric Chopin	22.	Jomo Kenyatta
23.	Mother Theresa	24.	Yasser Arafat

---

* The Seven Deadly Sins is not a concept found in the Bible but is attributable to Pope Gregory the Great in the sixth century AD. The concept was popularised by Dante in *The Divine Comedy* and by many artists of the fourteenth century and since.

† The Academy of Motion Picture Arts and Sciences was founded in 1927 and annually hosts the world's most prestigious artistic awards ceremony. Winners are chosen according to an annual vote of all members which is carried out in the utmost secrecy. Until the envelopes are opened, only two people know the results of the vote (the two assigned accountants from Price Waterhouse) and the counting of votes is performed by six assistants who are given random selections from each category. Two sets of winning envelopes are sealed in a safe and on the day of the awards ceremony are driven to the location by two different routes. They arrive two hours before the ceremony where they are guarded until they are ready to be given to the presenters.

EVENTS IN THE HEPTATHLON Name the *seven* events of the heptathlon. Find the solution on page 278. [**Target: 5**]

SOLOMON GRUNDY Recall the *seven* landmarks in the life of Solomon Grundy as told in the nursery rhyme. Turn to page 298 for the solution. [**Target: 6**]

FIRST LINES OF POP SONGS II Deduce the titles of these songs from the first lines below. (The year each song was a hit in the UK is given.) For advanced play, name the performers as well. You will find the solutions on page 317. [**Target: 12**]

1. 'There's a lady who's sure all that glitters is gold.' (1971)
2. 'I remember when, I remember, I remember when I lost my mind.' (2006)
3. 'We skipped the light fandango.' (1967)
4. 'Some people call me the space cowboy.' (1973)
5. 'As I walk through the valley of the shadow of death.' (1995)
6. 'It's close to midnight and something evil's lurking in the dark.' (1983)
7. 'Please, please, tell me now.' (1983)
8. 'They say we're young and we don't know.' (1965)
9. 'I'm coming up.' (2002)
10. And you may find yourself living in a shotgun shack.' (1981)
11. 'I met a gin-soaked bar-room queen in Memphis.' (1969)
12. 'Yes! So crazy right now.' (2003)
13. 'You were working as a waitress in a cocktail bar when I met you.' (1981)
14. 'Hello? Is there anybody in there?' (1979)
15. 'I heard you on the wireless back in '52.' (1979)
16. 'Well you're dirty and sweet, clad in black, don't look back, and I love you.' (1971)
17. 'Well, I don't know why I came here tonight.' (1973)
18. 'Now there's a backstreet lover that is always undercover.' (1986)
19. 'Holding you closer it's time that I told you everything's going to be fine.' (2000)
20. 'Ever seen a blind man cross the road?' (2001)

21. 'Every night I grab some money and I go down to the bar.' (1981)
22. 'In my imagination, there is no complication, I dream about you all the time.' (1988)
23. 'You were my sun, you were my earth.' (2003)
24. 'Sweetness, sweetness I was only joking when I said I'd like to smash every tooth in your head.' (1986)

CATHOLIC CHURCH HIERARCHY List the *seven* ranks of the clerical hierarchy of the Roman Catholic Church. Turn to page 337 for the solution. [**Target: 5**]

VIRTUES Name the *Seven* Virtues (counterparts to the Seven Deadly Sins). Look for the solution on page 214. [**Target: 4**]

FIRST LINES OF POPULAR NOVELS III Identify the novels from these first lines. For advanced play, name the authors as well. The solutions are on page 235. [**Target: 10**]

1. 'All children, except one, grow up.'
2. 'Dorothy lived in the midst of the great Kansas prairies, with Uncle Henry, who was a farmer, and Aunt Em, who was the farmer's wife.'
3. 'Garp's mother, Jenny Fields, was arrested in Boston in 1942 for wounding a man in a movie theater.'
4. 'Mr Phileas Fogg lived, in 1872, at No. 7, Savile Row, Burlington Gardens, the house in which Sheridan died in 1814.'
5. 'Once upon a time there were four little Rabbits, and their names were – Flopsy, Mopsy, Cotton-tail, and Peter.'
6. 'A squat grey building of only thirty-four stories. Over the main entrance the words, CENTRAL LONDON HATCHERY AND CONDITIONING CENTRE, and, in a shield, the World State's motto, COMMUNITY, IDENTITY, STABILITY.'
7. 'By now the other warriors, those that had escaped head-long ruin by the sea or in a battle, were safely home.'
8. 'It was three hundred forty-eight years, six months, and nineteen days ago today that the citizens of Paris were

awakened by the pealing of all the bells in the triple precincts of the City, the University and the Town.'

9. 'Miss Brooke had that kind of beauty which seems to be thrown into relief by poor dress.'

10. 'My father's family name being Pirrip, and my christian name Philip, my infant tongue could make of both names nothing longer or more explicit than Pip.'

11. 'The great fish moved silently through the night water, propelled by short sweeps of its crescent tail.'

12. 'The sweat wis lashing oafay Sick Boy; he wis trembling.'

13. 'These two very old people are the father and mother of Mr Bucket.'

14. 'When Mrs Frederick C. Little's second son arrived, everybody noticed that he was not much bigger than a mouse.'

15. 'As Gregor Samsa awoke one morning from uneasy dreams he found himself transformed in his bed into a gigantic insect.'

16. 'Lyra and her daemon moved through the darkening Hall, taking care to keep to one side, out of sight of the kitchen.'

17. 'Amerigo Bonasera sat in New York Criminal Court Number 3 and waited for justice; vengeance on the men who had so cruelly hurt his daughter, who had tried to dishonour her.'

18. 'Except for the Marabar Caves – and they are twenty miles off – the city of Chandrapore presents nothing extraordinary.'

19. 'It was seven o'clock of a very warm evening in the Seeonee hills when Father Wolf woke up from his day's rest, scratched himself, yawned, and spread out his paws one after the other to get rid of the sleepy feeling in their tips.'

20. 'You better not never tell nobody but God.'

21. 'Whether I shall turn out to be the hero of my own life, or whether that station will be held by anybody else, these pages must show.'

22. 'It was the day my grandmother exploded.'

23. 'The studio was filled with the rich odour of roses, and when the light summer wind stirred amidst the trees of the garden, there came through the open door the heavy scent of the lilac, or the more delicate perfume of the pink-flowering thorn.'

24. 'The *Nellie*, a cruising yawl, swung to her anchor without a flutter of the sails, and was at rest.'

LIBERAL ARTS List the *seven* Liberal Arts*. The solution is on page 255. [**Target: 2**]

NOVELS BY E.M. FORSTER Name the *seven* novels by E.M. Forster. You will find the solution on page 294. [**Target: 3**]

SEVEN SEAS List the *seven* seas. Find the solution on page 278. [**Target: 5**]

MISCELLANY X Answer these questions of a miscellaneous nature. Turn to page 298 for the solutions. [**Target: 12**]

1. Who wrote the words, 'All animals are equal but some animals are more equal than others'?
2. Which numbered road was designated by the Ministry of Transport in 1921 following the route of the Great North Road?
3. A drawer contains ten red socks and ten blue socks. Without looking, how many socks would have to be picked to be absolutely sure of having a pair of red socks?
4. Which medical condition takes its name from the French word for 'yellow'?
5. For which global competition was Kiri Te Kanawa's 'World in Union', with which she had her only UK chart hit in 1991, the theme music?
6. Which word, meaning 'to destroy', is derived from the Roman practice of punishing mutinies by killing every tenth person?
7. *The Rime of the Ancient Mariner* is told at what social gathering?
8. What was the name of the store founded by Richard Block and David Quayle in Southampton in 1969?
9. What does the *Mona Lisa* have on her left hand?
10. In which American city would one find the Liberty Bell?
11. How many letters are there in the Greek alphabet?

---

* The Liberal Arts of antiquity describe the pursuit of knowledge by free men, as distinct from activities carried out by working men such as trades or crafts (the servile arts). The Liberal Arts represented the intellectual capital of the social élite, those people who did not have to work for a living.

12. Which muscle in the human body is capable of exerting the greatest force?

13. Which two teams compete in the Potteries Derby?

14. Which artistic movement were Goya, Munch and Van Gogh said to belong to?

15. Who is the Princess Royal married to?

16. Which form of government was introduced to England by Simon de Montfort in 1265?

17. When was the Jules Rimet Trophy last awarded?

18. The word used to describe bulk, unsolicited email is thought to derive from a sketch by which comedy performers?

19. Who was shot by Denis 'Sonny' O'Neill in County Cork in 1922?

20. Which two nations compete for the Bledisloe Cup?

21. Which London landmark was designed by David Marks and Julia Barfield?

22. Which TV weather presenter has a famous footballing father?

23. Which was the first film that Alfred Hitchcock made in Hollywood and the only of his films to win a Best Picture Oscar?

24. A snail is at the bottom of a well. The well is thirty feet deep. The snail can climb three feet during the day, but always slides back two feet during the night. How long will it take the snail to reach the top of the well?

WONDERS OF THE NATURAL WORLD Name the *seven* wonders of the natural world. Find the solution on page 318. [Target: 3]

COUNTRIES IN CENTRAL AMERICA Name the *seven* countries in Central America*. Turn to page 338 for the solution. [Target: 6]

AIRPORT CODES II Identify the cities that are served by these airports from the three-letter IATA codes listed. The solutions are on page 214. [Target: 18]

1.	LHR	2.	MIA
3.	ATL	4.	SYD

---

* Note that Mexico is technically part of North America.

5.	LTN	6.	MAD
7.	ZRH	8.	MAN
9.	FRA	10.	PEK
11.	SIN	12.	STN
13.	CPH	14.	DUB
15.	DEN	16.	HAV
17.	PHX	18.	NCE
19.	GIG	20.	BFS
21.	SCL	22.	FCO
23.	HND	24.	YYZ

CHARACTERISTICS OF LIVING THINGS Identify the *seven* characteristics common to all living things. Turn to page 235 for the solution. [**Target: 5**]

HEPTARCHY Name the *seven* ancient kingdoms that gave rise to the Kingdom of England. Find the solution on page 255. [**Target: 4**]

AMERICANISMS I For each of these words, give the equivalent word or words that would be used in the US*. Look for the solutions on page 278. [**Target: 18**]

1.	Flat (place to live)	2.	Trousers
3.	Chips	4.	Autumn

---

* Anyone who has ever operated a modern computer will have noticed that the native language of these islands is no longer English but 'English (UK)'. As early as the start of the eighteenth century, British commentators were noting a divergence in the language either side of the Atlantic and making disparaging remarks about how Americans were misusing the mother tongue. Ironically, many of the differences could be accounted for by changes to the language in Britain rather than in America. Words such as 'trash' (rubbish), 'loan' (instead of lend) and 'gotten' (got) are all found in Shakespeare but have since fallen out of use in Britain. Shakespearian English is in many respects closer to American English than it is to English (UK). English in America differs still further because of its acceptance of words from the indigenous population (such as canoe, barbecue, savannah, hickory) and also from Spanish colonists (canyon, ranch, stampede). There has been no pattern or logic to the way the language has developed in either of the two countries. A fact that led Bill Bryson to once observe: 'How else could the American Postal Service deliver the mail when in Britain the Royal Mail delivers the post?'

5.	Nappy	6.	Solicitor
7.	Postcode	8.	Biscuit
9.	Aubergine	10.	Torch
11.	Jelly	12.	Handbag
13.	Estate car	14.	Boot (of a car)
15.	Spanner	16.	Chemist
17.	Dressing gown	18.	Windscreen
19.	Saloon car	20.	Estate agent
21.	Love bite	22.	Suitcase
23.	Music hall	24.	Paraffin

NOVELS BY THE BRONTË SISTERS Recall the titles of the *seven* novels* written by the Brontë sisters. Find the solution on page 298. [**Target: 3**]

CHART-TOPPING SINGLES BY KYLIE MINOGUE Name the titles of the *seven* chart-topping singles by Kylie Minogue. Turn to page 318 for the solution. [**Target: 3**]

LINKED MISCELLANY VI Answer these questions and deduce the theme that links them. Look for the solution on page 338. [**Target: 7**]

1. Which was the second James Bond film to star Roger Moore?
2. Which title is usually given to the second son of a British monarch?
3. Which actress and star of *The Night Porter* and *Angel Heart* was once married to Jean-Michel Jarre?
4. What did Sir Richard Branson offer to buy from British Airways on 10 April 2003?

---

* In the nineteenth century novels were being published in greater numbers than ever before. Often they were serialised in newspapers and magazines which were becoming increasingly popular, giving the public real access to literature for the first time. Victorian novels, unlike the romantic adventures of the previous century (such as Defoe's *Robinson Crusoe* or Swift's *Gulliver's Travels*), tended to be grounded in the social reality of the times and largely reflected the morals and aspirations of the middle classes who were now the most prolific writers. Reflecting the social changes taking place in Britain, literature by female writers rose to prominence for the first time in history, particularly the works of Jane Austen at the beginning of the century, and the Brontë sisters and George Eliot in the mid-nineteenth century.

5. Which 1934 novel was set in a school called Brookfield?
6. In which maritime fire disaster did 167 men lose their lives in July 1988?
7. Which historical figure had the nickname of 'Longshanks'?
8. Which Phil Collins album featured the tracks 'Sussudio', 'One More Night' and 'Don't Lose My Number'?
9. Which island has a patron saint called St Helier?
10. Which 1970 film starred Donald Sutherland and Elliot Gould?

CLASSICAL PLANETS Name the *seven* classical planets (celestial bodies that appear in classical astrology, alchemy, etc.). Find the solution on page 215. [**Target: 5**]

THE MAGNIFICENT SEVEN List the *seven* actors who played the title roles in the 1960 film. Turn to page 235 for the solution. [**Target: 4**]

NICKNAMES OF FOOTBALL TEAMS I Identify the English League football teams according to these nicknames. You will find the solutions on page 255. [**Target: 10**]

1.	Red Devils	2.	Saints
3.	Hammers	4.	Cottagers
5.	Addicks	6.	Baggies
7.	Gills	8.	Foxes
9.	Railwaymen	10.	Owls
11.	Canaries	12.	Potters
13.	Hornets	14.	The 'O's
15.	Seagulls	16.	Dale
17.	The Pool	18.	Valiants
19.	Lillywhites	20.	Shakers
21.	Cherries	22.	Shrimpers
23.	Quakers	24.	Glovers

COUNTRIES ENDING WITH ' ~ STAN' Name the *seven* countries with names which end in '-stan*. Go to page 278 for the solution. [**Target: 4**]

---

* 'Stan' is the Persian word for country.

COLOURS OF THE VISIBLE SPECTRUM Name the *seven* colours of the visible spectrum of light. The solution is on page 299. [Target: 7]

CHARACTERS IN LITERATURE II Identify the works of literature that feature these characters. For advanced play, name the authors as well. You will find the solutions on page 318. [Target: 12]

1.	Ebenezer Scrooge	2.	Ford Prefect
3.	Tess Durbeyfield	4.	Henry Higgins
5.	Bigwig	6.	Mr Rochester
7.	Emma Woodhouse	8.	Edwin Drood
9.	Atticus Finch	10.	Fitzwilliam Darcy
11.	Napoleon the Pig	12.	Lucy Honeychurch
13.	Jack Aubrey	14.	Ben Gunn
15.	Holly Golightly	16.	Titus Groan
17.	Dolores Haze	18.	Lyra Belacqua
19.	Wilkins Micawber	20.	Natasha Rostova
21.	Arthur 'Boo' Radley	22.	Widow Douglas
23.	Count Vronsky	24.	Gussie Fink-Nottle

TAXONOMY OF LIVING THINGS List the *seven* hierarchical categories into which living things are classified. Turn to page 338 for the solution. [Target: 3]

LONDON GATES List the *seven** historic gates to the City of London. Find the solution on page 215. [Target: 3]

MISCELLANY XI Answer these questions of a miscellaneous nature. Go to page 235 for the solutions. [Target: 14]

1. Which soap opera takes place in Weatherfield?
2. Which country begins with the letter 'O'?
3. Who were Juanito in 1970, Gauchito in 1978, Striker in 1994 and Footix in 1998?

---

* An eighth gate, Bridgegate, was not traditionally included in the list as it was outside of London; this allowed access to the city from the south at the southern end of London Bridge.

4. Cleopatra's four children were fathered by which two men?
5. How many hurdles does a competitor jump in the men's 110m hurdles race?
6. 'Voices rant on' is an anagram of which twelve-letter word?
7. Which sport features in the NATO phonetic alphabet?
8. How many people went on to Noah's Ark?
9. Pulmonology is associated with the study of diseases of which organ?
10. In which direction does the Severn Bore travel, upstream or downstream?
11. Which steam locomotive recorded a speed of 126mph in 1938, the fastest ever by a steam engine?
12. What is significant about a place that lies just east of Church Flatts Farm, approximately one mile south-east of Coton in the Elms, Derbyshire?
13. In which UK cathedral is the Whispering Gallery?
14. 'And when God saved the Queen she turned a whiter shade of pale' is a line from which 2006 hit?
15. What is the literal translation of the Latin phrase 'lapsus linguae'?
16. What does the F7 key do in Microsoft Word?
17. How is the aurora australis better known?
18. What instrument did Glenn Miller play?
19. What links Ian Lavender and Wendy Richard?
20. In which film does the character Popeye Doyle first appear?
21. A farmer keeps a number of geese and a number of pigs. If there are 32 eyes and 46 legs, how many pigs and how many geese are there?
22. In which year did ITV start broadcasting?
23. Who signs his letters with his Christian name, followed by the word 'Ebor'?
24. Two days ago I was fifteen years old. Next year I will be eighteen years old. What is today's date, and when is my birthday?

RUTSHIRE CHRONICLES List the *eight* novels by Jilly Cooper in the Rutshire chronicles. The solution may be found on page 255. [Target: 6]

CHANNEL ISLANDS Name the *eight* inhabited islands making up the group known as the Channel Islands. Find the solution on page 279. [Target: 4]

BRAT PACK Name the *eight* members of the Brat Pack*. The solution is on page 278. [**Target: 5**]

SPORTS GOVERNING BODIES II Identify the sports represented by these governing bodies. Go to page 299 for the solutions. [**Target: 14**]

1.	FA	2.	WBC
3.	UEFA	4.	USPGA
5.	NFL	6.	RFU
7.	IOC	8.	IRB
9.	ICC	10.	IRFB
11.	LPGA	12.	RYA
13.	RL	14.	CONMEBOL
15.	LTA	16.	IJF
17.	FIH	18.	IBA
19.	ISA	20.	WBB
21.	IWF	22.	FIDE
23.	FIVB	24.	TWIF

IVY LEAGUE Name the *eight* Ivy League institutions. Turn to page 319 for the solution. [**Target: 4**]

BRITISH FILM CLASSIFICATIONS Name the *eight* film ratings issued by the British Board of Film Classification. Find the solution on page 338. [**Target: 6**]

FIRST LINES OF POP SONGS III Identify the titles of these songs from the first lines below. (The year each song was a hit in the UK is given.) For advanced play, name the performers as well. Turn to page 215 for the solutions. [**Target: 12**]

1. 'Right about now.' (1998)
2. 'Enjoy this trip, enjoy this trip – and it is a trip.' (1988)

---

* The Brat Pack was a group of young actors and actresses who appeared together in the 1980s, mainly in teen-orientated films. Brat Pack films include *The Breakfast Club* (1985), *St Elmo's Fire* (1985), *Weird Science* (1985), *About Last Night* (1986), *Pretty in Pink* (1986) and *The Lost Boys* (1987).

3. 'Why do birds suddenly appear?' (1970)
4. 'There lived a certain man in Russia long ago.' (1978)
5. 'Got to get up, got to get up, got to get up.' (1989)
6. 'Hell is gone and heaven's here.' (1998)
7. 'What you want, baby I got.' (1967)
8. 'One, two, three, four, five, everybody in the car, so come on let's ride.' (1999)
9. 'I make it alone.' (1980)
10. 'Poor old Johnny Ray.' (1982)
11. 'I am just a poor boy though my story's seldom told.' (1969)
12. 'Yo listen up here's a story about a little guy that lives in a blue world.' (1999)
13. 'Street's like a jungle so call the police.' (1994)
14. 'I feel so extraordinary something's got a hold on me.' (1987)
15. 'There must be some kind of way out of here.' (1968)
16. 'Holly came from Miami FLA.' (1973)
17. 'I'll sing it onc last time for you.' (2004)
18. 'Once upon a time not so long ago.' (1986)
19. 'I was searchin' on a one-way street.' (1978)
20. 'Who knows what tomorrow brings?' (1983)
21. 'You never close your eyes any more when I kiss your lips.' (1965)
22. 'We walked in the cold air, freezing breath on the window-pane.' (1981)
23. 'On your mark, ready, set, let's go.' (1998)
24. 'If you like to gamble, I tell you I'm your man.' (1980)

WARSAW PACT Name the *eight* nations which were signatories of the Warsaw Pact*. Find the solution on page 236. [**Target: 6**]

---

* The Warsaw Pact was drafted by Russian President Nikita Khrushchev in response to the formation of NATO and it was signed in Warsaw in 1955. Although during the Cold War East and West never came into direct conflict, the Warsaw Pact often had to use military force to crush uprisings in member states (notably in Hungary in 1956 and Czechoslovakia in 1968). The Soviet policy towards the member countries was ominously stated in the so-called Brezhnev Doctrine: 'When forces that are hostile to socialism try to turn the development of some socialist country towards capitalism, it becomes not only a problem of the country concerned, but a common problem and concern of all socialist countries.'

AUSTRALIAN STATES AND TERRITORIES Name the *eight**
territories and states in Australia. Look for the solution on page 256.
[Target: 6]

INNOVATIONS I Identify the technical innovations† which were
created by these individuals or organisations. Turn to page 279 for
the solutions. [Target: 12]

1.   Alexander Graham Bell (1876)
2.   Orville and Wilbur Wright (1903)
3.   Johannes Gutenberg (1455)
4.   Charles Macintosh (1823)
5.   Guglielmo Marconi (1901)
6.   Sony (1979)
7.   John Boyd Dunlop (1888)
8.   Linus Yale (1848)
9.   IBM (1981)
10. James Watt (1769)
11. Michael Faraday (1831)
12. Alfred Nobel (1863)
13. Nikolaus Otto (1876)
14. Charles Pathé (1909)
15. Nestlé (1937)
16. Jacques and Joseph Montgolfier (1783)
17. Christiaan Barnard (1967)
18. Alessandro Volta (1800)
19. Joseph Lister (1867)
20. Otto Frisch, Niels Bohr and Rudolf Peierls (1939)
21. Frank Whittle (1937)
22. Christopher Cockerell (1959)
23. The Roslin Institute (1997)
24. Gabriel Fallopius (1560)

---

* There are two territories and six states in Australia.
† An innovation may be described as an invention or process for which a practical
use or application has been found. It is often said that necessity is the mother of
invention, which goes some way to explaining the huge leaps in technology that are
produced during periods of warfare (for example radar, modern computing, atomic
energy, rocket technology and the jet engine were all advanced by the Second World
War). But this is not always the case. It is noteworthy that the parachute was
invented some 300 years before the first powered flight.

UNITED NATIONS SECRETARIES GENERAL Name the *eight* people* to have held the position of UN Secretary General. The solution is on page 299. [**Target: 4**]

RESERVOIR DOGS Name the *eight* characters in the film *Reservoir Dogs*. You will find the solution on page 319. [**Target: 6**]

QUOTATIONS FROM POPULAR FILMS I Identify the films from which these quotations† are taken. (The date of the film is provided.) Look for the solutions on page 339. [**Target: 16**]

1. 'Escape is not his plan. I must face him. Alone.' (1977)
2. 'A census taker once tried to test me. I ate his liver, with some fava beans and a nice Chianti . . .' (1991)
3. 'At my signal, unleash hell.' (2000)
4. 'If my calculations are correct, when this baby hits eighty-eight miles per hour you're gonna see some serious shit.' (1985)
5. 'I remember the days of Sputnik and Yuri Gagarin, when the world trembled at the sound of our rockets. Now they will tremble again, at our silence.' (1990)
6. 'Your ego is writing checks your body can't cash.' (1986)
7. 'Look at that! Look how she moves! It's just like jello on springs.' (1959)
8. 'Stupid is as stupid does.' (1994)
9. 'Pay no attention to the man behind the curtain . . .' (1939)

---

* The list does not include Gladwyn Jebb of the UK, Acting Secretary General from 24 October 1945 to 2 February 1946, who supervised the election of the first incumbent.

† 'Bond. James Bond' is a likely candidate for the most memorable film quotation of all time and a phrase that would be recognisable to the estimated 3 billion people that the Bond franchise has reached. The line was first used in *Dr No* (1962) to introduce the character of Bond (played by Sean Connery) to cinema audiences. Bond is in a casino playing baccarat with Sylvie Trench (played by Eunice Gayson, the first Bond girl). Director Terence Young set the scene up with Connery's back to the camera. When Bond is addressed by Trench, his face is seen for the first time as he lights a cigarette and introduces himself:

James Bond: I admire your courage, Miss . . . ?
Sylvia Trench: Trench. Sylvia Trench. I admire your luck, Mr . . . ?
James Bond: Bond. James Bond.

10. 'Don't worry, princess. I used to be afraid of the dark until . . . No, wait. I'm still afraid of the dark.' (2001)

11. 'I'm sorry I ate your fish, OK?' (1988)

12. 'Your clothes, give them to me.' (1984)

13. 'It's a very difficult job and the only way to get through is we all work together as a team. And that means you do everything I say.' (1969)

14. 'Is it safe?' (1976)

15. 'You're crazy. You oughta be locked up. You, too. Two hundred and fifty guys just walking down the road, just like that?' (1963)

16. 'Failure is not an option.' (1995)

17. 'Me? I'm dishonest, and a dishonest man you can always trust to be dishonest. Honestly.' (2003)

18. 'I want you to hit me as hard as you can.' (1999)

19. 'One minute you're defending the whole galaxy, and, suddenly, you find yourself sucking down Darjeeling with Marie Antoinette and her little sister.' (1995)

20. 'The man is the head, but the woman is the neck. And she can turn the head any way she wants.' (2002)

21. 'I was born a poor black child.' (1979)

22. 'She's so deliciously low. So horribly dirty.' (1964)

23. 'I feel like I've been in a coma for the past twenty years. And I'm just now waking up.' (1999)

24. 'I'm walking here! I'm walking here!' (1969)

PLANETS List the *eight* planets in the solar system. Find the solution on page 216. [**Target: 8**]

REINDEER Name the *nine* reindeer that belong to Santa Claus. The solution is on page 236. [**Target: 4**]

QUOTATIONS FROM SHAKESPEARE II Identify the plays of Shakespeare* from which these quotations are taken. (Note the same

---

* *Macbeth*, one of Shakespeare's best known plays, tells the story of the eponymous king who ruled Scotland from 1040 until 1057. In the play Macbeth, encouraged by his devious and ambitious wife and the predictions of three witches, murders Duncan and becomes King in his place. Having gained the throne, Macbeth *cont'd over!*

play may be the solution to more than one of the quotations.) If you wish, also name the character who is quoted. Go to page 256 for the solutions. [**Target: 12**]

1. 'Et tu, Brutè?'
2. 'Cry, "God for Harry! England and Saint George!"'
3. 'Now is the winter of our discontent / Made glorious summer by this son of York'
4. 'Friends, Romans, countrymen, lend me your ears'
5. 'A pair of star-cross'd lovers take their life'
6. 'We will have rings, and things, and fine array / And kiss me Kate, we will be married o' Sunday'
7. 'O beware, my lord, of jealousy: / It is a green-eyed monster which doth mock the meat it feeds on'
8. 'A sad tale's best for winter'
9. 'A plague o' both your houses'
10. 'Once more unto the breach, dear friends, once more'
11. 'But soft! What light through yonder window breaks?'
12. 'A woman moved is like a fountain troubled, / Muddy, ill-seeming, thick, bereft of beauty'
13. 'Yet who would have thought the old man to have had so much blood in him?'
14. 'Murder most foul, as in the best it is'
15. 'By the pricking of my thumbs, / Something wicked this way comes'
16. 'You call me misbeliever, cut-throat, dog, / And spit upon my Jewish gabardine'
17. 'The course of true love never did run smooth'

---

cont'd   becomes increasingly paranoid, committing further crimes against those he believes are plotting against him. He eventually receives his comeuppance at the hands of Macduff and Malcolm (Duncan's son) is proclaimed King. As always, Shakespeare took small liberties with historical accuracy, wise, as he was, to the political sensibilities of the time and, more importantly, to make a better story. There is no evidence to suggest Macbeth was a particularly bad man (nor that Duncan was a particularly strong or wise king as the play portrays; the historical evidence is that he was weak and ineffective). Duncan was killed in battle rather than in cold blood and although Malcolm did defeat Macbeth in the Battle of Dunsinnan in 1054, it was Malcolm not Macduff that killed Macbeth and actually in battle at Lumphanan in 1057. This is, however, academic given *Macbeth*'s status as one of the greatest plays ever written.

18. 'The lady doth protest too much, methinks'
19. 'All that glisters is not gold'
20. 'I know a bank where the wild thyme blows / Where oxlips and the nodding violet grows / Quite over canopied with luscious woodbine / With sweet musk-roses and with eglantine'
21. 'But I will wear my heart upon my sleeve, for daws to peck at'
22. 'What's in a name? That which we call a rose / By any other word would smell as sweet'
23. 'Very tragical mirth'
24. 'This blessèd plot, this earth, this realm, this England'

FORBIDDEN IN SWIMMING POOLS Recall the *nine* activities traditionally forbidden in public swimming pools*. Look for the solution on page 299. [**Target: 7**]

MISCELLANY XII Answer these questions of a miscellaneous nature. You will find the solutions on page 319. [**Target: 14**]

1. What word means favouring of relatives or friends?
2. What links gazpacho soup with revenge?
3. Which famous building, completed in 1648, contains the tomb of Queen Mumtaz Mahal?
4. What runs approximately 270 miles from Edale in Derbyshire to Kirk Yetholm, just inside the Scottish border?
5. What links Uriah Heep and Claudia Schiffer?
6. How many sides does a standard pencil have?
7. 'Tossed Salad and Scrambled Eggs' is the closing tune to which long-running comedy?
8. If your geographical position was 0 latitude, 0 longitude, where in the world would you be?
9. Where was the body of George Mallory found in 1999, seventy-five years after his death?
10. Which well-known building burnt down in 675, 1087, 1136 and 1666?

---

* And specifically according to the well-known safety poster displayed in swimming pools in the 1970s and 1980s.

11. Which honour has been accorded once to Neil Amstrong and Winston Churchill, twice to Dwight D. Eisenhower and John Glenn, and seven times to the New York Yankees?

12. In which English county would you find the towns of Bolsover, Buxton and Bakewell?

13. What was the Wales Empire Swimming Pool demolished to make way for in 1999?

14. Which literary character had a housekeeper called Mrs Hudson?

15. 'W' is the symbol for which chemical element?

16. Who would normally carry a crosier?

17. Who was the first female DJ on Radio 1?

18. Who was the first Soviet leader to have been born after the 1917 revolution?

19. Which main character dies in *Harry Potter and the Half-Blood Prince*?

20. In which war were the battles of Bunker Hill and Brandywine Creek fought?

21. You have two hourglass timers; one runs for exactly two minutes, the other for exactly five minutes. Using only these devices, how could you time an egg to cook for exactly three minutes?

22. Which type of beans are used to make baked beans?

23. The Hindu god Ganesha is depicted with the head of which animal?

24. A woman goes into four shops. In each shop she pays an entry fee of £1, spends half of her money and on the way out puts £1 in the charity box. After leaving the fourth shop she has no money left. How much money did she begin with?

COUNTRIES ENDING WITH ' ~ LAND' Name the *nine* sovereign countries in the world whose names end in '-land'. Find the solution on page 339. [**Target:** 7]

BOOKS BY GEORGE ORWELL Name the *nine* books written by George Orwell*. Go to page 216 for the solution. [**Target:** 3]

---

* George Orwell was the pen name of Eric Arthur Blair.

RECENT HISTORY II Identify the correct year from each of these clues. Find the solutions on page 236. [**Target: 10**]

1. Dr Harold Shipman is sentenced to life imprisonment for killing fifteen people, although the total number of victims is feared to be much higher; New Zealand retains the America's Cup; the Tate Modern opens at Bankside; Concorde crashes in Paris and all Concorde flights are immediately suspended; the Russian submarine, the Kursk, sinks in the Barents Sea; George W. Bush is controversially elected US President, the result comes down to disputed votes in Florida; police foil an attempt to steal the Millennium Star diamond from an exhibition at the Millennium Dome; fears of worldwide failures to computer systems prove unfounded.

2. Peter Mandelson resigns from the Cabinet* for the second time; foot-and-mouth disease breaks out in the UK; Crown Prince Dipendra murders his father and other members of the Nepalese royal family before killing himself; the Labour Party is elected for a second term in government; Jeffrey Archer is imprisoned for perjury; 3,000 people are killed in the 9/11 terrorist attacks on the World Trade Center and the Pentagon; US and UK forces overthrow the Taliban in Afghanistan; Apple release the iPod; Enron files for bankruptcy; the film *The Fellowship of the Ring* is released.

3. Al-Qaeda bomb US embassies in Nairobi and Dar es Salam killing 224 people; the Good Friday Agreement is signed in Northern Ireland; Bill Clinton is challenged with impeachment over his affair with Monica Lewinsky; the number of AIDS sufferers reaches 33 million worldwide; *Titanic* wins eleven Oscars and becomes the highest-ever grossing film; the US

---

* Although it has no legal powers as such, the Cabinet, a committee of Secretaries of State and other senior government positions, has a collective responsibility to Parliament for the decisions taken by the government. The modern history of the Cabinet had its beginnings with the Privy Council, a small group of men who gave advice to the monarch. Sir Robert Walpole, the first British Prime Minister, further developed the concept by holding meetings of the King's Ministers. The 1832 Reform Act emphasised the need for the government to have the confidence of Parliament, thus causing the convention of collective Cabinet responsibility to develop. The Cabinet meets once a week, usually on Thursday morning.

Department of Justice file an antitrust case against Microsoft; Cornershop top the charts with 'Brimful of Asha'; France beat Brazil 3–0 to win the World Cup.

4. Yitzhak Rabin is assassinated; O.J. Simpson is found not guilty of murder; Timothy McVeigh bombs an Oklahoma government building killing 168 people; the war in Bosnia ends; Pierce Brosnan plays James Bond for the first time; Blackburn Rovers win the Premiership; Nick Leeson is arrested over his role in the collapse of Barings Bank; DVD format is defined; the European Court of Justice announces the Bosnan Ruling in relation to football transfers; Princess Diana talks openly about her marriage in an interview broadcast on *Panorama*.

5. Deep Blue, an IBM computer, beats Garry Kasparov at a game of chess; beach volleyball debuts as an Olympic sport; eight climbers die in bad weather on Mount Everest; the Prince and Princess of Wales divorce; Kabul falls to the Taliban; Bill Clinton is elected for a second term; the Spice Girls top the charts with 'Wannabe'.

6. Louise Brown becomes the world's first test-tube baby; John Paul II is named as Pope; the Camp David treaty between Egypt and Israel is brokered by President Jimmy Carter; Sid Vicious murders Nancy Spungen; the *Amoco Cadiz* runs aground off the coast of Brittany, Argentina hosts the World Cup and also wins it.

7. Apollo 11 astronauts Neil Armstrong and Buzz Aldrin are the first men to set foot on the moon; British troops are sent to Northern Ireland; El Salvador and Honduras go to war over a football match; Concorde* makes its maiden flight; the

---

* Concorde 001 flew from Toulouse in March of this year and Concorde 002 from Bristol in April with regular passenger services beginning in 1976 (the British Airways Concorde made its maiden passenger flight from Heathrow to Bahrain, the Air France Concorde from Paris to Rio de Janeiro). Concorde was capable of cruising at a speed of Mach 2 and in 1983 set the record for the fastest flight from New York to London at two hours and fifty-six minutes. Sadly, the economics of air travel always worked against Concorde and the early promise of orders from other countries dried up. Only twenty Concordes were ever built: two prototypes, two pre-production and sixteen production models, split equally between Air France and British Airways. In spite of huge increases in the demand for air travel in the last thirty years, it has been for cheap rather than quick flights and the Boeing 747 has emerged as the world's leading passenger aircraft. The Paris crash *cont'd over/*

Woodstock music festival takes place; the Harrier jump jet enters service with the RAF, John Lennon and Yoko Ono marry.

8. Palestinian terrorists murder eleven Israeli athletes at the Munich Olympics; the Watergate building is burgled in Washington; the Bloody Sunday shootings take place in Derry; Jane Fonda tours North Vietnam; the pocket calculator is introduced; Richard Nixon visits China; *The French Connection* wins the Oscar for Best Picture; Bobby Fischer defeats Boris Spassky to become world chess champion.

9. Allied forces land in Normandy on D-Day; a German counter-offensive takes place resulting in the Battle of the Bulge; the Siege of Leningrad is finally relieved by Russian forces; the Bretton Woods conference takes place to establish a framework for post-war economic development; Rome and Paris are liberated; Anne Frank and her family are discovered in hiding by the Gestapo.

10. Terry Waite is taken hostage in Lebanon; 193 people lose their lives when the *Herald of Free Enterprise* capsizes; southern England is hit by hurricane force winds causing widespread damage; President Reagan admits the Iran Contra affair; a fire at King's Cross underground station kills thirty-six people; Coventry City win the FA Cup; West German pilot, Mathias Rust, lands a private plane in Red Square in Moscow; Lester Piggott is jailed for tax evasion.

11. The Winter Olympics take place in Lillehammer; the first female priests are ordained by the Church of England; Nelson Mandela becomes President of South Africa; the Channel Tunnel opens; *Schindler's List** wins seven Oscars; Ayrton Senna dies at the San

---

cont'd saw Concorde jump from being statistically the safest aircraft in the world (with no fatal accidents in thirty years – a single incident of a blown tyre in 1979) to one of the most dangerous, due to the relatively few number of flights it had made (less than 100,000). This, combined with the 2001 terror attacks which depressed the airline industry, led to the retirement of Concorde in 2003 leaving jet-setters at the mercy of no-frills travel.

* The book on which the film was based was *Schindler's Ark*, written by Thomas Keneally. In October 1980, while en route to the airport, Keneally visited a luggage shop in Beverly Hills to buy a new briefcase. The shop was owned by Leopold Pfefferberg, one of the 1,200 people saved by Oskar Schindler, who would tell his story to any writer, producer or director who came into his store. Pfefferberg (who produced two filing cabinets of documents backing up his claims) was able to convince Keneally to tell his story and it became his next book.

Marino Grand Prix; Tony Blair becomes leader of the Labour Party; Wet Wet Wet top the charts with 'Love Is All Around'; Al Gore chairs the Superhighway Summit to discuss the growing importance of the Internet.

12. The Panama Canal opens; the Home Rule Act is passed to enable Irish self-government; Archduke Franz Ferdinand of Austria is assassinated; Babe Ruth makes his debut for the Boston Red Sox; St Petersburg changes its name to Petrograd; the first successful blood transfusion is made.

13. Britain joins the EEC; coal strikes force the British Government to declare a three-day working week; Richard Nixon is sworn in for a second term; Arab oil producers blockade oil supplies to the West, leading to a global energy crisis; the US completes its withdrawal from Vietnam; *The Godfather* wins the Oscar for Best Picture; Pink Floyd release *The Dark Side of the Moon*; the Sydney Opera House is opened by the Queen.

14. Hong Kong falls to the Japanese; Germany invades Russia; Japanese air forces mount a surprise attack on the US naval base at Pearl Harbor; the *Bismarck* is sunk by the British Navy; penicillin is used for the first time; Orson Welles directs *Citizen Kane**.

15. North Vietnam mounts the Tet Offensive; Martin Luther King and Robert Kennedy are assassinated; Russia sends tanks into Czechoslovakia; astronauts orbit the moon for the first time in Apollo 8; mass student protests take place in Paris.

16. Margaret Thatcher is elected leader of the Conservative Party, *The Rocky Horror Picture Show* opens in New York, the Birmingham Six are sentenced to life imprisonment, Queen release 'Bohemian Rhapsody', *One Flew Over a Cuckoo's Nest* wins five Oscars including Best Film, Best Actor and Best Director.

17. Queen Victoria dies; President William McKinley is assassinated; the Boxer Rebellion ends in China; the Royal Navy launches its first submarine; Marconi receives the first transatlantic radio communication†.

18. Indira Gandhi becomes Prime Minister of India; the Cultural Revolution begins in China; Luna 6 makes the first soft landing

---

* The film is based on William Randolph Hearst, who was so angered that he accused Orson Welles of being a communist in an unsuccessful bid to prevent its release.

† A transmission of the letter 's' in Morse code (i.e. three dots).

on the moon; Ronnie Kray murders George Cornell in the Blind Beggar pub; John Lennon makes the controversial comment that the Beatles are 'more popular than Jesus'; the Beach Boys release *Pet Sounds*; Moors Murderers Myra Hindley and Ian Brady are sentenced to life imprisonment; the Beatles play their last ever concert at Candlestick Park in San Francisco.

19. King George V dies; Edward VIII abdicates in order to marry American divorcée Wallis Simpson; Germany occupies the Rhineland; the Spanish Civil War begins; Mao Tse-tung begins the Long March; Hitler purges the Nazi Party in 'the night of the long knives'.

20. Yuri Gagarin becomes the first man in space; Cuban rebels assisted by US forces land at the Bay of Pigs; the Berlin Wall is raised; John F. Kennedy is inaugurated as US president; UN General Secretary Dag Hammarskjöld is killed in a plane crash.

21. Alaska and Hawaii join the United States, becoming the forty-ninth and fiftieth states; Fidel Castro seizes power in Cuba; the Dalai Lama is forced to flee Tibet; the first section of motorway opens in Britain.

22. Peace is achieved between the combatants in the Balkan War but tensions in the region continue to simmer; Emily Davison is killed at the Derby when she throws herself under the King's horse; the first ever crossword is published in *New York World*; the Seventeenth Amendment allows American Senators to be elected for the first time; Vincencio Peruggia tries to sell the stolen *Mona Lisa* in Florence and is arrested.

23. San Francisco is destroyed by a severe earthquake; the Simplon tunnel is opened between Italy and Switzerland to become the world's longest tunnel; 'SOS' becomes an international distress signal; Rolls-Royce is founded; HMS *Dreadnought* is launched, revolutionising battleship design and leading to a major arms race in the build up to the First World War.

24. Ernest Rutherford proposes the theory of atomic structure; Roald Amundsen reaches the South Pole; Standard Oil is broken up under antitrust laws; the first coast-to-coast flight of the US is made by Calbraith Rogers (with sixty-nine stops and sixteen crash landings); Italy declares war on Turkey in its attempt to conquer Tripolitania (Libya); Machu Picchu is discovered in the Peruvian Andes.

THE FELLOWSHIP OF THE RING Name the *nine* characters who made up the Fellowship of the Ring in the novel by J.R.R. Tolkien. Go to page 256 for the solution. [**Target: 8**]

POKER HANDS List the *nine* types of hand in poker. Find the solution on page 280. [**Target: 8**]

CHARACTERS IN LITERATURE III Identify the works of literature in which these characters appear. For advanced play, name the authors as well. The solutions are on page 300. [**Target: 12**]

1.	Phileas Fogg	2.	The Queen of Hearts
3.	Ratty	4.	The Miller
5.	Bob Cratchit	6.	Captain Ahab
7.	Uriah Heep	8.	Dorian Gray
9.	Oliver Mellors	10.	Alexey Karenin
11.	Bill Sikes	12.	Catherine Earnshaw
13.	Charles Chipping	14.	Tonya Gromeko
15.	Lord Sebastian Flyte	16.	Pinkie Brown
17.	Meggie Cleary	18.	Christopher Boone
19.	Pandora Braithwaite	20.	Alex DeLarge
21.	Stephen Wraysford	22.	Aunt Polly
23.	Blind Pew	24.	Fanny Price

LOSING WORLD CUP FINALISTS Name the *nine* countries that have lost in the final of the World Cup. Turn to page 319 for the solution. [**Target: 7**]

MOST OSCAR-NOMINATED ACTORS Name the *ten* actors who have received seven or more Oscar* nominations in their careers. You can find the solution on page 339. [**Target: 5**]

---

* The Oscar statuette was designed in 1927 by Cedric Gibbons, MGM Art Director, who was to win the award himself eleven times. The first Oscars were made of bronze although plaster was substituted during the war. Today they are fashioned from gold-plated Britannium (an alloy of tin, copper and antimony). The statuette is 13½ inches tall and weighs 8lb.

LINKED MISCELLANY VII In providing the correct solutions to these questions, deduce the connecting theme that links them. Go to page 216 for the solution. [**Target: 5**]

1. Which BBC soap opera was axed in July 1993 after only a year of production?
2. Which product is advertised with the tagline 'Bow chicka wah wah'?
3. With which team did Walter Payton and William 'The Refrigerator' Perry win Super Bowl XX in 1986?
4. Of which society are Isaac Asimov, Sir Clive Sinclair, Charles Ingram and Carol Vorderman all members?
5. Which Michael Crichton novel recounts the story of an outbreak of an extraterrestrial micro-organism which causes in its victims sudden and deadly clotting of the blood?
6. Which river runs from the Tibetan Plateau, through Kashmir, and emerges in the Arabian Sea near Karachi?
7. Which mountain range, located between Southern Turkey and Northern Syria, has a pass known in antiquity as the Cilician Gates, through which the armies of Alexander the Great and the Crusaders both passed?
8. Oncology is the medical term for the study and treatment of which disease?
9. The name of which performing artist provides the cockney rhyming slang for a prolonged drinking session?
10. Which four-engine turboprop aircraft is the main transport aircraft of the RAF?

PLAGUES OF EGYPT Name the *ten* plagues of Egypt, as told in Exodus in the Old Testament. You will find the solution on page 236. [**Target: 5**]

TYPES OF CLOUD List the *ten* types of naturally forming* clouds. Go to page 256 for the solution. [**Target: 7**]

---

* Additionally, the condensation trails left across the sky by aeroplanes (contrails) are technically classified as a type of cloud.

PHOBIAS Identify the stimuli which trigger these phobias. Turn to page 280 for the solutions. [**Target: 12**]

1.	Claustrophobia	2.	Technophobia
3.	Arachnophobia	4.	Xenophobia
5.	Bacteriophobia	6.	Agoraphobia
7.	Aviophobia	8.	Ornithophobia
9.	Haemophobia	10.	Acrophobia
11.	Heliophobia	12.	Demophobia
13.	Coitophobia	14.	Noctiphobia
15.	Ablutophobia	16.	Androphobia
17.	Bathophobia	18.	Brontophobia
19.	Spermaphobia	20.	Ophidiophobia
21.	Sesquipedalophobia	22.	Pentheraphobia
23.	Triskaidekaphobia	24.	Hexakosioihexekontahexaphobia

DOCTORS WHO Name the *eleven* actors to have played Doctor Who in the long-running BBC television series*. Find the solution on page 300. [**Target: 7**]

COUNTRIES WITH FOUR-LETTER NAMES Name the *ten* countries which have four-letter names. The solution is on page 319. [**Target: 6**]

ARTISTS Identify the artists† who created these works. You will find the solutions on page 339. [**Target: 12**]

---

* Peter Cushing starred as the Doctor in the films *Dr Who and the Daleks* (1965) and *Daleks' Invasion Earth: 2150 A.D.* (1966)

† Many artists have called on a mathematical idea known as the Golden Ratio in their work. It is a number that approximates to 1.618 and is normally represented by the Greek letter phi (f) but has some unusual mathematical properties. In antiquity it was believed that shapes derived using the ratio were aesthetically pleasing; this is evident in many examples of ancient architecture, including occurrences in the Parthenon in Athens and the Great Pyramid at Giza. The idea resurfaced during the Renaissance after the publication in 1509 of the *Divina Proportione* by Luca Pacioli which greatly influenced contemporary artists. A golden ratio can be found in the face of the *Mona Lisa* as well as in the dimensions of the painting itself.

1. *Mona Lisa (La Giaconda,* 1503–6), *The Last Supper (c.*1495–8)
2. *Starry Night* (1889), *Sunflowers* (1888), *The Potato Eaters* (1885)
3. *The Haywain* (1821), *Salisbury Cathedral* (1823)
4. *The Creation of Adam** (1508–12), *David* (1501–4)
5. *Water-Lilies* (1914), *Gare Saint Lazare, Paris* (1877), *Impression: Sunrise* (1873)
6. *The Birth of Venus (c.*1485), *Primavera (c.*1482)
7. *Guernica* (1937), *Three Dancers* (1925), *Les Demoiselles d'Avignon* (1907)
8. *Campbell's Soup Can* (1964), *Marilyn* (1964)
9. *The Scream* (1893)
10. *Christ of St John of the Cross* (1951), *The Persistence of Memory* (1931)
11. *The Fighting Temeraire* (1838), *Rain, Steam and Speed* (1844)
12. *The Milkmaid (c.*1658–60), *Girl with a Pearl Earring (c.*1665)
13. *A Bar at the Folies-Bergère* (1882), *Olympia* (1863)
14. *Luncheon of the Boating Party* (1881), *La Moulin de la Galette* (1876), *Umbrellas* (1883)
15. *Bacchus and Ariadne* (1520–2), *The Assumption* (1516–18)
16. *As I Opened Fire* (1964), *Whaam!* (1963)
17. *The Snail* (1953), *Blue Nude IV* (1952)
18. *The Kiss* (1908), *Danae* (1907–8)
19. *Dance Class* (1874), *Orchestra Musicians* (1870–1)
20. *The Betrothal of the Arnolfini* (1434)
21. *The Night Watch* (1642), *The Feast of Belshazzar (c.*1635)
22. *The Ambassadors* (1533), *Portrait of Sir Thomas More* (1527)
23. *Garden of Earthly Delights (c.*1510), *The Ship of Fools* (1490–1500)
24. *The Hunters in the Snow* (1565), *Children's Games* (1560)

CRICKETING DISMISSALS Name the *ten* ways in which a batsman may be dismissed in a game of cricket. Go to page 216 for the answer. [**Target: 8**]

COMMANDMENTS Recall the *Ten* Commandments. Find the solution on page 236. [**Target: 5**]

---

* Fresco in the Sistine Chapel.

MISCELLANY XIII Answer these questions of a miscellaneous nature. Go to page 257 for the solutions. [**Target: 8**]

1. Which word for madman is derived from a French word meaning 'moonstruck'?
2. Which is the nearest planet to earth?
3. Which sculptor created *The Thinker*?
4. What links the brand names of Nike, Flora and Mars?
5. Which British coin ceased to be legal tender in 1984?
6. The flag of which country includes a blue wheel at its centre known as Ashoka Chakra?
7. What name is given to the line that darts players must stand behind when they throw?
8. Which spice comes from the crocus?
9. With which London street is Sweeney Todd associated?
10. In 2005, whose ashes were fired from a cannon on top of a 150-foot tower to the sound of Bob Dylan's 'Mr Tambourine Man'?
11. In humans, which sex possesses both X and Y chromosomes?
12. Apart from London, which three other cities in Britain have an underground railway system?
13. Which two sequels have won a Best Picture Oscar?
14. Who said to whom, 'You're a drunk, a tramp, and an unfit mother'?
15. Who composed *Carmen*?
16. In the context of geography, what is the opposite of oriental?
17. Which famous book, published in 1816, is subtitled *The Modern Prometheus*?
18. Which British city hosted the 1958 Commonwealth Games?
19. In which city would you find an arch called 'The Gateway to India'?
20. The supporters of which deposed British king were known as Jacobites?
21. Who played Tony Manero in a 1978 film?
22. During the course of a party, everybody shook hands with everybody else. There were sixty-six handshakes. How many people were there at the party?

23. What happened in Britain between 3 and 13 September 1752?

24. On Wednesday, when Sally is visiting Molly's house, she remarks that the clock is five minutes slow. Molly says that it loses five minutes every hour. The following week, Sally visits Molly and notices the clock is telling the right time. 'You've fixed your clock,' says Sally. 'No I haven't,' says Molly. What day is it?

TEST CRICKET NATIONS Name the *ten* nations that play test cricket. (That is, nations which have had test status conferred by the International Cricket Council.) You will find the solution on page 280. [**Target: 9**]

MEMBERS OF ASEAN List the *ten* members of the Association of Southeast Asian Nations. The solution is on page 300. [**Target: 6**]

POLITICAL QUOTATIONS Identify the authors of these quotations of a political* nature. Note that more than one of these quotations may be attributable to the same author. The solutions may be found on page 319. [**Target: 16**]

1. 'You turn if you want to. The lady's not for turning.'
2. 'I did not have sexual relations with that woman.'
3. 'Today, in the world of freedom, the proudest boast is, "Ich bin ein Berliner."'
4. 'I have a dream that one day this nation will rise up and live out the true meaning of its creed.'
5. 'There can be no whitewash at the White House.'
6. 'Read my lips. No new taxes.'
7. 'A week is a long time in politics.'

---

* The political soundbite has gained major importance in the media age. A soundbite is a short excerpt – usually one line – from a longer delivery which very simply encapsulates the message which its author is attempting to put across. Although politicians (and their spin doctors) try to deliver soundbites in every speech they write, the ones that truly resonate can often do so inadvertently and may even have negative connotations.

8. 'Now this is not the end. It is not even the beginning of the end. But it is, perhaps, the end of the beginning.'
9. 'England expects every man will do his duty.'
10. 'Ask not what your country can do for you; ask what you can do for your country.'
11. 'I came, I saw, I conquered.'
12. 'Religion is the opium of the people.'
13. '. . . government of the people, by the people, for the people.'
14. 'I know I have the body but of a weak and feeble woman; but I have the heart and stomach of a king.'
15. 'From Stettin in the Baltic to Trieste in the Adriatic, an iron curtain has descended across the Continent.'
16. 'It is true that you may fool all of the people some of the time; you can even fool some of the people all of the time; but you can't fool all of the people all of the time.'
17. 'Let us be frank about it. Most of our people have never had it so good.'
18. 'Who will rid me of this turbulent priest?'
19. 'This is the second time in our history that there has come back from Germany to Downing Street peace with honour. I believe it is peace for our time.'
20. 'The buck stops here.'
21. 'Power is the ultimate aphrodisiac.'
22. 'Power grows out of the barrel of a gun.'
23. 'We will bury you.'
24. 'Trust in God and keep your powder dry.'

EVENTS IN THE DECATHLON Recall the *ten* events in the decathlon. Find the solution on page 340. [**Target: 8**]

OLOGIES II Describe the subjects that are studied in each of these disciplines. Look for the solutions on page 237. [**Target: 10**]

1.	Arachnology	2.	Parapsychology
3.	Seismology	4.	Gastroenterology
5.	Osteology	6.	Etymology
7.	Palaeontology	8.	Hippology

9.	Ophthalmology	10.	Topology
11.	Toxicology	12.	Cryptology
13.	Lexicology	14.	Allergology
15.	Pharmacology	16.	Oncology
17.	Mycology	18.	Epistemology
19.	Pedology	20.	Dendrochronology
21.	Graphology	22.	Angiology
23.	Speleology	24.	Vexillology

MAJOR WINE REGIONS OF FRANCE List the *ten* major French wine regions. Find the solution on page 280. [**Target: 6**]

LINKED MISCELLANY VIII Answer these questions and deduce the connecting theme that links them. Find the solution on page 301. [**Target: 5**]

1. Which 1979 film starring Dustin Hoffman and Meryl Streep won the Oscar for Best Picture?
2. Which US state is named after an English queen?
3. Which group released albums called *Borbolletta*, *Amigos* and *Abraxus*?
4. Who wrote *Doctor Zhivago*?
5. In the original film, who is the Terminator sent to kill?
6. Aside from the moon, what is the brightest object in the night sky?
7. Which German 'Pocket Battleship' was scuttled after the Battle of the River Plate?
8. Which group had a UK hit with 'Erasure-ish' following Erasure's hit with 'Abba-esque'?
9. How is fermented pear juice better known?
10. Which was the only song from Michael Jackson's *Thriller* album to go to number one in the UK?

WEALTHIEST FOOTBALL CLUBS Name the *ten* wealthiest football clubs in the world. Turn to page 320 for the solution. [**Target: 8**]

ROYAL PARKS Name the *ten* public parks* in London which are managed by the Royal Parks. You can find the solution on page 340. [**Target: 5**]

BRITISH OLYMPIANS I Identify these British Olympians† from their medal honours. The solutions are on page 217. [**Target: 8**]

1. Rower winning gold in the Coxed Fours at Los Angeles in 1984; gold in Coxless Pairs and bronze in the Coxed Pairs at Seoul in 1988; gold in the Coxless Pairs at Barcelona in 1992; gold in the Coxless Pairs at Atlanta in 1996; gold in the Coxless Fours at Sydney in 2000.
2. Ice dancers winning gold in the Ice Dance at Sarajevo in 1984 and bronze in the Ice Dance at Lillehammer in 1994.
3. Athlete winning gold in the Decathlon at Moscow in 1980 and gold in the Decathlon at Los Angeles in 1984.
4. Athlete winning gold in the 1500m and silver in the 800m at Moscow in 1980 and gold in the 1500m and silver in the 800m at Los Angeles in 1984.
5. Athlete winning gold in the Heptathlon at Sydney in 2000 and bronze in the Heptathlon at Atlanta in 1996.
6. Athlete winning gold in the 800m and silver in the 1500m at Moscow in 1980.
7. Cyclist winning gold in the 1km time trial in Athens in 2004 and gold in the Team Sprint, Keirin and Sprint at Beijing in 2008.

---

* In Victorian times the capital's parks were known as the 'Lungs of London' and for good reason. The city was permanently shrouded in smoke and soot and the green spaces not only gave Londoners places to escape the grime but were actually able to clean the air of its pollutants. The Victorians were deliberate in their widespread planting of the London plane tree, which can be seen today in virtually every green space in the municipality. London plane trees have distinctive flaky bark which is continually renewed, preventing their trunks from becoming caked in soot. Their leaves are covered in minute hairs which attract dust and smoke particles, removing them from the air to be washed away by the next rain shower. Given that each of the giant trees has an estimated total leaf area of around 900m^2, their capacity to remove pollution from the air is significant.

† At the inaugural modern Olympics in Paris in 1896, there were 245 competitors from fifteen different countries. This figure has grown every year since – the 2004 Athens Olympics featured 11,099 competitors from 202 countries.

8. Athlete winning gold in the 100m and silver in the 200m, Moscow 1980.
9. Swimmer winning gold in the 400m Freestyle and gold in the 800m Freestyle in Beijing in 2008.
10. Athlete winning silver in the Javelin at Seoul in 1988 and bronze in the Javelin at Los Angeles 1984.
11. Athlete winning silver in the 1500m at Los Angeles in 1984.
12. Athlete winning silver in the 400m and silver in the 4x400m Relay at Atlanta in 1996 and bronze in the 4x400m Relay at Barcelona in 1992.
13. Swimmer winning gold in the 100m Breaststroke at Seoul in 1988.
14. Competitor* winning bronze in the Middleweight Judo at Munich in 1972.
15. Athlete winning silver in the 4x100m Relay at Seoul in 1988 and bronze in the 4x400m Relay at Barcelona in 1992.
16. Athlete winning bronze in the 10,000m at Montreal in 1976.
17. Athlete winning gold in the Long Jump at Tokyo in 1964.
18. Athlete winning gold in the Javelin at Los Angeles in 1984.
19. Athlete winning silver in the 10,000m at Seoul in 1988.
20. Boxer winning bronze in the Light Middleweight Boxing at Munich in 1972.
21. Athlete winning gold in the 20km Walk at Tokyo in 1964.
22. Swimmer winning gold in the 200m Breaststroke, and silver in the 100m Breaststroke at Montreal in 1976 and silver in the 200m Breaststroke at Munich in 1972.
23. Athlete winning gold in the 100m and silver in the 4x100m Relay at Paris in 1924.
24. Athlete winning gold in the 50km Walk at Rome in 1960.

1966 WORLD CUP WINNERS Name the *eleven* English players who appeared in the final of the World Cup in 1966. The solution is on page 237. [**Target: 8**]

TRAGEDIES BY SHAKESPEARE List the *eleven* tragedies written by Shakespeare. The solution is on page 216. [**Target: 6**]

---

* Participants in judo are known as Judoka.

FILMS STARRING GRACE KELLY Name the *eleven* films in which Grace Kelly* starred. Find the solution on page 257. [Target: 3]

CAPITAL CITIES IV Identify the countries which have these capital cities. The solutions can be found on page 280. [Target: 12]

1.	Vienna	2.	Kingston
3.	Teheran	4.	Beirut
5.	Kathmandu	6.	Islamabad
7.	Damascus	8.	Manila
9.	La Paz	10.	Kabul
11.	Tallinn	12.	Dar es Salaam
13.	Kampala	14.	Vilnius
15.	Asunción	16.	Bridgetown
17.	Port-of-Spain	18.	Skopje
19.	Freetown	20.	Muscat
21.	Managua	22.	Yaoundé
23.	Suva	24.	Santo Domingo

WACKY RACERS Recall the *eleven* teams who competed in the Wacky Races. Look for the solution on page 301. [Target: 4]

MINERALS List the *eleven* minerals that are required as part of a healthy human diet. Find the solution on page 320. [Target: 5]

MISCELLANY XIV Answer these questions of a miscellaneous nature. The solutions may be found on page 340. [Target: 14]

1. In electronics, what does LED stand for?
2. What links London, Avonmouth and paper?
3. Who was the first person to be pictured on a postage stamp?
4. How did chemists John Lea and William Perrins achieve fame?
5. In which sport would you go to a Basho?
6. What device, invented in 1817 by Sir David Brewster, was given a name from Greek meaning 'viewer of beautiful shapes'?

---

* Later Princess Grace of Monaco.

---

7. What Japanese word means 'loveable egg'?

8. Which national daily paper has the Crusader as its logo?

9. Where is the Simpson Desert?

10. Who was the last English king to die in battle?

11. Which two teams compete in the 'Old Farm Derby'?

12. What landmark would you find in La Place de la Concorde in Paris, Central Park in New York and Victoria Embankment in London?

13. Where in the human body would you find loops and whorls?

14. Who wrote *Under Milk Wood*?

15. What was unusual about Holly Hunter's Oscar-winning performance?

16. A drawer contains six red socks and six blue socks. Without looking, how many socks would have to be picked out of the drawer to be absolutely sure of having a pair the same colour?

17. What does 'Vorsprung durch Technik' mean in English?

18. Which country has a flag consisting of a single colour?

19. What does P&O stand for?

20. Which two words are pronounced the same but do not share any common letters? (two possibilities)

21. Where is Parkhurst prison?

22. Which musician was the first to be awarded a gold disc, for sales of over a million records?

23. Which science fiction character took his name from a 1950s British car?

24. A right-handed glove is inverted and worn on the left hand. Which part of the hand (i.e. the palm or the back) is now in contact with the palm of the glove?

SCOTTISH FOOTBALL CHAMPIONS Name the *eleven* Scottish football teams to have won the title of Scottish League* Champions. Find the solution on page 217. [**Target: 8**]

---

* The Scottish Football League was formed in 1890, two years after the English League, in Holten's Hotel in Glasgow. A second division was added in the 1893/4 season and the league has since grown to four divisions. During the 1963/4 campaign in the old Scottish second division a meeting between Forfar Athletic and East Fife produced the following scoreline: Forfar 5, East Fife 4

CONFEDERACY Name the *eleven* Southern States which made up the Confederacy* of 1861 to 1865. The solution may be found on page 237. [**Target: 7**]

SCANDALS Identify the individuals at the centre of these scandals. Turn to page 257 for the solutions. [**Target: 14**]

1. British pop star arrested for committing a 'lewd act' in a public toilet in Beverly Hills.
2. Government minister who resigned after rumours circulated about his affair with a call-girl Christine Keeler and her relationship, in turn, with Soviet naval attaché, Yevgeny Ivanov.
3. Athlete who was stripped of his Olympic 100m gold medal after failing a drugs test.
4. Pop star alleged to have engaged in sexual activities with teenage boys during sleepovers at his house, but who was acquitted of all charges at trial.
5. Cabinet Minister who resigned for using his position to assist a passport application for his girlfriend's nanny.
6. Film star who was arrested by Los Angeles Police for indecent conduct in a car with prostitute Divine Brown.
7. Cabinet minister who was revealed to have had an affair with his diary secretary, Tracey Temple.
8. Pop star who experienced a 'wardrobe malfunction' during the half-time show of the Super Bowl, generating thousands of complaints from viewers.
9. Cabinet minister who resigned in 1998 for accepting an interest-free loan from Geoffrey Robinson, the Paymaster General.
10. Government minister who resigned in 1986 after allegations were made of his relationship with a prostitute and who was jailed in 2001 for committing perjury in the subsequent libel case.
11. Cabinet minister who resigned after fathering a child with his secretary, Sarah Keays.

---

* The Confederate States of America declared their independence from the United States of America following the election of Abraham Lincoln with a policy of abolition of slavery. The CSA was never formally recognised by the Union which held its existence as illegal and the Confederacy collapsed following the surrender of General Robert Lee to Union forces in April 1965.

---

12. Film director who separated from his partner after she discovered he had taken nude photos of his adopted daughter (whom he later married).

13. Cabinet minister who resigned after 'kiss-and-tell' allegations were made by actress Antonia de Sancha.

14. Footballer who was sent home from the 1994 World Cup after playing only two matches, following a positive test for ephedrine.

15. Liberal Democrat Home Affairs spokesman who resigned in 2006 after he was revealed to have had an affair with a male prostitute.

16. Television news and sports presenter whose career ended after revelations of a private life that involved wearing lingerie and taking cocaine at sex parties.

17. Biological weapons expert who committed suicide after talking to journalist Andrew Gilligan about the validity of the British Government's claims about Iraq's military capability.

18. Cabinet minister who resigned in 1998 after a 'moment of madness' on Clapham Common.

19. Liberal Party leader who resigned after allegations were made of his involvement in a plot to kill his gay lover, Norman Scott.

20. Olympic ice skater involved in a conspiracy to harm fellow competitor Nancy Kerrigan at the US Figure Skating Championships in 1994, causing an injury which forced Kerrigan to withdraw.

21. Television evangelist who lost his ministry after being photographed meeting prostitutes in 1988.

22. Conservative MP found dead in his flat wearing women's stockings reportedly as a result of auto-erotic asphyxiation.

23. Government minister who resigned in 1973 after photographs of him in bed with prostitute Norma Levy were published in the *News of the World.*

24. British society figure, known as the 'Dirty Duchess' after explicit pictures of her and a 'Headless Man' became public during her 1963 divorce case.

COUNTRIES ON THE EQUATOR Name the *eleven* countries through which the Equator passes. Look for the solution on page 280. [**Target: 5**]

WORDS CONTAINED IN 'THEREIN' Identify the *twelve* words that are contained in the word 'therein' (without rearranging or separating any letters). Find the solution on page 257. [**Target: 9**]

SIGNS OF THE ZODIAC Name the *twelve* signs of the zodiac (of Western astrology). Go to page 301 for the solution. [**Target: 12**]

FORMS OF ADDRESS Identify the correct forms of spoken address for each of these social ranks. (For example, one would address a Marquess as 'My Lord'.) The solutions may be found on page 320. [**Target: 8**]

1. An Anglican priest
2. A Roman Catholic priest
3. A knight
4. A circuit judge (when addressed in court)
5. The Queen (when addressed for the first time)
6. The Queen (when addressed subsequently)
7. A prince (when addressed for the first time)
8. A prince (when addressed for the second time and subsequently)
9. An ambassador
10. The Pope
11. A princess (when addressed for the second time and subsequently)
12. An archbishop
13. A male High Court judge (when addressed in court)
14. A bishop
15. A secretary of state
16. A countess
17. A duke
18. A baroness
19. A duchess
20. A cardinal
21. A baron
22. An earl
23. A female High Court judge (in court)
24. An archdeacon

GREEK GODS Name the *twelve* gods of the Dodekatheon: those gods who, according to Greek mythology, resided on Mount Olympus. Find the solution on page 341. [**Target: 6**]

MEMBERS OF OPEC List the *twelve* members of the Organisation of Petroleum Exporting Countries (OPEC). Turn to page 257 for the solution. [**Target: 6**]

NICKNAMES OF FOOTBALL TEAMS II Identify the English Football League teams which have these nicknames. The solutions may be found on page 237. [**Target: 8**]

1. Boro
2. Pompey
3. Black Cats
4. Toffeemen
5. Blades
6. Rams
7. Tractor Boys
8. Sky Blues
9. Citizens
10. Lions
11. Eagles
12. Villains
13. Dons
14. Pilgrims
15. Hatters
16. Irons
17. Minsters
18. Tangerines
19. Pirates
20. Royals
21. Silkmen
22. Swans
23. Trotters
24. Bluebirds

RUSSIAN HERO CITIES Name Russia's *twelve* Hero Cities*. Go to page 301 for the solution. [**Target: 5**]

ORIGINAL MEMBERS OF THE FOOTBALL LEAGUE Name the *twelve* original and founding members of the English Football League. Turn to page 320 for the solution. [**Target: 6**]

MISCELLANY XV Answer these questions of a miscellaneous nature. Find the solutions on page 341. [**Target: 14**]

1.   Which American state has previously been under French, Spanish and Mexican control?
2.   Thespis, in 535BC, is thought to be the first member of which profession?
3.   What were Juno, Sword and Gold?
4.   Which is the most common street name in Britain?
5.   Which American institution has its headquarters in Langley, Virginia?
6.   Which was the first colour film to win the Oscar for Best Picture?
7.   In snooker, what colour is the ball placed in the middle of the straight side of the 'D'?
8.   What links Copenhagen with the Battle of Waterloo?
9.   What cargo was carried by the *Cutty Sark*?
10. Which singer was once married to Renata Blauel?
11. In which publication would you find the columns 'Street of Shame' and 'Rotten Boroughs'?
12. What type of military hardware is associated with the designers Mikoyan and Gurevich?
13. What colour is a CO_2 fire extinguisher?
14. Which are the only two English words containing the letter group 'sthm'?
15. Illustrated on its logo, the product Marmite is named after a French word meaning what?

---

* 'Hero City' is an honorary title awarded by the Soviet Union in recognition of mass acts of heroism in some its cities during the Second World War (the Great Patriotic War). The Hero City is issued with the Order of Lenin and the Gold Star Medal. An obelisk is also erected in the city to mark the achievement.

16. Which extra terrestrial was the nemesis of Dan Dare?
17. Charing Cross is the name of a station in London and which other British city?
18. A rope ladder hangs over the side of a ship with rungs that are one metre apart. The incoming tide rises at the rate of 80cm an hour. If, at low tide, water just covers the bottom rung, how many rungs are covered three hours later?
19. Who directed *Alien*?
20. Which English letter corresponds with the letter 'c' in Cyrillic?
21. From which flower are vanilla pods obtained?
22. Who is the only person to have won both an Oscar and a Nobel Prize?
23. What comes next in the following sequence: red, blue, white, black, orange, _____?
24. You have a three-gallon jug, a five-gallon jug and an ample supply of water. How can you measure four gallons of water?

CREATURES IN CHINESE ASTROLOGY Name the *twelve* creatures in Chinese* astrology. Find the solution on page 217. [**Target: 10**]

CHRISTMAS GIFTS Name the *twelve* gifts sent by 'My True Love' in 'The Twelve Days of Christmas'. The solution is on page 237. [**Target: 10**]

COOKING TERMS II Identify the cooking terms and dishes from the descriptions provided. Find the solutions on page 258. [**Target: 10**]

1. Small cubes of fried bread used as a garnish for soups.
2. A Mexican dip made from avocado, garlic and lime juice.
3. Chicken stuffed with garlic, butter and chives, covered in breadcrumbs and fried.
4. Small pasta squares stuffed with meat or vegetables.
5. French sauce made from egg yolk, butter and vinegar; served with eggs benedict.

---

* Chinese horoscopes relate to the twelve-year cycle of the Chinese calendar and the association of an animal with each year of the cycle.

6. A style of Indian cooking (literally meaning 'bucket') where dishes are cooked in a karahi (a small, two-handled wok-shaped pan).

7. The French term for a clear soup.

8. The Italian term for toasted bread brushed with oil and garlic and served with a variety of toppings.

9. A spicy pork sausage from Spain or Mexico.

10. A green Italian pasta sauce made from olive oil, pine nuts, garlic and basil.

11. A French term meaning 'cooked slowly in the oven with cream and garlic'.

12. The French term for vegetables cut into thin strips.

13. The food flavouring made from sodium salt and glutamic acid.

14. A French term meaning 'between the ribs' usually applied to steak.

15. A Provençal fish stew cooked in a strongly flavoured stock, usually with saffron and tomatoes.

16. Oysters wrapped in bacon.

17. The French term for a smooth and thick fruit or vegetable purée (literally 'strained').

18. The French term for custard.

19. Bow-tie- or butterfly-shaped pasta.

20. Italian omelette usually made with meat, cheese and vegetables.

21. Spiral-shaped pasta.

22. Soya-bean paste used in Japanese cooking.

23. Paste made from black olives, anchovies and capers often served on crostini or bruschetta.

24. A French white sauce flavoured with onion.

LINES ON THE LONDON UNDERGROUND List the *twelve* lines of the London Underground*. Find the solution on page 280. [**Target: 11**]

APOSTLES Name the *twelve* Apostles. Look for the solution on page 301. [**Target: 5**]

---

* Note that the list does not include the Docklands Light Railway, national rail lines or tramlines.

DICTATORS Identify the dictators* of these countries from the period of their rule. The solutions are on page 320. [**Target: 16**]

1. Germany 1933–45
2. USSR 1924–53
3. Iraq 1979–2003
4. Cuba 1959–present
5. Zimbabwe 1980–present
6. Uganda 1971–9
7. Italy 1922–43
8. Cambodia 1976–9
9. China 1935–76
10. Iran 1979–89
11. Spain 1939–75
12. Serbia / Yugoslavia 1989–2000
13. Chile 1973–1990
14. Panama 1983–9
15. North Korea 1994–present
16. Romania 1965–89
17. Philippines 1965–86
18. Yugoslavia 1945–80
19. Ethiopia 1930–6; 1941–74
20. Democratic Republic of Congo 1997–2001
21. Liberia 1997–2003
22. Fiji 2000
23. Malawi 1963–97
24. Nigeria 1993–8

---

* The first use of the term dictator was to describe a temporary executive of the Roman Republic, invested with absolute power as an emergency measure deployed during wartime. Probably the best known of these was Lucius Quinctius Cincinnatus, a farmer, who was called to the Senate in 460BC when the Roman Army had got itself into difficulty with the neighbouring Aequi. Although invited to rule for a six-month period, Cincinnatus took just two weeks to defeat the Aequi and sixteen days after taking office was able to return to his farm. The modern use of the word describes an autocratic or tyrannical leader who usually controls a brutal or oppressive regime. Regardless of where in the world they set up their rule, dictatorships have many common characteristics: a swift and often violent rise to power, a preoccupation with remaining in power as long as naturally possible and a tendency to amass huge fortunes and/or to kill a lot of people. Some dictators fall from power as swiftly and violently as they ascended, but a surprising number manage to live out their entire lives in relative comfort.

CHART-TOPPING SINGLES BY MADONNA Name the *thirteen* singles by Madonna* which have topped the UK charts. Go to page 341 for the solution. [**Target: 5**]

CHARACTERS IN DAD'S ARMY Name the *twelve* main characters that regularly featured in *Dad's Army*. Look for the solution on page 217. [**Target: 9**]

LINKED MISCELLANY IX Answer these questions and deduce the connecting theme that links them. Find the solution on page 238. [**Target: 8**]

1.   Who is Belfast City Airport named after?
2.   What do farriers make?
3.   Who played Pamela Ewing in *Dallas*?
4.   What is another name for an apiary?
5.   Which glamour model first found fame at the age of sixteen when she was runner-up as the 'Face and Shape of 1983'?
6.   In which sport would you find googlies and yorkers?
7.   What is the US intercity bus service called?
8.   What in Britain is the equivalent of the dauphin in France?
9.   What is the name of the Japanese flag?
10. Where is the British Prime Minister's country residence?

SGT. PEPPER'S LONELY HEARTS CLUB BAND Recall the *twelve* tracks on *Sgt. Pepper's Lonely Hearts Club Band*, the acclaimed Beatles album. (Note there are thirteen actual tracks but one is repeated.) You will find the solution on page 258. [**Target: 7**]

FILMS BY STANLEY KUBRICK Name the *thirteen* feature films directed by Stanley Kubrick. Go to page 281 for the solution. [**Target: 5**]

---

* Born Madonna Louise Ciccone in Bay City, Michigan, in 1958, Madonna first broke into the US charts in 1983 and appeared in the British charts the following year. Her lengthy and consistently successful career can in part be attributed to her ability to reinvent herself and her careful selection of writers and producers with whom she collaborates.

TAGLINES OF POPULAR FILMS II Identify the films from their taglines and dates of release. The solutions are on page 302. [**Target: 16**]

1. 'Houston, we have a problem.' (1995)
2. 'They're on a mission from God.' (1980)
3. 'He's having the day of his life . . . over and over again.' (1993)
4. 'Twelve is the new eleven.' (2004)
5. 'The list is life.' (1993)
6. 'Five criminals. One line up. No coincidence.' (1995)
7. 'How far does a girl have to go to untangle her tingle?' (1972)
8. 'A comedy about the greatest love story almost never told . . .' (1998)
9. 'Come to laugh, come to cry, come to care, come to terms.' (1983)
10. 'Revenge is a dish best served cold.' (2004)
11. 'Collide with destiny.' (1997)
12. 'An undercover cop in a class by himself.' (1990)
13. 'A hero will rise.' (2000)
14. 'On the air, unaware.' (1998)
15. 'One dream. Four Jamaicans. Twenty below zero.' (1993)
16. 'Boy, have we got a vacation for you . . .' (1973)
17. 'An epic of miniature proportions.' (1998)
18. 'How the West was lost!' (1965)
19. 'They're not just getting rich . . . they're getting even.' (1983)
20. 'Flesh seduces. Passion kills.' (1992)
21. 'An assassin on the loose. A president in danger. Only one man stands between them . . .' (1993)
22. 'Introducing the plans for a new business venture.' (1969)
23. 'Love is in the hair.' (1998)
24. 'What's a little murder among friends?' (1984)

EUROZONE List the *sixteen* member states of the Eurozone, that is, countries which have adopted the Euro* as their currency. The solution is on page 321. [**Target: 10**]

---

* There are more than 600 billion euros in circulation.

COUNTRIES WITH NAMES CONTAINING ADJECTIVES List the *thirteen* countries with names that contain adjectives (but excluding adjectives in the titles of countries, for example 'Democratic'). Turn to page 341 for the solution. [**Target: 7**]

NOTORIOUS SHIPS II Identify each of these ships from the clues provided. Find the solutions on page 218. [**Target: 12**]

1. Vessel that sailed from Plymouth to Cape Cod in Massachusetts in 1620 carrying pilgrim fathers who founded the first colony in New England.
2. Argentine warship controversially sunk during the Falklands Conflict with the loss of 323 lives.
3. Vessel on which Columbus first sailed to the New World in 1492.
4. Cross-channel ferry that capsized near Zeebrugge in 1987 with the loss of 187 lives.
5. Clipper built in 1869, currently a museum ship in Greenwich.
6. Ship whose final voyage was from Hong Kong in 1997 carrying Chris Patten and Prince Charles, after which she was decommissioned.
7. Russian attack submarine that sank in 2000 with the loss of her entire crew.
8. German battleship sunk in 1941 after an engagement with the British Navy in which HMS *Hood* was sunk.
9. Supertanker that ran aground off the coast of Alaska in 1989 causing widespread environmental damage.
10. Ship completed in 2003 and currently the largest passenger liner in the world.
11. English warship sunk in Portsmouth Harbour, possibly due to poor seamanship, in 1545.
12. US aircraft carrier on which the Japanese surrender in the Second World War was officially taken in 1945.
13. British battleship launched in 1906 that so revolutionised battleship design that existing vessels became regarded as obsolete.
14. Vessel that sank after becoming trapped in pack ice on Shackleton's ill-fated Antarctic expedition of 1914–16.

15. Supertanker that ran aground off Land's End in 1967.
16. Warship decommissioned in 1838 and the subject of a painting by Turner.
17. Warship captained by Francis Drake during the attack of the Spanish Armada.
18. Captain Pugwash's pirate ship.
19. Italian cruise liner sunk by a collision with another liner, the *Stockholm*, in fog in the Atlantic in 1956.
20. The first iron-hulled warship, built in 1861.
21. Captain Ahab's whaling vessel in *Moby-Dick*.
22. The first ever iron-clad and turreted warship, which took part in the Battle of Hampton Roads on 9 March 1862 during the American Civil War.
23. British battleship commissioned in 1946 and the last battleship to be built by the British Navy.
24. American battleship commissioned in 1916 and sunk during the Japanese attack on Pearl Harbor in 1941.

PUNCTUATION Identify the *thirteen* types of punctuation marks used in written English. Turn to page 238 for the solution. [**Target: 10**]

CANADIAN PROVINCES AND TERRITORIES Name the *thirteen* provinces and territories of Canada. Find the solution on page 258. [**Target: 4**]

MISCELLANY XVI Answer these questions of a miscellaneous nature. Turn to page 281 for the solutions. [**Target: 8**]

1. If it rains on St Swithin's Day, for how many more days is it supposed to rain?
2. In which city would you find the Spanish Steps?
3. In a modern three-pin electrical plug, what is the colour of the live wire?
4. Montezuma II was the last Emperor of which civilisation?
5. What international standard measures 210mm x 297mm?
6. What type of cheese do competitors chase in the annual Coopers Hill Cheese Run and Wake in Gloucestershire?
7. What common English word is derived from the phrase 'God be with you'?

8. According to the song, what did Molly Malone sell on the streets of Dublin?
9. What links England, Portugal and Georgia?
10. What links the death of Henry VI with telephone caller identification?
11. Which fabric is woven from metallic yarns and has a name deriving from the Latin 'lamina' meaning a thin layer of metal?
12. Which English county gave its name to a geological era?
13. Which character is the female lead in *Chitty Chitty Bang Bang*?
14. In which organ of the body is insulin produced?
15. How much is a monkey?
16. On which island is Osbourne House, the former home of Queen Victoria?
17. Who wrote the novel *A Parliamentary Affair*?
18. Which television character lived at Number 52, Festive Road?
19. The assault on which D-Day beach is depicted in *Saving Private Ryan*?
20. Who was king of England in 1065?
21. A clock chimes to signal six o'clock (with six chimes) in five seconds. How long will it take for the same clock to signal twelve o'clock?
22. Which family* have produced three generations of Oscar-winners?
23. The town of Ytterby in Sweden is unique in having given its name to four types of what?
24. When the day after tomorrow is yesterday, then today is as far away from Saturday as the day that was today when the day before yesterday was tomorrow. What day is it tomorrow?

VITAMINS Name the *thirteen* vitamins that are required as part of a healthy diet. Find the solution on page 302. [**Target: 6**]

COUNTRIES IN SOUTH AMERICA Name the *thirteen* countries in the continent of South America. Turn to page 321 for the solution. [**Target: 11**]

---

* Two families have achieved this, name either.

IMPERIAL UNITS Identify the single imperial unit* that measures each of the quantities presented. The solutions are on page 342. [Target: 12]

1.	12 inches	2.	3 feet
3.	16 ounces	4.	1/36 yard
5.	1/8 gallon	6.	14 pounds
7.	5,280 feet	8.	4 quarts
9.	20 hundredweight	10.	1/20 pint
11.	4,840 square yards	12.	1/8 mile
13.	16 drams	14.	4 inches
15.	2 yards	16.	112 pounds
17.	3 nautical miles	18.	1/10 furlong
19.	2 pints	20.	5 fluid ounces
21.	6,076 feet	22.	120 acres
23.	18 inches	24.	8 gallons

NATIONAL PARKS Name the *thirteen* national parks in England and Wales. Go to page 218 for the solution. [Target: 8]

COUNTRIES BORDERING CHINA List the *fourteen* countries that border China. Turn to page 238 for the solution. [Target: 9]

LAST LINES OF POPULAR FILMS I Identify each film from its concluding line of dialogue. (The date of the film is provided to assist you.) Find the solutions on page 258. [Target: 10]

1. 'The name's Bond . . . James Bond.' (2006)
2. 'I'm not gonna leave here ever, ever again because I love you all! And oh, Auntie Em, there's no place like home!' (1939)
3. 'I do wish we could chat longer, but I'm having an old friend for dinner.' (1991)

---

* The imperial system of units originated in Britain and is so called because of its export and use in the colonies of the British Empire. The system has been largely abandoned in the UK and the Commonwealth, losing its legal status in the UK in 1995 (although the use of pints, miles, acres and troy ounces is still permitted). Imperial units, in spite of their irregularity, are still in widespread use in the United States.

4. 'Louis, I think this is the beginning of a beautiful friendship.' (1942)
5. 'The greatest trick the Devil ever pulled was convincing the world he didn't exist. And like that, he's gone.' (1995)
6. 'I hope I can make it across the border. I hope to see my friend and shake his hand. I hope the Pacific is as blue as it has been in my dreams. I hope.' (1994)
7. 'It was Beauty killed the Beast.' (1933)
8. 'Roads? Where we're going, we don't need roads.' (1985)
9. 'Hey, I don't have all the answers. In life, to be honest, I failed as much as I succeeded, but I love my wife, I love my life, and I wish you my kind of success.' (1996)
10. 'He's my brother.' (1983)
11. 'Way to go, Paula! Way to go!' (1982)
12. 'The horror. The horror.' (1979)
13. 'Mein führer! I can walk!' (1964)
14. 'Good. For a moment there, I thought we were in trouble.' (1969)
15. 'Alright Mr De Mille. I'm ready for my close-up.' (1950)
16. 'It will be a love story . . . for she will be my heroine for all time. And her name will be . . . Viola.' (1998)
17. 'You be careful John Book, out among them English!' (1985)
18. 'The old man was right, only the farmers won. We lost. We'll always lose.' (1960)
19. 'Some men get the world, others get ex-hookers and a trip to Arizona.' (1997)
20. OK folks, nothin' to worry about. Just a little illness. We'll be in Miami in just a few minutes.' (1969)
21. 'Oh, yes, I believe in friends, I believe we need them, but if, one day, you find you can't trust them any more, well, what then, what then? (1994)
22. 'This is Hollywood. Always time to dream, so keep on dreamin'.' (1990)
23. 'This was the story of Howard Beale, the first known instance of a man who was killed because he had lousy ratings.' (1976)
24. 'Madness. Madness.' (1957)

PEOPLE PICTURED ON BANK NOTES Name the *fourteen* people to have been pictured on bank notes issued by the Bank of England. The solution is on page 282. [**Target: 10**]

MARX BROTHERS FILMS Name the *fourteen* Marx Brothers films. You will find the solution on page 302. [**Target: 4**]

AMERICANISMS II Supply the equivalent word or words that would be used in the US. The solutions are on page 321. [**Target: 18**]

1.	Confectionery	2.	Lift (in a building)
3.	Crisps	4.	Petrol
5.	Curriculum vitae	6.	Draughts (game)
7.	Cupboard	8.	Curtains
9.	Tap (for water)	10.	Motorway
11.	Queue	12.	Pavement
13.	Underground (metro)	14.	Dinner jacket
15.	Courgette	16.	Jam
17.	Noughts and crosses (game)	18.	Sweet potato
19.	Cashier	20.	Refrigerator
21.	Braces	22.	Pushchair
23.	Budgerigar	24.	Undertaker

BRITISH NOBILITY Identify the *fourteen* titles of the British nobility. (Note the list includes both masculine and feminine variants.) Find the solution on page 342. [**Target: 10**]

COUNTRIES BORDERING RUSSIA List the *fourteen* countries that have borders with Russia. Go to page 218 for the solution. [**Target: 9**]

CHARACTERS IN CHILDREN'S TELEVISION I Name the children's television programmes that featured these characters. The solutions are on page 238. [**Target: 16**]

1. Bungle, George, Zippy
2. Brian, Florence, Mr Rusty
3. Tomsk, Bungo, Wellington

4. Madeleine, Gabriel, Emily
5. Benny the Ball, Choo Choo, Spook
6. Colonel K, Agent 57, Baron Silas Greenback
7. Dai Station, Owen the Signal, Idris the Dragon
8. Getafix, Vitalstatistix, Dogmatix
9. Ethel Meaker, Fred Mumford, Nadia Popov
10. Willo, Mavis Cruet, the Moog
11. Tripitaka, Sandy, Yu Lung
12. Bella, Fizz, Milo
13. Gulliver, Scampi, Flash
14. Sir Basil, Lady Rosemary, Constable Knapweed
15. Colonel White, Captain Magenta, Lieutenant Green
16. Posie, Perkins, Pootle
17. Princess, Jason, 7-Zark-7
18. Chas, Gillespie, Delilah
19. Mrs Goggins, Mrs Hubbard, PC Selby
20. Mr Spoon and his family
21. Lord Belborough, Brackett, Mr Clutterbuck
22. Hector, Zsa Zsa, Kiki
23. Hercules, Astrea, Mercury
24. Mummy, Daddy, Spotty Dog

POSITIONS IN A RUGBY UNION TEAM Name the *fourteen* unique positions in a rugby union side (there are fifteen positions but one is duplicated). Go to page 259 for the solution. [**Target: 12**]

MUSICALS BY ANDREW LLOYD WEBBER Name the *fourteen* musicals composed by Andrew Lloyd Webber. The solution is on page 282. [**Target: 8**]

'ISMS' I Identify the philosophies, beliefs, concepts or practices from the descriptions provided. (Note that all of the solutions contain the suffix '-ism'.) You will find the solutions on page 303. [**Target: 14**]

1. The practice of exclusion of meat and fish from diet.
2. An eponymous ideological theory or practice based on the works of Karl Marx and Friedrich Engels.

3. A doctrine defined separately as either the entire Christian religion or the branch of the Christian religion distinct from Protestantism and Eastern Orthodoxy.

4. The belief in the non-existence of God.

5. A hostility or institutionalised prejudice against Jews.

6. The promotion of the rights of women and of gender equality.

7. The practice of deriving pleasure from the combination of inflicting and receiving physical or emotional abuse.

8. The economic system in which capital and the means of production are privately owned and not subject to Government intervention.

9. The favouritism shown to relatives by those in positions of power.

10. A political ideology that emerged in Europe in the 1920s emphasising the power of the State, the right of a self-constituted élite to run it, the desirability of war to advance it and the ruthless exclusion of political ideologies, religions or ethnic groups deemed not to fit with the vision of the State.

11. The doctrine founded by Prince Siddhartha Gautama, known as 'The Enlightened One', in which a cycle of lives leading to nirvana is a central belief.

12. A political system in which Governmental power is divided between a centre and autonomous regional units.

13. The view that matter and material items are the only reality and emotions and mental experiences can be described in material terms; the desire for material or monetary items over spiritual or ethical pursuits.

14. The advocacy of the abolition of Government and State apparatus and the rule of law.

15. An ambiguous term meaning either a general opposition to change or a political ideology incorporating beliefs such as advocacy of minimal Government intervention, tight fiscal control and protection of existing social conventions.

16. The oldest of the three desert monotheist religions, from which both Christianity and Islam developed.

17. An eponymous political and ethical ideology inspired by the teaching of Confucius.

18. A social system in which serfs are bound to work for landowners in return for security and justice.

19. The doctrine that all human beings are equal and the advocacy of equality through political means.

20. The moral philosophy proposed by John Stuart Mill and Jeremy Bentham that the greatest happiness of the greatest number of people is the central criterion to morality.

21. A belief, in contrast to the doctrine of free will, which asserts all actions and events are pre-determined and causally linked and that only a single set of outcomes is possible in the future.

22. A philosophical movement asserting the meaning of the human state should be derived from the beliefs, experiences and choices of the individual and in contradiction to classical philosophy which sought to understand the meaning of the human state and derive from this how humans should behave. The movement was promoted particularly by the work of Jean-Paul Sartre, Friedrich Nietzsche and Albert Camus*.

23. The philosophical view that the world and all human experience is without meaning.

24. The belief that statements are only meaningful so long as they are empirical (measurable) or tautological (true or false by definition); a statement such as 'God exists' being neither measurable by human experience nor provable by logic would be irrelevant in this philosophy.

HOST COURSES OF THE OPEN CHAMPIONSHIP List the *fourteen* golf courses† that have hosted the Open Championship. Go to page 321 for the solution. [**Target: 5**]

ENGLAND FOOTBALL MANAGERS Name the *fifteen* people to have managed the England football team. Find the solution on page 342. [**Target: 8**]

MISCELLANY XVII Answer these questions of a miscellaneous nature. The solutions are on page 218. [**Target: 10**]

1. In geometry, what type of line bisects a circle?
2. Who wrote *The Blue Danube*?

---

* Camus played in goal for Algeria until tuberculosis cut short his football career. He once said: 'All I know most surely about morality and obligations, I owe to football.'
† Of these, nine are currently in regular rotation.

3. In *A Christmas Carol*, what did the Cratchits have for their Christmas dinner?
4. Which year followed 1BC?
5. Who wrote the novels *The Invisible Man* and *The Island of Doctor Moreau*?
6. What links the M1 with the A74?
7. In which city is the European Central Bank?
8. Which is the only London tube line to connect with every other tube line?
9. What is Spider-Man's real name?
10. Which fictional football team did Roy of the Rovers play for?
11. What would a sitting MP need to do to be appointed to the position of Steward of the Chiltern Hundreds?
12. What links Scott of the Antarctic with a 'Maneater'?
13. Which international footballer described English defenders as 'the noblest in the world'?
14. What is Adam's Ale?
15. What does VSOP on a brandy bottle stand for?
16. Which fabric is so named because it originally came from the French town of Nîmes?
17. Scotia was the Roman name for which region of the UK?
18. Which fictional character was based on the exploits of a mutinous Scottish sailor named Alexander Selkirk?
19. Which major American city is named after a British Prime Minister?
20. 'Tanner' was the slang term for which pre-decimal British coin?
21. If you were born on the Feast of Epiphany, which star sign would you be?
22. Which five cities beginning with the letter 'M' have hosted the Summer Olympic Games?
23. Whose catchphrase was 'Heavens to Murgatroid'?
24. A tramp discovers that he can roll a new cigarette from the tobacco of seven discarded cigarette butts. He picks up forty-nine butts and decides to smoke all the cigarettes he can make from them. How many cigarettes did he smoke?

COMIC OPERAS BY GILBERT AND SULLIVAN Name the *fourteen* comic operas by Gilbert and Sullivan. Find the solution on page 239. [**Target:** 5]

UNION OF SOVIET SOCIALIST REPUBLICS Recall the *fifteen* member nations of the USSR*. Turn to page 259 for the solution. [**Target: 10**]

FORMER NAMES OF COUNTRIES What are these countries called today? The solutions may be found on page 282. [**Target: 10**]

1. Rhodesia
2. Persia
3. Ceylon
4. Siam
5. Kampuchea
6. Mesopotamia
7. Dutch East Indies
8. Abyssinia
9. Tripolitania
10. Transjordan
11. East Pakistan
12. Outer Mongolia

---

* When the Cold War was at its height, the Soviet Union and United States employed a military defence strategy known as Mutually Assured Destruction. Under this strategy, a large nuclear capability was amassed in order to deter an opponent from launching a pre-emptive strike; although certain to be destructive, such a strike would effectively be suicidal as it would ensure an equally destructive retaliation. A potential flaw in the strategy was that it placed a good deal of faith in electronic detection and early warning systems and in the individuals who operated them. One such individual was a Russian colonel named Stanislav Petrov who worked in a military bunker just outside Moscow. Just past midnight on the morning of Monday 26 November 1983, Colonel Petrov was alerted by a warning of the approach of an incoming American ICBM. This was followed by further warnings consistent with a pre-emptive nuclear strike against the Soviet Union. The correct procedure for Petrov was to alert the Soviet high command who may have ordered a counter-strike against NATO. Petrov's intuition was not to trust his computer system and as such he did not respond to the warnings as he should. When the expected strike failed to materialise, while Petrov's judgement was proved to be correct, his failure to follow orders resulted in him being taken for questioning and reassigned and he left the military soon after. The events of that September day came to light in 1998 after the break-up of the Soviet Union and, although his mother country never recognised the significance of his actions, Petrov received recognition of sorts from a California-based organisation called the Association of World Citizens who in 2004 honoured him with its World Citizen Award. He received a trophy and $1,000.

13. Formosa
14. British Honduras
15. South West Africa
16. Upper Peru
17. New France
18. Aden
19. Upper Volta
20. Gold Coast
21. Trucial States*
22. Basutoland
23. Bessarabia
24. Seven Sisters

WORLD CUP HOST NATIONS Name the *sixteen* countries to have hosted the World Cup. The solution is on page 303. [**Target: 11**]

FILMS BY DAVID LEAN Recall the *sixteen* films directed by David Lean. Find the solution on page 321. [**Target: 4**]

METRIC UNITS Identify the physical quantities that are measured by these SI units†. Turn to page 342 for the solutions. [**Target: 10**]

1.	Celsius (C)	2.	Decibel (dB)
3.	Ampere (A)	4.	Joule (J)
5.	Kelvin (K)	6.	Hertz (Hz)
7.	Watt (W)	8.	Pascal (Pa)
9.	Ohm (W)	10.	Newton (N)
11.	Volt (V)	12.	Candela (cd)
13.	Coulomb (C)	14.	Mole (mol)
15.	Radian (rad)	16.	Becquerel (Bq)

---

* So called because of a truce Britain had with a number of Arab sheiks in the nineteenth century.

† The metric system is analogous to the SI system of units which is widely adopted by the international scientific community. SI is an abbreviation of Système International d'Unités, the governing body for the system. The system defines a small number of base units; all other quantities (derived units) are derived from these units. Consequently under this system most measurable quantities that occur in nature are readily comparable and interchangeable. The base units are: metre, kilogram, second, ampere, Kelvin, mole and candela.

17.	Lux (lx)	18.	Steradian (sr)
19.	Tesla (T)	20.	Farad (F)
21.	Roentgen (R)	22.	Henry (H)
23.	Weber (Wb)	24.	Siemens (S)

NOVELS BY CHARLES DICKENS Name the *sixteen* novels written by Charles Dickens*. Turn to page 218 for the solution. [**Target: 8**]

FOOTBALL TEAMS UNITED List the *sixteen* British League Football† clubs that have the word 'United' in their name. The solution is on page 283. [**Target: 6**]

PERFORMERS OF JAMES BOND THEMES Name the *eighteen* performers who have sung the theme music to James Bond films‡. The solution may be found on page 239. [**Target: 10**]

---

* Charles Dickens was born in 1812 and endured an unsettled and impoverished childhood. At the age of sixteen, having taught himself shorthand, Dickens found a job as a court reporter and later as a parliamentary reporter. It was during this period that his twin passions for writing and social reform were to develop, and he started to contribute articles urging reform to radical publications (pressure from Dickens and other campaigners helped bring about the Reform Act of 1832). Dickens also began writing fiction and in 1833 had a story published in the *Monthly Magazine* under the pen-name of Boz. He continued to write stories and was commissioned to write his first novel in 1836. Dickens kept up his outspoken campaign for social change by continuing to write articles for journals, but in the end it was his fiction that was probably most effective in drawing attention to the problems of the times in which he lived. He died in 1870.

† Including English and Scottish Premier Leagues.

‡ The James Bond theme is one of the most recognisable pieces of music in the world, but the credit for writing it has been a subject of controversy. Monty Norman, who wrote the soundtrack for *Dr No* in 1962, is credited with the composition, but it has often been claimed that the theme itself was written by John Barry, brought in by producers Cubby Broccoli and Harry Saltzman to work on it for a one-off fee. The matter was settled in the High Court when Norman successfully sued *The Sunday Times*, who had made such an allegation, for libel in 2001, and was awarded £30,000 in damages.

LINKED MISCELLANY X Answer the questions below and ascertain the connecting theme linking them. The solution is on page 259. [**Target: 6**]

1. Which book, first published on 26 June 1997, has gone on to sell 90 million copies worldwide?
2. In which English National Park are the James Herriot books set?
3. Which 1941 film was inspired by the life of newspaper magnate William Randolph Hearst?
4. Which famous store has been trading in Piccadilly Circus since 1925?
5. Who won the Oscar for Best Actor for *Reversal of Fortune* in 1990?
6. Which social insect is a member of the genus Vespa and has species that include European, Oriental, Yellow and Giant Asian?
7. Which novel was written by John Bunyan while in prison* in 1675?
8. The all-time best-selling album in the US is by which group?
9. What was the name of the flag of the USSR?
10. In which island group is Tenerife found?

BOXING WEIGHT DIVISIONS Identify the *seventeen* weight categories† in the sport of boxing‡ (as defined by the World Boxing Association). Find the solution on page 283. [**Target: 6**]

---

* Bunyan was imprisoned for holding religious services that were not sanctioned by the Church of England in violation of the Conventicle Act.

† There are seventeen recognised weight divisions, although only eight of these are commonly used. Olympic fights have eleven weight divisions, including super heavyweight.

‡ The Queensberry Rules were drafted in 1857 by a boxer called John Chambers and patronised by John Douglas, the 8th Marquis of Queensberry. Prior to this, boxing had been dangerous, brutal and mostly illegal. The Queensberry rules mandated the use of gloves and divided matches into three-minute rounds with one-minute intervals between them. It remains the code governing professional boxing today.

CHART-TOPPING SINGLES BY THE BEATLES Recall the *seventeen* singles by the Beatles* that have topped the UK charts. The solution is on page 304. [**Target: 8**]

LATIN PHRASES I Identify the commonly used Latin phrase or its abbreviations from these English translations†. The solutions are on page 322. [**Target: 10**]

1.	Before midday	2.	The Year of Our Lord
3.	Written after	4.	Which was demonstrated
5.	The state which exists	6.	By year
7.	Interrupted intercourse	8.	That is
9.	Bountiful mother	10.	At first sight
11.	Around, approximately	12.	For a special purpose
13.	On behalf of	14.	For example
15.	Compare with	16.	Remarkable year
17.	A great work	18.	One thing for another
19.	With good faith	20.	In fact
21.	First among equals	22.	And other things
23.	In the act of a crime	24.	Said in passing

---

* Shortly after the Beatles signed to EMI in 1962, their producer George Martin was keen for them to release material written by other songwriters, as was the norm for commercial recording artists of the day. The song picked by Martin for the Beatles' first A-side was 'How Do You Do It' by Mitch Murray. Although they recorded the Murray song the group resisted the pressure put on them by the record company to release it. Martin eventually gave in to John and Paul's wish to release their own material and in September 1962 'Love Me Do', a credited Lennon/McCartney composition, hit the record stores and soon after the charts. The Beatles had created a sound that was fresh and stood out from the beat combo acts that filled the charts at the time. The success of the song assured the future of the Lennon/McCartney writing partnership and the release of many more songs of extraordinary originality and appeal. More significantly, the song broke the mould of the music industry and paved the way for thousands of talented artists to be able to record and release original work from which the world of music has greatly benefited.

† In 1844, General Charles Napier, in violation of his orders, led a British force to conquer Sind (nowadays the area of southern Pakistan containing Hyderabad). It is apocryphal that, after his conquest, Napier sent a one-word communication to his superiors; 'Pecavvi,' meaning: 'I have sinned.'

NOVELS BY THOMAS HARDY Recall the titles of the *seventeen* novels by Thomas Hardy*. The solution may be found on page 342. [**Target: 5**]

COUNTY CRICKET Name the *eighteen* County Cricket† teams. Turn to page 219 for the solution. [**Target: 12**]

ADVERTISING SLOGANS III Identify the products that were promoted with these advertising slogans. Go to page 240 for the solutions. [**Target: 14**]

1.   'The mild cigar'
2.   'Any time, any place, anywhere'
3.   '8 out of 10 owners said their cats preferred it'
4.   'Du pain, du vin, du _____ '
5.   'It does exactly what it says on the tin'
6.   'I liked it so much I bought the company'
7.   'If anyone can, _____ can'
8.   'We're getting there'

---

* Thomas Hardy was born in Dorset in 1840 and wrote novels depicting the harsh lives and bleak outlook of ordinary country people during the nineteenth century. For the early part of his career Hardy lived in London, but after his books became popular he moved back down to Dorset, where he settled with his first wife Emma Lavinia Gifford (whom he had married in 1874) at Max Gate in Dorchester, a house Hardy designed. In the latter part of his life, Hardy turned his attention to writing poetry, which had always been his great passion. After the death of Emma in 1912, he married his secretary, Florence Dugdale (who was forty years his junior) and died at the age of eighty-eight in 1928. After his death, Hardy's ashes were interred in Westminster Abbey, but his heart was buried in Stinsford in Dorset.
† The rules of cricket drawn up in 1744 defined a cricket pitch to measure exactly twenty-two yards between the two wickets (equivalent to a chain, the old imperial unit) and ten feet wide. The code of 1744 also stated that the wicket should be twenty-two inches tall and six inches wide and the ball should weigh between five and six ounces. Before the formation of the MCC in 1787, the custodians of the rules of cricket were Hambledon Cricket Club and, in spite of the perceived view of cricket being the most sporting of contests, players in the eighteenth and nineteenth centuries were continually employing underhand means to gain advantage. A rule change was required in 1771 after Thomas 'Shock' White took to the crease for Reigate with a bat that was wider than the wicket; the maximum width of the bat was set at $4\frac{1}{4}$ inches thereafter.

9. 'Drivers wanted'
10. 'It's got to be _____'
11. 'The bank that likes to say yes'
12. 'A drink's too wet without one'
13. 'How do you eat yours?'
14. 'See the face you love light up'
15. 'We all adore a _____'
16. 'Hand-built by robots'
17. 'No _____, no comment'
18. 'Where do you want to go today?'
19. 'Prolongs active life'
20. 'Grace . . . Space . . . Pace'
21. 'Nothing acts faster than _____'
22. 'You're never alone with a _____'
23. 'Laughing all the way to the _____'
24. 'Three in one protection for your family'

OLYMPIC HOST NATIONS Name the *eighteen* nations to have hosted the Olympic Games. Find the solution on page 259. [**Target: 10**]

MISCELLANY XVIII Answer these questions of miscellaneous nature. The solutions are on page 304. [**Target: 12**]

1. Which British Prime Minister won the Nobel Prize for Literature in 1953?
2. What links the characters of Banquo in *Macbeth* and Jacob Marley in *A Christmas Carol*?
3. The murder of Sandra Rivett on 9 November 1974 led to whose disappearance?
4. What is the sum of degrees in the internal angles in a triangle?
5. Which patterned textile of tear-shaped motifs takes its name from a town in Scotland?
6. Which mountain, until 1865, was known as Peak XV?
7. Which artistic movement are Degas, Renoir and Monet said to belong to?
8. From where are measured distances from London taken?
9. What colour is the bottom stripe of the Stars and Stripes?
10. What did Henry Beck famously map out in 1932?

11. How many funnels did the *Titanic* have?
12. Which organisation has the motto: 'Fidelity, Bravery, Integrity'?
13. What was first sold as the 'Pluto Platter', being known by its more familiar name in 1958?
14. What links Caesar Cardini, Philippe de Mornay and Anna Pavlova?
15. Who wrote *The Old Man of Lochnagar*?
16. Which two countries have names beginning with the letter 'A' but not ending with the letter 'A'?
17. Which musical features the Cole Porter song 'Who Wants to Be a Millionaire'?
18. Musky Muskrat is the sidekick of which cartoon character?
19. What is the title of the film about a Scottish village that awakens once every 100 years?
20. Which British Prime Minister is associated with a hot drink?
21. The cost of painting lines on a road to divide it into three lanes is £100. How much would it cost to divide the road into six lanes?
22. Which two countries fought the Football War in 1969?
23. Which English word originates from the practice in the French royal court of providing tickets to visiting dignitaries with written instructions describing the expected code of behaviour?
24. A bottle of wine costs £10. If the wine costs £9 more than the bottle, how much is the bottle worth?

STORIES BY ROALD DAHL Name the *eighteen* children's stories written by Roald Dahl. The solution is on page 322. [**Target: 10**]

CHART-TOPPING SINGLES BY ELVIS PRESLEY Name the *eighteen* singles by Elvis Presley* that have topped the UK charts. (Elvis has had twenty-one number ones to date but three of these were re-releases.) Find the solution on page 343. [**Target: 5**]

---

* Elvis Aaron Presley was born in Tupelo, Mississippi in 1935. By his death in 1977, he had outsold every other recording artist, then or since, with global record sales of over 1 billion copies. Over 130 of his albums and singles have received gold (sales of over 500,000 copies), platinum (sales of over 1 million) or multi-platinum status. He also made thirty-three films. Elvis has the most UK number one singles of any artist.

FILMS AND THEIR STARS IV Identify the films from these selected cast members and the date of release. Find the solutions on page 219. [Target: 14]

1. John Hurt, Ian Holm, Harry Dean Stanton, Sigourney Weaver (1979)
2. Julie Andrews, Christopher Plummer (1965)
3. Robert Shaw, Richard Dreyfuss, Roy Scheider (1975)
4. Harrison Ford, Robert Duvall, Martin Sheen, Dennis Hopper, Marlon Brando (1979)
5. Robert De Niro, Andy Garcia, Sean Connery, Kevin Costner (1987)
6. Antonio Banderas, Denzel Washington, Tom Hanks (1993)
7. Julianne Moore, Steve Buscemi, Jeff Bridges, John Goodman (1998)
8. Michelle Pfeiffer, Jeff Bridges, Beau Bridges (1989)
9. Daniela Bianchi, Robert Shaw, Sean Connery (1963)
10. Elizabeth Taylor, Rock Hudson, James Dean (1956)
11. Robert Redford, Dustin Hoffman (1976)
12. Omar Sharif, Julie Christie, Alec Guinness (1965)
13. Elizabeth Taylor, Paul Newman (1958)
14. Bill Murray, Scarlett Johansson, Giovanni Ribisi (2003)
15. David Hemmings, Vanessa Redgrave (1966)
16. Daniel Craig, Michael Gambon, Sienna Miller (2004)
17. James Mason, Julie Christie, Warren Beatty (1978)
18. Danny Glover, Whoopi Goldberg (1985)
19. Katie Johnson, Herbert Lom, Alec Guinness, Peter Sellers (1955)
20. Leo McKern, Jeremy Irons, Meryl Streep (1981)
21. Jude Law, Nicole Kidman, Renée Zellweger (2003)
22. Ray Winstone, Ben Kingsley, Ian McShane, Amanda Redman (2000)
23. Maggie Smith, Michael Gambon, Kristin Scott Thomas, Charles Dance, Kelly MacDonald, Clive Owen, Richard E. Grant, Helen Mirren, Eileen Atkins, Emily Watson, Derek Jacobi (2001)
24. Richard Attenborough, Terry-Thomas, Peter Sellers (1959)

ABBA HITS Recall the *nineteen* songs by Abba* that have been Top Ten hits in the UK. You can find the solution on page 240. [**Target: 14**]

BEATRIX POTTER TALES Identify the *nineteen* Beatrix Potter tales†. The solution‡ can be found on page 260. [**Target: 5**]

NICKNAMES OF MONARCHS Identify each of these British monarchs from their nicknames. You will find the solutions on page 283. [**Target: 10**]

1.	The Lionheart	2.	The Virgin Queen
3.	The Confessor	4.	The Great
5.	Bloody Mary	6.	Longshanks
7.	The Unready	8.	Bluff King Hal
9.	Crookback	10.	The Nine-day Queen
11.	The Bastard	12.	The Merry Monarch
13.	The Widow of Windsor	14.	Lackland
15.	Farmer George	16.	Rufus
17.	Brandy Nan	18.	Ironside

---

* Björn Ulvaeus, Benny Andersson, Agnetha Faltskog and Anni-Frid Lyngstad took the name Abba from the initials of their Christian names. Bjorn and Benny met in the mid-1960s when Benny was keyboard player for the Hep Stars (Sweden's biggest pop group at the time) and Bjorn was playing with a folk-rock band called the Hootennany Singers and the pair started writing songs together. Their girlfriends Agnetha and Anna-Frid, both accomplished singers in their own right, collaborated with them and the group was born. After a failed attempt to gain selection for Sweden's Eurovision entry in 1973 (with 'Ring Ring', they came third), the following year 'Waterloo' stormed to success and international acclaim. By 1978, Abba had overtaken Volvo as Sweden's most profitable export.

† Beatrix Potter was born in 1866 in Kensington, London. As a child she spent her summers in the Lake District where her love of nature developed and she would while away her time drawing and sketching the many animals that she brought back to the house. The sketches would eventually accompany the stories that she wrote in adulthood. In 1905 she bought Hill Top Farm, which has become the most visited house in the Lake District, and devoted the latter part of her life to farming and particularly to breeding Herdwick sheep. She died in 1943, aged seventy-seven, leaving £200,000, and more than 4,000 acres of land to the National Trust.

‡ Specifically titles beginning 'The Tale of . . .'; Beatrix Potter also penned *The Story of a Fierce Bad Rabbit*, *The Story of Miss Moppet*, *Appley Dapply's Nursery Rhymes*, and *Cecil Parlsey's Nursery Rhymes*.

19. Curtmantle	20. Beauclerc
21. Builder	22. Denmark
23. Empress Maud	24. The Sailor King

LARGE BODIES OF WATER List the *twenty* largest bodies of water* (for example oceans, seas, gulfs and bays) in the world. The solution can be found on page 304. [**Target: 10**]

POPULAR LANGUAGES Name the *twenty* most widely spoken languages in the world (including native speakers and second-language speakers). Turn to page 323 for the solution. [**Target: 10**]

FIRST LINES OF POP SONGS IV Identify the titles of these songs from the first lines below. (The year each song was a hit is supplied to assist you.) For advanced play, name the performers as well. Turn to page 344 for the solutions. [**Target: 10**]

1. 'There is a house in New Orleans.'(1964)
2. 'Get up, get on up.' (1970)
3. 'Oh baby baby, how was I supposed to know?' (1999)
4. 'Goodbye Norma Jean.' (1974)
5. 'Help me escape this feeling of insecurity.' (1993)
6. 'On a dark desert highway.' (1977)
7. 'We've got stars directing our fate.' (1998)
8. 'My baby don't mess around because she loves me so.' (2004)
9. 'Hey there, here I am, I'm the man on the scene.' (1968)
10. 'Get your motor running.' (1969)
11. 'You could have a steam train if you'd just lay down your tracks.' (1986)
12. 'Nobody on the road, nobody on the beach.' (1985)

---

* Two-thirds of the surface of the earth are covered by water but very little is actually known about the ocean floors (around 90% is unexplored). The deepest point in the world is the Challenger Deep of the Marianas Trench, at 10,924 metres (just shy of seven miles) below the surface of the Pacific Ocean off the Philippines. It has been visited only once by man: in 1960 by Jacques Piccard and Don Walsh in their bathyscaphe, *Trieste*. In spite of the staggering pressures, Walsh and Piccard were surprised to witness a strange flatfish swimming on the ocean floor but were unable to take pictures and the creature was lost to posterity. The cost and high risks of such dives has meant that the pair remain the only men to have been so deep.

13. 'Though I've tried before to tell her of the feelings I have for her in my heart.' (1981)
14. 'I'm the trouble starter, punkin' instigator.' (1996)
15. 'My tea's gone cold, I'm wondering why I got out of bed at all.' (2001/2000)
16. 'You've done it all, you've broken every code.' (1975)
17. 'Living on free food tickets.' (1983)
18. 'You've been around all night and that's a little long.' (1982)
19. 'There's no point in asking, you'll get no reply.' (1977)
20. 'I want to run, I want to hide.' (1987)
21. 'Down down, you bring me down.' (1992)
22. 'Time goes by so slowly.' (2005)
23. 'Come gather round people wherever you roam.' (1965)
24. 'Here comes Johnny Yen again.' (1996)

RIVERS OF THE UK Name the *twenty* longest rivers in the UK. Find the solution on page 219. [**Target: 8**]

BRITISH PRIME MINISTERS List the *twenty* British Prime Ministers* of the twentieth century. The solution is on page 240. [**Target: 12**]

---

* The term 'Prime Minister' was first documented during the premiership of Benjamin Disraeli but not used as an official title until 1905. Robert Walpole (whose tenure endured from 1721 to 1742) is generally regarded to have been the first Prime Minister although at no point was the position formally created; it came into being mainly because of the way that Walpole dominated politics at the time. Walpole, a Whig, used his influence on the dying Queen Anne to name the Hanoverian George as her successor (rather than the Catholic James Stewart, son of James II). When George arrived from Germany he had no experience of politics or of British life, and relied heavily on the Whigs who had arranged for his succession. He made Walpole his Chancellor of the Exchequer in 1715, and although Walpole briefly fell out of favour, he rose back to prominence as the only member of the government not to be tarnished by the scandal of the South Sea Bubble financial disaster. He subsequently became known as the King's 'First Minister'. It was widely expected that the succession of George II (in 1727) would be the end of Walpole's tenure, but Walpole had been courting the Waleses by becoming advisor to the Princess of Wales (the future Queen Caroline) and it was even rumoured that Mrs Walpole had become the Prince of Wales' mistress. Such political manoeuvrings ensured that after the succession of George II, Walpole remained as Prime Minister, a post he kept until 1742. Not only did he define the role of Prime Minister, he is remembered as one of the most skilful political operators ever to rise to high office.

BATTLES II Name the wars in which these battles were fought. (Note that the same answer may occur more than once.) Look for the solutions on page 260. [**Target: 10**]

1.	Britain	2.	Waterloo
3.	El Alamein	4.	Trafalgar
5.	Arnhem	6.	Naseby
7.	Ypres	8.	River Plate
9.	Rorke's Drift	10.	Kursk
11.	Ardennes	12.	Saratoga
13.	Newbury	14.	Monte Cassino
15.	Arbela	16.	Blenheim
17.	Dieppe	18.	Marathon
19.	Antioch	20.	Austerlitz
21.	Isandhlwana	22.	Alma
23.	Aegospotami	24.	Thermopylae

BEST-SELLING ALBUMS Identify the *twenty* best-selling albums of all time in the UK. Find the solution on page 283. [**Target: 6**]

LARGE ISLANDS Name the *twenty* largest islands in the world (not including continental land masses). The solution can be found on page 305. [**Target: 8**]

PSEUDONYMS II Identify the pseudonyms by which these people are famously known. You will find the solutions on page 323. [**Target: 12**]

1.	Cherilyn Sarkisian La Pierre	2.	Gerry Dorsey
3.	Ernest Wiseman	4.	Eric Blair
5.	Jennifer Anastassakis	6.	Vladimir Ilyich Ulyanov
7.	Cassius Clay	8.	Richard Starkey
9.	Edda Hepburn van Heemstra	10.	Priscilla White
11.	Demetria Gene Guynes	12.	Reginald Dwight
13.	Mary Ann Evans	14.	Greta Gustaffson
15.	Prince Nelson	16.	Sophia Scicolini
17.	Lesley Hornby	18.	Walter Matuschanskayasky

19.	Harry Crosby	20.	Lee Yuen Kam
21.	Martha Jane Burke	22.	Carlos Estevez
23.	Maurice Micklewhite	24.	Vera Welch

FREQUENTLY OCCURRING WORDS List the *twenty* most frequently occurring words in written English. Turn to page 344 for the solution. [**Target: 10**]

LARGE LAKES Name the *twenty* largest lakes* in the world. The solution may be found on page 220. [**Target: 6**]

MISCELLANY XIX Answer these questions of a miscellaneous nature. Go to page 241 for the solutions. [**Target: 8**]

1. What links Vienna, Budapest and *2001: A Space Odyssey*?
2. Which well-known film is an anagram of 'Long Fridge'?
3. In what type of auction does the price of an item reduce until a bid is received?
4. What was the Warren Commission established in 1963 to investigate?
5. What did the Thirteenth Amendment to the US Constitution of 1865 prohibit?
6. Who wrote: 'You're a better man than I am, Gunga Din!'?
7. How many sides does a Stop sign have?
8. Which two cities are referred to in Charles Dickens' *Tale of Two Cities*?
9. Which country's presidency was offered to but declined by Albert Einstein?
10. Which sport was established at the Hurlingham Club in London in 1874?
11. Whose birth followed the Immaculate Conception?
12. How many holes are major golf tournaments played over?
13. What was the name of Rosco P. Coltrane's dog in *The Dukes of Hazzard*?
14. The 1905 mutiny on which Russian battleship was the subject

---

* The word lake is a generic term and refers to an area of water surrounded by land, usually of considerable size. See the footnote of the solution (page 220) for a discussion of some candidates that have not been included in the list.

of an eponymous, ground-breaking and highly influential silent film of 1925?

15. Who was the last British monarch to lead an army into battle?
16. Which English football team has a name which starts with five consonants in a row?
17. A man dies leaving £10,000 to be shared between his widow, five sons and four daughters. According to his will, each daughter should receive an equal amount, each son should receive twice as much as each daughter and his widow should receive three times as much as each son. How much did the widow receive?
18. Which is the only underground station whose name appears on both the London and Paris systems?
19. What were Eugene Cernan and Harrison Schmitt the last men to do?
20. Which two American football teams compete annually in a game known as 'The Game'?
21. Which character did Quentin Tarantino play in *Reservoir Dogs*?
22. Who wrote *The Railway Children*?
23. What is the medical name for the collarbone?
24. How many times do the hour and minute hands of an ordinary clock cross in any twelve-hour period of time?

METRIC PREFIXES Name the *twenty* metric prefixes. (Metric prefixes are words which are put before quantities such as scientific units or units of computing capacity to indicate their scale.) The solution is on page 261. [**Target: 10**]

WEALTHY COUNTRIES Identify the *twenty* wealthiest countries in the world, based on per capita Gross Domestic Product. Turn to page 323 for the solution. [**Target: 12**]

ETYMOLOGY OF ROCK AND POP NAMES I Identify the name of the groups or artists from the etymology of their names. The solutions can be found on page 306. [**Target: 16**]

1. After a character in the film *Barbarella* (and also the name of the club in Birmingham where the band first performed).

2. From 'Boys Entering Anarchistic States Towards Inner Excellence'.
3. A shock name referring to the assassination of two prominent US politicians.
4. From 'Ladies Love Cool James'.
5. After a medieval torture instrument.
6. Inspired by the answer to the meaning of life (according to Douglas Adams).
7. From the name of a famous agriculturalist and author of *Horse-Hoeing Husbandry*.
8. After the band's home town in Somerset
9. Taken from a French magazine title and meaning 'fast fashion'.
10. After a German art movement of the 1920s and 1930s.
11. After a pair of characters in the Tintin cartoons by Hergé.
12. Inspired by the band's cramped living conditions while working on their debut album.
13. Named after the Austrian whose assassination precipitated the First World War.
14. After a term for obsessive computer enthusiasts.
15. From a Muddy Waters song.
16. Inspired by the Velvet Underground and their song 'Venus in Furs'.
17. From the title of a 'video nasty' featuring a large number of enraged antagonists.
18. From a book by J.R.R. Tolkien.
19. Originally as a parody of Fats Domino's name.
20. After the silver ball in the Woody Allen film, *Sleeper*, which had a drug-like effect when touched.
21. Taken from the title of a Steely Dan song.
22. After the high priestess of Vulcan in *Star Trek*.
23. After the German word for 'power plant'.
24. From the names of the two founder members added to that of a trucking magazine.

LARGE COUNTRIES List the *twenty* largest countries in the world (by area). Turn to page 284 for the solution. [**Target: 10**]

WIT AND WISDOM II The following quotations are attributed to either Dorothy Parker, Mae West* or Joan Rivers. Identify the correct author of each quotation. The solutions are on page 221. [Target: 18]

1. 'When I'm good, I'm very good, but when I'm bad, I'm even better.'
2. 'I told my mother-in-law that my house was her house, and she said, "Get the hell off my property."'
3. 'One more drink and I'll be under the host.'
4. 'I used to be Snow White, but I drifted.'
5. 'My best birth control now is just to leave the lights on.'
6. 'It's not the men in my life; it's the life in my men.'
7. 'You can lead a horticulture, but you can't make her think.'
8. 'The first time I see a jogger smiling, I'll consider it.'
9. 'All I need is room enough to lay a hat and a few friends.'
10. 'Keep a diary, and someday it'll keep you.'
11. 'She runs the gamut of emotions from A to B.'
12. 'I hate housework. You make the beds, you wash the dishes and six months later you have to start all over again.'
13. 'It's so long since I've had sex I've forgotten who ties up who.'
14. 'It is better to be looked over than overlooked.'
15. 'If all the girls at the Yale Prom were laid end to end, I wouldn't be at all surprised.'
16. 'The one thing women don't want to find in their stockings on Christmas morning is their husband.'
17. 'I've never been a millionaire but I just know I'd be darling at it.'
18. 'When women go wrong, men go right after them.'

---

* Mae West is best known as a screen star but she was also a writer and penned the screenplays of many of the films she appeared in. Having experienced limited success writing a series of risqué Broadway plays (leading to an eight-day prison sentence on public obscenity charges) her breakthrough came in the 1932 film *Night after Night*. Although West only had a small role, she persuaded the producers to allow her to rewrite her lines and gave herself these classic words:

Cloakroom Girl: Goodness, what lovely diamonds!
Mae West: Goodness has nothing to do with it, dearie.

West's next roles would be starring ones and by 1935 she was the highest-earning woman in America. During the war, Allied soldiers gave her name to their inflatable lifejackets, inspired by her well-proportioned figure.

19. 'This is not a novel to be tossed aside lightly. It should be thrown with great force.'
20. 'When choosing between two evils I always like to take the one I've never tried before.'
21. 'Take care of the luxuries and the necessities will take care of themselves.'
22. 'If God wanted us to bend over he'd put diamonds on the floor.'
23. 'If you want to know what God thinks of money, just look at the people he gave it to.'
24. 'That woman speaks eight languages and can't say "no" in any of them.'

WELSH SURNAMES Name the *twenty* most common Welsh surnames. The solution is on page 242. [**Target: 12**]

FOOTBALL TEAM NAME ENDINGS Identify the *twenty-two* unique endings of English Football League teams*. You can find the solution on page 344. [**Target: 16**]

MEDITERRANEAN COUNTRIES Name the *twenty-one* countries that have coastlines on the Mediterranean Sea (excluding overseas territories). Turn to page 261 for the solution. [**Target: 16**]

LINKED MISCELLANY XI Answer these questions and determine the theme that links the solutions. Turn to page 285 for the solution. [**Target: 5**]

1. Which 1991 film won Oscars in each of the five major categories (Best Picture, Director, Screenplay, Actor and Actress), including an award for Jodie Foster?
2. Which Bob Dylan song has been covered by Eric Clapton, Bob Marley, Mark Knopfler and Guns N' Roses?

---

* Many English Football team names are made up of two words, a place name and a descriptive name (or nickname). 'Ham' as in West Ham and 'Bromwich' as in West Bromwich have not been included in the solution as they are part of the name of the location of the team.

3. What is the common name given to any species of insect of the order Diptera; a species which begins life as a maggot?
4. According to the Criminal Justice Act of 1988, what is defined as 'the unlawful application, intentionally or recklessly, of unlawful force'?
5. What term was coined by journalist and social commentator H.L. Mencken, in the early 1920s, to describe the geographical area of the US where evangelical Protestantism is a dominant part of the culture?
6. Ian and Janette Tough are better known as which double act?
7. Which river flows into the Great Ouse at Pope's Corner, just south of Ely?
8. Who had hits with 'This Town Ain't Big Enough for the Both of Us' and 'Beat the Clock'?
9. How is an intrauterine device better known?
10. Which former member of the Jeff Beck Group and the Faces was once married to Britt Ekland?

JAMES BOND FILMS Name the *twenty-two* (official*) James Bond films. The solution is on page 306. [**Target: 17**]

ROLLING STONES HITS Recall the *twenty-one* singles which have been Top Ten hits for the Rolling Stones† in the UK. Go to page 324 for the solution. [**Target: 10**]

---

* Unofficial films include *Never Say Never Again* (1983) and *Casino Royale* (1965).
† While the group enjoyed sustained commercial success throughout the 1960s their fortunes took a turn for the worse in 1969. With possible prison sentences already looming over the band members for drugs convictions, Brian Jones became resentful of the Jagger/Richards writing partnership and his loss of creative control of the band. He descended into a cycle of drink, drugs and ill-health which was only compounded by Anita Pallenberg, Jones's girlfriend, starting an affair with Richards (she would have two children by him). On 8 June, Jagger, Richards and Watts drove to Jones's Sussex mansion and sacked him from the band. On 3 July, Brian Jones was found dead in his swimming pool. In December of the same year at a concert in San Francisco, Meredith Hunter, the victim of a racially motivated attack, was hacked and stomped to death by members of the Hell's Angels whom the band had invited to provide security at the gig.

INNOVATIONS II Identify the innovations which were created by these individuals or organisations. The solutions may be found on page 344. [**Target: 12**]

1. John Logie Baird (1926)
2. Graf Ferdinand von Zeppelin (1900)
3. Igor Sikorsky (1939)
4. Boeing (1970)
5. Louis Pasteur (1867)
6. Mesopotamians (*c.*3500BC)
7. Alexander Fleming (1928)
8. Samuel Colt (1835)
9. Elisha Otis (1851)
10. Anders Celsius (1742)
11. Gottlieb Daimler (1884)
12. Jacques Cousteau (1943)
13. Tim Berners-Lee (1991)
14. Charles Babbage (1835)
15. Thomas Edison (1877)
16. Edward Jenner (1770)
17. Kenneth Wood (1947)
18. Percy Shaw (1934)
19. George Eastman (1889)
20. Tsai Lun (105)
21. Kirkpatrick Macmillan (1839)
22. David Bushnell (1776)
23. Hurley Machine Company (1907)
24. Dan Bricklin and Bob Frankston (1979)

FAMOUS FIVE STORIES Recall the *twenty-one* books in the *Famous Five* series by Enid Blyton*. Find the solution on page 221. [**Target: 2**]

---

* Enid Blyton was born in London in 1897. In her lifetime (she died in 1968) she wrote over 600 books including the *Noddy*, *Malory Towers* and *Secret Seven* series. Even though she was writing for a readership of a different era to that of today, her books are still popular with children and sell millions of copies annually.

EUROPEAN CLUB CHAMPIONS Name the *twenty-one* teams to have won the European Cup* or Champions League. You will find the solution on page 242. [Target: 12]

TAGLINES OF POPULAR FILMS III Name the films from the clues provided. The solutions are on page 261. [Target: 14]

1. 'Just when you thought it was safe to go back into the water . . .' (1978)
2. 'Check in. Relax. Take a shower.' (1960)
3. 'To enter the mind of a killer she must challenge the mind of a madman.' (1991)
4. 'The toys are back in town.' (1995)
5. 'Getting back was only the beginning.' (1989)
6. 'They dropped everything for a good cause.' (2003)
7. 'Five good reasons to stay single.' (1994)
8. 'The classic story of power and the press.' (1941)
9. 'With great power comes great responsibility.' (2002)
10. 'Protecting the earth from the scum of the universe.' (1997)
11. 'December 7, 1941 – a day that shall live in infamy.' (2001)
12. 'For anyone who's ever been set up, stood up or felt up.' (2001)
13. 'This is Benjamin . . . he's a little worried about his future.' (1967)
14. 'They're mean, green and on the screen.' (1990)
15. 'The year's most revealing comedy.' (1997)
16. 'Lust. Seduction. Revenge. See the game played as you've never seen it before.' (1988)

---

* In 1954, a friendly match took place between Wolverhampton Wanderers and the Hungarian side Honved (a side including several of the world's greatest players of the time, including Ferenc Puskas). Wolves won the game 3–2 and the victory led the Wolves manager Stan Cullis, along with most of the British press, to declare his team 'Champions of the World' (one report crowed: 'Even St George in his shining armour could not have fought more gallantly for England. And Wolves had all England, yes, and all the English-speaking world, behind them when they did it.'). The indignation suffered by Gabriel Hanot, a French newspaper editor, at these remarks was such that he started to lobby for the introduction of a new competition involving Europe's top teams. Two years later, the European Cup was born. The tournament involved the champion club in each European country competing in home and away ties in knockout rounds, climaxing in a one-off final. The format remained the same until 1992 when a league phase was introduced (to guarantee clubs greater earnings from the tournament) and the competition was renamed the Champions League.

17. 'For God's sake, get out of that house!' (1979)
18. 'Same Make. Same Model. New Mission.' (1991)
19. 'They're young . . . they're in love . . . and they kill people.' (1967)
20. 'If you don't remember the sixties, don't worry – neither did they.'(1987)
21. 'Everything you've heard is true.' (1999)
22. 'His story will touch you, even though he can't.' (1990)
23. 'In the middle of nowhere there is nowhere to hide.' (1989)
24. 'Some lines shouldn't be crossed.' (1990)

THE CANTERBURY TALES Name the *twenty-two* pilgrims' tales which make up *The Canterbury Tales**. Find the solution on page 285. [**Target: 4**]

MISCELLANY XX Answer these questions of a miscellaneous nature. The solutions are on page 324. [**Target: 12**]

1. Which is the most westerly country in Europe?
2. What mineral were the Seven Dwarfs mining for?
3. What links the words 'racecar' and 'kayak'?
4. Which Israeli-born celebrity was the first to be voted off the first series of *I'm a Celebrity Get Me Out of Here*?
5. 'Dieu et Mon Droit' appears on the header of which daily newspaper?
6. What links the plays *Who's Afraid of Virginia Woolf?* and *Waiting for Godot*?
7. Which two UK number ones have contained the word 'fandango' in their lyrics?
8. What was the first word spoken from the moon?
9. At what age was Adrian Mole when he started his diary?
10. Which English word originally used to describe a medieval mercenary is now applied to any professional hired for a specific piece of work without a long-term commitment to the employer?

---

* *The Canterbury Tales*, written by Geoffrey Chaucer, is a collection of stories told by pilgrims on their way to Thomas Becket's shrine in Canterbury. The pilgrims meet at the Tabard Inn, Southwark, where the tavern host, Harry Bailly, proposes they each tell stories on the road, the best of which will receive a free supper. The book was begun around 1387 and remains the most significant literary work of the fourteenth century.

11. Which American state is last alphabetically?
12. Which of the Dirty Dozen was also one of the Magnificent Seven?
13. In which city is Grampian TV based?
14. In the nursery rhyme, how was Jack's head treated after he had fallen down the hill?
15. Where is the hypo-centre of an earthquake in relation to its epicentre?
16. There are a certain number of children in a family. Each boy has the same number of brothers as he has sisters. Each girl has twice as many brothers as she has sisters. How many boys are there and how many girls?
17. Which two countries are connected by the Simplon Pass?
18. For the capture of which English king did Parliament offer a reward of £1,000?
19. What plant did Christopher Leyland name in 1888?
20. What links the supporters of Liverpool, Celtic, Feyenoord and FC Tokyo?
21. If you were born on St Swithin's Day, what star sign would you be?
22. What is the minimum number of strokes required to score 147 in a game of snooker?
23. Which blood vessel carries deoxygenated blood from the heart to the lungs?
24. Which number is equal to five times the sum of its digits?

TAROT CARDS List the *twenty-two* cards which make up the Major Arcana (or picture cards) of a deck of Tarot cards*. Find the solution on page 345. [**Target: 8**]

---

* A traditional Tarot deck consists of seventy-eight cards. There are fourteen cards in each of the four suits (Rods or Wands, Cups, Swords and Coins or Pentacles) and fifty-six cards which make up the Minor Arcana (Arcana derives from the Latin 'arcanum' meaning 'hidden things'). In addition, there are twenty-two picture cards which are illustrated with specific symbols and these are known as the Major Arcana. The precise origin of the Tarot deck is not well understood, but is often linked with ancient Egypt or India – although the earliest decks that we know about appeared in Italy in the fifteenth century. It is thought that the Tarot pre-dates the standard fifty-two-card deck and not vice versa, with Clubs corresponding to Rods, Hearts to Cups, Spades to Swords and Coins to Diamonds. Tarot has a fourth court card, the Knight, which has been dropped in the modern playing deck.

OLYMPIC HOST CITIES Recall the *twenty-two* cities to have hosted the Summer Olympic Games* in the modern era. The solution is on page 222. [**Target: 12**]

EVENTS IN HISTORY III Identify the century in which each of these historical events took place (be even more precise and name the year if you wish). Find the solutions on page 242. [**Target: 12**]

1. Christopher Columbus reaches America.
2. Charles Darwin publishes *The Origin of Species*.
3. Jesus of Nazareth is crucified in Jerusalem.
4. The Spanish Armada is defeated.
5. English prisoners die in the 'Black Hole of Calcutta'.
6. The Suez Canal opens.
7. Martin Luther nails his protest to a church door at Wittenberg.
8. Richard III is defeated by Henry Tudor at Bosworth.
9. The Gregorian calendar is adopted in Britain.
10. Marlborough defeats the French at Blenheim.
11. The American Civil War begins.
12. The formulation of the rules of cricket.
13. The Wars of the Roses begin.
14. *On the Revolutions of Heavenly Bodies* is published by Copernicus.
15. The *Daily Courant* becomes the first English newspaper.
16. Lloyds Coffee House becomes an insurance trading centre.
17. Michelangelo completes the painting of the Sistine Chapel.
18. Vasco da Gama reaches India.
19. Accession of James VI of Scotland as James I of England.
20. Marco Polo first visits China.
21. Duncan, King of Scotland, is killed by Macbeth.

---

* The Olympic Games were originally held every four years at Olympia in ancient Greece in honour of the god Zeus, and included competitions in literature, drama and music as well as sports. These events took place, with intervals, from 776BC until AD394. The modern Olympics began in 1896, appropriately enough, in Greece (the winter games were introduced in 1924). The founder of the modern games, Pierre de Coubertin, had a vision of amateur international athletes competing against each other for the love of sport, once famously saying: 'The most important thing in the Olympic Games is not to win but to take part.'

22. The Great Schism separates Christendom into Eastern Orthodox and Western Roman Catholic churches.
23. St Bartholomew's Day massacre takes place in Paris.
24. The Archbishopric of Canterbury is founded.

ARAB LEAGUE Identify the *twenty-two* members of the Arab League. You will find the solution on page 262. [**Target: 12**]

ENGLISH FOOTBALL LEAGUE CHAMPIONS Name the *twenty-three* clubs that have been League Champions (League or Premiership) since the inception of the Football League in 1888*. The solution may be found on page 285. [**Target: 16**]

NOVELTY RECORDS Identify the artists responsible for these novelty records. The solutions are on page 307. [**Target: 12**]

1. 'Can We Fix It?' (2000)
2. 'Combine Harvester (Brand New Key)' (1976)
3. 'Two Little Boys' (1969)
4. 'Ernie (The Fastest Milkman in the West)' (1971)
5. 'There's No-One Quite Like Grandma' (1980)
6. 'Livin' Doll' (1986)
7. 'Shaddap You Face' (1981)
8. 'Wand'rin' Star' (1970)
9. 'Grandad' (1971)
10. 'Spirit in the Sky' (2003)

---

* The Football League was the brainchild of William McGregor, a Scottish draper who had moved to Birmingham and become a director of Aston Villa. Administration of football in 1885 (when the game first became professional) was in disarray, with matches continually being cancelled and moved. McGregor wrote to the leading clubs of the time, proposing a League structure with home and away matches taking place over a single season. The League matches first kicked off in September 1888, with twelve member teams. Over the years, participating teams have grown in numbers and the League has seen the creation of separate divisions. A number of other developments have occurred; goal nets and the penalty kick were introduced in 1891; promotion and relegation in 1898; floodlit games in 1956; substitution in 1965; three points for a win in 1981 and play-offs in 1987. In 1992, the First Division broke away to form the Premiership. The Football League has been suspended twice in its history, during the First and Second World Wars.

11. 'Chocolate Salty Balls' (1999)
12. 'The Chicken Song' (1986)
13. 'Star Trekkin'' (1987)
14. 'Doctorin' the Tardis' (1988)
15. 'My Ding-a-Ling' (1972)
16. 'Goodness Gracious Me' (1960)
17. 'Let's Party' (1989)
18. 'Hoots Mon' (1958)
19. 'If' (1975)
20. 'Whispering Grass' (1975)
21. 'Itsy Bitsy Teeny Weeny Yellow Polka Dot Bikini' (1990)
22. 'Christmas Alphabet' (1955)
23. 'Amazing Grace' (1972)
24. 'Come Outside' (1962)

ENGLAND FOOTBALL CAPTAINS List the *twenty-three* players to have made ten or more appearances for England as Captain. Find the solution on page 325. [**Target: 10**]

LANGUAGES OF THE EUROPEAN UNION Name the *twenty-three* official languages of the European Union. The solution is on page 345. [**Target: 14**]

GOVERNMENTS Identify these types of government by the descriptions provided (the solutions are words ending in '-cracy' or '-archy'). Turn to page 222 for the solutions. [**Target: 8**]

1. Government by a single individual such as a king or queen, perpetuated through the right of inheritance
2. Government by officials or civil servants; implied inefficiency
3. Government by the people, via elections
4. Government by nobility or upper classes; a general term for the upper classes
5. Government by a single individual wielding unlimited power; a dictatorship
6. Government by men or fathers; any social system where men have authority
7. Government by those most deserving; any social system where rewards are earnt

8. Government by the Pope
9. Government according to a structured series of ranks or tiers; any organisation with a series of tiers
10. Government by the wealthy
11. Government by a few
12. Government by women or mothers; any social system where women have authority
13. Government by foreigners
14. Government by thieves
15. Government by technical experts
16. Government on the basis of religious law or by priests
17. Government by two people
18. Government by simple majority
19. Government by women
20. Government by men
21. Government by elders or the elderly
22. Government by children
23. Government by many people
24. Government by prostitutes

WORLD HERITAGE SITES IN THE UK Name the *twenty-four* World Heritage Sites* that are located in the UK†. Find the solution on page 243. [**Target: 7**]

FORBIDDEN DEGREES OF RELATIONSHIP Identify the *twenty-four* types of relative with whom sexual congress is forbidden for men‡ under UK law§. The solution may be found on page 262. [**Target: 16**]

---

* The World Heritage List was established by UNESCO (United Nations Educational, Scientific and Cultural Organisation) in 1972 to define and help protect cultural or natural sites of 'outstanding universal value'. In June 2007 there were 830 Heritage Sites listed in 138 countries; higher profile sites include the Grand Canyon National Park, the Great Wall of China, Machu Picchu, the Acropolis, the Pyramids at Giza and the Great Barrier Reef.
† Excludes World Heritage Sites located in British overseas territories, for example the town of St George in Bermuda.
‡ An equivalent and opposite list exists for women.
§ Note prohibitions apply to illegitimate as well as legitimate relationships; also note that it is permissible for a man to marry a cousin, but it is advisable to investigate family medical history if children are planned.

NICKNAMES OF PEOPLE II Identify the people famously associated with these nicknames. The solutions can be found on page 286. [**Target: 16**]

1.   Two Jags
2.   Ol' Blue Eyes
3.   The Lady with the Lamp
4.   The Boss
5.   Tarzan
6.   The Muscles from Brussels
7.   The Forces Sweetheart
8.   The Iron Duke
9.   Madame Sin
10. Eddie the Eagle
11. The Great White Shark
12. Hurricane
13. Razor
14. The Black Panther
15. The Rock Iguana
16. Her Madgesty
17. Lawrence of Arabia
18. The Liberator
19. Grocer
20. Supermac
21. The Human Riff
22. Twiggy
23. Uckers
24. The Jewish Elvis

QUEEN HITS Recall the *twenty-four* singles which have been Top Ten hits for Queen* in the UK. Go to page 307 for the solution. [**Target: 15**]

---

* Freddie Mercury was born Farrokh Bulsara in Zanzibar in 1946. He came to England when his family moved in 1963 and in 1971 teamed up with Roger Taylor, Brian May and bass player John Deacon to form Queen. Queen got their break in 1973 supporting Mott the Hoople on a UK tour; the year also saw them sign for EMI and release their first album. The band regularly appeared in the charts for the next twenty years, with their career perhaps peaking at the 1985 Live Aid concert when Freddie's charismatic performance stole the show. After persistent rumours about his health, on 22 November 1991 Freddie Mercury issued a statement confirming he had AIDS, a fact that he had known in private for many years. He died two days later at the age of forty-five.

GREEK ALPHABET Identify the *twenty-four* characters in the Greek alphabet. The solution may be found on page 325. [**Target: 10**]

UNTIMELY DEATHS Identify these well-known people whose untimely deaths are described as follows. Find the solutions on page 345. [**Target: 14**]

1. Rock and pop icon; heart failure caused by drugs use and over-eating, 1977.
2. Punk guitarist; drugs overdose after murdering his girlfriend in New York in 1978.
3. Rock star; shot by a delusional fan in New York in 1980.
4. Iconic movie actress; suicide by a drugs overdose, 1962.
5. Big Band leader; died in a plane crash in 1944.
6. Australian rock star; suicide or death by possible sexual misadventure in 1997.
7. Princess and former actress; killed in a car crash in Monaco in 1982.
8. Iconic movie actor; died in a car crash in 1955.
9. Mentally-ill Dutch artist; suicide by shooting himself in the chest, 1890.
10. Legendary rock guitarist; choked on vomit, 1970.
11. American grunge rock star; suicide by shotgun to the head in 1994.
12. West Coast gangsta rapper; killed in a drive-by shooting in Las Vegas in 1996.
13. Glam-rock star; killed in a car crash in south-west London in 1977.
14. British comedian; suicide by drugs overdose in an Australian hotel in 1968.
15. Soul singer; shot by his father during a row in 1984.
16. Female singer and songwriter; hit by speedboat while swimming off the coast of Mexico in 2000.
17. American poet; suicide by gassing herself in 1963.
18. Fashion mogul; shot by a serial killer in 1997.
19. American record producer, singer and politician; died in a skiing accident in 1998.
20. East Coast gangsta rapper; killed in a drive-by shooting in LA in 1997.

21. Author and feminist; drowned herself in the river Ouse, 1941.
22. Egyptian playboy; killed in a car crash in 1997.
23. Australian conservationist; killed by a stingray while filming in 2006.
24. Female American blues and folk singer; died following a drugs overdose in 1970.

FOOTBALL TEAMS WITH ONE-WORD NAMES Name the
twenty-five English League Football teams which have one-word names (ignoring FC or AFC). Turn to page 222 for the solution. [Target: 12]

ORDER OF SUCCESSION TO THE BRITISH THRONE
Name the *twenty-five* individuals closest in succession to the British throne. The solution may be found on page 243. [Target: 10]

MISCELLANY XXI Respond to these questions of a miscellaneous nature. Find the solutions on page 263. [Target: 14]

1. Which religion has Five Pillars?
2. In which city is the DVLA located?
3. In which English county would you find the site of the Battle of Bosworth, the town of Ashby-de-la-Zouch and Donington Park racing circuit?
4. Who played Hans Grüber in *Die Hard*?
5. Which two nations compete for the Calcutta Cup?
6. Which is the oldest university in the USA?
7. Which pub is associated with the fictional brewery Newton and Ridley?
8. Who was managed by Colonel Tom Parker?
9. Who wrote *The Old Man and the Sea*?
10. Which four American states are prefixed by the word 'New'?
11. How many curves are there on a standard paper clip?
12. What links Anne Boleyn, Lady Jane Grey, Robert Devereux Earl of Essex and the German spy, Josef Jakobs?
13. Where in the UK does the law forbid the Queen from

entering?

14. Who wrote *Heart of Midlothian, Ivanhoe* and *Rob Roy*?
15. Which country takes its name from the Latin word for 'southern'?
16. What is the chemical symbol for ozone?
17. What did John Sutter start in California in 1848?
18. If you were born on St Crispin's Day, what star sign would you be?
19. When was the last time a Wimbledon singles title was won by a British player?
20. How many people have walked on the moon?
21. In medicine, what is a lancet?
22. What is the largest number you can write in Roman numerals, using each character only once?
23. Which Teletubby has a triangular antenna on his/her head?
24. Which is the lowest number that, when written out, has its letters in alphabetical order?

POPULAR GIRLS' NAMES Name the *twenty-five* most popular girls' names (according to births registered in the UK in 2006). Find the solution on page 286. [**Target: 12**]

BUSY INTERNATIONAL AIRPORTS Identify the *twenty-five* busiest international airports* in the world (according to the number of international passengers carried in 2005). Turn to page 308 for the solution. [**Target: 10**]

---

* The demand for air travel is increasing at a remarkable rate. In the UK in the last twenty-five years, passenger volumes have risen 310% and the number of passengers using UK airports each year is projected to rise from 180 million in 2002 to 400 million in 2020. There are different measures for the quantity of traffic at airports. The world's busiest airport in terms of the total number of passengers (domestic and international) and the number of flights (departures and arrivals) is Atlanta with approximately 86,000 passengers in 2005 (until 1998, Chicago O'Hare held this title). Data for airports including domestic flights is dominated by the US due to the size of the domestic air transport industry. During the British Grand Prix, Silverstone is said to become the world's busiest airport with flights departing and arriving every few seconds.

RECENT HISTORY III Identify the year from the descriptions provided. The solutions may be found on page 326. [**Target: 10**]

1.   *The Return of the King* wins eleven Oscars; terrorist bombs explode during rush hour on the Madrid Metro killing 190 people; Vladimir Putin is elected for a second term as Russian President; Arsenal complete a whole season unbeaten in the Premiership; 335 people, many of them children, are killed in the Beslan school siege in Chechnya; Yasser Arafat dies; the Millau Viaduct, the world's tallest bridge, opens in France; 200,000 people are killed in Asia by tsunamis caused by a massive undersea earthquake, Athens hosts the Olympic Games.

2.   Adriana Iliescu at sixty-six becomes the oldest person to have given birth; the Kyoto Protocol to limit greenhouse gas emissions goes into effect without US participation; Pope John Paul II dies; Prince Charles marries Camilla Parker Bowles; the Labour Party wins a third general election; Liverpool win the Champions League, defeating AC Milan on penalties; the Live 8 concerts take place across the world, coinciding with the G8 summit at Gleneagles; terrorist bombs kill fifty-six people in London; London is awarded the 2012 Olympics; Lance Armstrong wins a seventh successive Tour de France; New Orleans is devastated by Hurricane Katrina.

3.   The Winter Olympics are held in Salt Lake City; the Queen confers an honorary knighthood on Rudolph Giuliani for his leadership in the aftermath of 9/11; traditional coins and notes cease to be legal tender in Eurozone member states and are replaced with the Euro; the Queen Mother dies at the age of 101; Switzerland joins the United Nations; Estonia hosts the Eurovision Song Contest; Roy Keane is sent home from the World Cup after an argument with Mick McCarthy, his manager; the Queen celebrates her Golden Jubilee.

4.   The SAS shoot dead three IRA members in Gibralta; Wimbledon win the FA Cup; Ayrton Senna wins his first Drivers' Championship after victory at the Japanese Grand Prix; George H.W. Bush is elected US President; Pan Am Flight 103 is blown up over Lockerbie killing 270 people; Ben Johnson is stripped of his Gold medal for failing a drugs test at the Seoul Olympics.

5. The FA Premier League is formed; Betty Boothroyd becomes the first female speaker of the House of Commons; race riots are sparked in Los Angeles after not-guilty verdicts are pronounced on Rodney King's attackers; Dan Quayle incorrectly spells the word 'potato'*; Linford Christie wins gold in the 100m at the Barcelona Olympics; the pound is withdrawn from the Exchange Rate Mechanism on Black Wednesday; Bill Clinton is elected US President for the first time; fire breaks out in Windsor Castle leading the Queen to describe the year as her 'annus horribilis'.

6. German reunification takes place; Nelson Mandela is released from prison; Margaret Thatcher resigns as Prime Minister; Iraq invades Kuwait, sparking the First Gulf War; Lithuania announces independence from the Soviet Union, the first Soviet Republic to do so; F.W. de Klerk begins to dismantle apartheid in South Africa, McDonald's opens its first fast-food outlet in Moscow; the Hubble telescope is launched aboard the space shuttle *Discovery*; England lose to Germany in the World Cup semi-final on penalties.

7. Jimmy Carter is sworn in as US President; EMI sack the Sex Pistols; *Star Wars* is released and quickly becomes the highest-grossing film to date; the Queen celebrates her Silver Jubilee; New York experiences a blackout for twenty-five hours; Elvis Presley dies.

8. Solidarity win the Polish elections; Communist governments collapse in Eastern Europe; the Berlin Wall is torn down; General Noriega is deposed by US troops in Panama; protests in Tiananmen Square in Beijing are crushed by the Chinese military, many demonstrators lose their lives; the Ayatollah Khomeini dies; the *Exxon Valdez* runs aground off Alaska, causing widespread environmental damage; Sky Television is launched; the poll tax is introduced in Scotland; ninety-six Liverpool supporters die in a crush at Hillsborough; *The Simpsons* airs for the first time in the US.

---

* While electioneering on a visit to a school in Trenton, New Jersey, Vice-President Dan Quayle corrected a schoolboy's spelling in front of the assembled media, placing an 'e' on the end of 'potato'. The error led to Quayle suffering widespread ridicule and greatly contributed to the media portrayal of the Vice-President as an intellectual lightweight. Quayle ran as a Republican Presidential candidate in 1999, but in the first contest finished in eighth (and last) place and withdrew from the race.

9. Winston Churchill replaces Neville Chamberlain as British Prime Minister; Germany invades the Low Countries with rapid assaults which become known as the 'Blitzkrieg'; the British expeditionary force is evacuated from Dunkirk; France surrenders to Germany and Vichy France is established; the Battle of Britain takes place in the skies over south-east England; Leon Trotsky is assassinated in Mexico.

10. The American Embassy in Tehran is seized by Islamic extremists and its occupants held hostage; Margaret Thatcher is elected British Prime Minister; Soviet troops invade Afghanistan; a radiation leak occurs at the Three Mile Island nuclear plant; Idi Amin is overthrown in Uganda but escapes into exile; fifteen sailors lose their lives during a freak storm hitting the Fastnet race; the first European Ariane rocket is launched.

11. Iraqi forces attack Iran leading to ten years of war; Zimbabwe gains independence from Britain and Robert Mugabe becomes President; Mount St Helens erupts spectacularly, killing fifty-seven people and causing widespread devastation; the SAS storm the Iranian Embassy in London; the Sony Walkman is introduced; John Lennon is shot dead in New York by a deranged fan; the US boycotts the Moscow Olympics in protest about the Soviet invasion of Afghanistan; millions watch *Dallas* to find out who shot JR.

12. Hillary and Tensing reach the summit of Mount Everest, the first men to do so; Stalin dies; the Korean War ends in stalemate; Elizabeth II is crowned in Westminster Abbey; Watson and Crick reveal the structure of DNA.

13. The first London Marathon is held; Pope John Paul II survives an assassination attempt by a Turkish gunman; the Penlee lifeboat and the *Union Star* are lost with all hands in a hurricane force storm off the south coast of Cornwall.

14. German forces surrender at Stalingrad; the Warsaw ghetto is attacked by German soldiers and the survivors are deported to concentration camps; the largest tank battle in history, the Battle of Kursk, takes place between Germany and Russia; Italy surrenders to Allied forces; *Casablanca* wins the Oscar for Best Picture.

15. The final episode of *M*A*S*H* airs in the US; Ronald Reagan announces the Strategic Defence Initiative, dubbed 'Star Wars';

Gandhi wins eight Oscars; *Stern* magazine publishes fabricated diaries of Adolf Hitler; Margaret Thatcher wins a second term in government; thirty-eight prisoners escape from Maze Prison in County Antrim.

16. Compact discs are first introduced; Argentina occupies the Falkland Islands; the *General Belgrano* is sunk by a British submarine; Leonid Brezhnev dies and is succeeded by Yuri Andropov; Mark Thatcher gets lost in the Sahara during the Paris–Dakar rally; Prince William is born; the *Mary Rose* is raised in the Solent; Channel 4 begins broadcasting.

17. The first Balkan War begins; the *Titanic* sinks on its maiden voyage after hitting an iceberg; the Chinese Republic is founded under Sun Yat-Sen; Lawrence Oates dies in an Antarctic blizzard.

18. Mata Hari is executed as a spy; Britain issues the Balfour Declaration for a Jewish homeland in Palestine; the Russian Revolution takes place; Tsar Nicholas II abdicates and Lenin assumes power; the US enters the First World War*.

---

* The entry of the United States into the First World War was primarily brought about by the frequent German attacks on American shipping (including the sinking of the *Lusitania*) but was hastened by the interception of a communication known as the Zimmermann Telegram. The telegram was a coded message sent by Arthur Zimmermann, the Foreign Secretary of the German Empire, to the German Ambassador in Mexico, Heinrich von Eckardt. The message contained instructions for von Eckardt to approach the Mexican Government, who at the time was involved in border conflicts with the US, to propose a military alliance with Germany. The message was sent from Berlin, first to the German Embassy in Washington via the submarine transatlantic cable (which the US had allowed Germany to use for encoded diplomatic communications), before being forwarded to the German Embassy in Mexico City. It was intercepted by British Naval Intelligence who were monitoring transmissions along the cable and decrypted using a code book acquired from a German agent captured in the Middle East. This posed a dilemma for the British: while it was important for British interests that the contents of the telegram were made known to the Americans, this would reveal to Germany the British capability in code-breaking, and reveal to the US that Britain had been monitoring her diplomatic communications. The solution presented itself when the British Government guessed that the telegram most probably reached Mexico City from Washington via the public telegraph system. An agent was dispatched to the telegraph office in Mexico City and in bribing a local official was able to retrieve a copy of the telegram. The telegram was presented to the US Ambassador in London as the work of British intelligence in Mexico without compromising the original source. Six weeks later, the US declared war on Germany.

19. The Vatican is established as an independent state; the St Valentine's Day Massacre occurs in Chicago; the Wall Street Crash takes place, followed by a period of economic depression; the British Labour Party wins its first general election and Ramsay MacDonald becomes Prime Minister.

20. Gandhi is assassinated; the State of Israel is created; the Berlin airlift takes place in response to a Soviet blockade; apartheid laws are passed in South Africa; the National Health Service is created in Britain.

21. Winston Churchill coins the term 'Iron Curtain' in a speech; the first meeting of the UN General Assembly takes place; the first programmable electronic computer becomes operational; Juan Perón becomes President of Argentina; the Fourth Republic begins in France.

22. Clinical trials of the contraceptive pill take place; the first Eurovision Song Contest takes place and is won by Switzerland; Britain and France are humiliated by the Suez Crisis, leading to Sir Anthony Eden's resignation the following year; the first transatlantic telephone cable is laid; Elvis Presley has his first hit in the US with 'Heartbreak Hotel'; Grace Kelly marries Prince Rainier III of Monaco.

23. The BBC begins radio broadcasts; Howard Carter opens Tutankhamen's tomb; the USSR is established; Mussolini seizes power in Italy; the Lloyd George government is bought down when Conservatives withdraw from the coalition, Bonar Law becomes Prime Minister; Michael Collins is assassinated in Dublin.

24. Ramsay MacDonald forms the first British Labour government but is defeated in a subsequent election over the Zinoviev Letter, linking him with communism; the first round-the-world flight takes 175 days (by the Army Air Service, precursor of the United States Air Force); Lenin dies and is buried in Red Square; Stalin begins purges against his rivals; the first Winter Olympic Games takes place in Chamonix in France.

POPULOUS COUNTRIES Name the *twenty-five* most populous countries* in the world. Turn to page 345 for the solution. [**Target: 14**]

PROLIFIC BATSMEN Name the *twenty-five* all-time leading run scorers† in test cricket‡. Find the solution on page 223. [**Target: 8**]

SINGERS AND BACKERS II Complete the names of these groups by identifying the singer most closely associated with the backing band. The solutions may be found on page 244. [**Target: 12**]

1. _____ and the Family Stone
2. _____ and the Comets
3. _____ and the Dominos
4. _____ and the Bunnymen
5. _____ and the MGs
6. _____ and the Supremes
7. _____ and the Heartbreakers
8. _____ and the Commotions
9. _____ and the New Power Generation
10. _____ and the Plastic Population
11. _____ and the Blowfish
12. _____ and the Mechanics

---

* The population of the world is growing at an enormous rate. The world's population first reached 1 billion in 1804 and took 123 years to add a second billion. It reached 3 billion thirty-three years later in 1960, 4 billion just fourteen years later in 1974 and 5 billion in 1987. In 1999 the 6 billionth person was born somewhere in the world. Encouragingly, the rate of population growth seems to have slowed from a peak of an annual addition of 87 million people in the late 1980s to 81 million a year by the 1990s and this is projected to have fallen to 50 million people a year in the 2040s. By that time, however, it is projected that the world population will have risen by 3 billion people on today's number and nobody is sure quite how many people the earth is capable of supporting.

† Donald Bradman, regarded by many as the greatest batsman there has ever been, scored 6,996 runs in his career, which is not quite enough to make this list. His test average, however, was 99.94 runs and but for an uncharacteristic duck in his final test innings would have been over 100. No other batsman who has played regularly for his country has even come close to this.

‡ A story has it that on one occasion, on being given out, W.G. Grace refused to walk. He glared at the official and snorted: 'They've not come to see you, umpire, they've come to see me bat.'

---

13. _____ and the Modern Lovers
14. _____ and Wizzard
15. _____ and His Jazzmen
16. _____ and the Stooges
17. _____ and the Tijuana Brass
18. _____ and the Impressions
19. _____ and the Magic Band
20. _____ and the Egyptians
21. _____ and the Bruvvers
22. _____ and the Famous Flames
23. _____ and the Luvvers
24. _____ and the Mindbenders

POPULAR BOYS' NAMES Identify the *twenty-five* most popular boys' names (according to births registered in the UK in 2006). Find the solution on page 263. [**Target: 12**]

NATO ALPHABET Recall the *twenty-six* words representing letters in the NATO phonetic alphabet*. The solution is on page 286. [**Target: 22**]

LINKED MISCELLANY XII Respond to the questions and work out the connecting theme that links them. The solution may be found on page 309. [**Target: 4**]

1. Who died after throwing herself under the King's horse in the 1913 Epsom Derby?
2. What is the common name for Petroselinum crispum, a plant used widely in European cooking, often as a garnish?
3. Which American company first produced the games of Monopoly, Risk, Cluedo and Trivial Pursuit?

---

* The development of radio communication gave rise for the need to be able to unambiguously convey letter sounds and as a result the British Army introduced the first phonetic alphabet in 1904. The original alphabet consisted of only six phonetic letter sounds but was expanded to a full alphabet in 1927. The entry of the United States into the Second World War led to the standardisation of the phonetic alphabet across all the Allied services, and, with the creation of NATO in 1953, the alphabet was changed into its current form.

4. Which Labour politician oversaw, as Postmaster General, the opening of the Post Office Tower and, as Minister of Technology, the development of Concorde?
5. Where would you see the Ponte Vecchio and Michelangelo's *David*?
6. What name is given to an advanced practitioner of yoga?
7. Who had hits in the 1980s with 'Doctor! Doctor!', 'You Take Me Up', and 'Hold Me Now'?
8. What dish consists of a filet of beef tenderloin coated in foie gras and chopped mushrooms and cooked in puff pastry?
9. Which river, the longest in Italy, connects Turin, Milan and the Adriatic Sea?
10. Who had a number five hit with 'I'm Free' in 1990?

COUNTRIES WITH FIVE-LETTER NAMES Recall the *twenty-six* countries that have five-letter names. Go to page 326 for the solution. [Target: 18]

TRACK-AND-FIELD EVENTS Name the *twenty-six* Olympic* athletics track-and-field events. Find the solution on page 346. [Target: 20]

ADVERTISING SLOGANS IV Identify the products or companies that were being advertised with these slogans. Go to page 223 for the solutions. [Target: 12]

1. 'The world's favourite airline'
2. 'When a man you've never met before suddenly gives you flowers'

---

* The 1908 London Olympics was the first (and not the last) games to be mired in controversy. Rome was originally due to host the 1908 Games, but was forced to withdraw when Mount Vesuvius erupted, throwing Italy into chaos. Animosity began at the opening ceremony when the American flag-bearer, Ralph Rose, refused to dip his flag to the royal box, greatly offending the British organisers. The rest of the games was characterised by a string of controversial judging decisions in which American athletes often came off second best. The final of the 400m was contested by four athletes, three Americans and a British runner Wyndham Halswelle. The race was ordered to be run again after J.C. Carpenter, the American 'winner', was judged to have interfered with the British athlete. The three Americans refused, and Halswelle competed on his own in the re-run, winning the event.

3. 'Fit the best'
4. 'Naughty but nice'
5. 'Let your fingers do the walking'
6. 'A newspaper, not a snoozepaper'
7. 'If it's on, it's in'
8. 'Because life's complicated enough'
9. 'Beats as it sweeps as it cleans'
10. 'It is. Are You?'
11. 'Is she or isn't she?'
12. 'Size matters'
13. 'You can't put a better bit of butter on your knife'
14. '_____ is good for you'
15. 'Loves the jobs you hate'
16. 'The ultimate driving machine'
17. 'Fluent in finance'
18. 'They're waffly versatile'
19. 'Let's make things better'
20. 'We won't make a drama out of a crisis'
21. 'It's everywhere you want to be'
22. 'Think small'
23. 'Free enterprise with every copy'
24. 'The longer-lasting snack'

MEMBERS OF NATO Name the *twenty-six* members of NATO*.
The solution is on page 244. [**Target: 14**]

BOOKS OF THE NEW TESTAMENT Name the *twenty-seven*
books of the New Testament†. Turn to page 263 for the solution.
[**Target: 6**]

---

* The North Atlantic Treaty Organization is a military alliance of twenty-six nations
which have made a commitment to their mutual defence. The commitment appears
in article 5 of the North Atlantic Treaty, which states that an attack on a single
alliance country is regarded as an attack against all the signatories. The treaty was
signed in Washington in 1949 by the twelve founding nations and other nations
have since joined the alliance. The break-up of the Soviet Union and Warsaw Pact
led to groups of Eastern Bloc countries joining in 1999 and 2004.
† The New Testament is made up of four books describing the ministry of Jesus
Christ (the Gospels, a narrative of the ministry of the Apostles), twenty-one letters
(the Epistles) and an apocalyptic prophecy.

QUOTATIONS FROM POPULAR FILMS II

Identify the films from which these quotations* are taken. (The date each film was released is given to assist you.) Look for the solutions on page 286. [**Target: 14**]

1. 'I know what you're thinking. Did he fire six shots or only five?' (1971)
2. 'The point is, ladies and gentlemen, that greed, for lack of a better word, is good. Greed is right. Greed works.' (1987)
3. 'Infamy! Infamy! They've all got it in for me!' (1964)
4. 'Broadsword calling Danny Boy.' (1968)
5. 'But, I'm funny how? Funny like a clown? I amuse you? I make you laugh?' (1990)
6. 'No Mr Bond. I expect you to die!' (1963)
7. 'Are you suggesting coconuts migrate?' (1975)
8. 'Meet you in Malkovich in one hour.' (1999)
9. 'Ten oughta do it, don't you think? Do you think we need one more? You think we need one more? All right, we'll get one more.' (2001)
10. 'Don't be stupid, be a smarty, come and join the Nazi Party!' (1968)
11. 'Who needs reasons when you've got heroin?' (1996)
12. 'Hello, my name is Inigo Montoya. You killed my father. Prepare to die.' (1987)
13. 'You either surf or you fight.' (1979)
14. 'I hate Illinois Nazis.' (1980)
15. 'Are you gonna bark all day, little doggy, or are you gonna bite?' (1992)
16. 'O pointy birds, O pointy pointy, anoint my head, anointy-nointy.' (1983)
17. 'I was a better man with you as a woman than I ever was with a woman as a man.' (1982)
18. 'They're coming outta the walls. They're coming outta the goddamn walls!' (1986)
19. 'Love is a many-splendoured thing, love is what makes the world go round, all you need is love.' (2001)

---

* In spite of being one of the most quoted movie lines, it is apocryphal that Humphrey Bogart delivered the line, 'Play it again, Sam' in *Casablanca*. In fact he never said it; Ingrid Bergman's Ilsa says the line: 'Play it, Sam. Play "As Time Goes By".' Other common movie misquotes include James Cagney's, 'You dirty rat,' and Mae West's, 'Is that a gun in your pocket, or are you just glad to see me?'

20. 'Fasten your seatbelts, it's going to be a bumpy night.' (1950)
21. 'One man's life touches so many others, when he's not there it leaves an awfully big hole.' (1946)
22. 'In Italy, for thirty years under the Borgias, they had warfare, terror, murder and bloodshed, but they produced Michelangelo, Leonardo da Vinci, and the Renaissance. In Switzerland, they had brotherly love; they had five hundred years of democracy and peace – and what did that produce? The cuckoo clock.' (1949)
23. 'I'm on this new diet for Paris. I don't eat anything until I feel like I'm about to faint, then I eat a cube of cheese. I'm one stomach flu away from reaching my goal weight.' (2006)
24. 'I don't train girls.' (2004)

STOPS ON THE CIRCLE LINE Name the *twenty-seven* stops on the Circle Line* of the London Underground. The solution may be found on page 309. [**Target: 12**]

FORMULA ONE WORLD CHAMPIONS Recall the *thirty* racing drivers to have become Formula One† World Champion (since the first Championship in 1950). The solution is on page 326. [**Target: 12**]

---

* Being an orbital railway, trains are always travelling in the same direction which causes uneven wear and tear on their wheels. To prevent this, trains are occasionally diverted via Aldgate East and Whitechapel, which turns the trains around.
† An average F1 engine produces 900 brake horsepower and can operate at over 19,000rpm (it idles at 4,000rpm) but weighs a mere 90kg. Although only about twice the capacity of an ordinary road car engine, this produces more than three times as many revs and eight times more power for less than half the weight (but at a cost of around £200,000 per engine). Brakes in F1 cars are made of carbon fibre and operate at temperatures in excess of 1,300 Celsius. Combined, these technologies allow the cars to be able to accelerate from 0 to 100mph and come back to a standstill in 6.6 seconds. Cornering speeds of F1 cars are increased using aerodynamic devices such as wings and barge boards which take advantage of the airflow over the car to create downforce and increase the car's grip on the road. The aerodynamics produce so much downforce that at over 100mph an F1 car could be driven upside down (if a suitable track existed). Fuel tanks in F1 consist of a Kevlar sack which is both crushable and strong enough to withstand the impact of a bullet. The refuelling rigs used in pit stops are able to refuel at a rate of approximately twelve litres a second; in this fashion, an ordinary road car with an empty tank could be completely refuelled in approximately three seconds. Drivers routinely experience forces of 5G (five times the force of gravity) when braking and cornering which means the driver's neck must be able to support five times the weight of his head and helmet combined – up to 25kg.

MISCELLANY XXII Answer these questions of a miscellaneous nature. Turn to page 346 for the solutions. [**Target: 14**]

1. From which military conflict do we get the balaclava and the cardigan?
2. In which English county would you find the castles of Bamburgh, Dunstanburgh and Alnwick?
3. Who left the Faces to join the Rolling Stones?
4. The first rule of Fight Club is: 'You do not talk about Fight Club.' What is the second rule of Fight Club?
5. How many players are there in a netball team?
6. Which 1962 novel featured a character called Alex and his gang of Droogs?
7. Who is Yogi Bear's girlfriend?
8. What links Jamrud in Pakistan with Torkham in Afghanistan?
9. Which type of character are *Julius Caesar*, *Richard III*, *Hamlet* and *Macbeth* the only of Shakespeare's plays to feature?
10. Who was the first man to exceed the speed of sound?
11. Which Olympic sport requires a planting box?
12. Which order of chivalry was founded by George I and derives its name from a purification ceremony undertaken by medieval knights?
13. Use of what costs $54,000 on average but has cost as much as $249,165 and as little as 36 cents?
14. A water lily growing in a circular pond doubles in size every day. If it takes ten days to cover the whole pond, how long does it take to cover half the pond?
15. Which is the only US state to have a border with only one other US state?
16. The first inter-racial kiss on American television took place in which series?
17. Who once said: 'I counted them all out and I counted them all back again'?
18. Which artistic term can be used to describe the painters Rembrandt, Caravaggio and Rubens and the composers Vivaldi, Handel and J.S. Bach?
19. Which is the only sea that has no contact with land?
20. How many pairs of ribs do humans have?
21. What makes a pink gin pink?

22. Which two chemical products result from burning pure methane?
23. Which Ministry did Winston Smith work for in *Nineteen Eighty-four*?
24. Martin has a clock that chimes every hour and every half hour. The clock chimes once at one o'clock, twice at two o'clock, three times at three o'clock, and so on. The clock also chimes once on the half hour. One day, Martin arrives home and hears the clock chime once. Half an hour later he hears it chime once again. Half an hour later it chimes once and another half an hour later it chimes once again. Given that the clock is functioning correctly, what time did Martin arrive home?

MONARCHIES Name the *twenty-eight* countries of the world that are governed by monarchs* (excluding Commonwealth Realms where the monarch is represented by a Governor General). Find the solution on page 223. [**Target: 12**]

RED, WHITE AND BLUE FLAGS Name the *twenty-nine* countries that have red, white and blue† flags (that is, in which the predominant colours are red, white and blue). Turn to page 244 for the solution. [**Target: 10**]

---

* A monarchy may be defined as an autocracy governed by a monarch who has usually inherited the title. In a monarchy, the monarch demands the service of their people, in contrast to a republic where the role of the leader is to serve the people. Examples of titles of monarchs are King, Emperor, Emir, Sultan, Sheik and Tsar. (Tsar is derived from Julius Caesar, the title first chosen by Ivan IV in 1547 to convey to his subjects a sense that he was a person with dictatorial powers. The German word Kaiser has the same derivation.)

† Colours have strong associations with psychology and emotion. These emotional characteristics are deliberately exploited in flag design, with colours chosen to represent qualities that the flag bearer wishes to endorse. Red is associated with passion, courage and energy as well as with ambition, anger and aggression. It has been used on the flags of the Russian Revolution, by the Nazis and by many communist dictatorships. White has associations with peace, purity, protection and healing. It is used as a symbolic colour by medical and peacekeeping organisations and the white flag is the recognised international symbol for calling a truce. Blue is the colour of harmony, reflection, truth and co-operation and has been adopted by the United Nations and European Union in their flags. Red, white and blue is a combination of colours that seemingly makes for an appealing package, being the most common colour combination appearing on national flags.

FILMS AND THEIR STARS V Name the films from these selected acting appearances and dates of release. The solutions are on page 263. [**Target: 8**]

1. Tom Hanks, Robin Wright, Gary Sinise (1994)
2. Jude Law, Haley Joel Osment (2001)
3. Judi Dench, Cate Blanchett, Bill Nighy (2006)
4. Hugh Grant, Toni Collette, Rachel Weisz (2002)
5. Clint Eastwood, Gene Hackman, Morgan Freeman, Richard Harris (1992)
6. Burt Reynolds, Roger Moore, Peter Fonda, Farrah Fawcett, Jackie Chan, Dean Martin, Sammy Davis Jr. (1981)
7. Sally Field, Dolly Parton, Daryl Hannah, Julia Roberts, Shirley MacLaine (1989)
8. Chow Yun-Fat, Michelle Yeoh, Zhang Ziyi (1999)
9. Rex Harrison, Richard Burton, Elizabeth Taylor (1963)
10. Linda Blair, Max von Sydow (1973)
11. Johnny Depp, Winona Ryder, Vincent Price (1990)
12. Julia Roberts, Denzel Washington (1993)
13. Tom Berenger, Willem Dafoe, Charlie Sheen, Forest Whitaker (1986)
14. Juliette Binoche, Carrie-Anne Moss, Judi Dench (2000)
15. Michael Douglas, Demi Moore, Donald Sutherland (1994)
16. Jon Voight, Bert Reynolds, Ned Beatty (1972)
17. Dustin Hoffman, Jessica Lange, Bill Murray (1982)
18. Forest Whitaker, Miranda Richardson, Stephen Rea (1992)
19. Christopher Walken, Andy Garcia, Christopher Lloyd, Steve Buscemi (1995)
20. Tom Cruise, Rebecca De Mornay (1983)
21. Denzel Washington, Kevin Kline (1987)
22. Meryl Streep, Shirley MacLaine, Dennis Quaid, Gene Hackman (1990)
23. Gwyneth Paltrow, Blythe Danner, Daniel Craig (2003)
24. Frank Sinatra, Laurence Harvey, Janet Leigh, Angela Lansbury (1962)

TOWNS NAMED AFTER RIVER MOUTHS Name the *twenty-nine* British towns that have the suffix '-mouth' as part of their names. Go to page 286 for the solution. [**Target: 10**]

NOTIFIABLE DISEASES Name the *thirty* notifiable diseases; that is, instances of diseases that general practitioners* in the UK are duty-bound to report†. The solution is on page 309. [**Target: 14**]

CATCHPHRASES II Identify the authors of these catchphrases (real or fictional). Turn to page 327 for the solutions. [**Target: 12**]

1. 'That's another nice mess you've got me into.'
2. 'You wouldn't let it lie!'
3. 'Listen very carefully; I will say zees only once.'
4. 'The truth is out there.'
5. 'Zoinks!'
6. 'No, no, no, no . . . yes.'
7. 'It's good but it's not right.'
8. 'My flabber has never been so gasted.'
9. 'Can we talk?'
10. 'Run around . . . now!'
11. 'You dirty old man!'
12. 'You dirty rotten swine, you.'
13. 'Silly old moo.'
14. 'You're my wife now!'
15. 'Shut it, you slaaagg!'
16. 'What do you think of it so far?'
17. 'I didn't get where I am today . . .'
18. 'Smoke me a kipper, I'll be back for breakfast!'
19. 'Nice 'ere, innit?'
20. 'Bite my shiny metal ass!'
21. 'Whatchoo talkin' 'bout, Willis?'
22. 'Ay thang you.'
23. 'Are you sitting comfortably?'
24. 'Mind how you go.'

---

* The medical profession owes much to Hippocrates, 'The Father of Medicine', who was a physician who was born in Greece in 460BC. He sought to find rational explanations for infirmity rather than look to superstitious explanations which were the norm at the time. He gave his name to the oath that underpins medical ethics and professionalism throughout the world today.

† In order to prevent the spread of infectious diseases, UK practitioners have a duty to report diseases designated as 'notifiable' to the consultant responsible for Communicable Disease Control.

CARRY ON FILMS Recall the *thirty Carry On* films*. You can find the solution on page 347. [**Target: 15**]

CHRISTIAN FEASTS Name the *thirty* feast days (or festivals) in the Christian calendar†. The solution is on page 224. [**Target: 6**]

NICKNAMES OF PLACES Identify these places from the nicknames that are presented. The solutions are on page 245. [**Target: 18**]

---

* The first *Carry On* film was made in 1958 by director Gerald Thomas and producer Peter Rogers, the pair who would go on to make all of the films in the series. After making his second successful *Carry On* film in 1959, Peter Rogers announced the regular *Carry On* team would consist of Kenneth Connor, Leslie Phillips, Kenneth Williams, Hattie Jacques, Terence Longden, Joan Sims, Charles Hawtrey and Bill Owen. (Sidney James would make his first appearance in a *Carry On* film later the same year.) The team were all offered a percentage of future takings but they each declined, preferring a fixed fee.

† Throughout history and across many societies religious practice and the calendar are interconnected. The link between gods and the names for the days of the week first appeared in about 300BC ('Before Christ') and the division of a week into seven days has its origins in Genesis. The modern calendar comes from the Romans, and particularly the Julian calendar adopted in 45BC. Julius Caesar arranged the days in months; every odd month having thirty-one days, even months having thirty and February having twenty-nine days or thirty in a leap year. The emperor Augustus insisted a day was taken from February and added to the month of August (which had taken his name) so it didn't have fewer days than any of the other months. The problem with the Julian calendar was that it erred from the solar calendar by about $11\frac{1}{2}$ minutes every year. By the sixteenth century this had created an error of ten days between the Julian and the solar calendars; the spring equinox had crept forward to 10 March. This was increasingly a problem for the Catholic Church as Easter Day, the most important day in the Christian calendar, was calculated according to the spring equinox. If the date of the equinox was wrong, Easter was being celebrated on the wrong day and, furthermore, most of the other movable feasts were calculated according to when Easter fell. Pope Gregory XIII fixed the problem in 1582 by moving the calendar forward by ten days, and removing leap years from century years that were not divisible by 400 (e.g. 1800, 1900, but not 2000). The Protestant countries of northern Europe took longer to switch to the Gregorian calendar, with Britain changing in 1752. Under the Julian calendar, New Year was celebrated on 1 April but was moved to 1 January with the introduction of the Gregorian calendar. People who continued to celebrate the New Year on 1 April, ignorant of the change, gave rise to the tradition of April Fools.

1.	The Big Apple	2.	The Big Smoke
3.	Tinseltown	4.	The Pond
5.	The Emerald Isle	6.	The Windy City
7.	The Roof of the World	8.	The Garden of England
9.	Motown	10.	City of Dreaming Spires
11.	Sin City	12.	The Big Easy
13.	The Granite City	14.	City of David
15.	The Gateway of India	16.	City of Light
17.	The Eternal City	18.	Mile High City
19.	City of Brotherly Love	20.	Bride of the Sea
21.	The Pink City	22.	The Mistake on the Lake
23.	The White City	24.	Pearl of the Orient

SHIPPING ZONES Recall the *thirty-one* shipping zones of the waters around the UK (that feature in weather forecasts* for shipping). Go to page 263 for the solution. [**Target: 8**]

IRISH COUNTIES Name the *thirty-two* counties in Ireland†. Find the solution on page 287. [**Target: 8**]

---

* The first scientific weather forecasts were made by Robert Fitzroy (1805–65) after his appointment as director of the new meteorological service for the Board of Trade in 1851. His reports (Fitzroy himself coined the term 'weather forecasts') were the first to be published (in *The Times*) and he is also credited with the invention of the Fitzroy Barometer, a maritime barometer which became essential to nineteenth-century mariners. In spite of this, history remembers Fitzroy for an altogether different reason. In 1831, Fitzroy invited the twenty-one-year-old Charles Darwin on his round-the-world expedition on HMS *Beagle*, ostensibly for his company as a dining companion, as society etiquette frowned on gentlemen fraternising with the lower ranks. It is a strange irony that Fitzroy's passion was creationism and his personal motivation for the voyage was to find evidence for the biblical interpretation of creation. He required a companion familiar with the scriptures to be able to discuss his ideas during the voyage and chose Darwin chiefly as he had just left Cambridge with a degree in divinity. Unsurprisingly, the two men quarrelled constantly throughout the five-year duration of the expedition. The publication of *The Origin of Species* was to be a bitter blow to Fitzroy from which he never recovered and he committed suicide in 1865.

† Historically, Ireland has consisted of four provinces: Munster in the South, Connaught in the West, Leinster in the East and Ulster in the North. Ulster is now divided between Northern Ireland and the Republic. Each province is sub-divided into counties.

CHARACTERS IN CHILDREN'S TELEVISION II

Recall the television programmes that featured these characters. The solutions are on page 309. [**Target: 14**]

1. Mr Burns, Ned Flanders, Principal Skinner
2. Cuthbert, Dibble, Grubb
3. Major, Tiny, the Soup Dragon
4. Scott, Tin-Tin, Grandma
5. Fred, Velma, Daphne
6. Boo Boo, Cindy, Ranger John Smith
7. Cut-throat Jake, Master Mate, Pirate Willy
8. The Slag Brothers, the Gruesome Twosome, Peter Perfect
9. PC Copper, Farmer Barleymow, Frank the Postman
10. Captain Haddock, the Thompson Twins, Professor Cuthbert Calculus
11. Tommy, Angelica, Phil
12. Edward, Henry, Gordon
13. Tortoise, Octavia, Pig
14. Mrs Dingle, PC McGarry (number 452), Captain Snort
15. Spot, Sgt. Flint, Rosemary
16. King Otto, Minister of Wheel Estate, Fenella the Kettle Witch
17. Bingo, Drooper, Fleegle
18. Nogbad the Bad, Olaf the Lofty, Grolliffe the Ice Dragon
19. Spud, Dizzy, Scoop
20. Dr Claw, MAD Cat, Chief Quimby
21. Robin, Rosie, Mr Ship
22. Muskie the Muskrat, Ty Coon, Vincent Van Gopher
23. Long Distance Clara, Mr Baskerville and Watson
24. Bubi Bear, Square Bear, Mr Peevley

THAMES CROSSINGS

Name the *thirty-two* Thames* crossings (bridges) in the tidal section of the river. Find the solution on page 327. [**Target: 16**]

---

* The river Thames emerges from the ground in a Gloucestershire field about three miles south-west of Cirencester. From here, it runs 215 miles to the sea (making it the longest river completely in England) and is navigable from Lechlade, 191 miles from the sea. The river is tidal from Kingston-upon-Thames.

GLADIATORS Name the *thirty-two* gladiators who appeared in the television series of the same name (running for eight series from 1992 to 1999). Look for the solution on page 348. [**Target: 12**]

ENTREPRENEURS II Identify the industry sectors most closely associated with these entrepreneurs. Turn to page 225 for the solutions. [**Target: 10**]

1.	Charles Merrill	2.	Milton Hershey
3.	Aristotle Onassis	4.	Hugh Hefner
5.	John Pierpont Morgan	6.	Donald Trump
7.	Martha Stewart	8.	Martha Lane Fox
9.	Michael Bloomberg	10.	John Rockefeller
11.	Howard Hughes	12.	Warren Buffet
13.	Paul Warburg	14.	Ted Turner
15.	George Soros	16.	Jean Paul Getty
17.	Cornelius Vanderbilt	18.	Andrew Carnegie
19.	John Harvey-Jones	20.	David Geffen
21.	Mark McCormack	22.	James Jerome Hill
23.	Theodore Vail	24.	Lord Beaverbrook

FILMS STARRING MARILYN MONROE Recall the *thirty-two* films in which Marilyn Monroe starred. Find the solution on page 245. [**Target: 5**]

TREES NATIVE TO THE BRITISH ISLES Name the *thirty-two* trees that are native* to the British Isles. You can find the solution on page 264. [**Target: 6**]

---

* Woodland has been a continuous feature of the British Isles since the last ice age receded around 10,000 years ago. At that time, Britain was connected to Europe by a land bridge, over which plant and animal species were able to slowly migrate as the ice moved north and the climate improved. The melting ice raised sea levels and flooded the English Channel which blocked this migration leaving the island with its small number of native trees. Many hundreds of new species have since been introduced by man. Native trees and woodland are richer in wildlife as they have had longer to build up client populations of insects which in turn provide food for other animals in the ecosystem.

MISCELLANY XXIII Respond to these questions of a miscellaneous nature. Look for the solutions on page 287.
[Target: 10]

1. What colour are the seats in the House of Lords?
2. *My Fair Lady* was based on which play by George Bernard Shaw?
3. The name for which English county is derived from a word meaning 'headland people'?
4. In which country would you find Sheriff's Courts?
5. What scientific discovery was made by Francis Crick and James Watson in 1953?
6. What is the key characteristic of a ship that is described as 'Post-Panamax'?
7. St Mary Mead is home to which fictional detective?
8. What links Charles Dickens, Laurence Olivier, Isaac Newton and Edward the Confessor?
9. What was developed by the Manhattan Project?
10. In 1988, who became the first footballer to be transferred for £2m between British clubs?
11. Specifically, what did Nelson lose on Tenerife in 1797?
12. What flower is alternatively known as the Lent Lily?
13. How many semitones are there in an octave?
14. Which TV family live at 742 Evergreen Terrace?
15. What does NAAFI stand for in the British military?
16. Which League Football team did Ian Botham play for?
17. Sir Anthony van Dyck was court painter to which English monarch?
18. Which slang word for a socially inept person first appeared in a Dr Seuss book?
19. In 1999, which two actresses received Oscar nominations for playing the same role, but in different films?
20. 'Yellow Submarine' was released as a double A-side with which other Beatles song?
21. Mr Smith weighs 40kg more than Mrs Smith. Together they weigh 130kg. How much do they each weigh?
22. What do Scots describe as Grahams, Corbetts and Munros?
23. In which sport are the team members known as lead, second, third and skip?

24. A bookworm encounters a ten-volume set of books on a shelf and starts eating them. Each book, pages and covers together, is 5cm thick. Each cover is ½ cm thick. If the bookworm eats at a rate of 1cm every hour, how long will it take the bookworm to eat its way from page one of the first volume to the last page of the last volume?

LONDON BOROUGHS Name the *thirty-three* London boroughs*. Find the solution on page 310. [**Target: 10**]

OFFICER RANKS IN THE BRITISH MILITARY Recall the *thirty-three* officer ranks† in the British armed forces (eleven ranks in each of the three services). Go to page 328 for the solution. [**Target: 14**]

---

* Greater London actually has three cities within it: Southwark, Westminster and London. The City of Westminster (home to the ruling monarch and the Government) and the City of London (home of the mercantile classes) historically have competed to gain the upper hand in the capital but one has never been wholly able to dominate the other. This rivalry can still be seen in the tradition of the Temple Bar ceremony whenever the reigning monarch visits the City. The London County Council was created in 1888 although it was subsequently weakened by the government of Lord Salisbury who established the London Boroughs and transferred most of the civic power to them. In 2000 a Greater London Authority was set up under an elected mayor but significant political power in the capital still rests with the boroughs.

† Rank-based command structure is first recorded in the second century BC when Roman forces under Gaius Marius were reorganised into a hierarchical structure. The restructure resulted in the creation of units of force called Legions (around 6,000 men commanded by a Legate), Cohorts (600 men) and Centuries (100 men commanded by a Centurion). Over time, military ranks have evolved to reflect changing military tactics and the emergence of new technologies (such as naval and air warfare). The Geneva Convention recognises three distinctions of military personnel; Commissioned Officers, Non-commissioned Officers (such as Sergeants and Petty Officers) and Other Enlisted Ranks (such as Privates). Commissioned Officer ranks are largely defined by the amount of force under their command and the degree of autonomy they are permitted. Flag officers (such as Generals and Admirals) are the most senior ranks and command large units such as brigades or fleets of ships and are expected to operate independently for long periods of time. Field officers (such as Colonels and Navy Captains) command individual units of force such as a regiment or a warship, and operate independently for shorter periods. Junior officers lead small units such as companies or watches, carrying out specific tasks and instructions with very little independence.

FIRST LINES OF POP SONGS V Recall the titles of these songs from the first lines provided. (The year each song was a hit is supplied to assist you.) If you wish, name the performers as well. Turn to page 348 for the solutions. [**Target: 14**]

1. 'Out on the wily, windy moors.' (1978)
2. 'In the deserts of Sudan.' (1978)
3. 'You've got a great car, yeah, what's wrong with it today?' (2001)
4. 'I met her in a club down in north Soho.' (1970)
5. 'I thought I saw a man brought to life.' (1997)
6. 'Sometimes I feel I've got to run away.' (1981)
7. 'DJ's got the party started there's no end in sight.' (2001)
8. 'She came from Greece, she had a thirst for knowledge.' (1995)
9. 'The lights are on, but you're not home.' (1986)
10. 'I made it through the wilderness.' (1984)
11. 'Look at the stars, look how they shine for you.' (2000)
12. 'Once I had a love and it was a gas.' (1979)
13. 'So if you're lonely you know I'm here waiting for you.' (2004)
14. 'How many times have you woken up and prayed for the rain?' (1986)
15. 'May I have your attention please?' (2000)
16. 'I'd rather be liberated, I find myself captivated.' (1998)
17. 'When the moon is in the seventh house and Jupiter aligns with Mars.' (1969)
18. 'Well I guess it would be nice if I could touch your body.' (1987)
19. 'I've been cheated by you since I don't know when.' (1975)
20. 'I've known a few guys who thought they were pretty smart.' (1999)
21. 'Oh, yeah, I'll tell you something.' (1963)
22. 'Sexy, everything about you so sexy.' (2002)
23. 'Get up in the morning, slaving for bread, sir.' (1969)
24. 'Are you gonna take me home tonight?' (1978)

SQUARES ON THE MONOPOLY BOARD Recall the *thirty-six** squares on the Monopoly† board, on which players may land. The solution is on page 225. [**Target: 28**]

PLAYS BY WILLIAM SHAKESPEARE Name the *thirty-seven* plays by William Shakespeare‡. You can find the solution on page 246. [**Target: 18**]

CHARACTERS IN LITERATURE IV Identify the works of literature in which each of these characters appears. Turn to page 264 for the solutions. [**Target: 14**]

1. Major Major Major Major
2. Aunt Spiker and Aunt Sponge
3. The Wife of Bath
4. Winston Smith

---

* There are actually forty squares on the board (ten along each side of the board) but some squares are duplicated.

† An American, Charles Darrow, conceived the game of Monopoly in 1934 based on properties in New York City and by the time of his death in 1967 was the world's first game-designer millionaire. The British version was released under licence in 1935 by Waddingtons, whose boss, Victor Watson, decided to change the properties to famous areas of London and the currency to pounds rather than dollars. Over the years, Monopoly has been released in different versions all over the world, and it is estimated that 200 million games have been sold to date (which equates to an estimated 5 billion little green houses).

‡ William Shakespeare was born in Stratford-upon-Avon in 1564 (the same year as his rival, Christopher Marlowe) but given his status today, surprisingly little is known about his life. He married Anne Hathaway, eight years his senior, when he was only eighteen, with Anne giving birth to their first child, Susanna, six months later (which may provide the reason for their union). Their twins Hamnet and Judith arrived two years later in 1585. Shakespeare is thought to have left Anne about this time to move to London to pursue a career as an actor and playwright, and probably began writing around 1588. Shakespeare acted with the Lord Chamberlain's Men (renamed the King's Men in 1603) along with Richard Burbage (the top celebrity actor of his day); their company had stakes in two London theatres, Blackfriars and The Globe. The first written reference to Shakespeare appears in a highly critical review by the playwright Robert Greene in 1592 which may coincide, ironically, with Shakespeare's first taste of commercial success. In 1596 Shakespeare's father, John, applied for a coat of arms, perhaps as a result of his son's accomplishments. Shakespeare died in 1616 after retiring to Stratford-upon-Avon but most of his plays were published posthumously in a volume called the First Folio in 1634, making it difficult to know the exact dates that the plays were written.

5.	Injun Joe	6.	Mr Tumnus
7.	Tweedledum and Tweedledee	8.	Abraham Van Helsing
9.	Rikki Tikki Tavi	10.	Holden Caulfield
11.	Mrs Malaprop	12.	Leopold Bloom
13.	Miss Havisham	14.	Maxim de Winter
15.	Mr Knightley	16.	Raskolnikov
17.	Pelagia Iannis	18.	Piggy
19.	Guy Montag	20.	Aunt Pittypat
21.	George Milton	22.	Anne Shirley
23.	Jack Torrance	24.	Bathsheba Everdene

PROLIFIC ENGLAND GOAL-SCORERS Name the *thirty-nine* players to have scored ten or more goals for England in the post-war period. Turn to page 287 for the solution. [**Target: 18**]

ACTORS APPEARING IN CARRY ON FILMS Recall the *thirty-eight* actors who have appeared in three or more *Carry On* films*. The solution is on page 310. [**Target: 12**]

---

* Talbot Rothwell joined the crew of the *Carry On* films in 1963 when he offered Peter Rogers (the producer of the series) a script entitled *Call Me a Cab*. Fortuitously for Rothwell, his offer coincided with the departure of the writer of the earlier *Carry On* films, Norman Hudis, to the United States. The script was renamed *Carry On Cabby* and Rothwell would remain with the series for a further nineteen films. Rothwell's writing took the series away from the slapstick of the Hudis scripts towards the seaside postcard bawdiness with which it is most associated. Some examples of Rothwell's dialogue include:

Det. Sgt. Bung: This ear was found in Slocombe woods.

Valeria: What, this ear?

Det. Sgt. Bung: Yes, that there.

Carry On Screaming (1966)

Biddle: Nurse I dreamt about you last night.

Nurse Clarke: Did you?

Biddle: No, you wouldn't let me.

Carry On Doctor (1967)

Captain Keene: Fire at will!

Brother Belcher: Poor old Will, why do they always pick on him?

Carry On Up the Khyber (1968)

LINKED MISCELLANY XIII Respond to these miscellaneous questions and deduce the connecting theme linking them. The solution is on page 328. [**Target: 7**]

1. Which country is the fifth largest in size in both area and population?
2. How is the constellation of Orion otherwise known?
3. What acronym was used to refer to the partners of the England football team at the 2006 World Cup?
4. Which group had hits with 'Wasteland', 'Tower of Strength' and 'Beyond the Pale'?
5. Who was the American First Lady from 1961 until 1963?
6. Which Ian Fleming novel, published in 1956, was the first in a series?
7. Which scientific quantity, by convention symbolised by Q, can be defined as 'energy in transit'?
8. Which famous city is overlooked by Table Mountain?
9. In golf, how is a Number 1 Wood more commonly known?
10. What term is given to the market conditions where investors have confident expectations of capital gains?

MICHAEL JACKSON HITS Name the *thirty-eight* solo Michael Jackson* singles to have reached the Top Ten in the UK. Turn to page 348 for the solution. [**Target: 12**]

HISTORIC ENGLISH COUNTIES Name the *thirty-nine* historic English counties; that is, the counties that existed from the sixteenth century until 1888 (and the Local Government Act†). The solution is on page 226. [**Target: 30**]

---

* Michael Jackson first started performing at the age of four and by the time he was ten, the Jackson 5 signed their first record deal with Motown Records in 1968. When MGM launched the solo career of Donny Osmond from rival band the Osmonds, Motown responded by launching Michael as a solo act. Hits followed, but it was his collaboration with producer Quincy Jones, on the *Off the Wall* album and then *Thriller*, that led to Jackson attaining superstardom.

† England has traditionally been composed of some thirty-nine counties, existing more or less unchanged from Norman times until the Victorian age. The Local Government Act of 1888 was the first legislation to alter the historical boundaries of English counties, and since then counties have regularly been created, changed and removed by successive governments. The most recent legislation has left England carved up into a variety of counties, districts and Unitary Authorities, greatly complicating the administrative map.

FOREIGN WORDS AND PHRASES II Identify the foreign word or phrase from the description provided. Each word or phrase is in common use in English but has been loaned from another language. Look for the answers on page 247. [**Target: 14**]

1. Outdoors (Italian)
2. Military takeover or a success (French)
3. Reason for being (French)
4. A zigzag course through obstacles (Norwegian)
5. The area adjacent to and behind the coast (German)
6. Ground floor balcony (Sanskrit)
7. Spirit of the times (German)
8. An incorrigible child (French)
9. A child prodigy (German)
10. Bugbear or pet fear (French)
11. A vast selection (Swedish)
12. Complete freedom to act, literally 'white card' (French)
13. An expert, especially one who gives a critical opinion (Hindi)
14. The lowest point (Arabic)
15. Appetite for travel (German)
16. Temporary lodging or small flat, literally 'a foothold' (French)
17. Pursuit of political interests ahead of ethical concerns (German)
18. Easy, without hard work (Hindi)
19. Out of control (Malay)
20. Type of mathematical notation, literally 'reunion of broken parts' (Arabic)
21. Taking pleasure in the misfortune of others (German)
22. Eager, zealous (Mandarin Chinese)
23. Strong criticism (German)
24. Government official responsible for investigating complaints (Swedish)

BOOKS OF THE OLD TESTAMENT Name the *thirty-nine* books of the Old Testament*. Find the solution on page 265. [**Target: 8**]

---

* The Bible is one of the oldest texts in existence and is also the world's best-selling book. The Old Testament is a collection of books believed to be written by around forty different authors between 1500BC and 400BC.

LONGEST RIVERS Name the *forty* longest rivers* in the world. You can find the solution on page 288. [**Target: 10**]

WIT AND WISDOM III The following quotations are attributed to either Groucho Marx or Woody Allen or Homer Simpson. Identify the correct author of each quotation. Look for the solutions on page 311. [**Target: 20**]

1. 'I don't care to belong to a club that accepts people like me as members.'
2. 'If you don't like your job you don't strike. You just go in there every day and do it really half-assed. That's the American way.'
3. 'I was raised in the Jewish tradition, taught never to marry a Gentile woman, shave on a Saturday night and, most especially, never to shave a Gentile woman on a Saturday night.'
4. 'Weaselling out of things is important to learn. It's what separates us from the animals . . . except the weasel.'
5. 'Outside of a dog, a book is man's best friend. Inside of a dog, it's too dark to read.'
6. 'It's not easy to juggle a pregnant wife and a troubled child, but somehow I managed to fit in eight hours of TV a day.'
7. 'I failed to make the chess team because of my height.'
8. 'What's the point of going out? We're just going to wind up back here anyway.'
9. 'He may look like an idiot and talk like an idiot but don't let that fool you. He really is an idiot.'
10. 'Getting out of jury duty is easy. The trick is to say you're prejudiced against all races.'

---

* Estimates for river lengths vary enormously for the following reasons: (i) seasonal fluctuations in precipitation; (ii) alternative interpretations of routes and particularly in the definition of tributaries; (iii) accuracy of measurement of length (for example, as measurement becomes more accurate river length will tend to increase as more directional fluctuations are included); (iv) definition of the river source may be arbitrary (for example, where many tributaries exist); (v) definition of the river mouth may be arbitrary (for example, where there is a large estuary which gradually opens into the sea). Figures tend to be inconsistent between different sources and must be treated as indicative.

11. 'I have had a perfectly wonderful evening, but this wasn't it.'
12. 'Money is better than poverty, if only for financial reasons.'
13. 'Either he's dead or my watch has stopped.'
14. 'I like my beer cold, my TV loud and my homosexuals flaming.'
15. 'I think crime pays. The hours are good, you travel a lot.'
16. 'A child of five would understand this. Get me a child of five!'
17. 'I took a speed-reading course and read *War and Peace* in twenty minutes. It involves Russia.'
18. 'I never forget a face, but in your case I'll make an exception.'
19. 'No one asked me to volunteer.'
20. 'How can I believe in God when just last week I got my tongue caught in the roller of an electric typewriter?'
21. 'Those are my principles. If you don't like them I have others.'
22. 'Why was I with her? She reminds me of you. In fact, she reminds me more of you than you do!'
23. 'I don't want to achieve immortality through my work. I want to achieve it through not dying.'
24. 'What if we chose the wrong religion? Each week we just make God madder and madder.'

ROYAL CONSORTS Name the *forty-one* consorts (that is, the husband or wife of the sovereign) of the kings and queens of England since 1066. You will be able to find the solution on page 329. [**Target: 7**]

FA CUP WINNERS Name the *forty-two* teams to have won the FA Cup*. The solution is on page 349. [**Target: 30**]

---

* The first Football Association Challenge Cup competition took place in 1872 and had fifteen entrants. Under the original format, the winner had the right to defend their title the following year, with all the remaining teams competing for the right to challenge the holder. This format was later dropped but the phrase 'Challenge Cup' was retained for the trophy. The first final was played at Kennington Oval, which hosted it a further twenty times. Between 1893 and 1923, the location of the final venue was unfixed until the completion of Wembley Stadium gave the competition its permanent home. The first Wembley final descended into chaos as 200,000 people, vastly more than the capacity, tried to squeeze into the new stadium. The following year it was made an all-ticket event.

MISCELLANY XXIV Respond to these questions of a miscellaneous nature. Go to page 226 for the solutions. [**Target: 12**]

1. A person experiencing a photic sneeze reflex sneezes in response to what external stimulus?
2. What does the flag of Belize have more of than any other national flag?
3. Which term for a period of isolation is derived from the biblical period of forty days?
4. In which month is the vernal equinox?
5. Who composed *Aida*?
6. From which television series was *Mork and Mindy* a spin-off?
7. Which singer has the middle name 'Hercules'?
8. In which town did the gunfight at the OK Corral take place?
9. A ship travelling along the Panama Canal from the Pacific Ocean to the Atlantic Ocean would be sailing in which general direction?
10. Which is the only US state with a one-syllable name?
11. What does the company founded in 1945 by Joseph Cyril Bamford produce?
12. In which human organ would you find aqueous humour and vitreous humour?
13. The name of which common cooking ingredient comes from the French meaning 'sour wine'?
14. In chess, what is the minimum number of moves a pawn must make to become a queen?
15. Which American University is located at New Haven, Connecticut?
16. What was the name of the blind Benedictine monk who, it is claimed, first produced champagne?
17. If it takes Belinda six hours to paint a fence and Janice three hours to paint the same fence, how long would it take to paint if they both worked at the same time?
18. What was the title of the first single released by the Beatles?
19. In *Alice's Adventures in Wonderland*, what did Alice use as a croquet mallet?
20. Which is the only Scottish League Football team to contain none of the letters of the word 'football' in its name?
21. Who wrote *Spycatcher*?

22. Africa was the Roman name for which modern-day country?
23. What links South Queensferry with North Queensferry?
24. Two trains are heading directly towards each other. One is moving at 70mph, the other at 50mph. How far apart will they be one minute before they meet?

ENGLISH MONARCHS Recall the *forty-three* sovereign rulers of England or Britain since 1066*. Go to page 265 for the solution. [Target: 32]

QUOTATIONS FROM POPULAR FILMS III Identify the films from which these quotations have been taken. (The date of the film is provided to assist you.) Look for the solutions on page 289. [Target: 12]

1. 'Of all the gin joints in all the towns in all the world, she walks into mine.' (1942)
2. 'This is an occasion for genuinely tiny knickers.' (2001)
3. 'Everybody listen! We have to put a barrier between us and the snakes!' (2006)
4. 'Go back to the shadow. You shall not pass!' (2001)
5. 'Fräulein, were you this much trouble at the Abbey?' (1965)
6. 'Cancel the kitchen scraps for lepers and orphans, no more merciful beheadings, and call off Christmas.' (1991)
7. 'They only see what they want to see. They don't know they're dead.' (1999)
8. 'A boy's best friend is his mother.' (1960)
9. 'With fronds like these, who needs anemones?' (2003)
10. 'You know I'm retired from hero work.' (2004)
11. 'Have you ever danced with the devil in the pale moonlight?' (1989)
12. 'I know you and Frank were planning to disconnect me, and I'm afraid that's something I cannot allow to happen.' (1968)
13. 'If your family circle joins my family circle, they'll form a chain. I can't have a chink in my chain.' (2004)

---

* Although England had kings prior to 1066, the Norman invasion defined and strengthened the institution of the monarchy. The succession of 1603 united the monarchies of England and Scotland, and all monarchs since have ruled the kingdom of Britain.

14. 'I got a feeling that behind those jeans is something wonderful just waiting to get out.' (1997)
15. 'Oh, I'm sorry. Did I break your concentration?' (1994)
16. 'Hope can drive a man insane.' (1994)
17. 'Joey, have you ever been to a Turkish prison?' (1980)
18. 'Keep your friends close, but your enemies closer.' (1974)
19. 'Would you like me to seduce you?' (1967)
20. 'If he invites us to stay, then we'll go . . . He's got to invite us to stick around.' (1969)
21. 'She cooks as good as she looks, Ted.' (1975)
22. 'The trick . . . is not minding that it hurts.' (1962)
23. 'If I'm not back in five minutes . . . just wait longer!' (1996)
24. 'It's awfully easy to lie when you know that you're trusted implicitly. So very easy, and so very degrading.' (1945)

LANDLOCKED COUNTRIES Name the *forty-three* landlocked countries* in the world; that is, countries which neither have direct access to an ocean nor to a sea that is accessible to an ocean†. Look for the solution on page 311. [**Target: 12**]

AMERICAN PRESIDENTS Recall the *forty-three* Presidents of the United States of America‡. The solution is on page 330. [**Target: 15**]

LATIN PHRASES II Identify each of these commonly used Latin§ phrases or their abbreviations from their English translations. The solutions are on page 349. [**Target: 14**]

---

* Landlocked countries are disadvantaged because of their reliance on the co-operation of neighbouring states for economic and military activity.
† Countries which have coastlines but on lakes or landlocked seas or which have access to the sea via inland waterways are still considered to be landlocked.
‡ American Presidents swear an oath on entering office, as specified in Article II, Section 1, of the Constitution: 'I do solemnly swear (or affirm) that I will faithfully execute the office of President of the United States, and will to the best of my ability, preserve, protect, and defend the Constitution of the United States.'
§ Latin has existed for around 2,500 years and although no longer spoken has provided the basis for the Romance languages of Italian, French, Spanish, Portuguese and Romanian. It has influenced English both directly and through words that have been incorporated from French. From the later Middle Ages until the nineteenth century, Latin was the language of religious, legal, administrative, scientific and academic texts, areas in which many Latin phrases are still in common use today.

1.	After midday	2.	And so on
3.	After death	4.	Unwelcome person
5.	With the order reversed	6.	By each head of population
7.	Way of operating	8.	Note well
9.	Other self	10.	Of sound mind
11.	Other things being equal	12.	Against
13.	For the time being	14.	Course of life
15.	In place of parents	16.	You must have the body
17.	My fault	18.	Under penalty
19.	From cause to effect	20.	It does not follow
21.	A god from a machine	22.	By fact itself
23.	Beneath one's dignity	24.	Among other things

PERFORMERS IN BAND AID Recall the *forty-four* artists who appeared on the original Band Aid single 'Do They Know It's Christmas?'*. The solution is on page 227. [**Target: 18**]

EUROPEAN CAPITAL CITIES Name the *forty-four* capital cities in the continent of Europe. The solution is on page 248. [**Target: 24**]

TAGLINES OF POPULAR FILMS IV Name the films from their taglines below. The solutions are on page 267. [**Target: 14**]

1. 'In space no one can hear you scream.' (1979)
2. 'He is afraid. He is alone. He is three million light years from home.' (1982)
3. 'Poultry in Motion.' (2000)
4. 'Seek the truth, seek the codes.' (2006)
5. 'What a feeling.' (1983)
6. 'A little pig goes a long way.' (1995)

---

* Bob Geldof collaborated with Midge Ure on the charity single after being appalled by news reports of the horrific Ethiopian famine of 1984. It quickly became the biggest-selling UK single ever with sales of 3.55 million copies taking it to the top of the charts for four weeks, including the Christmas number one spot. (Given the volume sold, this was a surprisingly short period, but was due to the rapid sales of the single.) Geldof rounded up many of the top recording artists of the time and instructed them to 'leave their egos at the door'.

7. 'And you thought your parents were embarrassing.' (2004)
8. 'Deadly. Silent. Stolen.' (1990)
9. 'A family comedy without the family.' (1990)
10. 'Sit back. Relax. Enjoy the fright.' (2006)
11. 'The future of law enforcement.' (1987)
12. 'Magic will happen.' (2001)
13. 'Marilyn Monroe and her bosom companions.' (1959)
14. 'His passion captivated a woman. His courage inspired a nation. His heart defied a king.' (1995)
15. '3.14159265358979' (1998)
16. 'Cute. Clever. Mischievous. Intelligent. Dangerous.' (1984)
17. 'A perfect assassin. An innocent girl. They have nothing left to lose except each other.' (1994)
18. 'Fridays will never be the same again.' (1980)
19. 'When he said I do, he didn't say what he did.' (1994)
20. 'The music is on his side.' (1984)
21. 'Does for rock and roll what *The Sound of Music* did for hills.' (1984)
22. 'Nice planet. We'll take it!' (1996)
23. 'Fifty million people watched, but no one saw a thing.' (1994)
24. 'The story that won't go away.' (1991)

CHURCH OF ENGLAND DIOCESES Name the *forty-four* Church of England Dioceses*. The solution can be found on page 290. [**Target: 30**]

COUNTRIES IN EUROPE List the *forty-four* countries in the continent of Europe†. Go to page 248 for the solution. [**Target: 34**]

SINGERS AND BACKERS III Complete the names of these groups by naming the singer most closely associated with these particular backing bands. Find the solutions on page 332. [**Target: 14**]

1. _____ and the Ants
2. _____ and the Sunshine Band

---

* A diocese is an administrative area which falls under the jurisdiction of a single bishop. Each diocese has a cathedral being the seat of the incumbent bishop and with which the diocese often shares its name.
† Europe has an area of 3.8 million square miles and a population of 567 million people, about 9% of the world's population.

3. _____ and Miami Sound Machine
4. _____ and the Pips
5. _____ and the Plastic Ono Band
6. _____ and the Wailers
7. _____ and the Gang
8. _____ and the News
9. _____ and the E Street Band
10. _____ and the Coconuts
11. _____ and the Dreamers
12. _____ and the Bad Seeds
13. _____ and the Crickets
14. _____ and Tubeway Army
15. _____ and the Drifters
16. _____ and the Mothers of Invention
17. _____ and the E-Train
18. _____ and the Miracles
19. _____ and the Rebelettes
20. _____ and the Refugee Allstars
21. _____ and the Dakotas
22. _____ and the Tremeloes
23. _____ and the Blue Flames
24. _____ and the Tuxedos

RED TRIANGULAR ROAD SIGNS Recall the *forty-nine* red triangular warning signs* that appear in the Highway Code. Turn to page 350 for the solution. [**Target: 20**]

MR MEN Name the *forty-nine* Mr Men in the series, originally created by Roger Hargreaves†. The solution is on page 247. [**Target: 20**]

---

* Red warning signs first appeared on the roads in 1944, consisting of a reflective triangle and a description of the hazard on a plate below. Symbolic signs were introduced in 1963 as recommended by the Worboys report. The Worboys committee was a much overdue attempt to consolidate and modernise the signs used on British roads which had been in a state of chaos since the Second World War when many were removed or re-positioned to confuse would-be invaders.

† Roger Hargreaves was once asked, 'What does a tickle look like?' by his young son. His response was to create the *Mr Men* series of books, the first of which was published in 1971. The books originally cost 15p each and were followed in 1981 by the *Little Miss* series. Roger Hargreaves died in 1988 at the age of fifty-five, but his son Adam has continued to write stories featuring his father's characters.

ASIAN CAPITAL CITIES Name the *fifty* capital cities in the continent of Asia. The solution is on page 228. [**Target: 26**]

MUSICAL TERMS Describe the meaning of each of these musical terms*. Find the solution on page 249. [**Target: 10**]

1.	Piano	2.	Crescendo
3.	Staccato	4.	Forte
5.	Allegro	6.	Accelerando
7.	Diminuendo	8.	Adagio
9.	A cappella	10.	Lento
11.	Vibrato	12.	Ritardando
13.	Largo	14.	Grave
15.	Legato	16.	Vivace
17.	Soave	18.	Con brio

---

* Musical notation originates with a Roman philosopher called Boethius (*c.*475–525AD) who first used letters to represent notes. The system was expanded in the twelfth century by Guido d'Arrezo, a Benedictine monk who came up with the idea of a staff on to which notes could be placed to indicate their pitch. Guido was also an inspirational teacher and to help his students devised a system using syllables to represent notes. He took these syllables from 'Ut queant laxis', a popular hymn of the time:

'*UT* queant laxis *RE*sonare fibri
*MI*ra gestorum *FA*muli tuorum
*SOL*ve polluti *LA*bii reatum
Sancte Ioannes'

The piece was notable because the first note of each musical phrase begins with a successively higher note, coinciding with the first six notes of the scale of C major, which Guido called 'UT', 'RE', 'ME', 'FA', 'SOL' and 'LA'. Since Guido's time, 'UT' has been replaced with the more sing-able 'DOH' and a seventh note, 'TE' has been added to complete the scale, leading to the familiar 'DOH-RE-ME' octave. (Guido represented the lowest line on his staff with the Greek letter gamma. Under his notation, the lowest note, 'UT' – which would now be called Middle C – became known as 'gamma ut' or 'gamut'. The word gamut later took on the connotation of describing the whole of the scale, from where it took on its current meaning of an entire range of anything.) During the Renaissance, devotional choral music gave way to new forms of music (such as opera) and composers started to write polyphonic arrangements for musical instruments as well as human voices. The use of Italian in musical notation is a legacy of the dominance of Italian composers and musicians in Western music during the seventeenth century.

19.	Al fine	20.	Presto
21.	Da capo	22.	Ma non troppo
23.	Tremolo	24.	Pizzicato

VALUABLE GLOBAL BRANDS Name the *fifty* most valuable brand* names in the world. Turn to page 229 for the solution.
[Target: 25]

AMERICAN STATES Recall the *fifty* states making up the United States of America†. Go to page 290 for the solution.
[Target: 40]

MISCELLANY XXV Respond to these questions of a miscellaneous nature. The solutions may be found on page 312.
[Target: 8]

1. What was banned in the US by the Eighteenth Amendment to the Constitution?
2. Which word was dropped from all British coins minted in 1982 and since?
3. Which harmful bacterium was first identified by Daniel Elmer Salmon?
4. Who played the Riddler in the 1995 film *Batman Forever*?
5. Which opera features Lieutenant Pinkerton?
6. Which government position is officially known as 'Second Lord of the Treasury'?
7. In *Star Trek*, what colour blood do Vulcans have?

---

* The advertiser David Ogilvy once defined brand as 'the intangible sum of a product's attributes: its name, packaging, and price, its history, its reputation, and the way it's advertised.'
† With a population of 280 million people and a GDP of $10 trillion, the United States of America is currently the world's only true superpower. The US spends more money on arms ($277bn) than the next twelve largest military spenders combined and consumes more energy than India, the Middle East, South America, Africa, South East Asia and Australasia combined. America became independent from Britain in 1776, and was recognised internationally as the United States of America by the Treaty of Paris in 1783. The original thirteen states were joined by thirty-seven others over the next two centuries as the settlers spread west.

8. What are Dunlin, Brent and Piper examples of?

9. Which two common fruits have names that are anagrams of each other?

10. Which is the only one of New York's five boroughs located on the mainland?

11. What was the name of Long John Silver's parrot in *Treasure Island*?

12. From which language does the word 'safari' originate?

13. In a town, 60% of the population speak English and 70% of the population speak French. Assuming these are the only languages spoken in the town, what proportion of the town is bilingual?

14. Whose body was exhumed from Westminster Abbey and subject to a posthumous execution?

15. What links the Vatican, Palestine and Taiwan?

16. How many possible opening moves are there in a game of draughts?

17. Which piece of sporting equipment measures 9' long by 5' wide and is 30" tall?

18. What are sodium thiopental, pancuronium bromide and potassium chloride, when administered in that order, used for?

19. In which city are the *Herald*, the *Evening Times* and the *Daily Record* newspapers printed?

20. What is the maximum number of match points that can be held at one time in a tennis* match at Wimbledon?

21. What is the collective name for the 'Nine Handmaidens of Odin'?

22. According to Genesis, on which day of creation did God make the sun, the moon and the stars?

---

* The scoring system of tennis is somewhat arcane and the origins are not well understood. It is likely tennis derives from a game played in medieval France in which a clock face was used to keep the score. Points in the games were incremented in multiples of fifteen (the 'forty' call is thought simply to be short for 'forty-five', and sixty, the top score, was never called as the game ended when this score was reached). Other peculiarities of tennis scoring include the term 'deuce', possibly a corruption of the French phrase 'à deux du jeu' meaning 'two points away from the (end of the) game'. The origins of the term 'love' are less clear. It may derive from 'l'oeuf' meaning 'egg' (which is the same shape as a zero), or from the idea that the player with zero points must be playing for love rather than money.

23. In *The Simpsons*, what is the name of Springfield's founder?
24. If it were two hours later, it would be half as long to midnight as if it were an hour later. What time is it now?

ASSASSINATIONS Identify the victims of these assassinations* from the clues. Find the solutions on page 232. [**Target: 14**]

1. Shot by Lee Harvey Oswald in Dallas in 1963.
2. Stabbed by Brutus and others in the Senate in 44BC.
3. Shot by actor John Wilkes Booth in Ford's Theatre, Washington, in 1865.
4. Shot by Mark Chapman outside his New York apartment in 1980.
5. Shot by Gavrilo Princip in Sarajevo; the assassination precipitated the First World War.
6. Murdered by four knights in Canterbury Cathedral in 1170.
7. Killed by an IRA bomb while sailing off County Sligo, Ireland, in 1979.
8. Murdered with an ice pick while in exile in Mexico in 1940.
9. Shot by James Earl Ray in Memphis, Tennessee, in 1968.
10. Shot by a Hindu fanatic in New Delhi in 1948.
11. Shot in the Hotel Ambassador, Los Angeles, in 1968.
12. Killed by an IRA car bomb in the House of Commons car park in 1979.
13. Murdered by members of her Sikh bodyguard in New Delhi in 1984.
14. King of Scotland, murdered by Malcolm III in 1057.
15. American Muslim leader, shot during a political rally in 1965.
16. Sinn Fein leader, killed in an ambush in the Irish Republic in 1922.
17. Swedish Prime Minister, shot walking home from the cinema by an unknown assassin in 1986.

---

* The word 'assassin' is derived from a word translating as 'hashish-eater', the name given to certain members of the Nizari Ismaili, a tribe originating in twelfth-century Syria. According to legend, the assassins carried out killings on behalf of the Nizari leader, who controlled them through the use of hashish. The word was brought into English by returning crusaders, where it entered common use as a noun meaning 'murderer'. Assassination has since come to its current meaning as the killing of a prominent person usually for a politically motivated reason.

18. Israeli Prime Minister, murdered by a Jewish extremist in 1995.
19. Roman Emperor, poisoned by his wife in AD54.
20. Russian dissident, poisoned with radionuclide polonium-210 in London in 2006.
21. King of England, murdered in Berkeley Castle in 1327.
22. British Prime Minister, shot entering the House of Commons by John Bellingham in 1812.
23. Roman Emperor, murdered by members of the Praetorian Guard in AD41.
24. US President, shot in a railway station by Charles Guiteau in 1881.

COUNTRIES IN ASIA Name the *fifty* countries in the continent of Asia*. Go to page 228 for the solution. [**Target: 36**]

POPULAR PUB NAMES List the *fifty* most common British pub names†. Find the solution on page 351. [**Target: 30**]

---

* Asia is the largest continent in the world, covering approximately 17 million square miles, a third of the world's total land area, and also the most populous; it is home to over 60% of the world's population. Asia is notable for its ethnic diversity: the sub-regions of Central Asia, South East Asia, the Middle East and India (particularly) are sometimes regarded as continents in their own right. The western boundaries of Asia are not well defined; Asia meets Africa somewhere near the Suez Canal. The European border could be said to include the Sea of Marmara, the Black Sea, the Caucasus, the Caspian Sea, the Ural River and the Ural Mountains.
† Although the term public house was coined by the Victorians, it was the under the Romans that the first pubs – or 'tabernae' - appeared in Britain. The continental custom was for the first proprietors to hang vine leaves outside their premises to indicate when the harvest was in. In Britain, although typically serving ale instead of wine, the custom of hanging foliage outside was adopted and would later evolve into the familiar pub sign (early pub names being 'The Grapes, 'The Bush' and even 'The Crooked Billet' referring to a bent tree-branch). In feudal times, village inns were the responsibility of the local landowner, often a lord or a religious official. As a result, many pubs were given names that reflect the political sensibilities of their owners, for example, using heraldic symbols of monarchs or religious imagery in order to demonstrate allegiance to the relevant authorities. Given the population was largely illiterate, publicans chose names for their establishments that could be easily illustrated and were visually recognisable. The pub name became mandatory in the fourteenth century under Richard II, who decreed that all pubs must display a sign (and as a result Richard's heraldic emblem is still one of the most common pub names today). Certain themes recur in pub names: heraldry, agriculture and religion were all common and, with the advent of industrialisation, engineering and sport also became widespread.

'ISMS' II Identify the philosophies, beliefs, concepts or practices from the descriptions provided. (Note that all of the solutions contain the suffix '~ism'.) You will find the solutions on page 229. [Target: 14]

1. The belief that a particular race is inherently superior or inferior to others; the discrimination against individuals based on their race.
2. The use of unlawful and often horrific violence against civilians in order to coerce or intimidate societies or governments for political or ideological purposes.
3. A term describing an extreme and excessive devotion to a cause or group but now more commonly applied to sexist males.
4. A general belief that things are bad and tend to become worse.
5. A political system in which all property belongs to the community and where all individuals have equal social and economic status.
6. The pursuit of pleasure as an end in itself.
7. A vague term for a cultural, artistic or philosophical movement that has moved beyond modernism.
8. An ancient polytheistic religion dating from 2000BC and the majority religion in India.
9. The practice of worship of the earth and nature, particularly by ancient European religions*; the term is often been used to imply a backward or culturally unsophisticated set of beliefs.
10. The practice of expansion by a nation through the annexation of foreign territories to create an empire.
11. The branch of communism in China associated with Mao Tse-tung which focused on the peasantry as the revolutionary force.
12. The religious movement founded by John Wesley in 1738.
13. A form of imperialism in which the mother country allows semi-autonomous legal and social institutions in the dependent states.

---

* For example Wicca, Druidism, Asatru and Shamanism.

14. A political system in which capital and the means of production are owned either collectively or by a central government that controls the economy.
15. A term describing adherence in religious groups to strict or literal interpretations of religious texts or ideas and often associated with belligerent and violent activities.
16. A religion meaning literally 'divine path', based on the worship of 'kami' – gods, ancestors and natural forces; the native religion of Japan.
17. The belief in more than one god.
18. The belief and proclamation of the Christian Gospel with particular emphasis on rebirth or conversion.
19. An extreme form of dictatorship under which all individuals are completely subject to the wishes of the State.
20. A term describing a belligerent or hawkish stance towards opposition supposed to be technically or culturally inferior.
21. The psychological method of studying the behaviour of individuals and how it changes in response to different stimuli.
22. A philosophy derived from Hegel's dialectics and Marx's materialism in which successive contradictory statements (thesis, antithesis, synthesis) are used to explain the evolution of human society.
23. A branch of Protestantism with the central tenet that people are predestined for either salvation or eternal damnation regardless of wealth or piety.
24. A philosophy that opposes the separation of Church and State, first recorded in 1858, but perhaps better known for being one of the longest English words.

COMMONWEALTH COUNTRIES Name the *fifty-three* members of the Commonwealth*. Find the solution on page 249. [**Target: 14**]

---

* The Commonwealth is a loose political union of former colonies of the British Empire. The term was coined by Lord Rosebery in 1884, referring to a 'commonwealth of nations' as the status of the British Colonies evolved into self-governing dominions (Canada in 1867, Australia 1900, New Zealand 1907, South Africa 1910, Irish Free State 1921). After the independence of India and Pakistan, in 1949 the Commonwealth took on its present form, with the word 'British' being dropped from the title.

ALFRED HITCHCOCK FILMS List the *fifty-four* films directed by Alfred Hitchcock*. The solution is on page 268. [**Target: 10**]

SCENTS Identify the producers of each of these scents†. (Note that the same producer may be the solution to more than one of these.) Go to page 290 for the solutions. [**Target: 7**]

1.	No. 5	2.	Polo
3.	CK One	4.	Coco
5.	Dune	6.	Opium
7.	Obsession	8.	Anaïs Anaïs
9.	Poison	10.	Chloé
11.	Jazz	12.	Eternity
13.	Fahrenheit	14.	Fifth Avenue

---

* The 'Master of Suspense' was born in Leytonstone in 1899 and, in a career that lasted over fifty years, almost single-handedly defined the movie-thriller genre. As a young film enthusiast, Hitchcock got a job as a title designer at the new Paramount studios in London and worked his way up to the position of Director, completing his first film in 1925. His films began to win international acclaim and Hitchcock himself was gaining notoriety for his trademark cameo appearances. In 1940 and with the outbreak of war, Hitchcock moved to the US and started working in Hollywood, and in the 1950s produced what many critics regard as his best work. Although recognised by the American Film Institute and receiving a knighthood in Britain, Hitchcock was largely ignored by the Oscars, never winning the award for Best Director. Hitchcock's work and his unique understanding of his audience was perhaps best summed up when he once said: 'There is no terror in the bang, only in the anticipation of it.' Alfred Hitchcock died in 1980.

† Modern perfume is made up of a mixture of essential oils, fixative and alcohol. The essential oils provide the scent, the fixative is used to bind the oils together and alcohol evaporates on contact with the skin leaving the fragrance behind to evaporate over a period of hours. Perfume consists mostly of alcohol (about 78% to 95%); the strength (and therefore cost) of a perfume is defined by the concentration of the essential oils in the alcohol. Concentrations of over 22% essential oils are called perfume, 15–22% eau de perfume, 8–15% eau de toilette and those under 8% are known as eau de cologne. Really subtle scents of 3% or less are called eau fraiche. Essential oils are produced through the distillation of plants and flowers or sometimes through a process called 'enfleurage' where they are absorbed into wax. Common organic products used include anise, bay leaf, bergamot, cardamom, cedar wood, eucalyptus, frankincense, gardenia, geranium, iris, jasmine, lavender, lemon, lilac, lily, lily of the valley, magnolia, moss, neroli, orange, orris, patchouli, pine, raspberry, rose, sage, sandalwood, tuberose, vanilla, violet and ylang-ylang.

15.	Poême	16.	So Pretty
17.	Passion	18.	Intuition
19.	Organza	20.	All About Eve
21.	La Nuit	22.	Xeryus
23.	Accenti	24.	Clandestine

COUNTRIES IN AFRICA List the *fifty-four* countries that make up the continent of Africa*. You can find the solution on page 312. [**Target: 25**]

OLYMPIC DISCIPLINES Name the *fifty-six* Olympic disciplines (in both the summer and winter games). Note that 'disciplines' are not necessarily synonymous with 'sports' or 'events', for example the sport of cycling has four associated disciplines for which eighteen medals are contested†. The solution is on page 332. [**Target: 40**]

LINKED MISCELLANY XIV In responding to these miscellaneous questions, deduce the connecting theme linking the solutions. The solution is on page 352. [**Target: 6**]

1. Which actress appeared in *Grease 2*, *Tequila Sunrise* and *Batman Returns*?
2. Which nocturnal and omnivorous mammal of the genus Procyon is naturally found throughout the Americas and is noted for its manual dexterity, for example an ability to open rubbish bins?
3. What nationality were the explorers Thor Heyerdahl and Roald Amundsen?
4. What common name is applied to the edible plants of the Capsicum genus?
5. Who was queen to Henry II of England?
6. Which singer has been romantically linked with John F. Kennedy Jr., Warren Beatty, Vanilla Ice and Sandra Bernhard?

---

* Africa is the second largest of the world's continents, with an area of 11.69 million square miles.
† The current Olympic programme consists of thirty-five sports and just shy of 400 events (for which each medal is awarded).

7. Which global federation was formed in 1922 and dissolved in 1991?
8. What is 2^6?
9. The title of which James Bond film is based on an advertising slogan?
10. Which poem by Lewis Carroll tells the story of its two eponymous characters taking a walk on a beach with some friendly oysters?

BRITISH RACECOURSES Name the *sixty* racecourses that stage national hunt and flat races* in Britain. The solution is on page 230. [Target: 16]

TUBE STATIONS IN ZONE 1 List the *sixty-two* stations in Zone 1 of the London Underground. Turn to page 249 for the solution. [Target: 36]

ETYMOLOGY OF ROCK AND POP NAMES II Identify the names of the groups or artists from these brief descriptions of their etymology. The solutions can be found on page 269. [Target: 18]

1. After the lead singer's bleached hair.
2. Taken from the name of an unemployment benefit form.
3. Changed their name from the 'Chicago Transit Authority' after legal action by the City of Chicago.
4. Prompted by a newspaper headline reporting Frank Sinatra's move to California.
5. Inspired by the term 'rhythmic gymnastics', a method of teaching music.

---

* Horse racing in Britain can be traced back to the time of the Crusades, when Arab horses were brought back and mixed with English stock to produce the first thoroughbreds, some pedigrees of which exist today. Racing gained popularity under the patronage of Charles II who established Newmarket as the centre of flat racing in the country. The popularity increased, leading to the staging of the Derby (first run in 1780) and the Grand National (1839). Today, there are two types of racing: national hunt racing and flat racing. National hunt racing is normally run over jumps and includes steeplechases, which have courses with large fixed fences and are so called because church steeples were once used as the start and finishing points of races.

6. From the desperate financial situation the band members once found themselves in.

7. After the French town and football team.

8. After a children's programme on French TV about a little boy and his dog.

9. From a slang term for the drug Dexedrine.

10. As a parody of many groups whose names start with 'the'.

11. Named after the river in Greek mythology that separates the earth from the underworld.

12. From a slang term for lesbian.

13. Taken from the name of a chain of cinemas.

14. Meaning 'beyond the voice' in Latin.

15. From a joke once made about the band's future prospects 'going down like a lead balloon'.

16. Based on the Italian phrase for 'political writings'.

17. Named after a character in the *Back to the Future* series of films.

18. The nickname for the bouffant hairstyle sported by its female members.

19. Originally named after a children's book called *Mr Crowe's Garden*.

20. Spanish for 'the Wolves'.

21. After a book written by Herman Melville, this artist's great-uncle.

22. From the nicknames of the two lead singers, Joseph Simmons and Darryl McDaniels.

23. After a slang term for a drug user who takes a lot of speed.

24. From a term for the detached gaze of a battle-weary or shell-shocked soldier.

NOVELS BY AGATHA CHRISTIE Name the *sixty-six* mystery novels written by Agatha Christie*. Go to page 291 for the solution. [Target: 10]

---

* Dame Agatha Christie was born in Torquay in 1890. By her death in 1976, she had written a total of sixty-six novels and several short-story collections. She also wrote more than a dozen plays, one of which, *The Mousetrap*, is the longest-running play in theatrical history, opening in London on 25 November 1952.

CITIES IN THE UK List the *sixty-six* cities in the United Kingdom, that is, cities which have had city status* conferred upon them. The solution may be found on page 313. [**Target: 50**]

MOTORWAYS Name the *sixty-nine* numbered motorways† in mainland Britain. (Note that the list excludes motorways located in Northern Ireland.) The solution can be found on page 307. [**Target: 25**]

---

* Until the arrival of the Romans, Britain had a rural population and those towns that existed were largely tribal and ceremonial centres. The Romans built fortresses across the country which became economic hubs in their own right, serving not only the legions based there but also the native population. Significantly, the Romans founded the city of London (Londinium) which has remained the economic centre of the country (if not always the capital) ever since. Surprisingly, after the Romans withdrew, fifth-century Britain went back to its rural roots and neglected its towns. Urban living did not return until 400 years later when Saxon Britain faced the new threat of Viking invasion and many Roman towns and their defences were resurrected. After the Norman invasion, the defensive rationale for living in a town gradually gave way to an economic one with a host of new towns appearing in this period; by 1300 there were over thirty towns in England with 5,000 inhabitants or more. Around this time, 'Charters of Incorporation' were issued by the monarchy, allowing a town to become an incorporated borough and be permitted to hold a market (effectively a licence to trade). The first recognition of city status appeared in 1189 in the Charters of Incorporation for Hereford and Worcester. The term 'city' has traditionally been synonymous with the location of diocesan cathedrals but the widespread urban population growth during the Victorian era led to many existing cities being dwarfed by the new industrial towns. Legislation was passed in 1888 allowing large towns (such as Birmingham) to be recognised as cities. City status is now conferred by Royal Charter. The Royal Charter is not defined by any specific criteria, nor does it bestow any benefits on the designated city; competition for city status is, however, fierce. In 1998, reorganisation of local authorities led to the status of some cities being threatened. Bath and Hereford both appointed Charter Trustees to protect their status but Rochester somehow neglected to and was subsequently demoted back to a humble town. To make matters worse, the Medway town, a city since 1211, only learnt of its fate four years later when the City of Rochester Society noticed its name missing from the Lord Chancellor's list of UK cities. The Mayor of Rochester, Ted Baker, was reportedly 'horrified'.

† The list excludes a motorway nominally called the M96 which is part of the Fire Service College, located near Moreton-in-Marsh in Gloucestershire and used for emergency rescue training. It is not a public highway.

BRITISH OLYMPIANS II Identify these British Olympians from their medal honours. Go to page 332 for the solutions. [**Target: 8**]

1. Athlete winning gold in the 800m and gold in the 1500m at Athens in 2004 and bronze in the 800m at Sydney in 2000.
2. Athlete winning gold in the 100m at Barcelona in 1992, silver in the 100m and silver in the 4x100m Relay at Seoul in 1988.
3. Rower winning gold in the Coxless Fours at Athens in 2004, gold in the Coxless Fours at Sydney in 2000, gold in the Coxless Pairs at Barcelona 1992 and gold in the Coxless Pairs at Atlanta in 1996.
4. Athlete winning gold in the Triple Jump at Sydney in 2000 and silver in the Triple Jump at Atlanta in 1996.
5. Athlete winning gold in the 400m Hurdles and silver in the 4x400m Relay at Barcelona in 1992.
6. Swimmer winning gold in the 100m Breaststroke and bronze in the 4x100m Medley Relay at Moscow in 1980.
7. Athlete winning silver in the Javelin at Sydney in 2000, silver in the Javelin at Atlanta in 1996 and bronze in the Javelin at Barcelona in 1992.
8. Ice skater winning gold in the Single Figure Skating at Lake Placid in 1980.
9. Boxer winning gold in the Super Heavyweight at Sydney in 2000.
10. Athlete winning gold in the 400m in Beijing in 2008.
11. Athlete winning silver at the 110m Hurdles in Seoul in 1988.
12. Ice skater winning gold in the Single Figure Skating at Innsbruck in 1976.
13. Cyclist winning gold in the 4000m Individual Pursuit at Barcelona in 1992 and bronze in the Road Time Trial at Atlanta in 1996.
14. Athlete winning silver in the 4x400m Relay at Los Angeles in 1984; bronze in the 400m Hurdles and bronze in the 4x400m Relay at Barcelona in 1992.
15. Athlete winning gold in the 4x100m Relay at Athens in 2004 and silver in the 200m at Sydney in 2000.
16. Rower winning gold in the Coxless Fours at Athens in 2004 and gold in the Coxless Fours at Sydney in 2000.
17. Athlete winning gold in the Pentathlon at Munich in 1972.

18. Athlete winning gold in the Long Jump, silver in the Pentathlon and bronze in the 4x100m Relay at Tokyo in 1964.
19. Rowing brothers winning gold in the Coxed Pairs at Barcelona in 1992, and bronze in the Coxless Fours at Atlanta in 1996.
20. Equestrian winning silver in the Three-day Event Team at Sydney in 2000, silver in the Three-day Event Team and silver in the Individual Three-day Event at Seoul in 1988 and silver in the Three-day Event Team at Los Angeles in 1984.
21. Bobsleigher winning silver in the Skeleton at Turin in 2006.
22. Cyclist winning gold in the 1 km Time Trial at Athens in 2004 and silver in the Team Sprint at Sydney in 2000.
23. Sailor winning gold in the Finn at Beijing in 2008, gold in the Finn at Athens in 2004, gold in the Laser at Sydney in 2000 and silver in the Laser at Atlanta in 1996.
24. Athlete winning gold in the 400m and bronze in the 200m at Paris in 1924.

SEAS Name the *seventy-one* seas of the world; that is, those bodies of water having the word 'Sea' as part of their name*. Go to page 353 for the solution. [**Target: 16**]

CONSTELLATIONS List the *eighty-eight* modern constellations†. The solution is on page 230. [**Target: 16**]

MISCELLANY XXVI Respond to these questions of a miscellaneous nature. The solution is on page 250. [**Target: 14**]

1. What was the first product to be advertised on Channel Five?
2. Which planet was reclassified as a Dwarf Planet on 24 August 2006?
3. Which artist is famous for painting a portrait of his mother?

---

* As defined by the International Hydrographical Association (IHO).
† The eighty-eight constellations align to distinct areas of the sky with precise boundaries defined by the International Astronomical Union. Every place in the sky belongs within one of these constellations. Stars which make up constellations may appear to be close together when viewed from Earth but in three-dimensional space have no relationship to one another and may be vast distances apart.

4. What was the name of the legislation passed in Britain in 1715 giving local authorities the power to declare any crowd of over twelve people an unlawful assembly and to disperse it accordingly?

5. By what name is the Gravelly Hill Interchange better known?

6. In medicine, how is Methicillin Resistant Staphylococcus Aureus more commonly known?

7. Who won the tennis 'Golden Slam' in 1988 by winning the Grand Slam of singles titles and winning a gold medal at the Olympic Games?

8. What links Edward III, Japan and the Animals?

9. What is the last word in the Bible?

10. In cricket, what is the score of 111 known as?

11. In the human body, what is the function of the endocrine system?

12. Which word, meaning an odd or whimsical person, is derived from the Greek, meaning literally 'out of centre'?

13. What banking 'first' did Reg Varney (of *On the Buses* fame) achieve in a branch of Barclays Bank in Enfield on 27 June 1967?

14. Who created the television series *Prime Suspect*?

15. Which two teams compete in the A23 Derby?

16. What is the official language of Pakistan?

17. In the US, what is celebrated on 2 February and was also the title of a popular film?

18. What does QANTAS stand for?

19. In a knock-out tennis tournament with 256 entrants, how many matches must be played to produce a winner?

20. Which English monarch was succeeded on her death by her husband?

21. Where would you find an American flag that has never been lowered?

22. What is the middle day in a (non-leap) year?

23. How many stars are there on the flag of the European Union?

24. A brick weighs 1kg and half a brick. How heavy is the brick?

CHEMICAL ELEMENTS List the *one hundred and eighteen* elements of the periodic table. Find the solution on page 270. [**Target: 25**]

GREATEST LIVING FOOTBALLERS Name the *one hundred and twenty-five* footballers selected by Pelé* for the FIFA 100, a list of the greatest living† footballers to mark the 100th anniversary of FIFA. The solution is on page 292. [**Target: 40**]

LAST LINES OF POPULAR FILMS II Identify the films from the closing lines. Find the solutions on page 353. [**Target: 12**]

1.   'Cargo and ship destroyed. I should reach the frontier in about six weeks. With a little luck, the network will pick me up. This is Ripley, last survivor of the *Nostromo*, signing off.' (1979)
2.   'After all, tomorrow is another day.' (1939)
3.   'Don Corleone.' (1972)
4.   'I do.' (1994)
5.   'I look up at the moon, and wonder: when will we be going back? And who will that be?' (1995)
6.   'Oh, now I suppose you're gonna say it's not enough. Well tough, Erin. Too goddamn bad. 'Cause this is absolutely, positively, where I draw the line.' (2000)
7.   'Th-th-th-that's all, Folks!' (1988)
8.   'I'm an average nobody. I get to live the rest of my life like a schnook.' (1980)
9.   'Sam . . . I'm glad you're with me.' (2001)
10. 'Gaff had been there, and let her live. Four years, he figured. He was wrong. Tyrell had told me Rachael was special: no termination date. I didn't know how long we had together. Who does?' (1982)
11. 'Asshole!' (1988)
12. 'That's right, that's right. Attaboy, Clarence.' (1946)
13. 'I'm the boss, I'm the boss, I'm the boss, I'm the boss, I'm the boss . . . boss, boss, boss, boss, boss, boss.' (1980)

---

* Pelé's list contains some surprising inclusions from around the world, and he was accused of being more representative of international diversity than of footballing pedigree; the list caused controversy in Pelé's homeland, particularly with the omission of many Brazilian players who felt they should have been included. The former Brazilian midfielder Gerson expressed his anger at the selection by tearing it up on Brazilian television.
† As of 2004; some have now expired.

14. 'Eliza? Where the devil are my slippers?' (1964)
15. 'Hey! What's this I see? I thought this was a party. Let's dance!' (1984)
16. 'It's Mrs Danvers. She's gone mad. She said she'd rather destroy Manderley than see us happy here.' (1940)
17. 'When I despair, I remember that all through history the way of truth and love has always won. There have been tyrants and murderers and for a time they can seem invincible, but in the end they always fall. Think of it. Always.' (1980)
18. 'Merry Christmas!' (1954)
19. 'Love means never having to say you're sorry.' (1970)
20. 'Well, nobody's perfect.' (1959)
21. 'Little girls, I am in the business of putting old heads on young shoulders, and all my pupils are the crème de la crème. Give me a girl at an impressionable age and she is mine for life.' (1969)
22. 'Say, friend – you got any more of that good sarsaparilla?' (1998)
23. 'Man, if this is their idea of Christmas, I gotta be here for New Year's.' (1988)
24. 'Now, where was I?' (2000)

SOLUTIONS

'Knowledge is the food of the soul.'

Plato

BRONTË SISTERS (from page 4)

Anne Brontë / Charlotte Brontë / Emily Brontë

CREAM (from page 7)

Eric Clapton .... Guitar
Jack Bruce .... Bass
Ginger Baker .... Drums

WIT AND WISDOM I (from page 9)

1. 'I have nothing to declare but my genius.' .... Wilde
2. '. . . and you, madam, are ugly . . .' .... Churchill
3. 'I can resist anything but temptation.' .... Wilde
4. 'The report of my death was an exaggeration.' .... Twain
5. 'It is better to keep your mouth closed . . .' .... Twain
6. 'There is only one thing in the world worse than . . .' .... Wilde
7. 'I have taken more out of alcohol . . .' .... Churchill
8. 'A classic is something that . . .' .... Twain
9. 'This is the sort of English up with which . . .' .... Churchill
10. 'Work is the curse of the drinking classes.' .... Wilde
11. 'He hadn't a single redeeming vice.' .... Wilde
12. 'I am ready to meet my Maker . . .' .... Churchill
13. 'Truth is more of a stranger than fiction.' .... Twain
14. 'He has all the virtues I dislike . . .' .... Churchill
15. 'I must decline your invitation . . .' .... Wilde
16. 'Man is the only animal that blushes. Or needs to.' .... Twain
17. 'A modest man, who has much . . .' .... Churchill*
18. 'If you tell the truth . . .' .... Twain
19. 'I am not young enough to know everything.' .... Wilde
20. 'I am always ready to learn . . .' .... Churchill
21. 'Familiarity breeds contempt – and children' .... Twain
22. 'It has been said that democracy . . .' .... Churchill
23. 'America is the only country to go from barbarism . . .' .... Wilde
24. 'Men stumble over the truth from time to time . . .' .... Churchill

CROQUET COLOURS (from page 12)

Black / Blue / Red / Yellow

MONOPOLY STATIONS (from page 15)

King's Cross / Marylebone / Fenchurch Street / Liverpool Street

---

* In reference to Clement Attlee.

MISCELLANY II (from page 20)

1. 273°; 2. The Hudson*; 3. The Restoration of the Monarchy (in 1660);
4. Cymbal; 5. The statement is false; 6. Richard Whiteley (in *Countdown*);
7. Wales; 8. 'In the beginning . . .'; 9. Sapphire; 10. Lee Harvey Oswald (in 1963);
11. Nicole Kidman; 12. Q and Z (worth ten points each); 13. Twenty-three;
14. Christopher Marlowe; 15. The Channel Tunnel†; 16. The Tongue; 17. (*The*)
Kama Sutra; 18. Yew; 19. Once; 20. Alaska; 21. Oedipus‡; 22. They have no
singular form; 23. Tia Maria; 24. Sergei Rachmaninov (Piano Concerto Number 2).

TELETUBBIES (from page 23)

Tinky Winky / Dipsy / Laa-Laa / Po

BONES OF THE LEG (from page 24)

Femur / Tibia / Fibula / Patella

EVENTS IN HISTORY I (from page 26)

1. 1666; 2. 1860; 3. 1086; 4. 1775; 5. 1815; 6. 1848; 7. 1876; 8. 1347;
9. 1642; 10. 1534; 11. 1415; 12. 1870; 13. 1688; 14. 1215; 15. 1620;
16. 1314; 17. 1066; 18. 1707; 19. 1453; 20. 597; 21. 1202; 22. 1206; 23. 625;
14. 1337.

CHARACTERISTICS OF DIAMONDS (from page 31)

Carat / Clarity / Colour / Cut

EVANGELISTS (from page 33)

Matthew / Mark / Luke / John

FILMS AND THEIR STARS II (from page 36)

1. *Pulp Fiction*; 2. *Kramer vs. Kramer*; 3. *The Da Vinci Code*; 4. *Wall Street*;
5. *Blade Runner*; 6. *Apollo 13*; 7. *The Constant Gardener*; 8. *The Bourne Identity*;
9. *Rebel without a Cause*; 10. *Fight Club*; 11. *Nine to Five*; 12. *Footloose*;
13. *Chinatown*; 14. *A Bridge Too Far*; 15. *The Hours*; 16. *Logan's Run*; 17. *The*
Pianist; 18. *National Velvet*; 19. *The African Queen*; 20. *It's a Wonderful Life*;
21. *Klute*; 22. *Dead Again*; 23. *North Country*; 24. *Eternal Sunshine of the Spotless*
Mind.

---

* The East River is a tidal strait rather than a river. It connects Upper New York
Bay to Long Island Sound.
† Cheriton, a district of Folkestone, is the site of the English Channel Tunnel
terminal, and Sangatte the French terminal. Folkestone and Sangatte are also linked
by the HVDC Cross Channel, a submarine power cable joining the French and
British electricity grids.
‡ The riddle was: 'What walks on four legs in the morning, two legs in the
afternoon, and three legs in the evening?' The answer is man; the riddle is referring
to a baby crawling, an adult walking and an old man bent over a stick.

JACKSON 5 (from page 38)

Jackie / Jermaine / Marlon / Michael / Tito

RAT PACK (from page 40)

Frank Sinatra / Dean Martin / Sammy Davis Jr.
Peter Lawford / Joey Bishop

CAPITAL CITIES II (from page 43)

1. Stockholm; 2. New Delhi; 3. Brasília; 4. Khartoum; 5. Phnom Penh; 6. Hanoi;
7. Reykjavik; 8. Caracas; 9. Algiers; 10. Riyadh; 11. Bucharest; 12. Lima;
13. Ottawa; 14. Tashkent; 15. Abuja; 16. Kuala Lumpur; 17. Minsk; 18. Nicosia;
19. Jakarta; 20. Monrovia; 21. Amman; 22. Ashgabat; 23. Lilongwe; 24. Maseru.

BOOKS OF MOSES (from page 44)

Genesis / Exodus / Leviticus / Numbers / Deuteronomy

ENGLISH CLASSIC HORSE RACES (from page 47)

The Derby / The Oaks / The St Leger
The One Thousand Guineas / The Two Thousand Guineas

SINGERS AND BACKERS I (from page 49)

1. Gerry; 2. Cliff Richard; 3. Ian Dury; 4. Siouxsie; 5. Paul McCartney; 6. Bruce
Hornsby; 7. Doctor; 8. Steve Harley; 9. Martha Reeves; 10. Elvis Costello;
11. Joan Jett; 12. Prince; 13. Katrina; 14. Frankie Valli; 15. Neil Young; 16. Gary
Byrd; 17. Lonnie Donegan; 18. Acker Bilk; 19. Elvis Presley; 20. Harold Melvin;
21. Dr Hook; 22. Johnny; 23. Terry Dactyl; 24. Eddie.

NEW ENGLAND STATES (from page 53)

Connecticut / Maine / Massachusetts
New Hampshire / Rhode Island / Vermont

ENGLISH ROMANTIC POETS (from page 56)

William Blake / Samuel Taylor Coleridge / George Gordon, Lord Byron
John Keats / Percy Bysshe Shelley* / William Wordsworth

COOKING TERMS I (from page 59)

1. Chilli con carne; 2. Lasagne; 3. Moussaka; 4. Paella; 5. Salsa; 6. Blini;
7. Gnocchi; 8. Couscous; 9. Calzone; 10. Escalope; 11. Jus; 12. Antipasto;
13. Bombay Duck; 14. Poussin; 15. Penne; 16. Prosciutto; 17. Tagine; 18. Devils
on Horseback; 19. Compote; 20. En croute; 21. Roux; 22. Marinière (à la);
23. Panna cotta; 24. Aioli.

---

* Husband of Mary Shelley, author of *Frankenstein* and also influential in the
Romantic movement.

WEAPONS IN CLUEDO (from page 63)

Candlestick / Dagger / Lead Piping

Rope / Revolver / Spanner

SYMBOLS IN ROMAN NUMERALS (from page 65)

I   V   X   L   C   D   M

MISCELLANY IX (from page 68)

1. Morphine (Morpheus); 2. Russia and France*; 3. lb†; 4. Roald Amundsen;
5. They both have the prefix 'Royal'; 6. Goat (cashmere goat); 7. *The Silence of the Lambs*; 8. The Bank of England; 9. Montreal; 10. *All's Well that Ends Well*;
11. Kidney; 12. Salvador Dalí (at the International Surrealist Exhibition);
13. Danny and Sandy; 14. Touché; 15. Iraq‡; 16. Angela Lansbury (*Murder, She Wrote*); 17. Indonesia; 18. 24; 19. Xylophone; 20. Brabinger; 21. Hindu§;
22. Today Is Saturday Watch And Smile; 23. London; 24. 54.

DEADLY SINS (from page 71)   VIRTUES¶ (from page 73)

Lust .... Chastity

Gluttony .... Temperance

Envy .... Charity

Sloth .... Diligence

Wrath .... Forgiveness

Avarice .... Generosity

Pride .... Humility

AIRPORT CODES II (from page 76)

1. London (Heathrow); 2. Miami; 3. Atlanta (Hartsfield-Jackson); 4. Sydney (Kingsford-Smith); 5. Luton; 6. Madrid (Barajas); 7. Zurich; 8. Manchester;
9. Frankfurt; 10. Beijing (formerly Peking); 11. Singapore (Changi); 12. London (Stansted); 13. Copenhagen; 14. Dublin; 15. Denver; 16. Havana (José Martí);
17. Phoenix (Sky Harbor); 18. Nice (Côte d'Azur); 19. Rio de Janeiro (Galeão);
20. Belfast; 21. Santiago (Arturo Merino Benítez); 22. Rome (Leonardo da Vinci);
23. Tokyo; 24. Toronto (Pearson).

---

* 'La Marseillaise' and 'God Save the Tsar!'

† Derived from Libra, the scales.

‡ Iraq invaded Kuwait in 1990.

§ Kumbh Mela is a Hindu pilgrimage that gathers in India four times every twelve years. It rotates between four locations and each cycle contains a Great Kumbh Mela at Prayag, which is attended by huge numbers. In 2001, this was attended by some 70 million people, a number greater than the population of the UK.

¶ An alternative list of the Seven Virtues is derived from a combination of the four Cardinal Virtues from Plato (Prudence, Justice, Temperance and Fortitude) and the three Theological Virtues (Faith, Hope and Love) from 1 Corinthians.

CLASSICAL PLANETS (from page 79)

Sun / Moon / Mercury / Venus / Mars / Jupiter / Saturn

FIRST LINES OF POP SONGS III (from page 82)

1. 'Rockafeller Skank' (Fatboy Slim); 2. 'Theme from S Express' (S Express);
3. '(They Long to Be) Close to You' (The Carpenters); 4. 'Rasputin' (Boney M*);
5. 'Ride on Time' (Black Box); 6. 'Let Me Entertain You' (Robbie Williams);
7. 'Respect' (Aretha Franklin); 8. 'Mambo No. 5' (Lou Bega); 9. 'One Day I'll Fly
Away' (Randy Crawford); 10. 'Come on Eileen' (Dexy's Midnight Runners);
11. 'The Boxer' (Simon and Garfunkel); 12. 'Blue (Da Ba De)' (Eiffel 65);
13. 'Girls and Boys' (Blur); 14. 'True Faith' (New Order); 15. 'All Along the
Watchtower' (Jimi Hendrix); 16. 'Walk on the Wild Side' (Lou Reed); 17. 'Run'
(Snow Patrol); 18. 'Livin' on a Prayer' (Bon Jovi); 19. 'Sweet Talkin' Woman'
(Electric Light Orchestra); 20. 'Up Where We Belong'† (Joe Cocker & Jennifer
Warnes); 21. 'You've Lost That Loving Feeling' (Righteous Brothers); 22. 'Vienna'‡
(Ultravox); 23. 'Getting Jiggy With It' (Will Smith); 24. 'The Ace of Spades'
(Motörhead).

LONDON GATES (from page 80)

Ludgate / Newgate / Aldersgate / Cripplegate
Moorgate§ / Bishopsgate / Aldgate

---

* Boney M was the creation of West German record producer Frank Farian. Farian
recruited the four members of the band as a vehicle for his own songwriting. He
courted controversy later in his career with the creation of Milli Vanilli. Farian used
Fab Morvan and Rob Pilatus to be the 'face' of the band, while having competent,
but 'unmarketable' singers supply the vocals on their recordings. By the time of their
second album, *Girl You Know It's True* Milli Vanilli had become enormously popular
and they were awarded the Grammy for Best New Artist in 1990. Rumours about
the contribution of Morvan and Pilatus began to circulate and led to Farian
admitting the truth in November of 1990. The band were stripped of their Grammy
award (the only group ever to suffer this indignity) and dropped by their record
company. A court ruling was even passed in the US entitling disgruntled fans a full
refund from any Milli Vanilli record they had purchased. After a disastrous attempt
to resurrect the act, Pilatus descended into drug addiction and petty crime. He died
of a drug overdose in 1998.

† The song was the theme to *An Officer and a Gentleman,* starring Richard Gere and
Debra Winger.

‡ 'Vienna' was kept from the number one spot by the Joe Dolce Music Theatre with
'Shaddap You Face'.

§ Moorgate was built in medieval times. The other gates were part of the original
Roman fortification of London.

PLANETS* (from page 86)

Mercury / Venus / Earth / Mars
Jupiter / Saturn / Uranus / Neptune

BOOKS BY GEORGE ORWELL (from page 89)

Down and Out in Paris and London	1933
Burmese Days	1934
A Clergyman's Daughter	1935
Keep the Aspidistra Flying	1936
The Road to Wigan Pier	1937
Homage to Catalonia	1938
Coming Up for Air	1939
Animal Farm	1945
Nineteen Eighty-four	1949

LINKED MISCELLANY VII (from page 96)

1. *Eldorado*†; 2. Lynx; 3. The Chicago Bears; 4. Mensa; 5. *The Andromeda Strain*; 6. River Indus; 7. The Taurus Mountains; 8. Cancer; 9. Leo Sayer (all-dayer); 10. Lockheed C-130 Hercules.

The link is constellations‡.

CRICKETING DISMISSALS (from page 98)

Bowled / Caught / Leg before wicket / Hit wicket
Run out / Stumped / Handled the ball / Hit the ball twice
Obstructing the field / Timed out

TRAGEDIES BY SHAKESPEARE (from page 104)

Antony and Cleopatra / Coriolanus / Hamlet / Julius Caesar
King Lear / Macbeth / Othello / Romeo and Juliet
Timon of Athens / Titus Andronicus / Troilus and Cressida

---

* In 2006, Pluto lost its planet status and was reclassified as a Dwarf Planet. At the time of writing, the International Astronomical Union, which adjudicates on astronomical nomenclature, has identified the Dwarf Planets of Ceres, Pluto and Eris in the Solar System although more are likely to be discovered.

† *Eldorado* was noted for its wooden acting and poor production values. Much of the filming took place in villas rather than studios which led to poor sound quality. The term 'Eldorado sound' is still used by the BBC to describe recordings that have too much echo.

‡ Dorado, Lynx, the Great Bear (Ursa Major), Mensa, Andromeda, Indus, Taurus, Cancer, Leo and Hercules.

BRITISH OLYMPIANS I (from page 103)

1. Steve Redgrave; 2. Jane Torville and Christopher Dean; 3. Daley Thompson;
4. Sebastian Coe; 5. Denise Lewis; 6. Steve Ovett; 7. Chris Hoy; 8. Alan Wells;
9. Rebecca Adlington; 10. Fatima Whitbread; 11. Steve Cram*; 12. Roger Black;
13. Adrian Moorhouse; 14. Brian Jacks; 15. John Regis; 16. Brendan Foster;
17. Lynn Davies; 18. Tessa Sanderson; 19. Liz McColgan; 20. Alan Minter;
21. Ken Matthews; 22. David Wilkie; 23. Harold Abrahams†; 24. Don Thompson.

SCOTTISH FOOTBALL CHAMPIONS‡ (from page 106)

Rangers / Celtic / Heart of Midlothian / Hibernian
Aberdeen / Dumbarton / Dundee / Dundee United
Kilmarnock / Motherwell / Third Lanark

CREATURES IN CHINESE ASTROLOGY (from page 112)

Rat§ / Ox / Tiger / Rabbit / Dragon / Snake
Horse / Sheep (or Goat) / Monkey / Rooster / Dog / Pig

CHARACTERS IN DAD'S ARMY (from page 115)

Captain Mainwaring¶	Arthur Lowe
Sergeant Wilson	John Le Mesurier
Lance-Corporal Jones	Clive Dunn
Private Walker	James Beck
Private Pike	Ian Lavender
Private Frazer	John Laurie
Private Godfrey	Arnold Ridley
Private Sponge	Colin Bean
ARP Warden Hodges	Bill Pertwee
Mrs Mavis Pike	Janet Davies
Reverend Farthing	Frank Williams
Maurice Yeatman**	Edward Sinclair

---

* Cram, Coe and Ovett have all held the record for the mile, Cram in 1985 and Ovett in 1980 and 1981. Coe broke it in 1979 and twice in 1981. In the summer of 1981, Coe and Ovett broke the record three times in just nine days (Coe on 19 August with 3:48.53s, Ovett on 26 August with 3:48.40s and Coe again on 28 August with 3:47.33s).

† Together with Eric Liddell was the subject of the film *Chariots of Fire*.

‡ The League Title has been won only on nineteen occasions since the first season in 1890 by clubs other than Rangers and Celtic.

§ In Chinese legend, the rat was given the task of assembling all the animals to be selected as zodiac signs by the Jade Emperor, the ruler of Heaven. The rat forgets to invite his friend the cat and cats have hated rats ever since. Another legend relates the order of the zodiac was determined by a race between the animals. The rat cheated by standing on the ox's head, jumping off at the last minute to win the race.

¶ Pronounced 'Mannering'.

** The verger.

NOTORIOUS SHIPS II (from page 117)

1. *Mayflower*, 2. *General Belgrano*, 3. *Santa Maria*, 4. *Herald of Free Enterprise*,
5. *Cutty Sark*, 6. HMY *Britannia*, 7. *Kursk*, 8. *Bismarck*; 9. *Exxon Valdez*,
10. *QMII*; 11. *Mary Rose*, 12. USS *Missouri*; 13. HMS *Dreadnought*,
14. *Endurance*, 15. *Torrey Canyon*, 16. HMS *Temeraire*, 17. *Revenge*; 18. *Black Pig*,
19. *Andrea Doria*, 20. HMS *Warrior*, 21. *Pequod*, 22. USS *Monitor*, 23. HMS
Vanguard, 24. USS *Arizona*.

NATIONAL PARKS (from page 120)

Peak District / Lake District / Snowdonia / Dartmoor
Pembrokeshire Coast / North Yorkshire Moors / Yorkshire Dales
Exmoor / Northumberland / Brecon Beacons
The Broads / New Forest / South Downs

COUNTRIES BORDERING RUSSIA (from page 122)

Azerbaijan / Belarus / China / Estonia / Finland / Georgia
Kazakhstan / Latvia / Lithuania[K] / Mongolia
North Korea / Norway / Poland[K] / Ukraine
[K] indicates a border with Kaliningrad, a Russian enclave in Eastern Europe

MISCELLANY XVII (from page 125)

1. The diameter; 2. Johann Strauss II; 3. Goose; 4. AD1 5. H.G. Wells; 6. The
M6; 7. Frankfurt; 8. Jubilee Line; 9. Peter Parker; 10. Melchester Rovers;
11. Resign; 12. Oates*; 13. Diego Maradona; 14. Water; 15. Very Special Old
Pale; 16. Denim; 17. Northern Ireland; 18. Robinson Crusoe; 19. Pittsburgh;
20. Sixpence; 21. Capricorn (6 January); 22. Melbourne, Mexico City, Munich,
Montreal and Moscow; 23. Snagglepuss; 24. Eight†.

NOVELS BY CHARLES DICKENS (from page 129)

The Pickwick Papers	1836–7
Oliver Twist	1837–9
Nicholas Nickleby	1838–9
The Old Curiosity Shop	1840–1
Barnaby Rudge	1841
A Christmas Carol	1843
Martin Chuzzlewit	1843–4
Dombey and Son	1846–8
David Copperfield	1849–50
Bleak House	1852–3
Hard Times	1854
Little Dorrit	1855–7

---

* Hall and Oates / Captain Lawrence Oates.

† He makes seven cigarettes from those he picks up and he makes another one from
the butts of these.

COUNTY CRICKET (from page 132)

Derbyshire / Durham / Essex / Glamorgan / Gloucestershire
Hampshire / Kent† / Lancashire / Leicestershire / Middlesex
Northamptonshire / Nottinghamshire / Somerset / Surrey
Sussex / Warwickshire / Worcestershire / Yorkshire

FILMS AND THEIR STARS IV (from page 135)

1. *Alien*; 2. *The Sound of Music*; 3. *Jaws*; 4. *Apocalypse Now*; 5. *The Untouchables*; 6. *Philadelphia*; 7. *The Big Lebowski*; 8. *The Fabulous Baker Boys*; 9. *From Russia with Love*; 10. *Giant*; 11. *All the President's Men*; 12. *Doctor Zhivago*; 13. *Cat on a Hot Tin Roof*; 14. *Lost in Translation*; 15. *Blow-up*; 16. *Layer Cake*; 17. *Heaven Can Wait*; 18. *The Color Purple*; 19. *The Ladykillers*; 20. *The French Lieutenant's Woman*; 21. *Cold Mountain*; 22. *Sexy Beast*; 23. *Gosford Park*; 24. *I'm All Right Jack*.

RIVERS OF THE UK (from page 138)

Severn	220 miles
Thames	215
Trent	185
Aire	161
Great Ouse	143
Wye	135
Tay	117
Spey	107
Nene	100
Clyde	98
Tweed	96
Eden (Cumbria)	90
Dee (Aberdeenshire)	85
Avon‡ (Warwickshire)	84

---

* Unfinished.

† Kent play at the St Lawrence Ground in Canterbury, a ground notable for having a lime tree inside the boundary. Shots that are blocked by the tree are awarded four runs; only four players in history have cleared the tree for a six. The tree was blown down in high winds in 2005 but a replacement was planted in the same year.

‡ 'Avon' is derived from the Celtish word for river ('afan') and gives its name to many rivers in the UK. As well as the Warwickshire Avon there are river Avons in Bigbury-on-Sea in Devon, in Hampshire through Salisbury and Christchurch, in Wiltshire and through Bath and Bristol; in Falkirk and in Strathspey.

Don (Aberdeenshire)	80
Bann*	76
Ribble	75
Tyne	73
Tees	70
Dee (Wales)	70

LARGE LAKES† (from page 140)

Caspian Sea ^{Asia}	143,250
Lake Superior $^{N. America}$	31,700
Lake Victoria ^{Africa}	26,560
Lake Huron $^{N. America}$	23,010
Lake Michigan $^{N. America}$	22,320
Lake Tanganyika ^{Africa}	12,700
Great Bear Lake $^{N. America}$	12,100
Lake Baikal‡ ^{Asia}	11,780
Lake Nyasa§ ^{Africa}	11,600
Great Slave Lake $^{N. America}$	11,030
Lake Erie $^{N. America}$	9,920
Lake Winnipeg $^{N. America}$	9,420
Lake Ontario $^{N. America}$	7,320
Lake Ladoga ^{Europe}	7,100
Lake Balkhash ^{Asia}	6,720
Aral Sea¶ ^{Asia}	6,620

---

* The Bann is the longest river in Northern Ireland. It rises in the Mourne Mountains in County Down, flowing through Lough Neagh and into the sea at Portstewart on the north-west coast.

† Other notable lakes include: Lake Maracaibo in Venezuela, a body of salt water connected to the Gulf of Venezuela by a narrow strait, is 5,100 square miles in size. Tonle Sap, a lake and river system in Cambodia, is subject to seasonal monsoon flooding which can cover an area of 11,000 square miles. Lake Vostok, a giant lake trapped under about 3km of ice has recently been discovered in Antarctica. It is thought to be about 4,000 square miles in size and 500 metres deep but further surveys are required to confirm this. Lake Chad (in North Africa) used to be about the same size as Lake Victoria in the 1960s, but reduced rainfall and increased irrigation have seen it shrink to a fraction of that size. Lake Michigan and Lake Huron are sometimes considered as a single lake as they are connected by a channel five miles wide.

‡ With a depth of 1,740m, Lake Baikal in Siberia is the deepest lake in the world. It contains more water than all of the North American Great Lakes combined and is estimated to contain 20% of the earth's fresh water.

§ Also known as Lake Malawi.

¶ The Aral Sea, in Central Asia, was the fourth largest lake in the world in 1960. It has since lost 80% of its volume of water due to the diversion of rivers for irrigation projects in the area (before 1960, 55 million cubic metres of water flowed into the Aral Sea, nowadays the annual flow is between 1 and 5 million cubic metres). It is expected to have dried up by 2015.

Lake Onega [Europe]	....	3,710
Lake Nicaragua [N. America]	....	3,330
Lake Titicaca [S. America]	....	3,220
Lake Athabaska [N. America]	....	3,060

All figures are in square miles and are approximate

WIT AND WISDOM II (from page 143)

1.	'When I'm good . . .'	West
2.	'I told my mother-in-law . . .'	Rivers
3.	'One more drink . . .'	Parker
4.	'I used to be Snow White . . .'	West
5.	'My best birth control now . . .'	Rivers
6.	'It's not the men in my life . . .'	West
7.	'You can lead a horticulture . . .'	Parker*
8.	'The first time I see a jogger smiling . . .'	Rivers
9.	'All I need is room enough to lay a hat . . .'	Parker
10.	'Keep a diary . . .'	West
11.	'She runs the gamut of emotions . . .'	Parker
12.	'I hate housework . . .'	Rivers
13.	'It's so long since I've had sex . . .'	Rivers
14.	'It is better to be looked over . . .'	West
15.	'If all the girls at the Yale Prom . . .'	Parker
16.	'The one thing women don't want to find . . .'	Rivers
17.	'I've never been a millionaire . . .'	Parker
18.	'When women go wrong . . .'	West
19.	'This is not a novel to be tossed aside lightly . . .'	Parker
20.	'When choosing between two evils . . .'	West
21.	'Take care of the luxuries . . .'	Parker
22.	'If God wanted us to bend over . . .'	Rivers
23.	'If you want to know what God thinks of money . . .'	Parker
24.	'That woman speaks eight languages . . .'	Parker

FAMOUS FIVE STORIES (from page 146)

Five . . .

. . . on a Treasure Island / . . . Go Adventuring Again
. . . Run Away Together / . . . Go to Smuggler's Top
. . . Go Off in a Caravan / . . . on Kirrin Island Again
. . . Go Off to Camp / . . . Get into Trouble
. . . Fall into Adventure / . . . on a Hike Together
. . . Have a Wonderful Time / . . . Go Down to the Sea
. . . Go to Mystery Moor / . . . Have Plenty of Fun
. . . on a Secret Trail / . . . Go to Billycock Hill

---

* While playing a word game, Dorothy Parker was asked to create a sentence which included the word 'horticulture'.

. . . Get into a Fix I . . . on Finniston Farm
. . . Go to Demon's Rocks I . . . Have a Mystery to Solve
. . . Are Together Again

OLYMPIC HOST CITIES (from page 150)

Amsterdam	1928
Antwerp	1920
Athens	1896, 2004
Atlanta	1996
Barcelona	1992
Beijing	2008
Berlin	1936
Helsinki	1952
London	1908, 1948, 2012
Los Angeles	1932, 1984
Melbourne	1956
Mexico City	1968
Montreal	1976
Moscow	1980
Munich	1972
Paris	1900, 1924
Rome	1960
Seoul	1988
St Louis	1904
Stockholm	1912
Sydney	2000
Tokyo	1964

GOVERNMENTS (from page 152)

1. Monarchy; 2. Bureaucracy; 3. Democracy*; 4. Aristocracy; 5. Autocracy;
6. Patriarchy; 7. Meritocracy; 8. Paparchy; 9. Hierarchy; 10. Plutocracy;
11. Oligarchy; 12. Matriarchy; 13. Xenocracy; 14. Kleptocracy; 15. Technocracy;
16. Theocracy; 17. Biarchy; 18. Arithmocracy; 19. Gynocracy; 20. Androcracy;
21. Gerontocracy; 22. Paedarchy; 23. Polyarchy; 14. Pornocracy.

FOOTBALL TEAMS WITH ONE-WORD NAMES (from page 156; as at the time of publishing)

Arsenal / Barnet / Barnsley / Blackpool / Brentford
Bournemouth / Burnley / Bury / Chelsea / Chesterfield
Darlington / Everton / Fulham / Gillingham
Liverpool / Middlesbrough / Millwall
Portsmouth / Reading / Rochdale / Southampton
Sunderland / Walsall / Watford / Wrexham

---

* The word 'democracy' comes from the Greek words demos, meaning 'common people' and kratos meaning 'rule' or 'strength'.

PROLIFIC BATSMEN (from page 163; as at the time of publishing)

Sachin Tendulkar [IND P]	12,696
Brian Lara [WI]	11,953
Alan Border [AUS]	11,174
Ricky Ponting [AUS P]	10,960
Steve Waugh [AUS]	10,927
Rahul Dravid [IND P]	10,728
Jaques Kallis [SA P]	10,277
Sunil Gavaskar [IND]	10,122
Graham Gooch [ENG]	8,900
Javed Miandad [PAK]	8,832
Inzamam-ul-Haq [PAK]	8,830
Matthew Hayden [AUS P]	8,625
Viv Richards [WI]	8,540
Shivnarine Chanderpaul [WI P]	8,502
Alex Stewart [ENG]	8,463
Mahela Jayawardene [SL P]	8,251
David Gower [ENG]	8,231
Geoffrey Boycott [ENG]	8,114
Garfield Sobers [WI]	8,032
Mark Waugh [AUS]	8,029
Michael Atherton [ENG]	7,728
Justin Langer [AUS]	7,696
Colin Cowdrey [ENG]	7,624
Gordon Greenidge [WI]	7,558
Mark Taylor [AUS]	7,525

P indicates currently still playing test cricket

ADVERTISING SLOGANS IV (from page 165)

1. British Airways; 2. Impulse; 3. Everest double glazing; 4. Cream cakes (National Dairy Council); 5. Yellow Pages; 6. *Mail on Sunday*; 7. *Radio Times*; 8. Abbey National; 9. Hoover; 10. *Independent*; 11. Harmony Hairspray; 12. Renault Clio; 13. Country Life butter; 14. Guinness; 15. Mr Muscle; 16. BMW; 17. Barclays Bank; 18. Birds Eye Potato Waffles; 19. Philips; 20. Commercial Union; 21. Visa; 22. Volkswagen; 23. *The Economist*; 24. Twix.

MONARCHIES* (from page 170; as at the time of publishing)

Andorra / Bahrain / Belgium / Bhutan / Brunei / Cambodia / Denmark
Japan / Jordan / Kuwait / Lesotho / Liechtenstein
Luxembourg / Malaysia / Monaco / Morocco
Netherlands / Norway / Oman / Qatar / Saudi Arabia
Spain / Swaziland / Sweden / Thailand
Tonga / United Arab Emirates / United Kingdom

---

* Note the Vatican is a theocracy in which the Supreme Pontiff is elected by a conclave of cardinals.

CHRISTIAN FEASTS (from page 173)

Solemnity of Mary, Mother of God	1 January
Epiphany	6 January
Baptism of Jesus	11 January
Conversion of Paul the Apostle	25 January
Candlemas Day	2 February
Ash Wednesday[M]	4 February–10 March
Chair of Peter the Apostle	22 February
Palm Sunday[M]	Sunday before Easter
Good Friday[M]	Friday before Easter
Holy Saturday[M]	Saturday before Easter
Easter[M*]	22 March–25 April
Annunciation of the Virgin Mary	25 March
Ascension[M]	30 April–3 June
Whit Sunday[M]	10 May–13 June
Trinity Sunday[M]	17 May–20 June
Corpus Christi[M]	21 May–24 June
Birth of John the Baptist	24 June
Transfiguration	6 August
Assumption of the Virgin Mary	15 August
Queenship of Mary	22 August
Birthday of the Virgin Mary	8 September
Exaltation of the Holy Cross	14 September
Guardian Angels	2 October
All Saints	1 November
All Souls	2 November
Presentation of the Virgin Mary	21 November
First Sunday in Advent[M]	Sunday nearest 30 November
Immaculate Conception	8 December
Christmas Day†	25 December
Holy Innocents	28 December

[M] indicates movable feast falling on or between the dates indicated

* Easter was originally a pagan festival which was adopted by Christianity as it spread through northern Europe. Bede, in his *Ecclesiastical History of the English People* (AD731) refers to a Saxon goddess called Eostre who was related to the dawn, to spring and fertility. The festival of Eostre was celebrated on the spring equinox, and the words 'Easter' and 'East' (the direction in which the sun rises) seem to derive from this. It became appropriate for the Christian Easter, which is about rebirth and renewal, to be celebrated on this day.

† Christmas derives from a pagan festival called Yule which celebrated the shortest day of the year. Many Christmas traditions date back to this pre-Christian festival such as holly, mistletoe, the Yule log and the twelve days.

ENTREPRENEURS II (from page 176)

1. Banking; 2. Food (chocolate); 3. Shipping; 4. Media (*Playboy* magazine);
5. Banking; 6. Property; 7. Broadcasting; 8. E-commerce (Lastminute.com);
9. Financial information; 10. Oil; 11. Oil, cinema, property; 12. Finance and
investment*; 13. Banking; 14. Media (CNN); 15. Finance and investment†;
16. Oil and property; 17. Railways‡; 18. Steel and railways§; 19. Chemicals (ICI);
20. Recording (Geffen Records); 21. Sports representation; 22. Railways;
23. Telecoms (AT&T); 24. Media and politics.

SQUARES ON THE MONOPOLY BOARD (from page 180)

Go / Old Kent Road[B] / Community Chest / Whitechapel Road[B]

Income Tax / King's Cross Station

The Angel, Islington [LB] / Chance / Euston Road[LB]

Pentonville Road[LB] / Jail / Pall Mall[P]

Electric Company / Whitehall[P] / Northumberland Avenue[P]

Marylebone Station / Bow Street[O] / Marlborough Street[¶][O]

Vine Street[**][O] / Free Parking / Strand[R]

---

* Warren Buffet has been nicknamed the 'Oracle of Omaha' and has amassed an
enormous fortune making him the world's second-richest man (after Bill Gates).
† Soros is best known for profiting to the tune of over $1bn at the expense of the
Bank of England on Black Wednesday. He later admitted '. . . when Norman
Lamont said just before the devaluation he would borrow nearly $15bn to defend
sterling, we were amused because that was about how much we wanted to sell.'
‡ Vanderbilt made his fortune as a steamship operator before moving into railways
relatively late in his life. A ruthless man, he once said to a competitor: 'You have
undertaken to cheat me. I won't sue you, for the law is too slow. I'll ruin you.'
§ The son of a Scottish weaver, Carnegie was born in 1835 and moved to America
in 1948 where he made his fortune with a series of companies including the
Carnegie Steel Company (which launched the steel industry in Pittsburgh and was
sold to J.P. Morgan for $480m). Carnegie believed that the rich had an obligation to
redistribute their wealth and formed the Carnegie Corporation which, among other
things, created 2,509 new libraries around the world.
¶ Victor Watson sent his secretary, Marjory Phillips, to scout out locations to be
included in the new game. She had lunch at the Angel, Islington and (possibly as a
result) omitted the word 'Great' from Great Marlborough Street in Soho, an error
which still appears in the game.
** The probability of landing on each property on the board is not equal. Given that Chance
and Community Chest cards and the Go to Jail square can send players to other locations,
some properties will on average be visited more often than others. Combining this with the
cost of development, which also varies around the board, an expected return on investment
may be calculated for each property. The top ten properties on the board in terms of expected
return are: 1. Vine Street; 2. Pentonville Road; 3. Bow Street; 4. Marlborough Street;
5. Mayfair; 6. The Angel, Islington; 7. Euston Road; 8. Trafalgar Square; 9. Northumberland
Avenue; 10. Piccadilly (this assumes the properties are developed with a hotel).

Fleet Street^R / Trafalgar Square^R / Fenchurch Street Station
Leicester Square^Y / Coventry Street^Y / Water Works
Piccadilly^Y / Go to Jail / Regent Street^G
Oxford Street^G / Bond Street^G / Liverpool Street Station
Park Lane^{DB} / Super Tax / Mayfair^{DB}
^{B} Brown ^{LB} Light Blue ^{P} Pink ^{O} Orange ^{R} Red ^{Y} Yellow ^{G} Green ^{DB} Dark Blue

HISTORIC ENGLISH COUNTIES (from page 182)

Bedfordshire / Berkshire / Buckinghamshire
Cambridgeshire / Cheshire^P / Cornwall / Cumberland
Derbyshire / Devon / Dorset / County Durham^P
Essex / Gloucestershire / Hampshire* / Herefordshire
Hertfordshire / Leicestershire / Huntingdonshire / Kent
Lancashire^P / Lincolnshire / Middlesex / Norfolk
Northamptonshire / Northumberland / Nottinghamshire
Oxfordshire / Rutland / Shropshire / Somerset
Staffordshire / Suffolk / Surrey / Sussex / Warwickshire
Westmorland / Worcestershire / Wiltshire / Yorkshire
^{P} indicates County Palatine†

MISCELLANY XXIV (from page 186)

1. Sunlight; 2. Colours; 3. Quarantine; 4. March; 5. Giuseppe Verdi; 6. *Happy Days*; 7. Elton John (Reginald Hercules Dwight); 8. Tombstone, Arizona; 9. Northwest; 10. Maine; 11. Mechanical diggers; 12. The eyes; 13. Vinegar‡; 14. Five; 15. Yale; 16. Dom Perignon; 17. Two hours§; 18. 'Love Me Do'; 19. A flamingo; 20. Dundee; 21. Peter Wright; 22. Tunisia; 23. The Forth Bridge; 24. Two miles¶.

---

* Including the Isle of Wight.
† County Palatines were areas with sovereign jurisdictions autonomous and independent from the rest of the kingdom. In medieval times, the king granted special authority to Palatines who controlled the county independently from the king but still owed him allegiance (for example, County Durham was ruled by the Prince Bishops of Durham). Palatines were a useful instrument of government as their powers allowed more effective defence of Welsh and Scottish border territories.
‡ Vin aigre.
§ In one hour Belinda can paint one sixth of the fence and Janice one third, one half of the whole fence in total. Therefore it will take two hours to paint the whole fence.
¶ The trains are travelling towards one another at a velocity of 120mph (their combined velocities). An object travelling at this velocity in one minute would travel a distance of two miles. The trains are therefore two miles apart one minute before they meet.

PERFORMERS IN BAND AID (from page 189)

Stuart Adamson	Big Country
Robert 'Kool' Bell	Kool & the Gang
Bono*	U2
David Bowie	Solo artist
Boy George†	Culture Club
Pete Briquette	The Boomtown Rats
Mark Brzezicki	Big Country
Tony Butler	Big Country
Adam Clayton	U2
Phil Collins	Solo artist
Chris Cross	Ultravox
Simon Crowe	The Boomtown Rats
Sarah Dallin	Bananarama
Siobhan Fahey	Bananarama
Johnny Fingers	The Boomtown Rats
Bob Geldof	The Boomtown Rats
Glenn Gregory	Heaven 17
Tony Hadley	Spandau Ballet
Holly Johnson	Frankie Goes to Hollywood
John Keeble	Spandau Ballet
Gary Kemp	Spandau Ballet
Martin Kemp	Spandau Ballet
Simon Le Bon	Duran Duran
Marilyn	Solo artist
Paul McCartney	Solo artist
George Michael‡	Wham!
Jon Moss	Culture Club
Steve Norman	Spandau Ballet
Rick Parfitt	Status Quo
Nick Rhodes	Duran Duran
Francis Rossi	Status Quo
Sting	Solo artist
Andy Taylor	Duran Duran
James 'J.T.' Taylor	Kool & the Gang
John Taylor	Duran Duran
Roger Taylor	Duran Duran
Dennis Thomas	Kool & the Gang
Midge Ure	Ultravox
Martyn Ware	Heaven 17
Jody Watley	Shalamar

* Fourth solo: 'Well, tonight, thank God it's them, instead of you . . .'

† Second solo: 'And in our world of plenty, we can spread a smile of joy . . .'

‡ Third solo: 'But say a prayer; pray for the other ones . . .'

Bruce Watson	Big Country
Paul Weller	Style Council
Keren Woodward	Bananarama
Paul Young*	Solo artist

COUNTRIES IN ASIA†
(from page 196)

ASIAN CAPITAL CITIES
(from page 192)

Afghanistan	Kabul
Armenia	Yerevan
Azerbaijan	Baku
Bahrain	Manama
Bangladesh	Dhaka
Bhutan	Thimphu
Brunei	Bandar Seri Begawan
Cambodia	Phnom Penh
China	Beijing
Cyprus	Nicosia
East Timor	Dili
Georgia	Tbilisi
India	New Delhi
Indonesia	Jakarta
Iran	Tehran
Iraq	Baghdad
Israel	Jerusalem
Japan	Tokyo
Jordan	Amman
Kazakhstan	Astana
Kuwait	Kuwait City
Kyrgyzstan	Bishkek
Laos	Vientiane
Lebanon	Beirut
Malaysia	Kuala Lumpur
Maldives	Malé
Mongolia	Ulaanbaatar
Burma	Rangoon
Nepal	Kathmandu
North Korea	Pyongyang
Oman	Muscat
Pakistan	Islamabad
Philippines	Manila
Qatar	Doha
Russia	Moscow

---

* First solo: 'It's Christmas time, there's no need to be afraid . . .'
† Note that parts of Russia and Turkey are in both Asia and Europe.

Saudi Arabia	Riyadh
Singapore	Singapore City
South Korea	Seoul
Sri Lanka	Colombo
Syria	Damascus
Taiwan	Taipei
Tajikistan	Dushanbe
Thailand	Bangkok
Turkey	Ankara
Turkmenistan	Ashkhabad
United Arab Emirates	Abu Dhabi
Uzbekistan	Tashkent
Vietnam	Hanoi
West Bank	Ramallah
Yemen	Sana

VALUABLE GLOBAL BRANDS* (from page 193, as at date of publishing)

Accenture[47] / American Express[15] / Apple[24] / BMW[13]
Budweiser[33] / Canon[36] / Cisco[17] / Citi[19] / Coca-Cola[1] / Dell[32]
Disney[9] / eBay[46] / Ford[49] / GE[4] / Gillette[14] / Goldman Sachs[38]
Google[10] / Gucci[45] / H&M[22] / Harley-Davidson[50]
Hewlett-Packard[12] / Honda[20] / HSBC[27] / IBM[2] / Ikea[35]
Intel[7] / JPMorgan[37] / Kellogg's[39] / Louis Vuitton[16] / Marlboro[18]
McDonald's[8] / Mercedes-Benz[11] / Merrill Lynch[34] / Microsoft[3]
Morgan Stanley[42] / Nescafé[28] / Nike[29] / Nintendo[40] / Nokia[5]
Oracle[23] / Pepsi[26] / Philips[43] / Samsung[21] / SAP[31] / Siemens[48]
Sony[25] / Thomson Reuters[44] / Toyota[6] / UBS[41] / UPS[30]

'ISMS' II (from page 197)

1. Racism; 2. Terrorism; 3. Chauvinism†; 4. Pessimism; 5. Communism‡;
6. Hedonism; 7. Postmodernism; 8. Hinduism; 9. Paganism; 10. Imperialism;
11. Maoism; 12. Methodism; 13. Colonialism; 14. Socialism; 15. Fundamentalism;
16. Shintoism; 17. Polytheism; 18. Evangelism; 19. Totalitarianism; 20. Jingoism§;

---

* The list is according to data from Interbrand and *Business Week* magazine. The list is limited to those organisations for which financial data is publicly available and does not include airlines.
† The term is named after Nicholas Chauvin, a French officer whose support for Napoleon Bonaparte was so enthusiastic as to be deemed embarrassing by his peers.
‡ Frank Zappa once said: 'Communism doesn't work because people like to own stuff.'
§ During the 1870s at the peak of the British Empire, Russia was in military conflict with the Ottoman Empire. Although Prime Minister Disraeli opposed British intervention, the mood in the country was more belligerent. A popular chorus at the time gave rise to the term: *cont'd over/*

21. Behaviourism; 22. Dialectical materialism; 23. Calvinism; 24. Antidisestablishmentarianism.

BRITISH RACECOURSES (from page 201)

Flat:

Bath / Beverley / Brighton / Chester / Epsom Downs*
Goodwood / Hamilton Park / Newmarket† / Nottingham
Pontefract / Redcar / Ripon / Salisbury / Thirsk
Windsor / Wolverhampton / Yarmouth / York

National Hunt:

Aintree‡ / Bangor-on-Dee / Cartmel / Cheltenham
Devon and Exeter / Fakenham / Fontwell Park
Hereford / Hexham / Huntingdon / Kelso / Ludlow
Market Rasen / Musselburgh / Newton Abbot / Perth
Plumpton / Sedgefield / Stratford-upon-Avon / Taunton
Towcester / Uttoxeter / Wetherby / Wincanton / Worcester

Flat and National Hunt:

Ascot / Ayr / Carlisle / Catterick Bridge / Chepstow
Doncaster§ / Ffos Las / Folkestone / Haydock Park / Kempton Park
Leicester / Lingfield Park / Newbury / Newcastle
Sandown Park / Southwell / Warwick

CONSTELLATIONS (from page 205)

Andromeda / Antlia / Apus / Aquarius / Aquila / Ara
Aries / Auriga / Boötes / Caelum / Camelopardalis
Cancer / Canes Venatici / Canis Major / Canis Minor
Capricornus / Carina / Cassiopeia / Centaurus / Cepheus
Cetus / Chamaeleon / Circinus / Columba / Coma Berenices
Corona Austrina / Corona Borealis / Corvus / Crater
Crux¶ / Cygnus / Delphinus / Dorado / Draco / Equuleus
Eridanus / Fornax / Gemini / Grus / Hercules / Horologium
Hydra / Hydrus / Indus / Lacerta / Leo / Leo Minor
Lepus / Libra / Lupus / Lynx / Lyra / Mensa
Microscopium / Monoceros / Musca / Norma / Octans
Ophiuchus / Orion / Pavo / Pegasus / Perseus
Phoenix / Pictor / Pisces / Piscis Austrinus / Puppis

---

cont'd   'We don't want to fight / But, by Jingo, if we do / We've got the ships / We've got the men / We've got the money, too.'

* Home of the Derby and the Oaks.

† Home of the One Thousand Guineas and the Two Thousand Guineas.

‡ Home of the Grand National.

§ Home of the St Leger.

¶ Commonly known as the Southern Cross.

Pyxis / Reticulum / Sagitta / Sagittarius / Scorpius
Sculptor / Scutum / Serpens / Sextans / Taurus
Telescopium / Triangulum / Triangulum Australe
Tucana / Ursa Major* / Ursa Minor† / Vela
Virgo / Volans / Vulpecula

ORIGINAL MEMBERS OF LEAGUE AND PREMIERSHIP (from page 4)
Aston Villa / Blackburn Rovers / Everton

LINKED MISCELLANY I (from page 7)
1. St Michael's Mount; 2. Bonnie Prince Charlie; 3. Victor Meldrew; 4. (30)
November; 5. Sierra Nevada; 6. India; 7. 'Echo Beach'; 8. Alpha; 9. Quebec City;
10. X-Rays.

The link is the NATO phonetic alphabet‡.

THE POLICE (from page 10)
Sting§ .... Bass
Andy Summers .... Guitar
Stewart Copeland .... Drums

THE MONKEES (from page 13)
Davy Jones / Micky Dolenz
Michael Nesmith / Peter Tork

ADVERTISING SLOGANS I (from page 15)
1. iPod (Nano); 2. Fry's Turkish Delight; 3. Gillette; 4. Cadbury's Milk Tray;
5. R. White's Lemonade; 6. Audi; 7. Nokia; 8. Opal Fruits; 9. Access; 10. *Daily
Mirror*; 11. Castrol GTX; 12. Honda; 13. Iceland; 14. Malibu; 15. IBM;
16. Bisto; 17. Club biscuit; 18. Zanussi; 19. Kellogg's Fruit and Fibre;
20. Monster Munch; 21. Goodyear Tyres (Grand Prix S); 22. Insignia; 23. DHL;
24. Croft Original.

ASSASSINATED US PRESIDENTS (from page 21)
Abraham Lincoln (1860) / James A. Garfield (1881)
William McKinley (1901) / John F. Kennedy (1963)

AMERICAN STATES BEGINNING WITH 'I' (from page 23)
Idaho / Illinois / Indiana / Iowa

---

* Or the Great Bear; colloquially known as the Plough or the Big Dipper.
† Or the Lesser Bear; colloquially known as the Plough or the Little Dipper.
‡ Mike, Charlie, Victor, November, Sierra, India, Echo, Alpha, Quebec and X-Ray.
§ Born Gordon Matthew Sumner and nicknamed Sting because of a black-and-
yellow-striped jumper he often wore.

ASSASSINATIONS (from page 195)

1. John F. Kennedy; 2. Julius Caesar; 3. Abraham Lincoln*; 4. John Lennon†;
5. Archduke Franz Ferdinand; 6. Thomas Becket; 7. Lord Mountbatten; 8. Leon
Trotsky; 9. Martin Luther King; 10. Mohandas Gandhi; 11. Robert F. Kennedy;
12. Airey Neave; 13. Indira Gandhi; 14. Macbeth; 15. Malcolm X; 16. Michael
Collins; 17. Olaf Palme; 18. Yitzhak Rabin; 19. Claudius; 20. Alexander Litvinenko;
21. Edward II‡; 22. Spencer Perceval; 23. Caligula; 24. James A. Garfield.

BALEARIC ISLANDS (from page 27)

Majorca (Mallorca) / Minorca (Menorca)
Ibiza (Eivissa) / Formentera

HORSEMEN OF THE APOCALYPSE§ (from page 31)

Pestilence / War / Famine / Death

MISCELLANY IV (from page 33)

1. The Fosbury Flop; 2. Robert Louis Stevenson; 3. France and Mexico; 4. Pixel;
5. Spandex; 6. Kenneth Clarke; 7. four; 8. i and j; 9. Lewis and Harris (in the
Outer Hebrides); 10. Liberace; 11. Hydrogen; 12. Dog licence; 13. Edinburgh;
14. Geoffrey Chaucer; 15. 28; 16. Charles de Gaulle; 17. Rover; 18. *Hi-de-Hi!*;
19. Red and yellow cards; 20. J.R.R. Tolkien; 21. 85 degrees; 22. The Black Sea;
23. *Treasure Island*; 24. Fourteen horses, eight men.

UNITED NATIONS SECURITY COUNCIL (from page 36)

China / France / Russia / United Kingdom / United States

HOUSE OF TUDOR¶ (from page 39)

Henry VII / Henry VIII / Edward VI / Mary I / Elizabeth I

CATCHPHRASES I (from page 41)

1. Victor Meldrew (*One Foot in the Grave*); 2. Captain Mainwaring (*Dad's Army***);
3. Alan Partridge (*Knowing Me, Knowing You*); 4. Frank Carson; 5. Leslie Phillips;
6. Hannibal Smith (*The A-Team*); 7. Kenneth Williams; 8. Joey Tribbiani (*Friends*);

---

* Wilkes Booth broke his leg as he leapt to the stage; it has been suggested that the
theatrical expression 'break a leg' derives from this.

† Lennon's killer, Mark Chapman, was carrying a copy of *Catcher in the Rye* when
he was arrested.

‡ Painfully, with a hot poker, according to one historical account.

§ The Four Horsemen of Apocalypse are described in Chapter 6 of the Book of
Revelation in the Bible.

¶ Lady Jane Grey reigned England for nine days during the Tudor period but was
never crowned. She was executed in the Tower of London in 1554.

** The show also gave us 'They don't like it up 'em' and 'Don't panic!' from the
belligerent and flappable Corporal Jones (played by Clive Dunn).

9. Alan Freeman; 10. Columbo; 11. Arthur Daley (*Minder*); 12. The Fonz (*Happy Days*); 13. Max Bygraves; 14. George Formby; 15. Horace Rumpole (*Rumpole of the Bailey*); 16. Mrs Doyle (*Father Ted*); 17. Dick Emery; 18. Andy (*Little Britain*); 19. Steve McGarrett (*Hawaii Five-O*); 20. Jack Regan (*The Sweeney*); 21.Cartman (*South Park*); 22. Tony Hancock; 23. Sgt. Joe Friday (*Dragnet*); 24. Tommy Trinder.

FAMOUS FIVE (from page 43)

Julian / Dick / Anne / George / Timmy the Dog

HALOGENS (from page 45)

Fluorine .... F
Chlorine Cl
Bromine .... Br
Iodine I
Astatine .... At*

FILMS AND THEIR STARS III (from page 47)

1. *The Godfather*; 2. *The Lord of the Rings: The Fellowship of the Ring*; 3. *Schindler's List*; 4. *Trading Places*†; 5. *Casablanca*; 6. *LA Confidential*; 7. *Driving Miss Daisy*; 8. *The Accused*; 9. *King Kong*; 10. *Lawrence of Arabia*; 11. *The Name of the Rose*; 12. *Erin Brockovich*; 13. *The Talented Mr Ripley*; 14. *Million Dollar Baby*; 15. *The Thomas Crown Affair*; 16. *Mystic River*; 17. *1984*; 18. *The People vs. Larry Flynt*; 19. *Sense and Sensibility*; 20. *Rear Window*; 21. *Walk the Line*; 22. *Fried Green Tomatoes at the Whistle Stop Café*; 23. *Brazil*; 24. *Hotel Rwanda*.

COLOURS OF THE RUBIK'S CUBE (from page 50)

Red / Yellow / Green / Blue / Orange / White

NUTRIENTS (from page 53)

Carbohydrate / Fat / Protein / Vitamins / Minerals / Fibre

DANCES (from page 56)

1. Limbo; 2. Twist; 3. Belly dance; 4. Flamenco; 5. Can-can; 6. Lap dance; 7. Conga; 8. Foxtrot; 9. Tango; 10. Paso doble; 11. Salsa; 12. Bolero; 13. Samba; 14. Bossa nova; 15. Jig; 16. Mexican hat dance; 17. Charleston; 18. Hula; 19. Waltz; 20. Bhangra; 21. Merengue‡; 22. Rumba; 23. Lambada; 24. Polka.

---

* Astatine is a naturally occurring radioactive element.
† The theme music is from Mozart's *The Marriage of Figaro*, a story in which a servant turns the tables on his master. The climax of the film may have been inspired by the Hunt brothers of Texas who lost $100m trying to corner the silver market during the 'Silver Thursday' crash on 27 March 1980.
‡ According to a story, during the civil war in the Dominican Republic a hero was wounded in the leg but escaped and arrived at a friendly village. A victory celebration was held, and so as not to offend the injured soldier, everybody danced with a limp. The dance became known as the merengue.

COURTS OF ENGLAND AND WALES (from page 60)

House of Lords* / Court of Appeal / High Court
Crown Court / County Court / Magistrates Court

WIVES OF HENRY VIII (from page 63)

Catherine of Aragon / Anne Boleyn / Jane Seymour
Anne of Cleves / Catherine Howard / Catherine Parr

FRUIT AND VEGETABLES (from page 65)

1. Potato†; 2. Orange; 3. Apple‡; 4. Grape; 5. Chilli; 6. Mushroom; 7. Tomato;
8. Broccoli; 9. Lettuce; 10. Plum; 11. Cabbage; 12. Aubergine; 13. Beetroot;
14. Cucumber; 15. Onion; 16. Pea; 17. Carrot; 18. Brussels spouts; 19. Cherry;
20. Parsnip; 21. Lemon; 22. Banana; 23. Grapefruit; 24. Pear.

SOVIET COMMUNIST PARTY LEADERS (from page 69)

Vladimir Lenin	1917–22
Joseph Stalin	1922–53
Nikita Khrushchev	1953–64
Leonid Brezhnev	1964–82
Yuri Andropov	1982–4
Konstantin Chernenko	1984–5
Mikhail Gorbachev	1985–91

* The House of Lords is the highest point of appeal in the UK although certain cases may be referred to the European Court of Justice. The House of Lords hears appeals regarding the meaning of the law rather than making judgements based on evidence.

† The potato was imported from South America in the sixteenth century. It was first grown by tribes in the foothills of the Andes in what today would be Peru and Bolivia and quickly became a staple food in Europe, so much so that failures to the potato crop soon would have devastating results. In 1845, 1846 and 1848 the Irish potato crop was devastated by the fungus phytophthora infestans, commonly known as 'potato blight'. In the ensuing famine, an estimated 1 million people died and between 1 and 2 million emigrated, mainly to Britain and the United States. Ireland's population would never recover from the famine. Nowadays, each person in the UK consumes around 110kg of potatoes per year (one quarter of which is in the form of chips). The largest world producer is now China, which grows 47 million tons of potatoes annually. The many hundreds of potato varieties that are available fall into two categories. Waxy potatoes (such as Charlotte or Pink Fir Apple) have a low starch and high moisture content. They hold their shape after cooking and are good for boiling or potato salads. Floury potatoes (such as Maris Piper or Golden Wonder) have a high starch and low moisture content making them better for mashing, roasting or frying.

‡ The Cox's Orange Pippin was created by Richard Cox in 1825 from a Ribston Pippin pollinated with a Blenheim Orange.

MOST OSCAR-NOMINATED ACTRESSES (from page 71; as at the time of publishing)

Meryl Streep	15 nominations (2 wins)
Katharine Hepburn	12 (4)
Bette Davis	11 (2)
Geraldine Page	8 (1)
Ingrid Bergman	7 (3)
Jane Fonda	7 (2)
Greer Garson	7 (1)

FIRST LINES OF POPULAR NOVELS III (from page 73)

1. *Peter Pan* (J.M. Barrie); 2. *The Wonderful Wizard of Oz* (Frank Baum); 3. *The World According to Garp* (John Irving); 4. *Around the World in 80 Days* (Jules Verne); 5. *The Tale of Peter Rabbit* (Beatrix Potter); 6. *Brave New World* (Aldous Huxley); 7. *The Odyssey* (Homer); 8. *The Hunchback of Notre Dame* (Victor Hugo); 9. *Middlemarch* (George Eliot); 10. *Great Expectations* (Charles Dickens); 11. *Jaws* (Peter Benchley); 12. *Trainspotting* (Irvine Welsh); 13. *Charlie and the Chocolate Factory* (Roald Dahl); 14. *Stuart Little* (E.B. White); 15. *Metamorphosis* (Franz Kafka); 16. *Northern Lights* (Philip Pullman); 17. *The Godfather* (Mario Puzo); 18. *A Passage to India* (E.M. Forster); 19. *The Jungle Book* (Rudyard Kipling); 20. *The Color Purple* (Alice Walker); 21. *David Copperfield* (Charles Dickens); 22. *The Crow Road* (Iain Banks); 23. *The Picture of Dorian Gray* (Oscar Wilde); 24. *Heart of Darkness* (Joseph Conrad).

CHARACTERISTICS OF LIVING THINGS (from page 77)

Movement / Respiration / Sensitivity / Growth
Reproduction / Excretion / Nutrition

THE MAGNIFICENT SEVEN (from page 79)

Yul Brynner	Chris Adams
Steve McQueen	Vin
Charles Bronson	Bernardo O'Reilly
James Coburn	Britt
Horst Buchholz	Chico
Brad Dexter	Harry Luck
Robert Vaughn	Lee

MISCELLANY XI (from page 80)

1. *Coronation Street*; 2. Oman; 3. World Cup mascots; 4. Julius Caesar and Mark Antony; 5. Ten; 6. Conversation; 7. Golf; 8. Eight; 9. The lungs; 10. Upstream; 11. The *Mallard*; 12. It is the furthest point from sea in Britain; 13. St Paul's; 14. 'I Wish I Was a Punk Rocker (with Flowers in My Hair)' by Sandi Thom; 15. Slip of the tongue; 16. Spelling and grammar check; 17. The Southern Lights; 18. Trombone; 19. They have both appeared in *EastEnders* and *Dad's Army*; 20. *The French Connection*; 21. 7 pigs and 8 geese; 22. 1955; 23. The Archbishop of York; 24. Today is 1 January and my birthday is on 31 December.

WARSAW PACT* (from 83)

Albania† / Bulgaria / Czechoslovakia / East Germany
Hungary / Poland / Romania / Soviet Union

REINDEER (from page 86)

Dasher / Dancer / Prancer / Vixen / Comet
Cupid / Donner / Blitzen / Rudolph

RECENT HISTORY II (from page 90)

1. 2000; 2. 2001; 3. 1998; 4. 1995; 5. 1996; 6. 1978; 7. 1969; 8. 1972;
9. 1944; 10. 1987; 11. 1994; 12. 1914; 13. 1973; 14. 1941; 15. 1968;
16. 1975; 17. 1901; 18. 1966; 19. 1936; 20. 1961; 21. 1959; 22. 1913;
23. 1906; 24. 1911.

PLAGUES OF EGYPT (from page 96)

Rivers turn to blood / Frogs / Lice / Flies / Pestilence
Boils / Hail and fire / Locusts / Darkness / Death of the first-born‡

COMMANDMENTS (from page 98)

First .... Thou shalt have no other gods before me
Second .... Thou shalt not make unto thee any graven image
Third .... Thou shalt not take the name of the Lord thy God in vain
Fourth .... Remember the Sabbath day, to keep it holy
Fifth .... Honour thy father and thy mother
Sixth .... Thou shalt not kill
Seventh .... Thou shalt not commit adultery
Eighth .... Thou shalt not steal
Ninth .... Thou shalt not bear false witness against thy neighbour
Tenth .... Thou shalt not covet thy neighbour's house, wife, ox, etc.

---

* Despite being part of Eastern Europe, Yugoslavia was never a member of the
Warsaw Pact.

† Withdrew in 1968.

‡ There is evidence to suggest a series of calamitous events did affect Egypt at
around this time (thought to be about 1300BC) and are recorded independently in
Egyptian and Hebrew texts. Attempts have been made to scientifically explain the ten
plagues. It has been suggested that a bloom of a toxic algae in the Nile (such as
physteria) would have the effect of turning the water red and killing all the fish. This
would bring about many of the other plagues, for example, frogs would leave the
poisonous river, and a lack of predators would increase insect populations, in turn
spreading disease to people and animals. Some historians have noted the events
described in Exodus could have coincided with the eruption of Thera, the largest
volcanic eruption in civilised history, and could also explain many of the phenomena
in the recorded accounts, for example fire and hail, darkness and poisoned rivers.

OLOGIES II (from page 101)

1. Spiders; 2. Mental phenomena; 3. Earthquakes; 4. Diseases of the stomach and intestine; 5. Bones; 6. The origin of words; 7. Life in the geological past; 8. Horses; 9. The eyes; 10. Mathematical connectedness; 11. Poisons; 12. Codes and ciphers; 13. Words; 14. Allergies; 15. The action of drugs on the body; 16. Cancers; 17. Fungi; 18. Knowledge; 19. Soil; 20. Age of trees by rings; 21. Handwriting; 22. The anatomy of blood and lymphatic systems; 23. Caves; 24. Flags.

1966 WORLD CUP WINNERS (from page 104)

1 Gordon Banks

5 Jack Charlton / 6 Bobby Moore (Capt.)

2 George Cohen / 3 Ray Wilson

4 Nobby Stiles / 16 Martin Peters

7 Alan Ball / 9 Bobby Charlton

10 Geoff Hurst / 21 Roger Hunt

CONFEDERACY* (from page 107)

South Carolina / Mississippi / Florida / Alabama

Georgia / Louisiana / Texas / Virginia

Arkansas / Tennessee / North Carolina

NICKNAMES OF FOOTBALL TEAMS II (from page 110)

1. Middlesbrough; 2. Portsmouth; 3. Sunderland; 4. Everton†; 5. Sheffield United; 6. Derby County; 7. Ipswich Town; 8. Coventry City; 9. Manchester City; 10. Millwall; 11. Crystal Palace; 12. Aston Villa; 13. M.K. Dons; 14. Plymouth Argyle; 15. Luton Town; 16. Scunthorpe; 17. York City; 18. Blackpool; 19. Bristol Rovers‡; 20. Reading; 21. Macclesfield Town; 22. Swansea City; 23. Bolton Wanderers; 24. Cardiff City.

CHRISTMAS GIFTS (from page 112)

Twelve drummers drumming / Eleven pipers piping

Ten lords a-leaping / Nine ladies dancing

Eight maids a-milking / Seven swans a-swimming

Six geese a-laying / Five golden rings

Four calling birds / Three French hens

Two turtle doves / A partridge in a pear tree

---

* Slavery was also permitted in the border states of Missouri and Kentucky although these states also had Union ties and were never under the control of the Confederacy.

† After the toffee mints produced in the Everton district of Liverpool.

‡ Also known as 'The Gas' due to the proximity of their old ground at Eastville to a gas works.

LINKED MISCELLANY IX (from page 115)

1. George Best; 2. Horseshoes; 3. Victoria Principal; 4. Beehive; 5. Samantha Fox;
6. Cricket; 7. Greyhound; 8. The Prince of Wales; 9. The Rising Sun;
10. Chequers.

The link is names of pubs*.

PUNCTUATION (from page 118)

Full stop	ends a sentence
Comma	to give additional information
Colon	before a list, summary or quotation
Semi-colon	to link two sentences that are related
Dash	for emphasis or parenthesis
Hyphen	to form compound words
Apostrophe	to indicate possession or missing letters
Question mark	to indicate that a response is expected
Exclamation mark	to add emphasis
Quotation marks	for direct speech, quotations, titles of short texts
Round brackets	for parenthesis
Square brackets	for editorial comments
Ellipsis (three dots)	to replace missing words

COUNTRIES BORDERING CHINA (from page 120)

Afghanistan / Bhutan / Myanmar (Burma) / India / Kazakhstan
North Korea / Kyrgyzstan / Laos / Mongolia / Nepal
Pakistan / Russia / Tajikistan / Vietnam

CHARACTERS IN CHILDREN'S TELEVISION I (from page 122)

1. *Rainbow*†; 2. *The Magic Roundabout*‡; 3. *The Wombles*; 4. *Bagpuss*; 5. *Boss Cat*§;
6. *Dangermouse*; 7. *Ivor the Engine*; 8. *Asterix the Gaul*; 9. *Rentaghost*; 10. *Willo the
Wisp*; 11. *Monkey*; 12. *Tweenies*; 13. *Fingerbobs*; 14. *The Herbs*; 15. *Captain Scarlet
and the Mysterons*; 16. *The Flumps*; 17. *Battle of the Planets*; 18. *The Amazing
Adventures of Morph*; 19. *Postman Pat*; 20. *Button Moon*; 21. *Chigley*; 22. *Hector's
House*; 23. *Space Sentinels*; 24. *The Woodentops*.

---

* The George, The Three Horseshoes, The Victoria, The Beehive, The Fox and
Hounds, The Cricketers, The Greyhound, The Prince of Wales, The Rising Sun,
The Chequers.

† The voices for George and Zippy were provided by Roy Skelton, who had
previously provided the voices for the Daleks in *Doctor Who*.

‡ Originally titled *Le Manège Enchanté* in France, and featuring Pollux (Dougal) who
spoke with a heavy English accent, Ambroise (Brian) Margot (Florence) and Zebulon
(Zebedee), the programme was imported and, rather than translate it, Eric Thompson
(father of actress Emma Thompson) wrote and narrated new stories.

§ Renamed from *Top Cat* in the UK because it shared its name with a popular cat
food; the characters in the programme were based on *The Phil Silvers Show*.

COMIC OPERAS BY GILBERT AND SULLIVAN (from page 126)

Thespis	1871
Trial by Jury	1875
The Sorcerer	1877
HMS Pinafore	1878
The Pirates of Penzance	1879
Patience	1881
Iolanthe	1882
Princess Ida	1884
The Mikado	1885
Ruddigore	1887
The Yeomen of the Guard	1888
The Gondoliers	1889
Utopia, Limited	1893
The Grand Duke	1896

PERFORMERS OF JAMES BOND THEMES* (from page 129; as at the time of publishing)

A-ha	*The Living Daylights*
Alicia Keys & Jack White	*Quantom of Solace*
Carly Simon	*The Spy Who Loved Me*
Chris Cornell	*Casino Royale*
Duran Duran	*A View to a Kill*
Garbage	*The World Is Not Enough*
Gladys Knight	*Licence to Kill*
Lulu	*The Man with the Golden Gun*
Madonna	*Die Another Day*
Matt Monro	*From Russia with Love*
Nancy Sinatra	*You Only Live Twice*
Paul McCartney and Wings	*Live and Let Die*
Rita Coolidge	*Octopussy*
Sheena Easton	*For Your Eyes Only*
Sheryl Crow	*Tomorrow Never Dies*
Shirley Bassey	*Goldfinger, Diamonds Are Forever, Moonraker*
Tina Turner	*Goldeneye*
Tom Jones	*Thunderball*

---

* The themes to *Dr No* and *On Her Majesty's Secret Service* were instrumentals composed by Monty Norman and John Barry respectively. Although not an official Bond film, the theme to *Never Say Never Again* was sung by Lani Hall.

ADVERTISING SLOGANS III (from page 132)

1. Hamlet; 2. Martini*; 3. Whiskas; 4. Boursin; 5. Ronseal; 6. Remington;
7. Canon; 8. British Rail; 9. Volkswagen; 10. Gordon's (gin); 11. TSB;
12. McVitie's Rich Tea biscuit†; 13. Cadbury's Creme Egg; 14. Terry's All Gold;
15. Kia-Ora; 16. Fiat Strada; 17. *FT* (*Financial Times*); 18. Microsoft; 19. Pal;
20. Jaguar; 21. Anadin; 22. Strand‡; 23. The Leeds; 24. Aquafresh.

ABBA HITS (from page 136; as at the time of publishing)

'Waterloo'	1974	(reaching no. 1)
'SOS'	1975	(6)
'Mamma Mia'	1975	(1)
'Fernando'	1976	(1)
'Dancing Queen'	1976	(1)
'Money Money Money'	1976	(3)
'Knowing Me, Knowing You'	1977	(1)
'The Name of the Game'	1977	(1)
'Take a Chance on Me'	1978	(1)
'Summer Night City'	1978	(5)
'Chiquitita'	1979	(2)
'Does Your Mother Know?'	1979	(4)
'Voulez-Vous'	1979	(3)
'Gimme Gimme Gimme (a Man after Midnight)'	1979	(3)
'I Have a Dream'	1979	(2)
'The Winner Takes It All'	1980	(1)
'Super Trouper'	1980	(1)
'Lay All Your Love on Me'	1981	(7)
'One of Us'	1981	(3)

BRITISH PRIME MINISTERS (from page 138)

The Marquess of Salisbury ^{Con}§	1895–1902
Arthur Balfour ^{Con}	1902–5
Sir Henry Campbell-Bannerman ^{Lib}	1905–8
Herbert Henry Asquith ^{Lib}	1908–16

---

* Cinzano, the rival brand to Martini, was forced to axe its popular adverts featuring Leonard Rossiter and Joan Collins after suffering extremely low brand recall; many viewers believed they had seen a Martini advert. This is known in advertising as the 'vampire effect', where the product becomes overshadowed by the celebrity who is endorsing it.

† Terry Wogan once described the Rich Tea as the 'Lord of all Biscuits'.

‡ Strand cigarettes went out of business as a result of this advert which portrayed a man in a trench coat on a dark, deserted street 'alone with his Strand'. The intention had been to promote a comforting association with the brand, but the negative connotation of being lonely and unpopular proved the stronger with consumers.

§ Also in office from 1885–6 and 1886–92.

David Lloyd George ^{Lib} 1916–22
Andrew Bonar Law ^{Con} 1922–3
Stanley Baldwin ^{Con} 1923, 1924–9, 1935–7
James Ramsay MacDonald ^{Lab} 1924, 1929–35
Neville Chamberlain ^{Con} 1937–40
Sir Winston Churchill ^{Con} 1940–5, 1951–5
Clement Richard Attlee ^{Lab} 1945–51
Sir Anthony Eden ^{Con} 1955–7
Harold Macmillan ^{Con} 1957–63
Sir Alec Douglas-Home ^{Con} 1963–4
Harold Wilson ^{Lab} 1964–70, 1974–6
Edward Heath ^{Con} 1970–4
James Callaghan ^{Lab} 1976–9
Margaret Thatcher ^{Con} 1979–90
John Major ^{Con} 1990–7
Tony Blair ^{Lab} 1997–2007

MISCELLANY XIX (from page 140)

1. The Danube*; 2. *Goldfinger*; 3. A Dutch auction; 4. The assassination of John F. Kennedy; 5. Slavery†; 6. Rudyard Kipling; 7. Eight; 8. London and Paris; 9. Israel; 10. Polo; 11. The Virgin Mary‡; 12. Seventy-two; 13. Flash; 14. *Potemkin*§; 15. George II¶; 16. Crystal Palace; 17. £3,000; 18. Temple; 19. Walk on the moon; 20. Harvard and Yale**; 21. Mr Brown; 22. Edith Nesbit; 23. Clavicle; 24. Eleven.

---

* *The Blue Danube* by Johann Strauss was famously used in the soundtrack to *2001: A Space Odyssey*.
† The Amendment was ratified in 1865 by the required three-quarters of states to allow it to pass into law, although some states opposed it. It was ratified by Kentucky in 1976 and by the state of Mississippi as recently as 1995.
‡ The Immaculate Conception is not to be confused with the Virgin Birth. In order to give birth to Jesus Christ, Catholic theologians believe that from the very first moment of her existence, Mary was free from sin, and therefore her conception was 'immaculate'.
§ The film was *The Battleship Potemkin*.
¶ Battle of Dettingen, 1743.
** 'The Game' of 1968 is generally considered to be the best; Harvard pulled back a 16-point deficit in the dying seconds including a touchdown pass with the final play to tie the match 29–29. The Harvard student newspaper later crowed: 'Harvard beats Yale 29–29'.

WELSH SURNAMES* (from page 144)

Jones / Williams / Davies / Evans / Thomas / Roberts / Hughes
Lewis / Morgan / Griffiths / Edwards / Owen / James / Morris
Price / Rees / Phillips / Smith / Harris / Lloyd

EUROPEAN CLUB CHAMPIONS (from page 147; as at the time of publishing)

Real Madrid	1956–60, 1966, 1998, 2000, 2002
AC Milan	1963, 1969, 1989, 1990, 1994, 2003, 2007
Liverpool	1977, 1978, 1981, 1984, 2005
Ajax	1971–3, 1995
Bayern Munich	1974–6, 2001
Barcelona	1992, 2006, 2009
Manchester United	1968, 1999, 2008
Benfica	1961, 1862
Inter Milan	1964, 1965
Juventus	1985, 1996
Nottingham Forest	1979, 1980
Porto	1987, 2004
Aston Villa	1982
Borussia Dortmund	1997
Celtic	1967
Feyenoord	1970
Hamburg	1983
Marseilles	1993
PSV Eindhoven	1988
Red Star Belgrade	1991
Steaua Bucharest	1986

EVENTS IN HISTORY III (from page 150)

1. 1492; 2. 1859; 3. *c.*AD30; 4. 1588; 5. 1756; 6. 1869; 7. 1517; 8. 1485;
9. 1752; 10. 1704; 11. 1861; 12. 1774; 13. 1455; 14. 1543; 15. 1702;
16. 1688†; 17. 1512; 18. 1498; 19. 1603; 20. 1271; 21. 1040; 22. 1054;
23. 1572; 24. 602.

---

* The Welsh share an extremely small number of surnames; it has been estimated
that around 95% of the population has one of fifty surnames. Historically, Wales has
used a patronymic naming system whereby a child would take the father's given
name to be their surname. Thus David Williams' son John would be called John
Davies. John Davies's son, Thomas, would be called Thomas Jones. Thomas Jones's
son, Ieuan, would be called Ieuan Thomas. And so on.
† Many of London's institutions began in coffee houses. The Stock Exchange
operated from coffee houses, most notably Jonathan's and Garraway's, until 1773.
Maritime traders frequented the house of Edward Lloyd at 16 Lombard Street and
the business of underwriting ships began there in 1727 (where it remained until the
foundation of Lloyds of London in 1771). Coffee houses in *cont'd over/*

WORLD HERITAGE SITES IN THE UK (from page 153; as at the time of publishing)

Castles and Town Walls of King Edward I in Gwynedd
Durham Castle and Cathedral
Giant's Causeway and Causeway Coast
Ironbridge Gorge
St Kilda
Stonehenge, Avebury and Associated Sites
Studley Royal Park including the Ruins of Fountains Abbey
Blenheim Palace
City of Bath
Frontiers of the Roman Empire (Hadrian's Wall)
Westminster Palace, Westminster Abbey and Saint Margaret's Church
Canterbury Cathedral, St Augustine's Abbey, and St Martin's Church
Tower of London
Old and New Towns of Edinburgh
Maritime Greenwich
Heart of Neolithic Orkney
Blaenavon Industrial Landscape
Derwent Valley Mills
Dorset and East Devon Coast
New Lanark
Saltaire
Royal Botanic Gardens, Kew
Liverpool, Maritime Mercantile City
Cornwall and West Devon Mining Landscape

ORDER OF SUCCESSION TO THE BRITISH THRONE (from page 156; as at the time of publishing)

1. HRH The Prince of Wales (b.1948)
2. HRH Prince William of Wales (b.1982)
3. HRH Prince Henry of Wales (b.1984)
4. HRH The Duke of York (b.1960)
5. HRH Princess Beatrice of York (b.1988)
6. HRH Princess Eugenie of York (b.1990)
7. HRH The Earl of Wessex (b.1964)
8. Lady Louise Windsor (b.2003)
9. HRH The Princess Royal (b.1950)
10. Peter Phillips (b.1977)

---

cont'd   Westminster catered for the political classes; the Tories would meet at the Cocoa Tree, the Whigs at the St James. Covent Garden coffee houses became popular with the literati (John Dryden would frequent Will's House on Russell Street) and the men of the Royal Society (such as Isaac Newton and Edmund Halley) preferred the Graecian on the Strand.

11. Zara Phillips (b.1981)

12. Viscount Linley (b.1961)

13. The Hon. Charles Armstrong-Jones (b.1999)

14. The Hon. Margarita Armstrong-Jones (b.2002)

15. Lady Sarah Chatto (b.1964)

16. Samuel Chatto (b.1996)

17. Arthur Chatto (b.1999)

18. HRH The Duke of Gloucester (b.1944)

19. Alexander Windsor, Earl of Ulster (b.1974)

20. Xan Windsor, Lord Culloden (b.2007)

21. Lady Davina Lewis (b.1977)

22. Lady Rose Windsor (b.1980)

23. HRH The Duke of Kent (b.1935)

24. Lady Marina-Charlotte Windsor (b.1992)

25. Lady Amelia Windsor (b.1995)

SINGERS AND BACKERS II (from page 163)

1. Sly; 2. Bill Haley; 3. Derek; 4. Echo; 5. Booker T; 6. Diana Ross; 7. Tom Petty; 8. Lloyd Cole; 9. Prince; 10. Yazz; 11. Hootie; 12. Mike; 13. Jonathan Richman; 14. Roy Wood; 15. Kenny Ball; 16. Iggy Pop; 17. Herb Alpert; 18. Curtis Mayfield; 19. Captain Beefheart; 20. Robyn Hitchcock; 21. Joe Brown; 22. James Brown; 23. Lulu; 24. Wayne Fontana.

MEMBERS OF NATO (from page 166; as at the time of publishing)

Belgium / Bulgaria / Canada / Czech Republic / Denmark
Estonia / France / Germany / Greece / Hungary / Iceland
Italy / Latvia / Lithuania / Luxembourg / Netherlands
Norway / Poland / Portugal / Romania / Slovakia / Slovenia
Spain / Turkey / United Kingdom / United States

RED, WHITE AND BLUE FLAGS (from page 170; as at the time of publishing)

Australia* / Cambodia / Chile / Costa Rica / Croatia / Cuba
Czech Republic / Dominican Republic / France / Iceland / Laos
Liberia / Luxembourg / Myanmar / Nepal / Netherlands
New Zealand / North Korea / Norway / Panama / Paraguay
Russia / Slovakia / Slovenia / Taiwan / Thailand
United Kingdom† / United States / Yugoslavia

---

* The flag features the constellation of the Southern Cross in the right hand half; the larger star in the bottom left quadrant is known as the Commonwealth Star.
† The Union Jack features the heraldic symbols of St George, St Andrew and St Patrick and was introduced in 1606 with the union of England, Scotland and Ireland. The Welsh dragon is not featured as at the time of the union the Welsh Principality was considered part of England.

NICKNAMES OF PLACES (from page 173)

1. New York*; 2. London; 3. Hollywood†; 4. Atlantic Ocean; 5. Ireland;
6. Chicago; 7. Tibet; 8. Kent; 9. Detroit; 10. Oxford‡; 11. Las Vegas; 12. New
Orleans; 13. Aberdeen; 14. Jerusalem; 15. Mumbai; 16. Paris; 17. Rome;
18. Denver; 19. Philadelphia; 20. Venice; 21. Jaipur; 22. Cleveland; 23. Belgrade;
24. Manila.

FILMS STARRING MARILYN MONROE (from page 176)

Dangerous Years	1947
Scudda Hoo! Scudda Hay!	1948
Ladies of the Chorus	1948
Green Grass of Wyoming	1948
You Were Meant for Me	1948
Love Happy	1949
A Ticket to Tomahawk	1950
The Asphalt Jungle	1950
The Fireball	1950
All About Eve	1950
Right Cross	1950
Home Town Story	1951
As Young as You Feel	1951
Love Nest	1951
Let's Make It Legal	1951
We're Not Married	1952
O. Henry's Full House	1952
Clash by Night	1952
Monkey Business	1952
Don't Bother to Knock	1952
Niagara	1953
Gentlemen Prefer Blondes	1953
How to Marry a Millionaire	1953
River of No Return	1954
There's No Business Like Show Business	1954
The Seven Year Itch	1955
Bus Stop	1956
The Prince and the Showgirl	1957

---

* The term probably stems from 'apple', musician's slang for a performing
engagement. A date in New York was the 'big apple'; New York is also known as
the Empire City.

† The name may stem from Oscar Levant's 1930s quote: 'Strip the phoney tinsel off
Hollywood and you'll find real tinsel underneath.'

‡ An ironic term, implying its inhabitants were not concerned with real issues,
coined by the poet Matthew Arnold (1822–88) in the poem 'Thyrsis', calling Oxford
the 'sweet city with her dreaming spires'.

PLAYS BY WILLIAM SHAKESPEARE (from page 180)

Dates are estimated

FOREIGN WORDS AND PHRASES II (from page 183)

1. Al fresco; 2. Coup d'état; 3. Raison d'être; 4. Slalom; 5. Hinterland;
6. Verandah; 7. Zeitgeist; 8. Enfant terrible; 9. Wunderkind; 10. Bête noir;
11. Smörgåsbord; 12. Carte blanche; 13. Pundit*; 14. Nadir; 15. Wanderlust;
16. Pied-à-terre; 17. Realpolitik; 18. Cushy; 19. Amok; 20. Algebra;
21. Schadenfreude; 22. Gung-ho; 23. Flak; 24. Ombudsman.

MR MEN† (from page 191)

Mr Birthday | Mr Bounce | Mr Brave | Mr Bump | Mr Busy
Mr Chatterbox | Mr Cheeky | Mr Cheerful | Mr Christmas
Mr Clever | Mr Clumsy | Mr Cool
Mr Daydream | Mr Dizzy | Mr Forgetful | Mr Funny
Mr Fussy | Mr Good | Mr Greedy | Mr Grumble | Mr Grumpy
Mr Happy | Mr Impossible | Mr Jelly | Mr Lazy
Mr Mean | Mr Messy‡ | Mr Mischief | Mr Muddle
Mr Noisy | Mr Nonsense | Mr Nosey | Mr Perfect
Mr Quiet | Mr Rude | Mr Rush | Mr Silly | Mr Skinny
Mr Slow | Mr Small | Mr Sneeze | Mr Snow
Mr Strong | Mr Tall | Mr Tickle | Mr Topsy-Turvy
Mr Uppity | Mr Worry | Mr Wrong§

---

* During the nineteenth century the empires of the two largest world powers, Russia and Great Britain, converged on the territories of central Asia. The struggle for political influence over this region lasted for most of the nineteenth century and became known as the Great Game. It became a strategic concern of the British that the lands to the north of India, such as Tibet, which were largely inaccessible to Westerners, were surveyed and mapped. These surveys were largely carried out by Indians recruited from the border provinces whose appearance would not automatically arouse suspicion beyond the Himalayas. They were trained as surveyors, disguised as lamas (Buddhist holy men) and in order to maintain their cover, used surveying tools that were disguised as objects that a lama would carry. The surveyors learned to make exactly 2,000 paces to a mile and in order to count these distances, their prayer beads were adapted from the usual 108 to a set of 100, with every tenth bead being slightly larger. Buddhist prayer wheels were also converted so that they could contain paper for making notes and drawing maps. Although it was dangerous work from which many failed to return, the surveys were completed with incredible accuracy. A measure of the high regard in which the surveyors were held is that they became known as pundits, from a Sanskrit word meaning an expert or a respected person.

† Mr Men created by Roger Hargreaves' son Adam are: *Mr Birthday, Mr Brave, Mr Cheeky, Mr Cheerful, Mr Christmas, Mr Cool, Mr Good, Mr Grumble, Mr Perfect, Mr Rude*.

‡ Features Mr Neat and Mr Tidy who do not themselves have eponymous stories.

§ Features Mr Right who does not himself have an eponymous story.

COUNTRIES IN EUROPE*
(from page 190)

EUROPEAN CAPITAL CITIES
(from page 189)

Albania .... Tirana
Andorra .... Andorra la Vella
Austria .... Vienna
Belarus .... Minsk
Belgium .... Brussels
Bosnia and Herzegovina .... Sarajevo
Bulgaria .... Sofia
Croatia .... Zagreb
Czech Republic .... Prague
Denmark .... Copenhagen
Estonia .... Tallinn
Finland .... Helsinki
France .... Paris
Germany .... Berlin
Greece .... Athens
Hungary .... Budapest
Iceland .... Reykjavik
Ireland .... Dublin
Italy .... Rome
Latvia .... Riga
Liechtenstein .... Vaduz
Lithuania .... Vilnius
Luxembourg .... Luxembourg
Macedonia .... Skopje
Malta .... Valletta
Moldova .... Chisinau
Monaco .... Monaco
Netherlands .... Amsterdam
Norway .... Oslo
Poland .... Warsaw
Portugal .... Lisbon
Romania .... Bucharest
Russia .... Moscow
San Marino .... San Marino
Serbia and Montenegro .... Belgrade
Slovakia .... Bratislava
Slovenia .... Ljubljana
Spain .... Madrid
Sweden .... Stockholm

---

* Note that Cyprus is sometimes considered to be in Europe. Geographically it is
part of Asia but politically it is closer to Europe. Also note that Turkey and Russia
are part of both Europe and Asia.

```
Switzerland .......................................................... Bern
Turkey ............................................................ Ankara
Ukraine ............................................................ Kiev
United Kingdom ................................................. London
Vatican City ................................................. Vatican City
```

MUSICAL TERMS (from page 192)

1. Softly; 2. Becoming louder; 3. Short and detached; 4. Loudly; 5. Fast or lively; 6. Getting gradually faster; 7. Becoming quieter; 8. Slowly; 9. Without instrumental accompaniment; 10. Very slowly; 11. Rapid fluctuation of the pitch of a note (vibrating); 12. Gradually slower; 13. Slowly and broadly; 14. Slowly and solemnly; 15. Smoothly; 16. Lively or uptempo; 17. Gently; 18. With vigour or spirit; 19. To the end; 20. Very quickly; 21. From the beginning; 22. Not too much; 23. Rapid repetition of one note (trembling); 24. Plucked (referring to a bowed instrument).

COMMONWEALTH COUNTRIES (from page 198; as at the time of publishing)

Antigua and Barbuda / Australia / Bahamas / Bangladesh
Barbados / Belize / Botswana / Brunei Darussalam
Cameroon / Canada / Cyprus / Dominica / Fiji Islands*
Gambia / Ghana / Grenada / Guyana / India
Jamaica / Kenya / Kiribati / Lesotho / Malawi / Malaysia
Maldives / Malta / Mauritius / Mozambique / Namibia
Nauru / New Zealand / Nigeria / Pakistan / Papua New Guinea
St Kitts and Nevis / St Lucia / St Vincent and the Grenadines
Samoa / Seychelles / Sierra Leone / Singapore / Solomon Islands
South Africa / Sri Lanka / Swaziland / Tonga
Trinidad and Tobago / Tuvalu / Uganda
United Kingdom / Tanzania / Vanuatu / Zambia

TUBE STATIONS IN ZONE 1 (from page 201)

Aldgate / Aldgate East / Angel / Baker Street / Bank / Barbican
Bayswater / Blackfriars / Bond Street / Borough / Cannon Street [L]
Chancery Lane [L] / Charing Cross / Covent Garden / Earl's Court
Edgware Road / Elephant & Castle† / Embankment / Euston
Euston Square / Farringdon / Gloucester Road / Goodge Street
Great Portland Street / Green Park / High Street Kensington
Holborn / Hyde Park Corner / King's Cross St Pancras
Knightsbridge / Lambeth North / Lancaster Gate
Leicester Square / Liverpool Street / London Bridge
Mansion House / Marble Arch / Marylebone / Monument

---

* Membership suspended following a coup in December 2006.
† Has largely replaced Newington as the name of this area of Southwark. After the pub name which derives from the corruption of the Spanish 'Infanta de Castilla'.

Moorgate / Old Street / Oxford Circus / Paddington
Piccadilly Circus / Pimlico / Queensway / Regent's Park
Russell Square / St James's Park / St Paul's / Sloane Square*
South Kensington / Southwark / Temple ^L
Tottenham Court Road / Tower Hill / Tower Gateway
Vauxhall / Victoria / Warren Street / Waterloo / Westminster

^L indicates limited opening hours

MISCELLANY XXVI (from page 205)

1. Chanel No. 5; 2. Pluto; 3. James Whistler; 4. The Riot Act†; 5. Spaghetti
Junction; 6. MRSA; 7. Steffi Graf; 8. The Rising Sun‡; 9. Amen; 10. Nelson;
11. Production of hormones; 12. Eccentric; 13. He was the first person to withdraw
cash from an ATM; 14. Lynda La Plante; 15. Brighton & Hove Albion and Crystal
Palace; 16. Urdu; 17. Groundhog Day; 18. Queensland and Northern Territory Aerial
Services; 19. 255; 20. Mary II; 21. On the moon; 22. 2 July; 23. Twelve; 24. 2kg.

CELEBRITY BABY NAMES (from page 12)

1. David & Victoria Beckham; 2. Bob Geldof & Paula Yates; 3. David & Angie
Bowie; 4. Michael Hutchence & Paula Yates; 5. Michael Jackson & Debbie Rowe;
6. Madonna & Carlos Leon; 7. Gwyneth Paltrow & Chris Martin; 8. Frank & Gail
Zappa; 9. Liam Gallagher & Patsy Kensit; 10. Madonna & Guy Ritchie;
11. Britney Spears & Kevin Federline; 12. Bob Geldof & Paula Yates; 13. Geri
Halliwell§; 14. Angelina Jolie & Brad Pitt; 15. Jamie Oliver & Jools Norton;
16. Frank & Gail Zappa; 17. Jude Law & Sadie Frost; 18. Simon & Yasmine Le
Bon; 19. Bruce Willis & Demi Moore; 20. Jason Lee & Beth Riesgraf; 21. Sharleen
Spiteri & Ashley Heath; 22. Bono & Alison Stewart; 23. Sylvester Stallone & Sasha
Czack; 14. Jonathan Ross & Jane Goldman.

MAGI¶ (from page 8)

Balthazar / Caspar** / Melchior

---

* A large pipe running diagonally across the ceiling at the western end of the
platforms of Sloane Square station is a conduit for the river Westbourne which flows
from the Serpentine to the river Thames at Chelsea.

† 'Our sovereign Lord the King chargeth and commandeth all persons, being assembled,
immediately to disperse themselves, and peaceably to depart to their habitations, or to
their lawful business, upon the pains contained in the act made in the first year of King
George, for preventing tumults and riotous assemblies. God save the King.'

‡ Heraldic symbol of Edward III, Japanese flag and 'The House of the Rising Sun'.

§ The identity of the father is not publicly known.

¶ The Wise Men were Zoroastrian astrologers who came to worship the infant Jesus
according to the Gospel of St Matthew (the only Gospel to mention the incident). The
Wise Men are not mentioned by name in the New Testament and the assumption that
there were three of them comes by association of the gifts of gold, frankincense and
myrrh. These names for the Wise Men became accepted around the seventh century AD.

** Alternatively Gasper.

250

BONES OF THE EAR* (from page 10)

Malleus (hammer) / Incus (anvil) / Stapes (stirrup)

FIRST LINES OF POP SONGS I (from page 13)

1. 'Stand By Your Man' (Tammy Wynette); 2. 'My Way' (Frank Sinatra); 3. 'Never Ever' (All Saints†); 4. 'All You Need Is Love' (The Beatles); 5. 'Brimful of Asha' (Cornershop); 6. 'I Heard It Through the Grapevine' (Marvin Gaye); 7. 'Walking on Sunshine' (Katrina and the Waves); 8. 'Wonderwall' (Oasis); 9. 'A Groovy Kind of Love' (Phil Collins); 10. 'Puppet on a String' (Sandie Shaw); 11. 'Danger High Voltage' (Electric Six); 12. 'I Don't Like Mondays'‡ (The Boomtown Rats); 13. 'Take Me Home, Country Roads' (John Denver); 14. 'These Boots Are Made for Walking' (Nancy Sinatra); 15. 'You Raise Me' (Westlife); 16. 'Somethin' Stupid' (Frank and Nancy Sinatra); 17. 'Going Underground' (The Jam); 18. 'Tubthumping' (Chumbawamba); 19. 'Song 2' (Blur); 20. 'Graceland' (Paul Simon); 21. 'West End Girls' (Pet Shop Boys); 22. 'Everything I Do (I Do It For You)' (Bryan Adams); 23. 'The Logical Song' (Supertramp); 24. 'Leave Right Now' (Will Young).

BLOOD GROUPS§ (from page 16)

A / B / O / AB

SEVEN SUMMITS (from page 64)

Kilimanjaro . . . . Africa/Tanzania
Vinson Massif . . . . Antarctica
Puncak Jaya¶ . . . . Australasia/Indonesia

---

* The ossicles amplify sounds received by the ear drum and transmit them to the cochlea, a coiled chamber filled with fluid (named from the Latin word for 'snail'). Tiny hairs inside this detect vibrations in the fluid and transmit them as nerve signals to the brain.
† The quartet took their name from the street in which their London recording studio was based.
‡ The song was inspired by Brenda Spencer who killed two people at her San Diego school on 29 January 1979. When questioned she said, 'I don't like Mondays'.
§ This is known as the AOB system which is determined by red blood-cell type. Each blood group may also be termed positive or negative depending on the existence or absence of the Rhesus D antigen. While it is always preferable to donate or receive blood from a member of the same blood group, compatibility is defined as follows: blood group O can donate blood to any other group but can only receive blood from other members of O; blood group A can donate to A and AB but can only receive blood from A or O; blood group B can donate to B and AB but can only receive blood from B and O; blood group AB can receive blood from any other group but can only donate blood to AB.
¶ An original list, postulated and first climbed by Richard Bass, included Mount Kosciuszko (2,228m) on mainland Australia. Most mountaineers prefer the Messner list as Puncak Jaya in New Guinea, at 4,884 metres, is technically the highest mountain in Australasia. It is also a much more difficult climb; until recently the summit of Mount Kosciuszko was accessible by car. It has *cont'd over/*

LINKED MISCELLANY II (from page 23)

1. Black Monday; 2. Daryl Hall and John Oates; 3. Lead; 4. The Green Berets;
5. Egg white; 6. The British Library; 7. Candlestick Park; 8. Mustard gas;
9. *Revolver*; 10. Scarlett Johansson

The link is Cluedo*.

INFORMATION SUPPLIED BY PRISONERS OF WAR (from page 25)

Name / Date of Birth / Rank / Service Number

LITTLE WOMEN (from page 27)

Amy / Beth / Jo / Meg

ADVERTISING SLOGANS II (from page 31)

1. Brut 33; 2. British Gas Share Flotation; 3. Pedigree Chum; 4. Ready Brek;
5. BT; 6. Shell oil; 7. Hofmeister; 8. Sugar Puffs; 9. De Beers; 10. Vodafone;
11. Alka Seltzer; 12. Michelin; 13. Ford; 14. Domestos; 15. Toyota; 16. Polycell;
17. Skoda; 18. Midland Bank; 19. Calgon; 20. *TV Times*; 21. Kellogg's Bran
Flakes; 22. Vauxhall Cavalier; 23. Peugeot; 24. Ariston.

BATMEN (from page 34; as at the time of publishing)

Adam West .... *Batman* (1966)
Michael Keaton .... *Batman* (1989), *Batman Returns* (1992)
Val Kilmer .... *Batman Forever* (1995)
George Clooney .... *Batman & Robin* (1997)
Christian Bale .... *Batman Begins* (2005), *The Dark Knight* (2008)

EVENTS OF THE MODERN PENTATHLON (from page 37)

Fencing / Running / Riding / Shooting / Swimming

AIRPORT CODES I (from page 39)

1. London (Gatwick); 2. New York (John F. Kennedy); 3. Los Angeles; 4. Hong
Kong; 5. Mexico City (Juarez); 6. Brussels; 7. Glasgow; 8. Barcelona; 9. Paris
(Charles De Gaulle); 10. Bangkok (Don Muang); 11. Edinburgh (Turnhouse);

---

cont'd   been observed that as a mountaineering challenge, climbing the second
highest summit on each continent presents a much greater challenge as in almost
every case the second highest peak is a technically harder climb and without a
significant reduction in height.

* Dr Black (the murder victim), Hall, Lead Piping, Reverend Green, Mrs White,
Library, Candlestick, Colonel Mustard, Revolver, Miss Scarlet.

12. Amsterdam (Schipol); 13. Liverpool (John Lennon); 14. Mumbai (formerly Bombay); 15. San Francisco; 16. Auckland; 17. Las Vegas; 18. Seattle (Tacoma); 19. Chicago (O'Hare) 20. Johannesburg (Jan Smuts); 21. Moscow (Sheremetyevo); 22. Berlin (Schonefeld); 23. Dubai; 24. Tokyo (Narita).

BONES OF THE SHOULDER AND ARM (from page 41)
Clavicle / Scapula / Humerus / Radius / Ulna

HOLLYWOOD FILM STUDIOS (from page 43)
20th Century Fox / Metro-Goldwyn-Mayer / Paramount Pictures
RKO Radio Pictures / Warner Brothers

MISCELLANY VI (from page 45)
1. Rio de Janeiro; 2. Adjacent to the kidneys; 3. The Eiffel Tower; 4. Kevin Keegan, Stanley Matthews and Bobby Charlton; 5. Donald Campbell; 6. Meg Ryan; 7. (A pink) Rolls Royce*; 8. Kenya; 9. Twelve; 10. Beagle; 11. Guilty, Not Guilty and Not Proven; 12. SARS; 13. Boy George; 14. *Cutty Sark*; 15. The House of Commons; 16. Motorcycle racing†; 17. Fyodor Dostoevsky; 18. Brazil, Colombia, Ecuador; 19. Pompeii and Herculaneum; 20. Middle Earth‡; 21. Toyota Corolla; 22. They both killed presidential assassins§; 23. Earl Grey tea; 24. Twenty-four days.

CINQUE PORTS¶ (from page 48)
Dover / Hastings / Hythe / New Romney / Sandwich

NOVELS BY GEORGE ELIOT (from page 65)

Adam Bede	1859
The Mill on the Floss	1860
Silas Marner	1861
Romola	1863
Felix Holt, the Radical	1866
Middlemarch	1872
Daniel Deronda	1876

---

* Lady Creighton Ward is also known as Lady Penelope from *Thunderbirds*.
† The Isle of Man TT Race.
‡ The Mediterranean is named from the Latin, 'medius' meaning middle and 'terra' meaning earth. Middle Earth is the fantasy setting for *The Hobbit* and *Lord of the Rings*.
§ Boston Corbett shot John Wilkes Booth and Jack Ruby shot Lee Harvey Oswald. The shooting of Lee Harvey Oswald occurred live on American television.
¶ The 'Ancient Towns' of Rye and Winchelsea are often included in this list. The Confederation of Cinque Ports was originally established for military and trade purposes.

FIRST LINES OF POPULAR NOVELS II (from page 53)

1. *Bridget Jones's Diary* (Helen Fielding); 2. *Moby-Dick* (Herman Melville); 3. *The Hitchhiker's Guide to the Galaxy* (Douglas Adams); 4. *Harry Potter and the Philosopher's Stone* (J.K. Rowling); 5. *The Hound of the Baskervilles* (Sir Arthur Conan Doyle); 6. *A Christmas Carol* (Charles Dickens); 7. *Don Quixote* (Miguel de Cervantes); 8. *Anna Karenina* (Leo Tolstoy); 9. *Goldfinger* (Ian Fleming); 10. *Chitty Chitty Bang Bang* (Ian Fleming); 11. *The War of the Worlds* (H.G. Wells); 12. *Watership Down* (Richard Adams); 13. *Jane Eyre* (Charlotte Brontë); 14. *Tom Sawyer* (Mark Twain); 15. *Frankenstein* (Mary Shelley); 16. *The Go-Between* (L.P. Hartley); 17. *The Curious Incident of the Dog in the Night-time* (Mark Haddon); 18. *Dracula* (Bram Stoker); 19. *Fahrenheit 451* (Ray Bradbury); 20. *The Secret Garden* (Frances Hodgson Burnett); 21. *The Great Gatsby* (F. Scott Fitzgerald); 22. *The Old Man and the Sea* (Ernest Hemingway); 23. *Jude the Obscure* (Thomas Hardy); 24. *Catch-22* (Joseph Heller).

MONOPOLY TOKENS (from page 58)

Boat / Boot / Car / Dog / Hat / Iron

WOODWIND INSTRUMENTS (from page 60)

Piccolo / Flute / Oboe / Cor Anglais / Clarinet / Bassoon

TAGLINES OF POPULAR FILMS I (from page 63)

1. *Star Wars*; 2. *Forrest Gump*; 3. *Se7en*; 4. *Austin Powers: International Man of Mystery*; 5. *Shaun of the Dead*; 6. *Erin Brockovich*; 7. *The Wizard of Oz**; 8. *The Magnificent Seven*; 9. *Mission: Impossible*; 10. *Jurassic Park*; 11. *Three Men and a Baby*; 12. *The Perfect Storm*; 13. *Meet the Parents*; 14. *The Sixth Sense*; 15. *Saving Private Ryan*†; 16. *Scream*; 17. *The Shawshank Redemption*; 18. *Misery*; 19. *The Piano*; 20. *The Matrix*; 21. *Speed*; 22. *Mrs Doubtfire*; 23. *Brokeback Mountain*; 24. *Saturday Night Fever*.

SPACE SHUTTLES (from page 66)

Columbia‡	Destroyed 2003
Challenger	Destroyed 1986
Discovery§	Active

---

* Production of the film had to be stopped and the set repainted when the yellow brick road appeared green in the first colour prints. *The Wizard of Oz* pioneered the use of Technicolor film.

† To enhance the look and feel of the film Steven Spielberg reduced the colour saturation of the print in the laboratory by 60% to mirror the colour film reels produced during the war. When the film was later aired on cable channels in the US, the broadcasters were forced to increase the colour saturation after they were inundated with complaints from subscribers about their picture quality.

‡ *Columbia* was the first shuttle to enter space on 12 April 1981.

§ *Discovery* has flown the most missions of any shuttle, and flew both of the 'return to flight' missions following the *Challenger* and *Columbia* disasters. *Discovery* was the shuttle which launched the Hubble telescope.

Atlantis .... Active

Endeavour .... Active

Enterprise .... Atmospheric test flights

Pathfinder .... Ground test simulator

VON TRAPP CHILDREN (from page 69)

Liesl / Friedrich / Louisa / Kurt / Brigitta / Marta / Gretl

EPONYMOUS AIRPORTS (from page 71)

1. New York; 2. Paris; 3. Rome; 4. Liverpool; 5. Tehran; 6. Delhi; 7. New Orleans; 8. Venice; 9. Istanbul; 10. Tel Aviv; 11. Pisa; 12. Salzburg; 13. Chicago; 14. Montreal; 15. Washington DC; 16. Houston; 17. Mexico City; 18. Gdansk; 19. Krakow; 20. Boston; 21. Warsaw; 22. Nairobi; 23. Tirana; 24. Rafah (Gaza Strip).

LIBERAL ARTS (from page 75)

Grammar / Logic / Rhetoric*

Arithmetic / Geometry / Music / Astronomy†

HEPTARCHY (from page 77)

Northumbria / Mercia / East Anglia

Essex / Kent / Sussex / Wessex

NICKNAMES OF FOOTBALL TEAMS I (from page 79)

1. Manchester United; 2. Southampton; 3. West Ham United; 4. Fulham; 5. Charlton Athletic‡; 6. West Bromwich Albion; 7. Gillingham; 8. Leicester City; 9. Crewe Alexander; 10. Sheffield Wednesday; 11. Norwich City; 12. Stoke City; 13. Watford; 14. Leyton Orient; 15. Brighton; 16. Rochdale; 17. Hartlepool United; 18. Port Vale; 19. Preston North End; 20. Bury; 21. Bournemouth; 22. Southend United; 23. Darlington; 24. Yeovil.

RUTSHIRE CHRONICLES§ (from page 81)

Riders 1986

Rivals¶ 1988

Polo 1991

The Man Who Made Husbands Jealous 1993

Appassionata 1996

---

* Grammar, logic and rhetoric were collectively known as the Trivium.

† Arithmetic, geometry, music and astronomy were collectively known as the Quadrivium.

‡ 'Addick' derives from the word 'haddock'.

§ Although not set in Rutshire, *Pandora* and *Wicked!* include some of the characters from other books in the series, notably the Campbell Blacks.

¶ Also known as *Players*.

AUSTRALIAN STATES AND TERRITORIES (from page 84)
Australian Capital Territory* / New South Wales
Northern Territory / Queensland / South Australia
Tasmania / Victoria / Western Australia

QUOTATIONS FROM SHAKESPEARE II (from page 86)
1. *Julius Caesar* (Caesar); 2. *Henry V* (King Harry); 3. *Richard III* (King Richard); 4. *Julius Caesar* (Antony); 5. *Romeo and Juliet* (Chorus); 6. *The Taming of the Shrew* (Petruchio); 7. *Othello* (Iago); 8. *The Winter's Tale* (Mamillius); 9. *Romeo and Juliet* (Mercutio); 10. *Henry V* (King Harry); 11. *Romeo and Juliet* (Romeo); 12. *The Taming of the Shrew* (Katherine); 13. *Macbeth†* (Lady Macbeth); 14. *Hamlet* (Ghost); 15. *Macbeth* (Second Witch); 16. *The Merchant of Venice* (Shylock); 17. *A Midsummer Night's Dream* (Lysander); 18. *Hamlet* (Queen Gertrude); 19. *The Merchant of Venice* (Prince of Morocco); 20. *A Midsummer Night's Dream* (Oberon); 21. *Othello* (Iago); 22. *Romeo and Juliet* (Juliet); 23. *A Midsummer Night's Dream* (Lysander); 24. *Richard II* (John of Gaunt).

THE FELLOWSHIP OF THE RING (from page 95)
Frodo / Sam / Merry / Pippin
Gandalf / Aragorn / Legolas / Gimli / Boromir

TYPES OF CLOUD (from page 96)
Cirrus	high level
Cirrocumulus	high level
Cirrostratus	high level
Altostratus	medium level
Altocumulus	medium level
Nimbostratus	medium level
Stratocumulus	low level

---

* The Australian Capital Territory is an inland enclave in New South Wales and the smallest self-governing territory or state in Australia. Following federation in 1901, land was ceded by the state of New South Wales in 1911 and construction of the capital, Canberra, began in 1913.

† The play has gained a reputation in the theatre for being unlucky although no one seems to know why – members of the acting profession often refer to it only as 'The Scottish Play'. The link with witchcraft is an obvious answer. It is equally possible that the numerous fight scenes in the play have led to injuries to cast members over the years which have caused shows to be postponed or cancelled. It has also been suggested that being a popular play, *Macbeth* was often staged as a replacement for failing plays, giving it the association with bad luck.

Stratus	low level
Cumulus	low level
Cumulonimbus	vertically developed

MISCELLANY XIII (from page 99)

1. Lunatic; 2. Venus; 3. Auguste Rodin; 4. All named after gods; 5. Halfpenny;
6. India*; 7. Oche (pronounced 'ocky'); 8. Saffron; 9. Fleet Street; 10. Hunter S.
Thompson; 11. Male; 12. Glasgow, Liverpool, Newcastle; 13. *The Godfather, Part
II* and *Lord of the Rings: The Return of the King*; 14. J.R. Ewing to Sue Ellen;
15. Georges Bizet; 16. Occidental; 17. *Frankenstein*; 18. Cardiff; 19. Mumbai
(formerly Bombay); 20. James II; 21. John Travolta (*Saturday Night Fever*);
22. Twelve; 23. Nothing†; 24. Tuesday.

WORDS CONTAINED IN 'THEREIN' (from page 109)

The / There / He / I / In / Rein / Her / Here / Er / Ere / Herein / Therein

FILMS STARRING GRACE KELLY (from page 105)

Fourteen Hours	1951
High Noon	1952
Mogambo	1953
Dial M for Murder	1954
Green Fire	1954
Rear Window	1954
The Country Girl	1954
The Bridges at Toko-Ri	1954
To Catch a Thief	1955
The Swan	1956
High Society	1956

SCANDALS (from page 107)

1. George Michael; 2. John Profumo; 3. Ben Johnson; 4. Michael Jackson; 5. David
Blunkett; 6. Hugh Grant; 7. John Prescott; 8. Janet Jackson; 9. Peter Mandelson;
10. Jeffrey Archer; 11. Cecil Parkinson; 12. Woody Allen; 13. David Mellor;
14. Diego Maradona; 15. Mark Oaten; 16. Frank Bough; 17. Dr David Kelly;
18. Ron Davies; 19. Jeremy Thorpe; 20. Tonya Harding; 21. Jimmy Swaggart;
22. Stephen Milligan; 23. Lord Lambton; 24. Margaret Campbell, Duchess of Argyll.

MEMBERS OF OPEC (from page 110; as at the time of publishing)

Algeria / Angola / Indonesia / Iran
Iraq / Kuwait / Libya / Nigeria / Qatar
Saudi Arabia / United Arab Emirates / Venezuela

---

* The Wheel of Law. Ashoka the Great ruled India in the second century BC.
† After 2 September, the next day was 14 September, due to the change from the
Julian to the Gregorian calendar.

COOKING TERMS II (from page 112)

1. Croutons; 2. Guacamole; 3. Chicken Kiev; 4. Ravioli; 5. Hollandaise; 6. Balti;
7. Consommé; 8. Bruschetta; 9. Chorizo; 10. Pesto; 11. Dauphinoise (à la);
12. Julienne; 13. Monosodium glutamate (MSG); 14. Entrecôte; 15. Bouillabaisse;
16. Angels on Horseback; 17. Coulis; 18. Crème anglaise; 19. Farfalle; 20. Frittata;
21. Fusilli; 22. Miso; 23. Tapenade; 24. Béchamel.

SGT. PEPPER'S LONELY HEARTS CLUB BAND (from page 115)

'Sgt. Pepper's Lonely Hearts Club Band'	McCartney
'With a Little Help from My Friends'	Lennon and McCartney
'Lucy in the Sky with Diamonds'	Lennon
'Getting Better'	McCartney
'Fixing a Hole'	McCartney
'She's Leaving Home'	Lennon and McCartney
'Being for the Benefit of Mr Kite!'	Lennon
'Within You Without You'	Harrison
'When I'm Sixty-Four'	McCartney
'Lovely Rita'	McCartney
'Good Morning Good Morning'	Lennon
'Sgt. Pepper's Lonely Hearts Club Band' (Reprise)	McCartney
'A Day in the Life'	Lennon and McCartney

CANADIAN PROVINCES AND TERRITORIES (from page 118)

Alberta / British Columbia / Manitoba / New Brunswick
Newfoundland and Labrador / Northwest Territories[T]
Nova Scotia / Nunavut[T] / Ontario / Prince Edward Island
Quebec / Saskatchewan / Yukon[T]

[T] indicates a territory

LAST LINES OF POPULAR FILMS I (from page 120)

1. *Casino Royale*; 2. *The Wizard of Oz*; 3. *The Silence of the Lambs*; 4. *Casablanca**;
5. *The Usual Suspects*; 6. *The Shawshank Redemption*; 7. *King Kong*; 8. *Back to the Future*; 9. *Jerry Maguire*; 10. *Return of the Jedi*; 11. *An Officer and a Gentleman*;
12. *Apocalypse Now*; 13. *Dr Strangelove*; 14. *Butch Cassidy and the Sundance Kid*;
15. *Sunset Boulevard*; 16. *Shakespeare in Love*; 17. *Witness*; 18. *The Magnificent Seven*; 19. *LA Confidential*; 20. *Midnight Cowboy*; 21. *Shallow Grave*; 22. *Pretty Woman*; 23. *Network*; 24. *The Bridge on the River Kwai*.

---

* The budget for *Casablanca* was so small that in the airport scene at the end of the film, a cardboard cut-out of the plane was used with midgets playing the ground crew to give the illusion it was a full-sized aircraft.

POSITIONS IN A RUGBY UNION TEAM (from page 123)

Loosehead Prop / Hooker / Tighthead Prop
Lock* (x 2)
Blindside Flanker / Number Eight / Openside Flanker
Scrum Half / Fly Half†
Left Wing / Inside Centre / Outside Centre / Right Wing
Full Back

UNION OF SOVIET SOCIALIST REPUBLICS (from page 127)

Armenia / Azerbaijan / Belarus / Estonia / Georgia / Kazakhstan
Kyrgyzstan / Latvia / Lithuania / Moldova / Russia
Tajikistan / Turkmenistan / Ukraine / Uzbekistan

LINKED MISCELLANY X (from page 130)

1. *Harry Potter and the Philosopher's Stone*; 2. The Dales; 3. Citizen Kane;
4. Lillywhites; 5. Jeremy Irons; 6. Hornet; 7. *The Pilgrim's Progress*; 8. The Eagles‡;
9. The Hammer and Sickle; 10. The Canary Islands.
The link is nicknames of football teams§.

OLYMPIC HOST NATIONS (from page 133)

Australia	1956, 2000
Belgium	1920
Canada	1976
China	2008
Finland	1952
France	1900, 1924
Germany	1936, 1972
Greece	1896, 1906, 2004
Italy	1960
Japan	1964
Mexico	1968
Netherlands	1928
South Korea	1988
Spain	1992
Sweden	1912
UK	1908, 1948, 2012

---

* Alternatively known as Second Row.

† Alternatively known as Stand Off or Outside Half.

‡ Their *Greatest Hits*, released in 1976, has sold 29 million copies in the US and 41 million copies worldwide.

§ Potters (Stoke City), Dale (Rochdale), Citizens (Manchester City), Lillywhites (Preston North End), Irons (Scunthorpe), Hornets (Watford), Pilgrims (Plymouth Argyle), Eagles (Crystal Palace), Hammers (West Ham United) and Canaries (Norwich City).

BEATRIX POTTER TALES (from page 136)

*The Tale of Peter Rabbit**
The Tale of Squirrel Nutkin
The Tale of Tailor of Gloucester
The Tale of Benjamin Bunny
The Tale of Two Bad Mice
The Tale of Mrs Tiggy-Winkle†
The Tale of Mr Jeremy Fisher
The Tale of Tom Kitten
The Tale of Jemima Puddle-Duck
The Tale of the Flopsy Bunnies
The Tale of Mrs Tittlemouse
The Tale of Timmy Tiptoes
The Tale of Johnny Town-Mouse
The Tale of Mr Tod
The Tale of Pigling Bland
The Tale of Samuel Whiskers
The Tale of the Pie and the Patty Pan
The Tale of Ginger and Pickles
The Tale of Little Pig Robinson

BATTLES II (from page 139)

1. Second World War (1940); 2. Napoleonic Wars (1815); 3. Second World War (1942); 4. Napoleonic Wars (1805); 5. Second World War (1944); 6. English Civil War (1645); 7. First World War (1914 and 1915); 8. Second World War (1939); 9. Zulu War (1879)‡; 10. Second World War (1943)§; 11. Second World War (1945)¶; 12. War of American Independence (1777); 13. English Civil War (1643); 14. Second World War (1944); 15. Wars of Alexander the Great (331BC); 16. War of Spanish Succession (1704); 17. Second World War (1942); 18. Greco-Persian Wars (490BC); 19. First Crusade (1098); 20. Napoleonic Wars (1805); 21. Zulu

---

* Having been rejected by several publishers, Beatrix Potter published her first book, *The Tale of Peter Rabbit*, herself in 1901.

† Inspired by her childhood pet hedgehog.

‡ At Rorke's Drift, a small number of British troops repelled a numerically superior force of Zulus. Eleven Victoria Crosses were awarded after the battle.

§ The Battle of Kursk was the largest tank battle in history with German forces comprising some 2,700 tanks, 1,800 aircraft and 900,000 personnel and Russian forces estimated at 3,600 tanks, 2,400 aircraft and 1.3 million men.

¶ Also known as the Battle of the Bulge as it was nicknamed by Churchill.

War (1879); 22. Crimean War (1854); 23. Peloponnesian War (405BC); 24. Greco-Persian Wars (480 BC)*.

METRIC PREFIXES (from page 141)

Yetta- (Y)	1 000 000 000 000 000 000 000 000
Zetta- (Z)	1 000 000 000 000 000 000 000
Exa- (E)	1 000 000 000 000 000 000
Peta- (P)	1 000 000 000 000 000
Tera- (T)	1 000 000 000 000
Giga- (G)	1 000 000 000
Mega- (M)	1 000 000
Kilo- (K)	1 000
Hecto- (H)	100
Deca- (da)	10
Deci- (d)	0.1
Centi- (c)	0.001
Milli- (m)	0.0 001
Micro- (μ)	0.000 001
Nano- (n)	0.000 000 001
Pico- (p)	0.000 000 000 001
Femto- (f)	0.000 000 000 000 001
Atto- (a)	0.000 000 000 000 000 001
Zepto- (z)	0.000 000 000 000 000 000 001
Yocto- (y)	0.000 000 000 000 000 000 000 001

MEDITERRANEAN COUNTRIES (from page 144)

Spain / France / Monaco / Italy / Malta / Slovenia / Croatia
Bosnia and Herzegovina / Montenegro / Albania / Greece
Turkey / Cyprus / Syria / Lebanon / Israel / Egypt / Libya
Tunisia / Algeria / Morocco

TAGLINES OF POPULAR FILMS III (from page 147)

1. *Jaws 2*; 2. *Psycho*†; 3. *The Silence of the Lambs*; 4. *Toy Story 2*; 5. *Back to the Future II*;

---

* At Thermopylae a small force of around 1,000 Greeks (Spartans and Thespians) led by King Leonidas of Sparta held a pass through which the Persian Army under Xerxes I and numbering hundreds of thousands of men, needed to travel. In one of the most infamous last stands in history, the Persians sustained heavy and disproportionate losses before overcoming the defenders, while Leonidas, in the certain knowledge that he and his force would all be killed, bought enough time for the retreating Greek armies to recover and regroup for the next battle.

† The film is famous for its shower scene and particularly the sinister music that accompanies it. Originally Hitchcock wished the shower scene to play silently. In spite of this the composer Bernard Hermann went ahead and scored it; on hearing the soundtrack Hitchcock immediately changed his mind. The 'blood' used in the scene was chocolate sauce.

6. *Calendar Girls*; 7. *Four Weddings and a Funeral*; 8. *Citizen Kane*; 9. *Spider-Man*; 10. *Men in Black*; 11. *Pearl Harbor*; 12. *Bridget Jones's Diary*; 13. *The Graduate*; 14. *Teenage Mutant Ninja Turtles*; 15. *The Full Monty*; 16. *Dangerous Liaisons*; 17. *The Amityville Horror*; 18. *Terminator 2: Judgment Day**; 19. *Bonnie and Clyde*; 20. *Withnail and I*; 21. *The Blair Witch Project*; 22. *Edward Scissorhands*; 23. *Dead Calm*; 24. *Flatliners*.

ARAB LEAGUE† (from page 151; as at the time of publishing)

Algeria / Bahrain / Comoros / Djibouti / Egypt [F]

Iraq [F] / Jordan [F] / Kuwait / Lebanon [F] / Libya [F] / Mauritania

Morocco / Oman / Palestine / Qatar / Saudi Arabia [F] / Somalia

Sudan / Syria [F] / Tunisia / United Arab Emirates / Yemen [F]

[F] indicates founder member

FORBIDDEN DEGREES OF RELATIONSHIP (from page 153)

Mother
Step-mother or former step‡-mother
Mother-in-law or former mother-in-law
Adoptive mother or former adoptive mother
Daughter
Step-daughter or former step-daughter
Daughter-in-law or former daughter-in-law
Adoptive daughter or former adoptive daughter
Sister
Half-sister
Father's mother (grandmother)
Mother's mother (grandmother)
Father's father's former wife (step-grandmother)
Mother's father's former wife (step-grandmother)
Son's daughter (granddaughter)
Daughter's daughter (granddaughter)
Wife's son's daughter (step-granddaughter)
Wife's daughter's daughter (step-granddaughter)
Son's son's wife (grandson's wife)
Daughter's son's wife (grandson's wife)
Father's sister (aunt)
Mother's sister (aunt)
Brother's daughter (niece)
Sister's daughter (niece)

---

* Arnold Schwarzenegger earned $15m for the film and delivered 700 words of dialogue; or $21,429 per word.

† Eritrea, India and Venezuela are observer states.

‡ Step-relatives may marry in certain circumstances (provided they are both at least twenty-one years of age and the younger of the pair was at no point a minor living in the household of the elder).

MISCELLANY XXI (from page 156)

1. Islam; 2. Swansea; 3. Leicestershire; 4. Alan Rickman; 5. England and Scotland;
6. Harvard; 7. The Rovers Return; 8. Elvis Presley; 9. Ernest Hemingway;
10. New York, New Jersey, New Hampshire, New Mexico; 11. Three; 12. They
have all been executed in the Tower of London; 13. House of Commons; 14. Sir
Walter Scott; 15. Australia; 16. O$_3$; 17. The Gold Rush; 18. Scorpio*; 19. 1977
(Virginia Wade); 20. Twelve; 21. Scalpel; 22. (1,666) MDCLXVI; 23. Tinky
Winky; 24. Forty.

POPULAR BOYS' NAMES (from page 164)

Jack / Thomas / Oliver / Joshua / Harry / Charlie / Daniel
William / James / Alfie / Samuel / George / Joseph
Benjamin / Ethan / Lewis / Mohammed / Jake / Dylan
Jacob / Luke / Callum / Alexander / Matthew / Ryan

BOOKS OF THE NEW TESTAMENT (from page 166)

Matthew / Mark / Luke / John / Acts / Romans / 1 Corinthians
2 Corinthians / Galatians / Ephesians / Philippians / Colossians
1 Thessalonians / 2 Thessalonians / 1 Timothy / 2 Timothy
Titus / Philemon / Hebrews / James / 1 Peter / 2 Peter
1 John / 2 John / 3 John / Jude / Revelation

FILMS AND THEIR STARS V (from page 171)

1. *Forrest Gump*; 2. *Artificial Intelligence: A.I.*; 3. *Notes on a Scandal*; 4. *About a Boy*; 5. *Unforgiven*; 6. *The Cannonball Run*; 7. *Steel Magnolias*; 8. *Crouching Tiger, Hidden Dragon*; 9. *Cleopatra*; 10. *The Exorcist*; 11. *Edward Scissorhands*; 12. *The Pelican Brief*; 13. *Platoon*; 14. *Chocolat*; 15. *Disclosure*; 16. *Deliverance*; 17. *Tootsie*; 18. *The Crying Game*; 19. *Things to Do in Denver When You're Dead*; 20. *Risky Business*; 21. *Cry Freedom*; 22. *Postcards from the Edge*; 23. *Sylvia*; 24. *The Manchurian Candidate*.

SHIPPING ZONES (from page 174)

Bailey / Biscay / Cromarty / Dogger / Dover / Faeroes
Fair Isle / Fastnet / Fitzroy† / Fisher / Forth / Forties
German Bight / Hebrides / Humber / Irish Sea
Lundy / Malin / North Utsire / Plymouth / Portland
Rockall / Shannon / Sole / South Utsire / South-east Iceland
Thames / Trafalgar / Tyne / Viking / Wight

---

* St Crispin's day falls on 25 October.

† Formerly Finisterre but renamed in commemoration of the meteorologist Robert Fitzroy.

TREES NATIVE TO THE BRITISH ISLES (from page 176)

Alder .... Alnus glutinosa
Crab Apple .... Malus sylvestris
Common Ash .... Fraxinus excelsior
Aspen .... Populus tremula
Common Beech .... Fagus sylvatica
Downy Birch .... Betula pubescens
Silver Birch .... Betula pendula
Box .... Buxus sempervirens
Bird Cherry .... Prunus padus
Wild Cherry .... Prunus avium
Wych Elm .... Ulmus glabra
Common Hawthorn .... Crataegus monogyna
Midland Hawthorn .... Crataegus laevigata
Hazel .... Corylus avellana
Holly .... Ilex aquifolium
Hornbeam .... Carpinus betula
Juniper .... Juniperus communis
Large Leaved Lime .... Tilia platyphyllos
Small Leaved Lime .... Tilia cordata
Field Maple .... Acer campestre
Pedunculate Oak (Common Oak)* .... Quercus robur
Sessile Oak .... Quercus petraea
Scots Pine .... Pinus sylvestris
Black Poplar .... Populus nigra
Wild Service Tree .... Sorbus torminalis
Common Whitebeam .... Sorbus aria
Rowan (Mountain Ash) .... Sorbus aucuparia
Bay Willow .... Salix pentandra
Crack Willow .... Salix fragilis
Goat Willow (Sallow) .... Salix caprea
White Willow .... Salix alba
Yew† .... Taxus baccata

CHARACTERS IN LITERATURE IV (from page 180)

1. *Catch-22* (Joseph Heller)‡; 2. *James and the Giant Peach* (Roald Dahl); 3. *The Canterbury Tales* (Geoffrey Chaucer); 4. *Nineteen Eighty-four* (George Orwell);

---

* A mature oak will produce about 250,000 leaves each year and 50,000 acorns.
† The yew has pagan associations with longevity and was thought to ward off malevolent spirits. Traditionally it is planted in graveyards. The oldest tree in Europe is the 2,000-year-old Fortingall Yew near Loch Tay in Scotland.
‡ In the story, the character received the name Major as both of his given names by his father as a cruel joke. A computer error then resulted in Major being promoted to Major.

5. *Tom Sawyer* (Mark Twain); 6. *The Lion, the Witch and the Wardrobe* (C.S. Lewis); 7. *Through the Looking-glass and What Alice Found There* (Lewis Carroll); 8. *Dracula* (Bram Stoker); 9. *The Jungle Book* (Rudyard Kipling); 10. *The Catcher in the Rye* (J.D. Salinger); 11. *The Rivals* (Richard Brinsley Sheridan)*; 12. *Ulysses* (James Joyce); 13. *Great Expectations* (Charles Dickens); 14. *Rebecca* (Daphne du Maurier); 15. *Emma* (Jane Austen); 16. *Crime and Punishment* (Fyodor Dostoyevsky); 17. *Captain Corelli's Mandolin* (Louis de Bernières); 18. *Lord of the Flies* (William Golding); 19. *Fahrenheit 451* (Ray Bradbury); 20. *Gone With the Wind* (Margaret Mitchell); 21. *Of Mice and Men* (John Steinbeck); 22. *Anne of Green Gables* (Lucy M. Montgomery); 23. *The Shining* (Stephen King); 24. *Far from the Madding Crowd* (Thomas Hardy).

BOOKS OF THE OLD TESTAMENT (from page 183)

Law:

Genesis† / Exodus / Leviticus / Numbers / Deuteronomy

History:

Joshua / Judges / Ruth / 1 Samuel / 2 Samuel / 1 Kings / 2 Kings

1 Chronicles / 2 Chronicles / Ezra / Nehemiah / Esther‡

Poetry:

Job§ / Psalms / Proverbs / Ecclesiastes / Song of Solomon

Major Prophets:

Isaiah / Jeremiah / Lamentations / Ezekiel / Daniel

Minor Prophets:

Hosea / Joel / Amos / Obadiah / Jonah / Micah / Nahum

Habakkuk / Zephaniah / Haggai / Zechariah / Malachi¶

ENGLISH MONARCHS (from page 187)

Anne[S] .... ruled 1702–14

Charles I[S] 1625–49

Charles II**[S] 1660–85

---

* The character was continually mixing up her words, for example: 'He is the very pineapple of politeness' (instead of pinnacle). She gave her name to malapropism – the jumbling of words in a comic fashion.

† Genesis is a Greek word meaning 'origin' or 'creation'. The name comes from the translation of the Hebrew 'bereshith' meaning 'in the beginning', which are the first words of the text. The oldest character in the Bible is Methuselah, described in Genesis 5:27, who lived to the age of 969.

‡ The Book of Esther does not include the word 'God'.

§ Job is believed to be the oldest book, dating from around 1500BC.

¶ Malachi is the most recently written book of the Old Testament, believed to date from around 400BC.

** Charles II ascended to the throne following the Restoration of the Monarchy. From 1649 until 1659, England was a republic governed by Oliver Cromwell, Lord Protector (1653–8) and Richard Cromwell, Lord Protector (1658–9).

Edward I^P 1272–1307
Edward II^P 1307–27
Edward III^P 1327–77
Edward IV^Y .... 1461–70 and 1471–83
Edward V^Y 1483
Edward VI^T 1547–53
Edward VII^{SC} 1901–10
Edward VIII^{W Abd} 1936
Elizabeth I^T 1558–1603
Elizabeth II^W 1952–present
George I^H 1714–27
George II^H 1727–60
George III^H 1760–1820
George IV^H 1820–30
George V*^W 1910–36
George VI^W 1936–52
Henry I^N 1100–35
Henry II^{P Dep} 1154–89
Henry III^P 1216–72
Henry IV^L 1399–1413
Henry V^L 1413–22
Henry VI^{L Dep} .... 1422–61 and 1470–1
Henry VII^T 1485–1509
Henry VIII^T 1509–47
James I^S 1603–25
James II^{S Dep} 1685–8
Jane† ^{Disp} 1553

---

* The name of the House of Windsor was adopted by the monarchy in 1917 in preference to Saxe-Coburg due to public anti-German sentiment.

† Jane was never crowned and the circumstances of her accession and reign have meant her qualification as a legitimate monarch is disputed. Jane's predecessor, Edward VI, died of tuberculosis on 6 July 1553 at the age of fifteen. Edward had received a staunch Protestant upbringing and, encouraged by his adviser the Duke of Northumberland, had no desire for his Catholic half-sister Mary to succeed him. Edward first fell ill in January 1553 but when, by May of that year, it had become clear that the King would not recover, Northumberland had Edward sign a redrafted will naming Jane Grey, great-granddaughter of Henry VII (and Northumberland's own daughter-in-law) as his heir. Jane was proclaimed queen on 10 July; although much of the English establishment backed the accession (concerned at the prospect of a Roman Catholic sovereign) the public supported Mary, the natural heir according to the Act of Succession of 1544. Mary rallied her supporters and on 19 July rode into London to be proclaimed Queen. Jane is alternatively known as the Nine-day Queen (or the Thirteen-day Queen if her reign was assumed to begin at the death of her predecessor). Jane Grey was executed a year later in 1554 at the age of only sixteen.

John^P 1199–1216
Mary I^T 1553–8
Mary II*^S 1688–94
Matilda† ^{Disp} 1141
Richard I^P 1189–99
Richard II^{P Dep} 1377–99
Richard III^Y 1483–5
Stephen^N 1135–54
Victoria^H 1837–1901
William I^N 1066–87
William II^N 1087–1100
William III‡ ^S 1688–1702
William IV^H 1830–7

Monarchs indicated as: ^NNorman; ^PPlantagenet; ^LLancaster; ^Y York; ^TTudor; ^SStuart; ^HHanover; ^{SC}Saxe-Coburg; ^WWindsor; ^{Disp} Disputed; ^{Dep} Deposed; ^{Abd} Abidicated

TAGLINES OF POPULAR FILMS IV (from page 189)

1. *Alien*; 2. *E.T. the ExtraTerrestrial*; 3. *Chicken Run*; 4. *The Da Vinci Code*; 5. *Flashdance*; 6. *Babe*; 7. *Meet the Fockers*; 8. *The Hunt for Red October*; 9. *Home Alone*; 10. *Snakes on a Plane*; 11. *Robocop*; 12. *Harry Potter and the Philosopher's Stone*; 13. *Some Like It Hot*; 14. *Braveheart*; 15. *Pi*; 16. *Gremlins*; 17. *Léon*;

---

* Mary ruled jointly with William III until her death in 1694.

† A maritime accident in 1120 had ramifications that would impact the course of English history for centuries to come. *The White Ship*, sailing overnight from Barfleur in France bound for England, hit rocks and capsized, drowning all crew and passengers bar one, but including seventeen-year-old William Adelin, the only legitimate son of King Henry I. As a result, Henry named his daughter Matilda as his heir with the consequence that, for the first time in its history, England would have a queen. When Henry I died in 1135, his nephew Stephen of Blois acted quickly in claiming the throne. In spite of Henry's barons swearing allegiance to Matilda, their doubts about the suitability of a female sovereign helped Stephen to become accepted as successor. Matilda, however, was incensed and raised an army to enforce her claim, plunging England into a period of bitter civil war which became known as the Anarchy. Matilda eventually defeated Stephen in February 1141 at the Battle of Lincoln, proclaiming herself Queen with Stephen captured and imprisoned. Matilda struggled to win public acceptance and only a few months later their fortunes were reversed when Stephen escaped and she herself was imprisoned. A deal was eventually struck allowing Stephen to rule as King, but for Matilda's son Henry to succeed him as Henry II. The succession crisis of 1135 increased baronial power, ultimately leading to the creation of the Magna Carta, and greatly influenced future monarchs, most notably Henry VIII four centuries later, in the lengths they would go to secure a male succession. Matilda's qualification as a legitimate English monarch is disputed.

‡ William ruled jointly with Mary II following the Glorious Revolution of 1688.

18. *Friday the 13th;* 19. *True Lies;* 20. *Footloose;* 21. *This Is Spinal Tap;* 22. *Mars Attacks!;* 23. *Quiz Show;* 24. *JFK.*

ALFRED HITCHCOCK FILMS (from page 199)

The Pleasure Garden	1925
The Mountain Eagle	1927
The Lodger	1927
Downhill	1927
Easy Virtue	1927
The Ring	1927
Champagne	1928
The Farmer's Wife	1928
The Manxman	1929
Blackmail	1929
Juno and the Paycock	1930
Murder!	1930
Mary	1931
The Skin Game	1931
Number Seventeen	1932
Rich and Strange	1932
The Man Who Knew Too Much	1934
Waltzes from Vienna	1934
The Thirty-Nine Steps	1935
Sabotage	1936
Secret Agent	1936
Young and Innocent	1937
The Lady Vanishes	1938
Jamaica Inn	1939
*Rebecca**	1940
Foreign Correspondent	1940
Mr and Mrs Smith	1941
Suspicion	1941
Saboteur	1942
Shadow of a Doubt	1943
Lifeboat†	1944
Spellbound	1945
Notorious	1946
The Paradine Case‡	1948

---

* Hitchcock's first film after moving to Hollywood. It won the Oscar for Best Picture.

† Hitchcock appears in the 'before' and 'after' pictures in the newspaper advert for a weight-loss product.

‡ Hitchcock is seen disembarking from a train at Cumberland Station, carrying a cello.

ETYMOLOGY OF ROCK AND POP NAMES II (from page 201)

1. Blondie; 2. UB40; 3. Chicago; 4. Frankie Goes to Hollywood; 5. Eurythmics; 6. Dire Straits; 7. St Etienne; 8. Belle and Sebastian; 9. Dexy's Midnight Runners; 10. The The; 11. Styx; 12. Scissor Sisters; 13. Roxy Music; 14. Ultravox; 15. Led Zeppelin; 16. Scritti Politti; 17. McFly; 18. The B52s; 19. The Black Crowes; 20. Los Lobos; 21. Moby; 22. Run DMC; 23. Motörhead; 24. Thousand Yard Stare.

---

* Hitchcock appears on the left side of a class reunion photo.

† Hitchcock is seen winding a clock in the songwriter's apartment.

‡ Remake of the 1934 film.

§ Hitchcock is seen missing a bus during the opening credits.

¶ *Psycho* was unusual in that Hitchcock killed off his major star (Janet Leigh in the famous shower scene) a third of the way into the film – immensely shocking to audiences at the time. In 1960s America, cinema-goers were sometimes prone to drifting into showings some time after the start of the film, but Hitchcock insisted that audiences could only watch his film from the start so as not to ruin this surprise. Hitchcock appears in the film wearing a ten-gallon hat outside Janet Leigh's office.

** Hitchcock is seen leaving a pet shop with two white terriers.

†† Hitchcock is seen rising from a wheelchair, shaking hands with a man and walking off.

‡‡ Hitchcock appears in the middle of a crowd, the only one not applauding the speaker.

CHEMICAL ELEMENTS* (from page 206; as at the time of publishing)

---

* Note that elements with atomic numbers 43, 61 and 95–118 can only be synthesised and do not exist naturally. Elements with atomic numbers 112–18 are placeholder names only. Chemistry as a distinct science is often said to date from 1661 and the publication by Robert Boyle of *The Sceptical Chymist*, a book which brought the subject into the open for the first time. Until that time chemical experiments were largely conducted in secrecy by alchemists. Boyle's main achievement was to define an element, being a substance that cannot be broken down into anything simpler, a discovery which represented a major breakthrough in the understanding of chemistry. The subject was further advanced by a French aristocrat, named Antoine-Laurent Lavoisier who, along with his wife, discovered that a rusting object gains weight as it rusts (and not loses it as everyone had assumed) and led for the first time to an understanding about the way matter behaves in chemical reactions. Throughout the late eighteenth and early nineteenth centuries there was a huge increase in the number of known elements with chemists in open competition to make new discoveries. Humphry Davy was more prolific than most, claiming potassium, sodium, magnesium, calcium, strontium and aluminium. When a Swedish chemist, J.J. Berzelius, suggested the use of abbreviations of Latin or Greek names to create chemical symbols, the notation of the science was born. Hence lead (plumbum) is Pb, tin (stannum) is Sn and mercury (hydrargyrum) is Hg. The biggest breakthrough was achieved by a young professor from St Petersburg in 1869, Dmitri Mendeleev, who was interested in the problem of how to correctly arrange the elements. At the time, elements were either grouped according to atomic weight or according to similar chemical properties but Mendeleev realised that these could be represented in a single arrangement. When elements were ordered by weight, certain physical and chemical properties appeared to repeat every eighth place. Mendeleev arranged these elements of similar properties in vertical rows which he called Groups, and horizontal rows of ascending atomic weight, called Periods, showing one set of relationships when read across and another when read down. Mendeleev's real genius was in the blank spaces he left in the table. At the time, only sixty-three elements were known to exist, but Mendeleev's Periodic Table predicted the elements that were still waiting to be found; predictions that turned out to be accurate as the missing elements were subsequently discovered.

* Named after Dmitri Mendeleev.

^Y indicates an element named after the village of Ytterby near Stockholm

PRIMARY COLOURS* (from page 6)
Red / Yellow / Blue

TRIANGLES† (from page 8)
Equilateral / Isosceles / Scalene

MISCELLANY I (from page 10)
1. Food processor or mixer; 2. Yom Kippur; 3. Nine ('Peter Piper picked a peck of pickled peppers'); 4. Shropshire; 5. El Salvador; 6. Six; 7. Bromine and mercury; 8. The Fifth Amendment; 9. Puccini; 10. Anti-clockwise; 11. They both died at the same address (12 Curzon Place, Mayfair, London); 12. Ash Wednesday;

---

* Traditionally primary colours refer to the coloured pigments used by artists to produce all other colours. In the modern context, primary colours are used in subtractive colour mixing (where the colour source relies on reflected light, for example in print) and additive colour mixing (where the colour source uses emitted light, for example in television). The subtractive primary colours are cyan, magenta, yellow and black (known as the CMYK colour space). The additive colours are red, green and blue (known as the RGB colour space).
† All of the sides of an equilateral triangle are of equal length and all its internal angles are 60°; an isosceles triangle has two sides are of equal length and two equal internal angles; a scalene triangle has all sides have different lengths and its three internal angles are different.

13. *Breakfast at Tiffany's*; 14. The A–Z of London; 15. Tug of war; 16. The M60; 17. 10 Downing Street (it is a title held by the Prime Minister); 18. Paul Young; 19. Eight; 20. *Nineteen Eighty-four*, 21. Hammersmith Bridge; 22. A; 23. Melon; 14. 1km per hour*.

TEA-PARTY IN WONDERLAND (from page 14)

Alice / The Dormouse / The Hatter† / The March Hare

RAF FIGHTER AIRCRAFT (from page 16)

Harrier / Tornado / Typhoon (Eurofighter)

BOY BANDS (from page 21)

1. Take That; 2. The Jackson 5; 3. Boyzone; 4. Duran Duran; 5. The Monkees; 6. The Osmonds; 7. The Bay City Rollers; 8. Bros; 9. Wham!; 10. Westlife; 11. Blue; 12. Busted; 13. New Kids on the Block; 14. N Sync; 15. 5ive; 16. McFly; 17. Backstreet Boys; 18. East 17; 19. New Edition; 20. Boyz II Men; 21. The Temptations; 22. Village People; 23. Big Fun; 24. A1

PAC-MAN GHOSTS (from page 24)

Inky / Pinky / Blinky / Clyde

HOUSES AT HOGWARTS (from page 25)

Gryffindor‡ .... courage
Ravenclaw .... intellect
Hufflepuff .... hard work and fair play
Slytherin .... cunning

---

* This problem is simpler than it first seems. The current in the stream acts on the bottle and the man in the same way. Therefore if the man swims away from the bottle for half an hour it will take half an hour for the man to swim back to the bottle. (The problem would be the same if the bottle and the water were stationary; assuming the swimmer has a constant speed, having swum away from the bottle for a fixed amount of time, it would take the same amount of time to swim back.) Given the bottle and the man reach the bridge at the same time, the bottle has travelled 1 kilometre in one hour. The speed of the current is therefore 1km per hour.
† The Hatter is reportedly based on Theophilus Carter, an eccentric inventor, top-hat wearer and proprietor of an Oxford furniture shop who was known locally as 'The Mad Hatter'. Sir John Tenniel who illustrated the story used Carter for his sketches. The association of madness with hatters came from the practice of using mercury in the process of curing felt. Mercury is a toxic substance which causes neurological damage, although this was unknown for a long time.
‡ Harry and his friends Ron and Hermione are sorted into Gryffindor.

ASTRONOMERS, MATHEMATICIANS AND PHYSICISTS (from page 27)

1. Albert Einstein; 2. Isaac Newton*; 3. Archimedes; 4. Nicolaus Copernicus;
5. Galileo Galilei†; 6. Edwin Hubble; 7. Edmond Halley; 8. Pythagoras;
9. Christian Doppler; 10. René Descartes; 11. Alan Turing‡; 12. Erwin
Schrödinger; 13. Florence Nightingale; 14. Michael Faraday; 15. Euclid; 16. Max
Planck; 17. Charles Babbage; 18. Werner Heisenberg; 19. Blaise Pascal;
20. Wilhelm Herschel; 21. Ptolemy; 22. Ernest Rutherford; 23. Niels Bohr§;
24. Robert Hooke.¶

GANG OF FOUR (from page 32)

Roy Jenkins / David Owen / Bill Rodgers / Shirley Williams

NORDIC COUNCIL (from page 34)

Denmark / Finland / Iceland / Norway / Sweden

---

* Newton's *Principia* is a candidate for the greatest scientific work of all time, but
without the actions of Edmond Halley would quite possibly never have been
published at all. In 1683, planets were known to have elliptical orbits but no one
was able to say why. Sir Christopher Wren offered a wager to Halley and Robert
Hooke, another prominent scientist of the day, to come up with a solution. The
following year Halley paid a visit to the Lucasian Professor in Cambridge and was
surprised to learn that Newton had solved the problem himself five years earlier.
Halley insisted that Newton publish his theories and after two years of frenetic work,
Principia was produced. Newton had absolutely no interest in contributing financially
to its publication; Halley, although by no means wealthy, somehow found the money
to fund it.

† Galileo was one of the first astronomers to benefit from the invention of the
telescope. As well as the rings of Saturn, he discovered the four largest moons of
Jupiter, the phases of Venus, sunspots and mountains and craters on the moon. He
discovered that the Milky Way was composed of stars, contrary to the thinking of
the time that it was a cloud of gas. There is evidence that he also observed the
planet Neptune, although he believed it to be a star. While away from stargazing,
Galileo found time to note that the velocity of a falling body was independent of its
mass and that a pendulum swing would always take the same time regardless of the
amplitude of the swing – a discovery that paved the way for accurate timekeeping.

‡ Turing predicted that artificial intelligence would one day be possible and devised a
test which could define a computer as being 'sentient'. In the Turing Test, a
computer and a human provide text-based answers to questions asked by a human
judge. If the judge cannot tell them apart, the machine is said to have passed the
test. So far, no computer has passed the test.

§ Commenting on the puzzling nature of quantum theory, Bohr once said: 'Anyone
who is not shocked by quantum theory has not understood it.'

¶ Possibly better known for his contribution to biological science, Hooke was the
first person to describe a cell.

LINKED MISCELLANY III (from page 37)

1. The Nolan Sisters; 2. *Indiana Jones and the Temple of Doom*; 3. Earl; 4. The Elgin Marbles; 5. Hell's Angels; 6. *Passport to Pimlico*; 7. The Black Friars; 8. Swiss; 9. Elephant; 10. *The Strange Case of Dr Jekyll and Mr Hyde*.
The link is London Underground stations*.

MARX BROTHERS (from page 39)

Chico / Groucho / Gummo / Harpo / Zeppo

PLATONIC SOLIDS (from page 41)

Tetrahedron / Hexahedron (Cube) / Octahedron
Dodecahedron / Icosahedron

OLOGIES I (from page 43)

1. Birds; 2. Ancestry; 3. Weather; 4. The nervous system; 5. Bees; 6. Skin and related diseases; 7. The universe; 8. Bells and bell ringing; 9. Old age; 10. Sounds in language; 11. The nose; 12. Dates; 13. Disease; 14. The heart and related diseases; 15. Blood; 16. Characteristics of rocks; 17. Insects; 18. Plant and animal cells; 19. Trees; 20. Aquatic mammals, especially whales; 21. Eggs; 22. Ants; 23. Fingerprints; 24. Life in outer space.

TASTES (from page 46)

Bitter / Salt / Sour / Sweet / Umami†

ELEMENTS WITH FOUR-LETTER NAMES (from page 48)

Gold / Iron / Lead / Neon / Zinc

MENTAL DISORDERS (from page 50)

1. Insomnia; 2. Kleptomania; 3. Anorexia nervosa; 4. Amnesia; 5. Bulimia nervosa; 6. Clinical depression; 7. Exhibitionism; 8. Nymphomania; 9. Post-traumatic stress disorder; 10. Pyromania; 11. Schizophrenia‡; 12. Dementia; 13. Tourette's syndrome; 14. Phobia; 15. Hypochondria; 16. Megalomania; 17. Narcolepsy; 18. Stockholm syndrome§; 19. Passive-aggressive disorder; 20. Obsessive-compulsive

---

* Seven Sisters, Temple, Earl's Court, Marble Arch, Angel, Pimlico, Blackfriars, Swiss Cottage, Elephant and Castle and Hyde Park Corner.

† Umami (a Japanese word) is triggered by monosodium glutamate in the same way that a sweet taste is triggered by sugar. This fact is well known to Chinese and Japanese chefs who use it extensively in their cooking.

‡ The term comes from the Greek 'schizo' (split or divide) and 'phrenos' (mind) and is often translated as 'shattered mind'.

§ Named after a bank robbery in Stockholm in August 1973 in which bank employees were held hostage for five days. Sometimes this is referred to erroneously in the popular media as 'Helsinki Syndrome' and notably in the film *Die Hard*. The syndrome may stem from the instinct of newborn babies to form an emotional attachment to the nearest powerful adult.

disorder; 21. Delusional disorder (or paranoia); 22. Bipolar disorder (or mania); 23. Munchausen's syndrome; 24. Munchausen's syndrome by proxy.

FIGHTERS OF THE BATTLE OF BRITAIN (from page 55)

Hawker Hurricane / Supermarine Spitfire
Boulton Paul Defiant / Bristol Blenheim
Gloster Gladiator / Bristol Beaufighter

NOBEL PRIZES (from page 58)

Physics / Chemistry / Medicine / Literature / Peace / Economics

MISCELLANY VIII (from page 60)

1. Narcissus; 2. Norfolk; 3. *The Hitchhiker's Guide to the Galaxy*; 4. Henry VIII; 5. Jim Rockford; 6. The M4; 7. The Presidential helicopter; 8. Corduroy; 9. Badminton; 10. Blood vessels; 11. 144; 12. Iwo Jima; 13. Montague and Capulet; 14. 'Mamma Mia'*; 15. The *Mona Lisa*; 16. Queen; 17. Machu Picchu; 18. Ben Cohen (the uncle is George Cohen); 19. 'Right Said Fred'†; 20. Campbells; 21. Herbert Asquith; 22. Ribena; 23. Miami‡; 24. 5p (the horse cost £1.05).

HOUSE OF STUART§ (from page 64)

James I / Charles I / Charles II / James II
Mary II¶ / William III** / Anne

WORLD CUP WINNERS†† (from page 67; as at the time of publishing)

Uruguay / Italy / Brazil / Germany
England / Argentina / France

---

* 'Mamma Mia' reached number one for Abba in February 1976.
† Bernard Cribbins had a hit in 1962 with 'Right Said Fred'; Richard Fairbrass was a member of the band Right Said Fred.
‡ 59% of Miami residents were born outside the United States.
§ The Stuarts presided over a period of significant upheaval for the monarchy and the country. The period saw the gunpowder plot, civil war, regicide, formation of a republic, restoration of the monarchy, deposition, the Glorious Revolution, the destruction and rebuilding of London and the creation of Great Britain.
¶ Ruled jointly with her husband William III.
** William of Orange, who married into the House of Stuart.
†† The World Cup trophy that Jules Rimet gave his name to weighed 3.8kg, stood 35cm tall and was made out of pure gold. After surviving some scrapes (it spent the Second World War hidden in a shoe box under the bed of a worried Italian football official, Ottorino Barassi; it was stolen from an exhibition in England in 1966 but recovered from a dustbin by a dog called Pickles) it was given permanently to the victorious Brazilian team of 1970 who had won the tournament for the third time. The trophy was stolen from the Brazilian FA in 1983 and has never been recovered.

ANIMAL ADJECTIVES (from page 70)

1. Horse; 2. Lion; 3. Bird; 4. Zebra; 5. Ape or monkey; 6. Cow* or ox; 7. Fish; 8. Pig; 9. Bull; 10. Dolphin; 11. Ostrich; 12. Bear; 13. Bee; 14. Goat; 15. Deer; 16. Goat; 17. Wolf; 18. Mouse; 19. Sheep; 20. Wasp; 21. Hare; 22. Fox; 23. Goose; 24. Dove.

EVENTS IN THE HEPTATHLON (from page 72)

100m hurdles / Long jump / High jump
200m / Shot put / Javelin / 800m

SEVEN SEAS (from page 75)

North Pacific / South Pacific
North Atlantic / South Atlantic
Arctic / Southern (Antarctic) / Indian

AMERICANISMS I (from page 77)

1. Apartment; 2. Pants; 3. French fries; 4. Fall; 5. Diaper; 6. Attorney†; 7. Zip code; 8. Cookie; 9. Eggplant; 10. Flashlight; 11. Jello; 12. Purse; 13. Station wagon; 14. Trunk; 15. Wrench; 16. Drug store; 17. Robe; 18. Windshield; 19. Sedan; 20. Realtor; 21. Hickey; 22. Valise; 23. Vaudeville‡; 24. Kerosene.

COUNTRIES ENDING WITH '~STAN' (from page 79)

Afghanistan / Kazakhstan / Kyrgyzstan / Pakistan
Tajikistan / Turkmenistan / Uzbekistan

BRAT PACK§ (from page 82)

Emilio Estevez / Anthony Michael Hall / Rob Lowe
Andrew McCarthy / Demi Moore / Judd Nelson
Molly Ringwald / Ally Sheedy

---

* 'The cow is of the bovine ilk; one end is moo, the other, milk.' Ogden Nash.
† In England, the word 'attorney' once referred to a qualified legal agent in the courts of Common Law who prepared cases for barristers to plead. An attorney was the Common Law equivalent of a 'solicitor' in the Chancery (the Chancery was a High Court under the jurisdiction of the Lord Chancellor; the Common Law courts relied on legal precedent). When the Judicature Act of 1873 merged the two courts, solicitor was assumed and attorney was dropped. In the United States, the term remained.
‡ The word describes the American variety shows of the nineteenth and early twentieth centuries. It is thought to derive from an area of France, Val de Vire, with a reputation for songs and entertainment. The term first appears in 1840 with the opening of the Vaudeville Theatre in Boston.
§ These eight actors are most commonly included in the Brat Pack. Other actors often associated with the Brat Pack are Kevin Bacon, Matthew Broderick, Phoebe Cates, Tom Cruise, Charlie Sheen and Kiefer Sutherland.

INNOVATIONS I (from page 84)

1. Telephone*; 2. Aeroplane; 3. Printing press; 4. Waterproof material; 5. Radio; 6. Walkman; 7. Pneumatic tyre; 8. Cylinder lock; 9. Personal computer; 10. Steam engine; 11. Electric generator; 12. Dynamite; 13. Internal combustion engine (four-stroke cycle)†; 14. Newsreel; 15. Instant coffee; 16. Hot-air balloon; 17. Heart transplant‡; 18. Electric battery; 19. Antiseptic surgery; 20. Atomic bomb; 21. Jet engine; 22. Hovercraft; 23. Genetic clone (Dolly the sheep); 24. Condom.

CHANNEL ISLANDS (from page 81)

Jersey / Guernsey / Alderney / Sark
Herm / Jethou / Brecqhou§ / Lihou

---

* The first speech to be transmitted by telephone was made by Bell on 1 July 1875. The first two-way speech (telephone conversation) was made by Bell and his assistant Watson, on 10 March 1876: 'Mr Watson, come here, I want to see you.'

† The first automobile appeared in 1886 but the idea was not a new one. An Italian inventor, Guido da Vigevano, produced a design for a wind-powered vehicle in 1335 and Leonardo da Vinci also proposed a clockwork-driven tricycle two centuries later. The eighteenth and nineteenth centuries saw many engineers experimenting with steam, electricity and even explosives to power an automobile engine but these attempts were largely unsuccessful. The invention of the internal combustion engine and the modern automobile was the result of the work of several men in the late nineteenth century. Jean Lenoir, a Belgian, patented a two-stroke petrol-powered engine in 1860. In 1862, a Frenchman, Alphonse Bear de Rochas worked out how to include a compression stroke into the cycle and the four-stroke cycle (intake–compression–power–exhaust) was born. De Rochas neglected to patent his invention but a German engineer named Nikolaus Otto did not. Otto had successfully developed a four-stroke engine which he patented in 1876 and as a result the four-stroke cycle is often known as the Otto Cycle. The invention of the automobile is credited with two German engineers, Gottlieb Daimler and Carl Benz who independently produced petrol-driven cars in 1885 based on Otto's engine and which they were able to improve on. Benz was able to patent his 'motorwagen' in 1886 and his invention was given much publicity when his wife Bertha drove it sixty-two miles from Mannheim to Pforzheim to visit her mother (without her husband's prior knowledge). Although Benz and Daimler never met, the companies they founded merged in 1926 to form Daimler-Benz or Mercedes-Benz as it is now known. The basic design of the internal combustion engine has remained the same ever since.

‡ Barnard performed the nine-hour operation on Louis Washkansky, fifty-five, who lived for eighteen days before dying of pneumonia.

§ Alternatively Brechou.

POKER HANDS (from page 95)

High card / Pair / Two pair / Three of a kind / Straight
Flush / Full house / Four of a kind / Straight flush*

PHOBIAS (from page 97)

1. Confined spaces; 2. Technology or computers; 3. Spiders; 4. Strangers or foreigners; 5. Bacteria; 6. Open spaces; 7. Flying; 8. Birds; 9. Blood or bleeding; 10. Heights; 11. Sunlight; 12. Crowds; 13. Sex; 14. Night-time; 15. Washing or bathing; 16. Men; 17. Depth; 18. Thunder and lightning; 19. Germs; 20. Snakes†; 21. Long words; 22. One's mother-in-law; 23. Friday the 13th or the number 13; 24. The number 666.

TEST CRICKET NATIONS (from page 100; as at the time of publishing)

Australia / England / South Africa / West Indies / New Zealand
India / Pakistan / Sri Lanka / Zimbabwe / Bangladesh

MAJOR WINE REGIONS OF FRANCE (from page 102)

Alsace / Beaujolais / Bordeaux / Burgundy / Champagne
Côtes du Rhône / Jura / Languedoc-Roussillon / Loire / Sud-Ouest

CAPITAL CITIES IV (from page 105)

1. Austria; 2. Jamaica; 3. Iran; 4. Lebanon; 5. Nepal; 6. Pakistan; 7. Syria; 8. Philippines; 9. Bolivia; 10. Afghanistan; 11. Estonia; 12. Tanzania; 13. Uganda; 14. Lithuania; 15. Paraguay; 16. Barbados; 17. Trinidad and Tobago; 18. Macedonia; 19. Sierra Leone; 20. Oman; 21. Nicaragua; 22. Cameroon; 23. Fiji. 24. Dominican Republic.

COUNTRIES ON THE EQUATOR‡ (from page 109)

Ecuador / Colombia / Brazil / São Tomé and Príncipe / Gabon
Republic of the Congo / Democratic Republic of Congo
Uganda / Kenya / Somalia / Indonesia

LINES ON THE LONDON UNDERGROUND (from page 113)

Bakerloo Line . . . . brown
Central Line . . . . red
Circle Line . . . . yellow

---

* A straight flush is a straight with all cards the same suit, for example 7♣ 6♣ 5♣ 4♣ 3♣ and is the highest hand in poker. A high straight flush, e.g. A♣ K♣ Q♣ J♣ 10♣ is called a royal flush, a low straight flush, e.g. 5♣ 4♣ 3♣ 2♣ A♣ is called a steel wheel.

† Indiana Jones was a sufferer of Ophidiophobia.

‡ The Equator passes through the Maldives and the Gilbert Islands, and part of Kiribati but does not make contact with land. Surprisingly, the Equator does not pass through Equatorial Guinea.

District Line .... green
East London Line .... orange
Hammersmith and City Line .... pink
Jubilee Line .... grey
Metropolitan Line .... purple
Northern Line .... black
Piccadilly Line .... dark blue
Victoria Line .... light blue
Waterloo and City Line .... turquoise

FILMS BY STANLEY KUBRICK (from page 115)

Fear and Desire 1953
Killer's Kiss 1955
The Killing 1956
Paths of Glory 1957
Spartacus 1960
Lolita 1962
*Dr Strangelove** 1964
2001: A Space Odyssey 1968
A Clockwork Orange 1971
Barry Lyndon 1975
The Shining 1980
Full Metal Jacket 1987
Eyes Wide Shut 1999

MISCELLANY XVI (from page 118)

1. Forty; 2. Rome; 3. Brown; 4. Aztec; 5. A4 paper; 6. Double Gloucester†;
7. Goodbye; 8. Cockles and mussels (alive alive-o); 9. St George is the patron saint;
10. 1471; 11. Lamé; 12. Devon (Devonian); 13. Truly Scrumptious; 14. Pancreas;
15. £500; 16. The Isle of Wight; 17. Edwina Currie; 18. Mr Benn; 19. Omaha;
20. Edward the Confessor; 21. Eleven seconds; 22. Huston or Coppola‡;
23. Elements (Yttrium [Y], Ytterbium [Yb], Terbium [Tb] and Erbium [Er]);
24. Sunday.

---

* Subtitled: *Or: How I Learned to Stop Worrying and Love the Bomb.*
† The cheese reaches speeds of up to 70mph.
‡ Walter Huston (Best Supporting Actor, *The Treasure of the Sierra Madre*, 1948),
John Huston (Best Director, *The Treasure of the Sierra Madre*, 1948) and Anjelica
Huston (Best Supporting Actress, *Prizzi's Honor*, 1985); Carmine Coppola (Best
Original Dramatic Score, *The Godfather, Part II*, 1974), Francis Ford Coppola (Best
Original Screenplay, *Patton*, 1970; Best Adapted Screenplay, *The Godfather*, 1972;
Best Picture, Best Director, Best Original Screenplay, *The Godfather, Part II*, 1974),
Nicolas Cage (Francis Ford Coppola's nephew) (Best Actor, *Leaving Las Vegas*,
1995), Sophia Coppola (Best Original Screenplay, *Lost in Translation*, 2003).

PEOPLE PICTURED ON BANK NOTES (from page 122; as at the time of publishing)

Queen Elizabeth II	All notes since Series C
Isaac Newton	£1 Series D
Duke of Wellington	£5 Series D
Florence Nightingale	£10 Series D
William Shakespeare	£20 Series D
Christopher Wren	£50 Series D
George Stephenson	£5 Series E
Charles Dickens	£10 Series E
Michael Faraday	£20 Series E
John Houblon*	£50 Series E
Elizabeth Fry	£5 Series E Revised
Charles Darwin	£10 Series E Revised
Edward Elgar	£20 Series E Revised
Adam Smith	£20 Series F

MUSICALS BY ANDREW LLOYD WEBBER (from page 123)

The Likes of Us	lyrics by Tim Rice
Joseph and the Amazing Technicolor Dreamcoat	Tim Rice
Jesus Christ Superstar	Tim Rice
Evita	Tim Rice
Tell Me on a Sunday†	Don Black
Cats	T.S. Eliot
Starlight Express	Richard Stilgoe
The Phantom of the Opera	Richard Stilgoe and Charles Hart
Aspects of Love	Don Black and Charles Hart
Sunset Boulevard	Don Black and Christopher Hampton
By Jeeves	Alan Ayckbourn
Whistle Down the Wind	Jim Steinman
The Beautiful Game	Ben Elton
The Woman in White	David Zippel

FORMER NAMES OF COUNTRIES (from page 127)

1. Zimbabwe; 2. Iran; 3. Sri Lanka; 4. Thailand; 5. Cambodia; 6. Iraq; 7. Indonesia;
8. Ethiopia; 9. Libya; 10. Jordan; 11. Bangladesh; 12. Mongolia; 13. Taiwan;
14. Belize; 15. Namibia; 16. Bolivia; 17. Canada; 18. Yemen; 19. Burkina Faso;
20. Ghana; 21. United Arab Emirates; 22. Lesotho; 23. Moldova; 24. Seychelles.

---

* The Bank of England's first governor, he held the post from 1694 to 1697.
† Written for Marti Webb and first performed in 1979, *Tell Me on a Sunday* became the first act of a show called *Song and Dance* produced in the West End in 1982; (the second act was a ballet choreographed to music by Lloyd Webber). *Tell Me on a Sunday* was updated and rewritten for a 2003 production starring Denise Van Outen. It features the song 'Take That Look Off Your Face'.

BOXING WEIGHT DIVISIONS* (from page 130)

Heavyweight .... >201lb
Cruiserweight 176–200lb
Light Heavyweight 169–75lb
Super Middleweight 161–8lb
Middleweight 155–60lb
Super Welterweight 148–54lb
Welterweight 141–7lb
Super Lightweight 136–40lb
Lightweight 131–5lb
Super Featherweight 127–30lb
Featherweight 123–6lb
Super Bantamweight 119–22lb
Bantamweight 116–18lb
Super Flyweight 113–15lb
Flyweight 109–12lb
Light Flyweight 106–8lb
Strawweight .... < 105lb

FOOTBALL TEAMS UNITED (from page 129; as at the time of publishing)

Airdrie United / Ayr United / Carlisle United
Colchester United / Dundee United / Hartlepool United
Hereford United / Leeds United / Manchester United
Newcastle United / Peterborough United / Rotherham United
Scunthorpe United / Sheffield United / Southend United
West Ham United

NICKNAMES OF MONARCHS (from page 136)

1. Richard I (1189–99); 2. Elizabeth I (1558–1603); 3. Edward (1042–66); 4. Alfred (871–99); 5. Mary I (1553–8); 6. Edward I (1272–1307); 7. Ethelred (978–1016); 8. Henry VIII (1509–47); 9. Richard III (1483–5); 10. Lady Jane Grey (1553); 11. William I (1066–87); 12. Charles II (1660–85); 13. Victoria (1837–1901); 14. John (1199–1216); 15. George III (1760–1820); 16. William II (1087–1100); 17. Anne (1702–14); 18. Edmund II (1016); 19. Henry II (1154–89); 20. Henry I (1100–35); 21. Henry III (1216–72); 22. Edward VII (1901–10); 23. Matilda (1141); 24. William IV (1830–7).

BEST-SELLING ALBUMS (from page 139; as at the time of publishing)

Greatest Hits .... Queen
Sgt. Pepper's Lonely Hearts Club Band .... The Beatles
(What's the Story) Morning Glory? .... Oasis
Brothers in Arms .... Dire Straits
Gold: Greatest Hits .... Abba

---

* Variations of these divisions are used by the WBO, WBC and the IBF.

The Dark Side of the Moon* .... Pink Floyd
Greatest Hits II .... Queen
Thriller .... Michael Jackson
Bad .... Michael Jackson
The Immaculate Collection .... Madonna
Stars .... Simply Red
Come on Over .... Shania Twain
Rumours .... Fleetwood Mac
Urban Hymns .... The Verve
No Angel .... Dido
Bridge over Troubled Water .... Simon and Garfunkel
Talk on Corners .... The Corrs
Back to Bedlam .... James Blunt
Spice .... Spice Girls
White Ladder .... David Gray

LARGE COUNTRIES (from page 142)

(from page 142)

Russia	6,592,800
Canada	3,855,100
United States	3,794,100
China	3,700,600
Brazil	3,287,600
Australia	2,969,900
India	1,183,400
Argentina	1,068,300
Kazakhstan	1,049,200
Sudan	967,500
Algeria	919,600
Democratic Republic of Congo	905,600
Saudi Arabia	849,400
Mexico	761,600
Indonesia	741,100
Libya	679,400
Iran	636,300
Mongolia	604,200
Peru	496,200
Chad	495,800

Figures are in square miles and are approximate

* In the United States, *The Dark Side of the Moon* spent a record 741 weeks on the Billboard Top 200 album chart.

LINKED MISCELLANY XI (from page 144)

1. *The Silence of the Lambs*; 2. 'Knockin' on Heaven's Door'; 3. Fly; 4. Battery; 5. The Bible Belt; 6. The Krankies; 7. The Cam; 8. Sparks; 9. Coil; 10. Rod Stewart.

The link is the internal combustion engine*.

THE CANTERBURY TALES† (from page 148)

The Knight's Tale / The Miller's Tale

The Reeve's Tale / The Cook's Tale

The Man of Law's Tale / The Wife of Bath's Tale

The Friar's Tale / The Summoner's Tale

The Clerk's Tale / The Merchant's Tale

The Squire's Tale / The Franklin's Tale

The Physician's Tale / The Pardoner's Tale

The Shipman's Tale / The Prioress's Tale

The Monk's Tale / The Nun's Priest's Tale

The Second Nun's Tale / The Canon's Yeoman's Tale

The Manciple's Tale / The Parson's Tale

ENGLISH FOOTBALL LEAGUE CHAMPIONS (from page 151; as at the time of publishing)

Liverpool / Manchester United / Arsenal / Everton / Aston Villa

Sunderland / Newcastle United / Sheffield Wednesday

Blackburn Rovers / Chelsea / Huddersfield Town / Leeds United

Wolverhampton Wanderers / Burnley / Derby County

Manchester City / Portsmouth / Preston North End

Tottenham Hotspur‡ / Ipswich Town / Nottingham Forest

Sheffield United / West Bromwich Albion

---

* Silencer, knocking, flywheel, battery, timing belt or fan belt, crankshaft, cam or cam shaft, spark plug, coil, piston rod.

† The group also included a guidesman, ploughman, carpenter, haberdasher, arrowmaker, dyer, weaver and Chaucer himself. There are two tales told by Chaucer, *The Tale of Sir Thopas* and *The Tale of Melibee*.

‡ The eldest son of the 1st Earl of Northumberland, Sir Henry Percy, was nicknamed 'Hotspur' for the speed with which he was able to attack Scots who ventured south across the border. Percy was instrumental in the deposition of Richard II and enthronement of Henry IV in 1399, but was himself killed by Henry IV in 1403. The seat of the Percys was in Northumberland Park in the Tottenham marshes of north London and this association having first been used by the local cricket club was taken in 1892 as the name of Hotspur Football Club, later becoming Tottenham Hotspur.

NICKNAMES OF PEOPLE II (from page 154)

1. John Prescott; 2. Frank Sinatra; 3. Florence Nightingale; 4. Bruce Springsteen; 5. Michael Heseltine; 6. Jean-Claude Van Damme; 7. Vera Lynn; 8. Duke of Wellington; 9. Cynthia Payne; 10. Eddie Edwards; 11. Greg Norman; 12. Alex Higgins; 13. Neil Ruddock; 14. Eusebio*; 15. Iggy Pop; 16. Madonna; 17. T.E. Lawrence; 18. Simon Bolivar; 19. Edward Heath; 20. Harold Macmillan; 21. Keith Richards; 22. Lesley Hornby; 23. Ludovic Kennedy; 24. Neil Diamond.

POPULAR GIRLS' NAMES (from page 157)

Grace / Ruby / Olivia / Emily / Jessica / Sophie
Chloe / Lily / Ella / Amelia / Lucy / Charlotte
Ellie / Mia / Evie / Hannah / Megan / Katie / Isabella
Isabelle / Millie / Abigail / Amy / Daisy / Freya

NATO ALPHABET (from page 164)

Alpha / Bravo / Charlie / Delta / Echo / Foxtrot / Golf / Hotel / India
Juliet / Kilo / Lima / Mike / November / Oscar / Papa / Quebec / Romeo
Sierra / Tango / Uniform / Victor / Whiskey / X-Ray / Yankee / Zulu†

QUOTATIONS FROM POPULAR FILMS II (from page 167)

1. *Dirty Harry*; 2. *Wall Street*; 3. *Carry On Cleo*; 4. *Where Eagles Dare*; 5. *Goodfellas*; 6. *Goldfinger*; 7. *Monty Python and the Holy Grail*; 8. *Being John Malkovich*; 9. *Ocean's Eleven*; 10. *The Producers*; 11. *Trainspotting*; 12. *The Princess Bride*; 13. *Apocalypse Now*; 14. *The Blues Brothers*; 15. *Reservoir Dogs*; 16. *The Man with Two Brains*; 17. *Tootsie*; 18. *Aliens*; 19. *Moulin Rouge*; 20. *All About Eve*; 21. *It's a Wonderful Life*; 22. *The Third Man*; 23. *The Devil Wears Prada*; 24. *Million Dollar Baby*.

TOWNS NAMED AFTER RIVER MOUTHS‡ (from page 171)

Lynmouth / Avonmouth / Monmouth§ / Barmouth
Cockermouth¶ / Lossiemouth / Grangemouth / Eyemouth
Tweedmouth / Burnmouth / Alnmouth / Lynemouth
Tynemouth / Monkwearmouth / Great Yarmouth
Creekmouth / Portsmouth / Yarmouth / Bournemouth
Weymouth / Charmouth / Axmouth / Sidmouth
Exmouth / Teignmouth / Dartmouth
East Portlemouth / Plymouth / Falmouth

---

* Also nicknamed the Black Pearl, Eusebio was the top scorer in the 1966 World Cup with nine goals, including four against North Korea and one in the semi-final against England.

† Also used by NATO armed forces to indicate Greenwich Mean Time.

‡ Moving clockwise around Britain starting from Land's End.

§ Monmouth is located inland where the river Monnow joins the river Wye.

¶ Cockermouth is located inland at the confluence of the river Cocker and the river Derwent.

IRISH COUNTIES (from page 174)

Antrim[UNI] / Armagh[UNI] / Carlow / Cavan[U] / Clare
Cork / Derry[UNI] / Donegal[U] / Down[UNI] / Dublin
Fermanagh[UNI] / Galway / Kerry / Kildare
Kilkenny / Laois / Leitrim / Limerick / Longford
Louth / Mayo / Meath / Monaghan / Offaly
Roscommon / Sligo / Tipperary / Tyrone[UNI]
Waterford / Westmeath / Wexford / Wicklow

[U] indicates county in Ulster; [NI] indicates county in Northern Ireland

MISCELLANY XXIII (from page 177)

1. Red; 2. *Pygmalion*; 3. Cornwall*; 4. Scotland; 5. The molecular structure of DNA; 6. It is too big to be able to fit through the Panama Canal; 7. Miss Marple; 8. They are all buried in Westminster Abbey; 9. The atom bomb; 10. Paul Gascoigne; 11. His right arm; 12. Daffodil; 13. Twelve; 14. *The Simpsons*; 15. Navy, Army and Air Force Institutions; 16. Scunthorpe; 17. Charles I; 18. Nerd; 19. Cate Blanchett (*Elizabeth*) and Judi Dench (*Shakespeare in Love*); 20. 'Eleanor Rigby'; 21. Mr Smith weighs 85kg and Mrs Smith weighs 45kg; 22. Mountains†; 23. Curling; 24. Forty-one hours‡.

PROLIFIC ENGLAND GOAL-SCORERS (from page 181; as at the time of publishing)

Bobby Charlton	49
Gary Lineker	48
Jimmy Greaves	44
Michael Owen[P]	40
Alan Shearer	30
Nat Lofthouse	30
Tom Finney	30
David Platt	27
Bryan Robson	26
Geoff Hurst	24
Stan Mortensen	23
Kevin Keegan	21

---

* From the Celtic word 'kernou' meaning 'headland' and the Old English word 'walh' meaning 'Celt' or 'Briton'. The word 'horn' meaning peninsular is from the same etymology.

† They describe mountain heights. Munros are mountains over 3,000ft, Corbetts are between 2,500 and 3,000ft, Grahams are between 2,000 and 2,500ft.

‡ When looking at a book on a shelf with the spine facing outwards, the first page is actually to the right and the last page is to the left. Therefore, if the bookworm eats from the first page of the first book to the last page of the last book, it actually eats a single cover of the first book, then eats completely through the next eight books and then eats through a single cover of the last book. The 'length of book' eaten is 41cm, which takes the bookworm forty-one hours.

Mick Channon	21
Wayne Rooney[P]	21
Martin Peters	20
Johnny Haynes	18
Roger Hunt	18
David Beckham[P]	17
Tommy Taylor	16
Tony Woodcock	16
Frank Lampard Jr.[P]	15
Paul Scholes	14
Peter Crouch[P]	14
Steven Gerrard[P]	14
Bobby Smith	13
Martin Chivers	13
Paul Mariner	13
Trevor Francis	12
Bryan Douglas	11
John Barnes	11
Stanley Matthews	11
Teddy Sheringham	11
Wilf Mannion	11
Allan Clarke	10
Dennis Wilshaw	10
Francis Lee	10
Jackie Milburn	10
Joe Cole	10
Ron Flowers	10

[P] indicates currently playing

LONGEST RIVERS (from page 184)

Nile	4,160
Amazon*	4,049
Chang (Yangtze)	3,964
Mississippi / Missouri	3,709
Ob / Irtysh	3,459
Yenisey / Angara / Selenga	3,448
Huang He (Yellow River)	3,395
Congo	2,900
Rio de la Plata / Parana	2,796
Mekong	2,749

* The Amazon discharges somewhere between 10 and 30 million gallons of water into the Atlantic Ocean every second and contains about one-fifth of the world's fresh river water. The Amazon changes the salt content and colour of the sea to a distance of about 200 miles from the coast.

Heilong Jiang /Argun	2,744
Lena / Kirenga	2,734
Mackenzie / Peace / Finlay	2,635
Niger	2,599
Murray / Darling	2,330
Volga	2,291
Purus	2,000
Madeira	1,988
Yukon	1,979
Indus	1,976
Syrdar'ya	1,913
St Lawrence	1,900
Rio Grande	1,899
São Francisco	1,802
Danube	1,770
Brahmaputra	1,765
Salween	1,750
Euphrates	1,749
Tocantins	1,708
Tarim He	1,708
Zambezi	1,700
Araguaia	1,632
Paraguay	1,615
Nelson / Saskatchewan	1,597
Nizhnaya Tunguska	1,590
Amudar'ya	1,578
Ural	1,575
Kolyma	1,562
Ganges	1,560
Orinocco	1,553

Figures are in miles and are approximate

QUOTATIONS FROM POPULAR FILMS III (from page 187)

1. *Casablanca*; 2. *Bridget Jones's Diary*; 3. *Snakes on a Plane*; 4. *Lord of the Rings: The Fellowship of the Ring*; 5. *The Sound of Music*; 6. *Robin Hood: Prince of Thieves*; 7. *The Sixth Sense*; 8. *Psycho*; 9. *Finding Nemo*; 10. *The Incredibles*; 11. *Batman*; 12. *2001: A Space Odyssey*; 13. *Meet the Fockers*; 14. *Boogie Nights*; 15. *Pulp Fiction*; 16. *The Shawshank Redemption*; 17. *Airplane*; 18. *The Godfather, Part II*; 19. *The Graduate**; 20. *Butch Cassidy and the Sundance Kid*; 21. *The Stepford Wives*; 22. *Lawrence of Arabia*; 23. *Ace Ventura: Pet Detective*; 24. *Brief Encounter*.

---

* The film's poster features Dustin Hoffman framed by Mrs Robinson's leg in an alluring pose. In reality the leg belonged to Linda Gray (rather than Anne Bancroft) who, an unknown model at the time, went on to play Sue Ellen in *Dallas* and later took on the role of Mrs Robinson on the London stage.

CHURCH OF ENGLAND DIOCESES (from page 190)

Bath and Wells / Birmingham / Blackburn / Bradford
Bristol / Canterbury / Carlisle / Chelmsford / Chester
Chichester / Coventry / Derby / Durham / Ely / Exeter
Gibraltar in Europe / Gloucester / Guildford / Hereford
Leicester / Lichfield / Lincoln / Liverpool / London
Manchester / Newcastle / Norwich / Oxford
Peterborough / Portsmouth / Ripon and Leeds
Rochester / Salisbury / Sheffield / Sodor and Man*
Southwark / Southwell and Nottingham / St Albans
St Edmundsbury and Ipswich / Truro / Wakefield
Winchester / Worcester / York

AMERICAN STATES† (from page 193)

Alabama / Alaska‡ / Arizona / Arkansas / California
Colorado / Connecticut^F / Delaware^F / Florida / Georgia^F
Hawaii§ / Idaho / Illinois / Indiana / Iowa / Kansas
Kentucky / Louisiana / Maine / Maryland^F
Massachusetts^F / Michigan / Minnesota / Mississippi
Missouri / Montana / Nebraska / Nevada
New Hampshire^F / New Jersey^F / New Mexico
New York^F / North Carolina^F / North Dakota / Ohio
Oklahoma / Oregon / Pennsylvania^F / Rhode Island^F
South Carolina^F / South Dakota / Tennessee / Texas
Utah / Vermont / Virginia / Washington
West Virginia^F / Wisconsin / Wyoming

^{F} indicates a founding state

SCENTS (from page 199)

1. Chanel; 2. Ralph Lauren; 3. Calvin Klein; 4. Chanel; 5. Christian Dior; 6. Yves St Laurent; 7. Calvin Klein; 8. Cacharel; 9. Christian Dior; 10. Lagerfeld; 11. Yves St Laurent; 12. Calvin Klein; 13. Christian Dior; 14. Elizabeth Arden; 15. Lancôme; 16. Cartier; 17. Elizabeth Taylor; 18. Estée Lauder; 19. Givenchy; 20. Joop!; 21. Paco Rabanne; 22. Givenchy; 23. Gucci; 24. Guy Laroche.

---

* The seat of the Bishop of Sodor and Man is Peel Cathedral on the Isle of Man.
† The US also includes Washington DC (District of Columbia), a district of sixty-eight square miles covering the city of Washington, the nation's capital. Washington DC is a federal area that is not part of any state. The district was formed on 16 July 1790, after disagreements arose over which state would contain the capital city. Consequently it was proposed to locate it on federal land rather than in a state and the states of Maryland and Virginia ceded territory along the Potomac River for the new city, which took the name of George Washington, the first President.
‡ The United States purchased Alaska from Imperial Russia for $7m in 1867. Alaska joined the Union in January 1959.
§ Hawaii was the most recent state to join the Union in August 1959.

NOVELS BY AGATHA CHRISTIE (from page 202)

[P] Hercule Poirot; [M] Miss Marple; [TT] Tommy Beresford and Tuppence Cowley

GREATEST LIVING FOOTBALLERS (from page 207)

(from page 207)

Michelle Akers[W] / Roberto Baggio / Michael Ballack
Gordon Banks / Franco Baresi / Gabriel Batistuta
Franz Beckenbauer / David Beckham / Emre Belozoglu
Dennis Bergkamp / Giuseppe Bergomi / George Best
Zbigniew Boniek / Giampiero Boniperti / Paul Breitner
Gianluigi Buffon / Emilio Butragueno / Cafu / Eric Cantona
Carlos Alberto / Jan Ceulemans / Bobby Charlton
Rui Costa / Hernan Crespo / Johan Cruijff
Teofilo Cubillas / Kenny Dalglish / Rinat Dasaev
Edgar Davids / Alessandro Del Piero / Marcel Desailly
Didier Deschamps / Alfredo Di Stefano / El Hadji Diouf
Djalma Santos / Luis Enrique / Eusebio / Giacinto Facchetti

---

* Written four decades earlier and stored securely, the book describes Poirot's last case. Agatha Christie authorised the novel for publication when she knew she would write no more novels.

† Published posthumously. The novel had been written four decades earlier and stored securely. Christie left instructions for the novel to be published in the event of her death. It relates Miss Marple's last case.

Falcão / Luis Figo / Elias Figueroa / Just Fontaine*
Enzo Francescoli / Ruud Gullit / Gheorghe Hagi
Mia Hamm^W / Thierry Henry / Junior / Oliver Kahn
Roy Keane / Kevin Keegan / Mario Kempes
Jurgen Klinsmann / Patrick Kluivert / Raymond Kopa
Brian Laudrup / Michael Laudrup / Gary Lineker
Sepp Maier / Paolo Maldini / Diego Maradona
Josef Masopust / Lothar Matthaus / Roger Milla
Gerd Muller / Hong Myung-Bo / Hidetoshi Nakata
Pavel Nedved / Johan Neeskens / Alessandro Nesta
Nilton Santos / Jay-Jay Okocha / Michael Owen
Jean-Pierre Papin / Daniel Passarella / Pelé / Abedi Pele
Jean-Marie Pfaff / Robert Pires / Michel Platini
Ferenc Puskas / Raul / Rustu Recber
Rob Rensenbrink / Frank Rijkaard / Rivaldo
Rivelino / Gianni Rivera / Roberto Carlos
Romario / Romerito / Ronaldinho / Ronaldo / Paolo Rossi
Karl-Heinz Rummenigge / Hugo Sanchez / Javier Saviola
Peter Schmeichel / Clarence Seedorf / Uwe Seeler / Alan Shearer
Andriy Shevchenko / Omar Sivori / Socrates / Hristo Stoichkov
Davor Suker / Lilian Thuram / Francesco Totti / Marius Trésor
David Trezeguet / Carlos Valderrama / Marco van Basten
Rene van de Kerkhof / Willy van de Kerkhof
Franky Van Der Elst / Ruud van Nistelrooy
Juan Sebastián Verón / Patrick Vieira / Christian Vieri
George Weah / Ivan Zamorano / Javier Zanetti
Zico / Zinedine Zidane / Dino Zoff

^{W} indicates a female player

NEWTON'S LAWS OF MOTION (from page 6)

1. Any object will remain in a state of rest or continue at a uniform velocity unless acted on by an external force.
2. The rate of change of momentum of a body is equal to the force impressed upon it and in the same direction†.
3. For every action there is an equal and opposite reaction.

CAPITAL CITIES I (from page 8)

1. Thailand; 2. South Korea; 3. Finland; 4. Czech Republic; 5. Bulgaria; 6. Ethiopia; 7. Kenya; 8. Libya; 9. Bosnia and Herzegovina; 10. Zimbabwe; 11. Sri Lanka; 12. Myanmar (Burma); 13. Azerbaijan; 14. Ukraine; 15. North Korea; 16. United

---

* Record holder for the most goals scored in a single World Cup final with thirteen goals in 1958.

† Newton's Second Law may be expressed as the equation $f=ma$, where f is force, m is mass and a is acceleration.

Arab Emirates; 17. Bahamas; 18. Bangladesh; 19. Armenia; 20. Democratic Republic of Congo; 21. Costa Rica; 22. Kazakhstan; 23. Montenegro; 24. Burkina Faso.

GHOSTS VISITING EBENEZER SCROOGE (from page 11)

The Ghost of Jacob Marley*
The Ghost of Christmas Past
The Ghost of Christmas Present
The Ghost of Christmas Yet to Come .

U2 (from page 14)

Adam Clayton .... Bass
Bono .... Vocals
Larry Mullen Jr. .... Drums
The Edge .... Guitar

RECENT HISTORY I (from page 16)

1. 2003; 2. 2006; 3. 1997; 4. 1945; 5. 1999; 6. 1984; 7. 1939; 8. 1986;
9. 1993; 10. 1976; 11. 1971; 12. 1963; 13. 1918; 14. 1991; 15. 1985;
16. 1915; 17. 1967; 18. 1964; 19. 1974; 20. 1916; 21. 1955; 22. 1957;
23. 1919; 24. 1910.

NOVELS BY E.M. FORSTER (from page 75)

Where Angels Fear to Tread .... published 1905
The Longest Journey 1907
A Room with a View 1908
Howards End 1910
A Passage to India 1924
Maurice† 1971
Arctic Summer‡ 1980

BIG FOUR RAILWAY COMPANIES (from page 24)

Great Western Railway§
London and North Eastern Railway
London, Midland and Scottish Railway
Southern Railway

---

* Jacob Marley was Scrooge's miserly business partner. The story begins with the death of Marley; Marley's tortured ghost appears to Scrooge, dragging the heavy chains he is now forced to carry as a penitence for the way he lived his life. Marley warns Scrooge a similar fate awaits him if he doesn't change his ways.

† Published posthumously, thought to be written in 1914.

‡ Unfinished, published posthumously.

§ In 1892, GWR accomplished one of the most extraordinary feats in the history of engineering, and probably the most unheralded. GWR had been *cont'd over/*

MISCELLANY III (from page 25)

1. Green; 2. Salop; 3. *The Magic Flute*; 4. The nucleus; 5. Belly button;
6. Twenty; 7. American football*; 8. *Brief Encounter*; 9. Orangutan; 10. The Blue
Peter; 11. Hadrian's Wall; 12. The Adam's apple; 13. Luxembourg; 14. 'Tonight I
Celebrate My Love'; 15. Jordan; 16. White; 17. Frog; 18. 300; 19. Big Ben (the
bell in the clock tower of the Palace of Westminster); 20. Watches at sea;
21. Rodgers and Hammerstein (from *Carousel*); 22. Taramasalata; 23. Hillsborough
Castle; 24. The five baboons would win.†

AMERICAN STATES BEGINNING WITH 'A' (from page 30)

Alabama / Alaska / Arizona / Arkansas

FAMILY HOMINIDAE (from page 32)

Chimpanzees / Gorillas / Humans / Orangutans

MEANINGS OF PLACE NAMES (from page 35)

1. Rio de Janeiro; 2. Essex; 3. Argentina; 4. Nova Scotia; 5. Baton Rouge;
6. Soweto; 7. Costa Rica; 8. Casablanca; 9. Puerto Rico; 10. SoHo‡;
11. Montenegro; 12. Munster; 13. Tripoli; 14. Sierra Nevada; 15. Belorussia;
16. Sierra Leone; 17. Bloemfontein; 18. Rajasthan; 19. Soho§; 20. Hawaii; 21. Las
Vegas; 22. Lagos; 23. Montreal; 24. Barbados.

NEW YORK BOROUGHS (from page 37)

The Bronx / Brooklyn / Manhattan / Queens / Staten Island

---

cont'd　　forced to convert its broad gauge tracks to conform to the rest of the
network which had standardised on the narrow gauge. In 1892, much of the
GWR network had already been converted, but the 177 miles of the main line
from London to Penzance remained. After an intense period of planning and
preparation, at dawn on Saturday 21 May 1892 over 4,000 workmen assembled
along the length of the line and commenced work. All remaining non-essential
engines and broad gauge stock travelled to Swindon, assembled in temporary
sidings in a vast collection of steam power on a scale which would never be seen
again. The conversion of the entire 177 miles of track was completed by 4.40 a.m.
on Monday 23 May – less than two days.

* Presented to the winners of the Super Bowl.

† Four baboons against two gorillas would result in a tie.

‡ Other New York acronyms are: NoHo (North of Houston) NoLIta (North of
Little Italy) TriBeCa (Triangle below Canal) and DUMBO (Down Under the
Manhattan Bridge Overpass).

§ In medieval times, Soho was an area of private parkland owned by the king and
used exclusively by royal hunting parties. The boundary of this area was marked by
blue posts, which endures to this day in the many Soho pubs named 'The Blue
Posts'.

CHILDREN IN CHARLIE AND THE CHOCOLATE FACTORY (from page 39)

Augustus Gloop / Veruca Salt / Violet Beauregarde
Mike Teavee / Charlie Bucket

EVENTS IN HISTORY II (from page 42)

1. 1789; 2. 1605; 3. 1812; 4. 1805; 5. 43; 6. 1789; 7. 1773; 8. 1807; 9. 1687;
10. 1506; 11. 1587; 12. 1600; 13. 476; 14. 1649; 15. 1653; 16. 1789;
17. 1519; 18. 79; 19. 122; 20. 1431; 21. 878; 22. 63; 23. 1065; 24. 312.

PILLARS OF ISLAM (from page 44)

The Testimony of Faith (Shahadah) / Prayer (Salah)*
Giving of Alms (Zakah) / Fasting (Sawm)†
The Pilgrimage to Mecca (Hajj)‡

SQUASH BALLS (from page 46)

Double Yellow	Extra Super Slow
Yellow	Super Slow
White	Slow§
Red	Medium
Blue	Fast

LINKED MISCELLANY IV (from page 49)

1. West Point; 2. *Dandy*; 3. *The Usual Suspects*; 4. 'It's My Party'; 5. Maori;
6. The Earth; 7. L'escargot; 8. *Papillon*; 9. Ben Nevis; 10. Rum.
The link is Grand National¶ winners**.

NOBLE GASES†† (from page 52)

Helium / Neon / Argon / Krypton / Xenon / Radon

---

* Muslims must pray five times per day, facing the direction of Mecca.
† During Ramadan.
‡ All Muslims who are financially and physically able must make the journey to Mecca once in their lifetime.
§ Slow balls may alternatively have a green dot.
¶ The Grand National was first run in 1837 at Maghull and moved to Aintree in 1839, where, with the exception of the First World War years (when it was held at Gatwick), it would remain to this day. The 1839 race involved the leading steeplechase jockey of the time, Captain Martin Becher who was thrown at the sixth fence and landed in the adjacent brook. After his fall, Becher is said to have commented, 'How dreadful water tastes without the benefit of whisky.'
** West Tip, Hallo Dandy, Last Suspect, Party Politics, Maori Venture, Earth Summit, L'Escargot, Papillon, Red Rum.
†† A seventh element in the series (temporarily called Ununoctium) was synthesised in 2006.

MOON LANDINGS (from page 55)

CAPITAL CITIES III (from page 58)

1. Canberra*; 2. Oslo; 3. Warsaw; 4. Cairo; 5. Lisbon; 6. Buenos Aires;
7. Santiago; 8. Ankara; 9. Bogota; 10. Havana; 11. Quito; 12. Tunis; 13. Taipei;
14. San Salvador; 15. Tirana; 16. Belgrade; 17. Montevideo; 18. Bratislava;
19. Riga; 20. Dakar; 21. Tbilisi; 22. Dushanbe; 23. Antananarivo; 24. Vaduz.

PINK PANTHER FILMS† (from page 61)

POSITIONS IN A NETBALL TEAM (from page 65)

Goal Attack / Goal Shooter / Wing Attack

Centre

Goal Defence / Goal Keeper / Wing Defence

QUOTATIONS FROM SHAKESPEARE I (from page 67)

1. *Hamlet* (Hamlet); 2. *Macbeth* (Three witches); 3. *Richard III* (King Richard);
4. *Hamlet* (Marcellus); 5. *Twelfth Night* (Orsino); 6. *Julius Caesar*§ (Soothsayer);
7. *Henry V* (King Harry); 8. *A Midsummer Night's Dream* (Puck); 9. *Hamlet*
(Hamlet); 10. *Antony and Cleopatra* (Cleopatra); 11. *Macbeth* (Macbeth);
12. *Hamlet* (Horatio); 13. *Henry V* (King Harry); 14. *Romeo and Juliet* (Juliet);

---

* Rivalry between Melbourne and Sydney led Australia to locate its capital city from
Melbourne to the neutral Canberra in 1913.

† *Inspector Clouseau* (1968) *Curse of the Pink Panther* (1983), *Son of the Pink Panther*
(1993) and the 2006 remake of *The Pink Panther* do not feature Peter Sellers.

‡ Sellers died in 1980. *Trail of the Pink Panther* features unused footage of Sellers as
Clouseau and flashbacks from earlier films. Lynne Frederick, the widow of Peter
Sellers, won a lawsuit against the film's makers claiming that it tarnished his
memory.

§ The 'Ides' was the Roman name for the fifteenth day in March, May, July, and
October and the thirteenth day of the other months. The Romans called the first
day of the month the 'Kalends' from which we get the word 'calendar'.

15. *King Lear** (Lear); 16. *The Tempest* (Prospero); 17. *Twelfth Night* (Malvolio); 18. *Romeo and Juliet* (Romeo); 19. *King Lear* (Lear); 20. *The Merchant of Venice* (Shylock); 21. *Hamlet* (Hamlet); 22. *King Lear* (Kent); 23. *Twelfth Night* (Feste); 24. *As You Like It* (Jacques).

CATHOLIC SACRAMENTS (from page 70)

Baptism / Confession / Confirmation / Eucharist
Matrimony / Ordination / Anointing the Sick

SOLOMON GRUNDY (from page 72)

Born .... Monday
Christened .... Tuesday
Married .... Wednesday
Took ill .... Thursday
Worse .... Friday
Died .... Saturday
Buried .... Sunday

MISCELLANY X (from page 75)

1. George Orwell (*Animal Farm*); 2. The A1; 3. Twelve; 4. Jaundice; 5. The 1991 Rugby World Cup; 6. Decimate; 7. A wedding; 8. B&Q; 9. Her right hand; 10. Philadelphia; 11. Twenty-four; 12. The jaw (or masseter); 13. Port Vale and Stoke City; 14. Expressionism; 15. Timothy Lawrence; 16. Democracy; 17. 1970 (to Brazil); 18. The Monty Python team (the spam sketch); 19. Michael Collins; 20. Australia and New Zealand; 21. The London Eye; 22. Suzanne Charlton; 23. *Rebecca*; 24. $28\frac{1}{2}$ days†.

NOVELS BY THE BRONTË SISTERS (from page 78)

Agnes Grey (1847) .... Anne
The Tenant of Wildfell Hall (1848) .... Anne
Jane Eyre (1847) .... Charlotte
Shirley (1849) .... Charlotte
Villette (1853) .... Charlotte
The Professor‡ (1857) .... Charlotte
Wuthering Heights (1847) .... Emily

---

* *King Lear* is based on a mythical king who is thought to have ruled somewhere in the south-west of England in pre-Roman times. The story of Lear was first told by Geoffrey of Monmouth in his *Historia Regum Britanniae* (*c.*1136).

† The snail reaches the top of the well halfway through the 28th day, that is, before nightfall on the 28th day.

‡ Published posthumously in 1857. The novel was written before *Jane Eyre* but had been rejected by many publishers.

COLOURS OF THE VISIBLE SPECTRUM* (from page 80)

Red / Orange / Yellow / Green / Blue / Indigo† / Violet

SPORTS GOVERNING BODIES II (from page 82)

1. Football Association; 2. World Boxing Council; 3. Union of European Football Associations; 4. United States Professional Golfers' Association; 5. National Football League; 6. Rugby Football Union; 7. International Olympic Committee; 8. International Rugby Board; 9. International Cricket Council; 10. International Rugby Football Board; 11. Ladies' Professional Golf Association; 12. Royal Yachting Association; 13. Rugby League; 14. *CON*federación Suda*ME*ricana de Fút*BOL*‡; 15. Lawn Tennis Association; 16. International Judo Federation; 17. Fédération Internationale de Hockey sur Gazon§; 18. International Baseball Association; 19. International Surfing Association; 20. World Bowls Board; 21. International Weightlifting Federation; 22. Fédération Internationale Des Echecs¶; 23. Fédération Internationale de Volleyball; 24. Tug of War International Federation.

UNITED NATIONS SECRETARIES GENERAL (from page 85; as at the time of publishing)

Trygve Lie	Norway
Dag Hammarskjöld	Sweden
U Thant	Myanmar
Kurt Waldheim	Austria
Javier Pérez de Cuellar	Peru
Boutros Boutros-Ghali	Egypt
Kofi Annan	Ghana
Ban Ki-moon	South Korea

FORBIDDEN IN SWIMMING POOLS (from page 88)

No Acrobatics or Gymnastics
No Bombing
No Ducking
No Petting
No Pushing
No Running
No Shouting

---

* Useful mnemonic: Richard Of York Gave Battle In Vain.
† The seven colours were originally cited by Sir Isaac Newton. The inclusion of indigo is questionable as most people cannot readily distinguish the colour on the spectrum from either blue or violet. Newton believed that light exhibited symmetry with musical notes and therefore there were seven rather than six distinct colours. The word 'indigo' is derived from a blue dye which came from India.
‡ That is, the South American Football Confederation.
§ Field Hockey (as opposed to Ice Hockey).
¶ I.e. the International Chess Federation.

No Smoking
No Swimming in the Diving Area

CHARACTERS IN LITERATURE III (from page 95)
1. *Around the World in Eighty Days* (Jules Verne); 2. *Alice's Adventures in Wonderland* (Lewis Carroll); 3. *The Wind in the Willows* (Kenneth Grahame); 4. *The Canterbury Tales* (Geoffrey Chaucer); 5. *A Christmas Carol* (Charles Dickens); 6. *Moby-Dick* (Herman Melville); 7. *David Copperfield* (Charles Dickens); 8. *The Picture of Dorian Gray* (Oscar Wilde); 9. *Lady Chatterley's Lover** (D.H. Lawrence); 10. *Anna Karenina* (Leo Tolstoy); 11. *Oliver Twist* (Charles Dickens); 12. *Wuthering Heights* (Emily Brontë); 13. *Goodbye Mr Chips* (James Hilton); 14. *Dr Zhivago* (Boris Pasternak); 15. *Brideshead Revisited* (Evelyn Waugh); 16. *Brighton Rock* (Graham Greene); 17. *The Thorn Birds* (Colleen McCullough); 18. *The Curious Incident of the Dog in the Night-time* (Mark Haddon); 19. *Adrian Mole* series (Sue Townsend); 20. *A Clockwork Orange* (Anthony Burgess); 21. *Birdsong* (Sebastian Faulks); 22. *Tom Sawyer* (Mark Twain); 23. *Treasure Island* (Robert Louis Stevenson); 14. *Mansfield Park* (Jane Austen).

DOCTORS WHO (from page 97)

First Doctor	William Hartnell
Second Doctor	Patrick Troughton
Third Doctor	Jon Pertwee
Fourth Doctor	Tom Baker
Fifth Doctor	Peter Davison
Sixth Doctor	Colin Baker
Seventh Doctor	Sylvester McCoy
Eighth Doctor	Paul McGann
Ninth Doctor	Christopher Eccleston
Tenth Doctor	David Tennant
Eleventh Doctor	Matt Smith

MEMBERS OF ASEAN (from page 100)
Brunei / Cambodia / Indonesia / Laos / Malaysia
Myanmar / Philippines / Singapore / Thailand / Vietnam

---

* In 1960 Penguin Books were charged under the Obscene Publications Act over *Lady Chatterley's Lover*, a book that according to the prosecuting counsel 'sets on a pedestal promiscuous intercourse, commends sensuality almost as a virtue, and encourages and even advocates coarseness and vulgarity of thought and language.' Penguin won what would become a landmark case, as much for exposing the attitudes of the judiciary as the legal precedent it set. During the trial, the crown prosecutor Mervyn Griffiths-Jones asked, 'Is it a book that you would even wish your wife or your servants to read?'

LINKED MISCELLANY VIII (from page 102)

1. *Kramer vs. Kramer*; 2. Virginia; 3. Santana; 4. Boris Pasternak; 5. Sarah Connor;
6. Venus; 7. *Graf Spee*; 8. Björn Again; 9. Perry; 10. Billie Jean.

The link is Wimbledon champions*.

WACKY RACERS (from page 105)

Dick Dastardly and Muttley	(driving) The Mean Machine
The Slagg Brothers	The Bouldermobile
The Gruesome Twosome	The Creepy Coupe
Prof. Pat Pending	The Convert-a-car
The Red Max	The Crimson Haybailer
Penelope Pitstop	The Compact Pussycat
Private Meekley and Sergeant Blast	The Army Surplus Special
The Anthill Mob	The Bulletproof Bomb
Luke and Blubber Bear	The Arkansas Chugabug
Peter Perfect	The Turbo Terrific
Rufus Ruffcut and Sawtooth	The Buzzwagon

SIGNS OF THE ZODIAC (from page 109)

Aries ♈ Taurus ♉ Gemini† ♊ Cancer ♋
Leo ♌ Virgo ♍ Libra‡ ♎ Scorpio ♏
Sagittarius ♐ Capricorn ♑ Aquarius ♒ Pisces ♓

RUSSIAN HERO CITIES (from page 111)

Leningrad§ / Odessa / Sevastopol / Stalingrad / Kiev / Moscow
Kerch / Novorossiysk / Minsk / Tula / Murmansk / Smolensk

APOSTLES (from page 113)

Andrew / Bartholomew¶
James son of Alphaeus / James son of Zebedee

---

* Jack Kramer, Virginia Wade, Manuel Santana, Boris Becker, Jimmy Connors,
Venus Williams, Steffi Graf, Björn Borg, Fred Perry and Billie Jean King.
† Gemini represents Castor and Pollux, twin sons of Leda and the brothers of
Clytemnestra and Helen of Troy.
‡ Libra is the only sign represented by a non-living thing (the scales).
§ Leningrad (now St Petersburg) was subjected to a siege by the German Army
lasting thirty months from September 1941 until January 1944. All food and power
supplies were cut off and the city was subject to continual artillery bombardment. By
the end of the siege an estimated 600,000 people had died of starvation or frozen to
death and 300,000 Russian soldiers were killed in the defence of the city and in
efforts to relieve it. Leningrad was the first city to have the Hero City title bestowed
upon it, in 1945.
¶ Alternatively Nathaniel.

John / Jude* / Judas Iscariot† / Matthew‡
Philip / Simon Peter / Simon the Zealot / Thomas

TAGLINES OF POPULAR FILMS II (from page 116)

1. *Apollo 13*; 2. *The Blues Brothers*; 3. *Groundhog Day*; 4. *Ocean's Twelve*;
5. *Schindler's List*; 6. *The Usual Suspects*; 7. *Deep Throat*; 8. *Shakespeare in Love*§;
9. *Terms of Endearment*; 10. *Kill Bill: Volume 2*; 11. *Titanic*; 12. *Kindergarten Cop*;
13. *Gladiator*; 14. *The Truman Show*; 15. *Cool Runnings*; 16. *Westworld*¶; 17. *A
Bug's Life*; 18. *Carry On Cowboy*; 19. *Trading Places*; 20. *Basic Instinct*; 21. *In the
Line of Fire*; 22. *The Italian Job***; 23. *There's Something about Mary*; 24. *Shallow
Grave*.

VITAMINS (from page 119; as at the time of publishing)

Vitamin A	Retinoids
Vitamin B1	Thiamine
Vitamin B2	Riboflavin
Vitamin B3	Niacin
Vitamin B5	Pantothenic acid
Vitamin B6	Pyridoxine
Vitamin B7	Biotin
Vitamin B9	Folic acid
Vitamin B12	Cyanocobalamin
Vitamin C	Ascorbic acid
Vitamin D	Ergocalciferol / Cholecalciferol
Vitamin E	Tocopherol / Tocotrienol
Vitamin K	Naphthoquinone

MARX BROTHERS FILMS (from page 122)

The Cocoanuts	1929
Animal Crackers	1930
Monkey Business	1931

---

* Alternatively Thaddeus.

† After his suicide, Judas was replaced by Mathias as the twelfth apostle.

‡ Alternatively Levi.

§ The film was co-written by Tom Stoppard, who also wrote *Rosencrantz and
Guildenstern Are Dead* (1990), another story in which the plot intertwines with actual
plot from Shakespeare.

¶ The script contains the first recorded use of the term 'computer virus'.

** There have been several theories on the 'great idea' Charlie Croker has in the bus
in the cliffhanger end of the film. Michael Caine has suggested the story would play
out as follows: they would turn the engine on and wait for the petrol to run out,
changing the balance of the bus. The characters are then able to jump from the bus,
which goes over the cliff (along with the gold) and into the hands of the mafia who
are waiting at the bottom.

'ISMS' I (from page 123)

1. Vegetarianism; 2. Marxism; 3. Catholicism; 4. Atheism; 5. Anti-Semitism;
6. Feminism; 7. Sado-masochism; 8. Capitalism; 9. Nepotism; 10. Fascism;
11. Buddhism; 12. Federalism; 13. Materialism; 14. Anarchism; 15. Conservatism;
16. Judaism; 17. Confucianism; 18. Feudalism*; 19. Egalitarianism;
20. Utilitarianism; 21. Determinism; 22. Existentialism; 23. Nihilism; 24. Logical positivism.

WORLD CUP HOST NATIONS† (from page 128; as at the time of publishing)

---

* Although feudalism disappeared in Britain around the start of the seventeenth century it endured in Japan until 1871 and in Russia until 1917. Slavery – feudalism by another name – persisted in the US until 1865 and the Thirteenth Amendment of the Constitution.
† South Africa will host in 2010.

CHART-TOPPING SINGLES BY THE BEATLES (from page 131; as at the time of publishing)

'From Me to You' .... April 1963
'She Loves You' .... August 1963
'I Want to Hold Your Hand' .... December 1963
'Can't Buy Me Love' .... March 1964
'A Hard Day's Night' .... July 1964
'I Feel Fine' .... December 1964
'Ticket to Ride' .... April 1965
'Help!' .... July 1965
'We Can Work It Out' / 'Day Tripper' .... December 1965
'Paperback Writer' .... June 1966
'Yellow Submarine' / 'Eleanor Rigby' .... August 1966
'All You Need Is Love' .... July 1967
'Hello, Goodbye' .... November 1967
'Lady Madonna' .... March 1968
'Hey Jude' .... August 1968
'Get Back' .... April 1969
'Ballad of John and Yoko' .... May 1969

MISCELLANY XVIII (from page 133)

1. Winston Churchill; 2. They both appear as ghosts; 3. Lord Lucan; 4. 180;
5. Paisley; 6. Everest; 7. Impressionism; 8. Trafalgar Square*; 9. Red; 10. The London Underground; 11. Four; 12. The FBI; 13. Frisbee; 14. They have each given their name to a dish†; 15. Prince Charles; 16. Azerbaijan, Afghanistan; 17. *High Society*; 18. Deputy Dawg; 19. *Brigadoon*; 20. Earl Grey; 21. £250; 22. El Salvador and Honduras; 23. Etiquette; 24. 50p.

LARGE BODIES OF WATER (from page 137)

Pacific Ocean 60,061,000
Atlantic Ocean 29,638,000
Indian Ocean 26,469,500
Southern Ocean‡ 7,848,500

---

* Distances from London are traditionally measured from the King Charles statue on the south side of Trafalgar Square, the original site of the Charing Cross. The Charing Cross was erected by King Edward I in what was then the hamlet of Charing, in memorial to his wife, Eleanor of Castile. The cross marked the point where Eleanor's coffin stopped overnight on its funeral procession from Lincolnshire to Westminster Abbey, her final resting place. In all, Edward erected twelve 'Eleanor Crosses' along the route, of which three remain today (at Waltham Cross, Northampton and Geddington). The Charing Cross was destroyed in 1647 and replaced with the statue of King Charles I in 1675; a replica was later built outside Charing Cross station.
† Caesar salad, mornay sauce and pavlova.
‡ The Southern Ocean (previously called the Antarctic Ocean) was defined in 2000 by the International Hydrographic Organization. It is now the fourth largest ocean.

Arctic Ocean	5,427,000
South China Sea	1,148,500
Caribbean Sea	971,500
Mediterranean Sea	969,000
Bering Sea	873,000
Gulf of Mexico	582,000
Arabian Sea	578,500
Sea of Okhotsk	537,500
Sea of Japan	391,000
Hudson Bay	282,000
East China Sea	256,500
Andaman Sea	218,000
Black Sea	196,000
Red Sea	175,000
North Sea	165,000
Baltic Sea	147,500

Figures are in square miles and are approximate

LARGE ISLANDS (from page 139)

Greenland	840,000
New Guinea	312,000
Borneo	288,000
Madagascar	226,500
Baffin Island Canada	196,000
Sumatra Indonesia	183,000
Honshu Japan	88,000
Great Britain	84,500
Victoria Island Canada	84,000
Ellesmere Island Canada	76,000
Sulawesi Indonesia	73,000
South Island New Zealand	58,500
Java Indonesia	51,000
North Island New Zealand	44,500
Cuba	43,000
Newfoundland Canada	42,000
Luzon Philippines	40,500
Iceland	39,500
Mindanao Philippines	36,500
Novaga Zemlya Russia	35,000

Figures are in square miles and are approximate

ETYMOLOGY OF ROCK AND POP NAMES I (from page 141)

1. Duran Duran; 2. Beastie Boys; 3. Dead Kennedys; 4. LL Cool J; 5. Iron Maiden; 6. Level 42; 7. Jethro Tull; 8. Portishead; 9. Depeche Mode; 10. Bauhaus; 11. The Thompson Twins; 12. Crowded House; 13. Franz Ferdinand; 14. The Propellerheads; 15. The Rolling Stones; 16. The Psychedelic Furs; 17. 10,000 Maniacs; 18. Marillion; 19. Chubby Checker; 20. The Orb; 21. Deacon Blue; 22. T'Pau; 23. Kraftwerk; 24. Bachman Turner Overdrive.

JAMES BOND FILMS (from page 145; as at the time of publishing)

Dr No [SC]	1962
From Russia with Love [SC]	1963
Goldfinger [SC]	1964
Thunderball[*] [SC]	1965
You Only Live Twice [SC]	1967
On Her Majesty's Secret Service [GL]	1969
Diamonds Are Forever [SC]	1971
Live and Let Die [RM]	1973
The Man with the Golden Gun [RM]	1974
The Spy Who Loved Me [RM]	1977
Moonraker [RM]	1979
For Your Eyes Only [RM]	1981
Octopussy [RM]	1983
A View to a Kill [RM]	1985
The Living Daylights [TD]	1987
Licence to Kill [TD]	1989
Goldeneye [PB]	1995
Tomorrow Never Dies [PB]	1997
The World Is Not Enough [PB]	1999
Die Another Day [PB]	2002
Casino Royale [DC]	2006
Quantom of Solace [DC]	2008

Bonds indicated as [SC] Sean Connery [GL] George Lazenby [RM] Roger Moore [TD] Timothy Dalton [PB] Pierce Brosnan [DC] Daniel Craig

---

* *Thunderball* was originally written as a screenplay collaboration between Fleming, filmmaker Kevin McClory and writer Jack Whittingham but the project stalled and Fleming went ahead and released the story as a novel. The publication became the source of a lengthy legal dispute between McClory and Fleming, and McClory was eventually awarded the film rights to *Thunderball*. McClory wanted to make the film independently, but after the success of Sean Connery and the first two films of the Broccoli/Saltzman franchise, he was forced to co-operate and took a share of the profits when Thunderball was made. McClory remade *Thunderball* as *Never Say Never Again* in 1983.

MOTORWAYS* (from page 203)

M1 / M2 / M3 / M4 / M5 / M6 / M6 Toll / M8 / M9 / M10 / M11 / M18
M20 / M23 / M25 / M26 / M27 / M32 / M40 / M42 / M45 / M48 / M49
M50 / M53 / M54 / M55 / M56 / M57 / M58 / M60 / M61 / M62 / M65
M66 / M67 / M69 / M73 / M74 / M77 / M80 / M90 / M180 / M181 / M271
M275 / M602 / M606 / M621 / M876 / M898 / A1(M) / A3(M) / A38(M)
A48(M) / A57(M) / A58(M) / A64(M) / A66(M) / A74(M) / A167(M) / A194(M)
A308(M) / A329(M) / A404(M) / A601(M) / A627(M) / A823(M) / A6144(M)

NOVELTY RECORDS (from page 151)

1. Bob the Builder; 2. The Wurzels; 3. Rolf Harris; 4. Benny Hill; 5. St
Winifred's School Choir; 6. Cliff Richard and the Young Ones; 7. Joe Dolce Music
Theatre; 8. Lee Marvin; 9. Clive Dunn; 10. Gareth Gates featuring the Kumars;
11. Chef; 12. Spitting Image; 13. The Firm†; 14. The Timelords; 15. Chuck
Berry; 16. Peter Sellers and Sophia Loren; 17. Jive Bunny; 18. Lord Rockingham's
XI; 19. Telly Savalas; 20. Windsor Davies and Don Estelle; 21. Bombalurina;
22. Dickie Valentine; 23. The Pipes and Drums and Military Band of the Royal
Scots Dragoons; 24. Mike Sarne with Wendy Richard.

QUEEN HITS (from page 154; as at the time of publishing)

'Seven Seas of Rhye'	1974	(reaching no. 10)
'Killer Queen'	1974	(2)
'Bohemian Rhapsody'	1975	(1)
'You're My Best Friend'	1976	(7)
'Somebody to Love'	1976	(2)
'We Are the Champions'	1977	(2)
'We Will Rock You'	1977	(3)
'Don't Stop Me Now'	1979	(9)
'Crazy Little Thing Called Love'	1979	(2)
'Another One Bites the Dust'	1980	(7)

---

* Road numbering in Britain is based on zones created by the major roads
running outwards from London, numbered clockwise from the A1 to the A6 and
from Edinburgh numbered clockwise from A7 to A9. For example, Zone 1 is the
area east of the A1 and north of the Thames; roads originating in Zone 1 are
allocated numbers beginning with 1. Zone 3 is the area north and west of the A3
and south of the A4; roads originating in Zone 3 are allocated numbers beginning
with 3. Roads can be named with one, two, three or four digits. In general,
arterial roads carry fewer digits (although exceptions exist, such as the A303).
When motorways were first built, many of them followed the routes of existing A
roads and as a result this numbering system has been adopted by them to a large
extent.

† 'There's Klingons on the starboard bow / It's life, Jim, but not as we know it / It's
worse than that, he's dead, Jim / We come in peace, shoot to kill / Ye cannae
change the laws of physics'.

'Flash'	1980	(10)
'Under Pressure'*	1981	(1)
'Radio Ga Ga'	1984	(2)
'I Want To Break Free'	1984	(3)
'It's a Hard Life'	1984	(6)
'One Vision'	1985	(7)
'A Kind of Magic'	1986	(3)
'I Want It All'	1989	(3)
'Breakthru'	1989	(7)
'Innuendo'	1991	(1)
'These Are the Days of Our Lives'†	1991	(1)
'Heaven for Everyone'	1995	(2)
'A Winter's Tale'	1995	(6)
'Let Me Live'	1996	(9)

BUSY INTERNATIONAL AIRPORTS (from page 157; as at the time of publishing)

London, Heathrow	62,099,000
Paris, Charles de Gaulle	54,904,000
Amsterdam, Schiphol	47,693,000
Frankfurt	47,088,000
Hong Kong	46,305,000
Singapore, Changi	35,221,000
Tokyo, Narita	34,237,000
Dubai	33,481,000
Bangkok, Don Mueang	31,633,000
London, Gatwick	31,140,000
Seoul, Incheon	30,753,000
Madrid, Barajas	28,951,000
Munich	23,915,000
Dublin	22,338,000
New York, John F. Kennedy	21,543,000
London, Stansted	21,202,000
Taipei, Taoyuan	20,855,000
Zurich	20,047,000
Milan, Malpensa	19,975,000
Copenhagen	19,328,000
Rome, Leonardo da Vinci	19,024,000
Manchester	18,665,000
Vienna	18,083,000

---

* With David Bowie.

† The song was released as a double A-side with 'Bohemian Rhapsody' in December 1991 following the death of Freddie Mercury. 'Bohemian Rhapsody' became a Christmas number one a second time.

| Brussels | 17,738,000 |
| Toronto, Pearson | 17,711,000 |

International passengers for 2007; figures are approximate

LINKED MISCELLANY XII (from page 164)

1. Emily Davison; 2. Parsley; 3. Parker Brothers; 4. Tony Benn; 5. Florence; 6. Yogi;
7. The Thompson Twins; 8. Beef wellington; 9. Po; 10. The Soup Dragons.
The link is children's television characters*.

STOPS ON THE CIRCLE LINE† (from page 168)

King's Cross St Pancras / Farringdon / Barbican / Moorgate
Liverpool Street / Aldgate / Tower Hill
Monument / Cannon Street / Mansion House / Blackfriars
Temple / Embankment / Westminster / St James's Park
Victoria / Sloane Square / South Kensington
Gloucester Road / High Street Kensington / Notting Hill Gate
Bayswater / Paddington / Edgware Road
Baker Street / Great Portland Street / Euston Square

NOTIFIABLE DISEASES (from page 172)

Acute encephalitis / Acute poliomyelitis / Anthrax
Cholera / Diphtheria / Dysentery (amoebic or bacillary)
Food poisoning / Leprosy / Leptospirosis / Malaria
Measles / Meningitis / Meningococcal septicaemia
Mumps / Ophthalmia neonatorum / Paratyphoid fever
Plague / Rabies / Relapsing fever / Rubella
Scarlet fever / Smallpox / Tetanus / Tuberculosis
Typhoid fever / Typhus / Viral haemorrhagic fever
Viral hepatitis / Whooping cough / Yellow fever

CHARACTERS IN CHILDREN'S TELEVISION II (from page 175)

1. *The Simpsons*; 2. *Trumpton*‡; 3. *The Clangers*; 4. *Thunderbirds*; 5. *Scooby Doo*;
6. *Yogi Bear*; 7. *Captain Pugwash*§; 8. *Wacky Races*; 9. *Bod*; 10. *The Adventures of*

---

* Emily (*Bagpuss*), Parsley the Lion (*The Herbs*), Parker (*Thunderbirds*), Mr Benn,
Florence (*The Magic Roundabout*), Yogi Bear, the Thompson Twins (*Tintin*),
Wellington (*The Wombles*), Po (*Teletubbies*) and the Soup Dragon (*The Clangers*).
† Travelling clockwise from King's Cross St Pancras.
‡ The full crew, led by Captain Flack were: Pugh, Pugh, Barney McGrew, Cuthbert,
Dibble and Grubb. The firemen's names were thought up by scriptwriter Alison Prince;
originally there was only one Pugh but Freddie Phillips who wrote the music for the
programme suggested adding a second Pugh to give the line-up a better rhythmic sound.
§ The series spawned a well-known urban myth which attached smutty names to the
characters and in 1991 the programme's creator, John Ryan, won a settlement from
the *Guardian* and the *Scotsman*, who had unwittingly reported it as fact.

Tintin; 11. *Rugrats*; 12. *Thomas the Tank Engine*; 13. *Pipkins*; 14. *Camberwick Green*; 15. *Hong Kong Phooey*; 16. *Chorlton and the Wheelies*; 17. *Banana Splits*; 18. *Noggin the Nog*; 19. *Bob the Builder*; 20. *Inspector Gadget*; 21. *Cockleshell Bay*; 22. *Deputy Dawg*; 23. *Pigeon Street*; 24. *The Hair Bear Bunch*.

LONDON BOROUGHS (from page 178)

Barking and Dagenham / Barnet / Bexley / Brent
Bromley / Camden[I] / Corporation of London
Croydon / Ealing / Enfield / Greenwich[I]
Hackney[I] / Hammersmith and Fulham[I] / Haringey
Harrow / Havering / Hillingdon / Hounslow
Islington[I] / Kensington and Chelsea [IR]
Kingston-on-Thames[R] / Lambeth[I] / Lewisham[I]
Merton / Newham / Redbridge / Richmond-on-Thames
Southwark [I] / Sutton / Tower Hamlets [I]
Waltham Forest / Wandsworth[I] / Westminster[I]
[I] indicates Inner Borough [R] indicates Royal Borough

ACTORS APPEARING IN CARRY ON FILMS (from page 181)

Kenneth Williams	25 films
Charles Hawtrey	23
Joan Sims	23
Sid James	19
Kenneth Connor	16
Bernard Bresslaw	14
Hattie Jacques	14
Peter Butterworth	14
Jim Dale	11
Barbara Windsor	9
Peter Gilmore	8
Patsy Rowlands	7
Cyril Chamberlain	6
Julian Holloway	6
Terry Scott	6
Jack Douglas	5
Angela Douglas	4
Bill Maynard	4
Bill Owen	4
Dilys Laye	4
Eric Barker	4
Jacki Piper	4
Joan Hickson	4
Jon Pertwee	4
Leslie Phillips	4
Liz Fraser	4

WIT AND WISDOM III (from page 184)

1. 'I don't care to belong to a club . . .' .... Marx

2. 'If you don't like your job you don't strike . . .' .... Simpson

3. 'I was raised in the Jewish tradition . . .' .... Allen

4. 'Weaselling out of things is important to learn . . .' .... Simpson

5. 'Outside of a dog, a book is man's best friend . . .' .... Marx

6. 'It's not easy to juggle a pregnant wife . . .' .... Simpson

7. 'I failed to make the chess team . . .' .... Allen

8. 'What's the point of going out . . .' .... Simpson

9. 'He may look like an idiot and talk like an idiot . . .' .... Marx

10. 'Getting out of jury duty is easy . . .' .... Simpson

11. 'I have had a perfectly wonderful evening . . .' .... Marx

12. 'Money is better than poverty . . .' .... Allen

13. 'Either he's dead or my watch has stopped.' .... Marx

14. 'I like my beer cold, my TV loud . . .' .... Simpson

15. 'I think crime pays . . .' .... Allen

16. 'A child of five would understand this . . .' .... Marx

17. 'I took a speed-reading course . . .' .... Allen

18. 'I never forget a face, but in your case . . .' .... Marx

19. 'No one asked me to volunteer.' .... Simpson

20. 'How can I believe in God when just last week . . .' .... Allen

21. 'Those are my principles . . .' .... Marx

22. 'Why was I with her? She reminds me of you . . .' .... Marx

23. 'I don't want to achieve immortality . . .' .... Allen

24. 'What if we chose the wrong religion . . .' .... Simpson

LANDLOCKED COUNTRIES (from page 188)

Afghanistan / Andorra / Armenia / Austria / Azerbaijan^{Casp}

Belarus / Bhutan / Bolivia / Botswana / Burkina Faso

Burundi / Central African Republic / Chad / Czech Republic

Ethiopia / Hungary / Kazakhstan^{Casp} / Kyrgyzstan / Laos

Lesotho / Liechtenstein ^{DL} / Luxembourg / Macedonia / Malawi

Mali / Moldova / Mongolia / Nepal / Niger / Paraguay
Rwanda / San Marino / Serbia / Slovakia / Swaziland
Switzerland / Tajikistan / Turkmenistan^{Casp} / Uganda
Uzbekistan ^{DL} / Vatican City / Zambia / Zimbabwe
^{Casp} indicates coastline on the Caspian Sea ^{DL} indicates doubly landlocked*

MISCELLANY XXV (from page 193)

1. Alcohol†; 2. New; 3. Salmonella; 4. Jim Carrey; 5. *Madame Butterfly*;
6. Chancellor of the Exchequer‡; 7. Green; 8. North Sea oil fields; 9. Lemon and
melon; 10. The Bronx; 11. Captain Flint; 12. Swahili; 13. 30%; 14. Oliver Cromwell;
15. They are not members of the United Nations; 16. Seven; 17. Table-tennis table;
18. They form the lethal injection used to execute prisoners in the US; 19. Glasgow;
20. Six§; 21. Valkyries; 22. The fourth day; 23. Jebediah Springfield; 24. 9 p.m.

COUNTRIES IN AFRICA (from page 200)

Algeria / Angola / Benin / Botswana / Burkina Faso
Burundi / Cameroon / Cape Verde / Central African Republic
Chad / Comoros / Congo / Congo, Dem. Republic
Côte d'Ivoire / Djibouti / Egypt / Equatorial Guinea
Eritrea / Ethiopia / Gabon / Gambia / Ghana / Guinea
Guinea-Bissau / Kenya / Lesotho / Liberia / Libya
Madagascar / Malawi / Mali / Mauritania / Mauritius
Morocco / Mozambique / Namibia / Niger / Nigeria
Rwanda / São Tomé and Príncipe / Senegal / Seychelles
Sierra Leone / Somalia / South Africa / Sudan
Swaziland / Tanzania / Togo / Tunisia / Uganda
Western Sahara¶ / Zambia / Zimbabwe

---

* Bordered only by landlocked countries; two international borders must be crossed
in order to reach the nearest coastline.
† It was repealed by the Twenty-first Amendment.
‡ The Exchequer was founded in the court of Henry I in 1110 to become England's
first Government department. The financial administration of Henry's kingdom was
carried out by officials of the Lower Exchequer, who collected taxes from the sheriffs
of the counties of England, and the Upper Exchequer who audited the taxes
centrally. Taxes received were counted using 'tallies' – strips of wood on which
notches were carved to correspond to the payment. (The tally would be split in half
on receipt, the taxpayer keeping one half and the tax collector the other.) The name
of the Exchequer derives from French (the language of Norman government)
meaning 'chequered'. In medieval times, maths and accounting was often carried out
using a table with a chequered pattern on it (the European equivalent of the abacus).
In Henry's court, 'the exchequer' was a large chequered table cloth that could be
placed on a table and used for this purpose by Henry's accountants.
§ 6–0 up in a tie-break.
¶ Disputed territory.

CITIES IN THE UK (from page 203)

Aberdeen / Armagh / Bangor / Bath / Belfast
Birmingham / Bradford / Brighton and Hove / Bristol
Cambridge / Canterbury / Cardiff / Carlisle / Chester
Chichester / Coventry / Derby / Dundee / Durham
Edinburgh / Ely / Exeter / Glasgow / Gloucester
Hereford / Inverness / Kingston-upon-Hull / Lancaster
Leeds / Leicester / Lichfield / Lincoln / Lisburn / Liverpool
London / Londonderry / Manchester / Newcastle-upon-Tyne
Newport / Newry / Norwich / Nottingham / Oxford
Peterborough / Plymouth / Portsmouth / Preston / Ripon
Salford / Salisbury / Sheffield / Southampton / St Albans
St David's / Stirling / Stoke-on-Trent / Sunderland / Swansea
Truro / Wakefield / Wells* / Westminster / Winchester
Wolverhampton / Worcester / York

NOTORIOUS SHIPS I (from page 6)

1. *Titanic*; 2. *Rainbow Warrior*; 3. HMS *Bounty*; 4. HMS *Victory*; 5. *Mary Celeste*;
6. *Marchioness*; 7. *QEII*; 8. *Golden Hind*; 9. *Great Britain*; 10. *Lusitania*†;
11. *Endeavour*; 12. *The Flying Dutchman*; 13. HMS *Beagle*; 14. *Amoco Cadiz*;
15. *Canberra*; 16. *Tirpitz*; 17. *Kon-Tiki*; 18. *Nautilus*; 19. *Archimedes*; 20. *Calypso*;
21. HMS *Conqueror*; 22. *Yamato*; 23. *Orca*; 14. HMHS *Britannic*.

STOOGES (from page 9)

Larry / Moe / Curly

GOLF MAJORS (from page 12)

The Masters / The US Open
The Open / The US PGA Championship

CHARACTERS IN LITERATURE I (from page 14)

1. *The Hobbit; Lord of the Rings* (J.R.R. Tolkien); 2. *Gone With the Wind* (Margaret Mitchell); 3. *Pride and Prejudice* (Jane Austen); 4. *Twenty Thousand Leagues Under the Sea* (Jules Verne); 5. *Treasure Island* (Robert Louis Stevenson); 6. *Tarzan of the Apes* (Edgar Rice Burroughs); 7. *Catch-22* (Joseph Heller); 8. *Bridget Jones's Diary* (Helen Fielding); 9. *The Count of Monte Cristo* (Alexandre Dumas); 10. *Don Quixote* (Miguel de Cervantes); 11. *A Streetcar Named Desire* (Tennessee Williams); 12. *The Graduate* (Charles Webb); 13. *Sense and Sensibility* (Jane Austen); 14. *Brave New World* (Aldous Huxley); 15. *Persuasion* (Jane Austen); 16. *Middlemarch* (George

---

* The population of the city of Wells was unaffected by industrialisation and its population has remained static at around 10,000; its relative size has declined significantly since the Middle Ages.
† Many of the victims of the sinking were Americans; the event hastened the entry of the United States into the First World War.

Eliot); 17. *The Name of the Rose* (Umberto Eco); 18. *The Great Gatsby* (F. Scott Fitzgerald); 19. *Great Expectations* (Charles Dickens); 20. *Matilda* (Roald Dahl); 21. *Vanity Fair* (William Makepeace Thackeray); 22. *Alice's Adventures in Wonderland* (Lewis Carroll); 23. *A Confederacy of Dunces* (John Kennedy Toole); 24. *Shogun* (James Clavell).

FOOTBALL TEAMS STARTING AND ENDING WITH THE SAME LETTER (from page 20)

Aston Villa / Charlton Athletic
Liverpool / Northampton Town

THE GOOD LIFE (from page 22)

Tom Good .... Richard Briers
Barbara Good .... Felicity Kendal
Margo Leadbetter .... Penelope Keith
Jerry Leadbetter .... Paul Eddington

NICKNAMES OF PEOPLE I (from page 24)

1. Graham Taylor; 2. Jane Fonda; 3. Joan of Arc; 4. Elle Macpherson; 5. Dave Lee Travis; 6. Ian Botham; 7. Mohandas Gandhi; 8. Alan Freeman*; 9. Arnold Schwarzenegger; 10. Steve Davis; 11. Emma Bunton; 12. John McEnroe; 13. Eric Bristow†; 14. Mark Wahlberg; 15. Jim Morrison; 16. Charlie Parker; 17. Muhammad Ali; 18. John Wayne; 19. Marvin Hagler; 20. Graham Kerr; 21. Martha Jane Burke‡; 22. Bette Midler 23. William Perry; 24. Billie Holiday.

AUTOMATIC EUROVISION QUALIFIERS (from page 26)

France / Germany / Spain / UK

CLASSICAL ELEMENTS§ (from page 30)

Air / Earth / Fire / Water

---

* Alan Freeman made famous a piece called 'At the Sign of the Swingin' Cymbal' (written by Brian Fahey and revamped in 1970 by Brass Incorporated), which he used for his chart countdowns. He was also the voice of Brentford Nylons in the 1960s and 1970s.
† Five times World Darts champion, Eric Bristow uses 22gms Harrows darts.
‡ Martha Jane Burke was expelled from General George Crook's Black Hills force when an officer discovered she was a woman. Her nickname is thought to derive from her frontier lifestyle and her propensity to help people who were facing disaster.
§ In China, there were five classical elements: metal, wood, earth, fire and water. The five visible planets were associated with these: Venus (metal), Jupiter (wood), Saturn (earth), Mars (fire) and Mercury (water). The Moon represented Yin and the Sun represented Yang. These themes appear in the *I Ching*, a classical Chinese text.

ENTREPRENEURS I (from page 32)

1. Remington; 2. Amstrad; 3. Body Shop; 4. Apple computers; 5. Ben and Jerry's;
6. MGM; 7. Microsoft; 8. Yahoo; 9. Coca-Cola; 10. Amazon.com; 11. Sony;
12. Ikea; 13. Starbucks; 14. Sun Microsystems; 15. Penguin Books; 16. Kodak;
17. Nokia; 18. McDonald's; 19. Nike; 20. Google; 21. eBay; 22. General Motors;
23. Wal-Mart; 24. Oracle (computer software).

TRAVELING WILBURYS (from page 35)

Bob Dylan / George Harrison / Jeff Lynne
Roy Orbison / Tom Petty

SPICE GIRLS (from page 37)

Victoria Adams (now Beckham) .... Posh
Melanie Brown .... Scary
Emma Bunton .... Baby
Melanie Chisholm .... Sporty
Geri Halliwell .... Ginger

MISCELLANY V (from page 39)

1. *The Angel of the North*; 2. Clint Eastwood; 3. Beefeaters; 4. John Smith; 5. Red;
6. Rudyard Kipling; 7. Charlie Chaplin; 8. Opossum; 9. 'The Owl and the
Pussycat'; 10. 'It's Not Unusual'; 11. Richard Trevithick*; 12. Cyprus; 13. Derby,
St Leger, Two Thousand Guineas; 14. £100; 15. The Suez Canal; 16. Vitamin D;
17. The two atom bombs dropped on Japan; 18. Dynamo; 19. Captain Ahab
(*Moby-Dick*); 20. White; 21. The America's Cup; 22. Splodgenessabounds;
23. (Large) diamonds; 24. 218.

DISNEY THEME PARKS (from page 42; as at the time of publishing)

Disneyland Resort (California)
Walt Disney World Resort (Florida)
Tokyo Disney Resort
Disneyland Resort Paris
Hong Kong Disneyland Resort

---

* Richard Trevithick, a Cornish mining engineer, unveiled Penydarren, the first high
pressure steam locomotive, in 1804. In producing this engine, Trevithick included
many design features that were to remain unchanged throughout the age of steam.
His locomotive had smooth wheels; up until that point engineers had relied on
cogged wheels believing a smooth contact to give insufficient traction to haul the
engine. Although a gifted engineer, Trevithick was not a good businessman and it
was the Stephensons (George, whose Stockton and Darlington Railway was the
world's first, opening to the public in 1825, and his son Robert, who with his father
designed the Rocket and saw it reach a record speed of 38mph in 1829) and others
like them who made their fortunes from the new railways.

THE LADYKILLERS (from page 44)

Alec Guinness .... Professor Marcus
Cecil Parker .... The Major
Herbert Lom .... Louis
Peter Sellers .... Harry
Danny Green .... One-Round

PSEUDONYMS I (from page 46)

1. Jordan; 2. Andy Garcia; 3. Eminem; 4. Eric Clapton; 5. Fatboy Slim; 6. Jean-Claude Van Damme; 7. Marilyn Monroe; 8. Pelé; 9. Tiger Woods; 10. Boy George; 11. David Walliams; 12. Dido; 13. Fred Astaire; 14. George Michael; 15. John Wayne; 16. Seal; 17. Tina Turner; 18. Van Morrison; 19. Big Daddy; 20. Bob Dylan; 21. Buffalo Bill; 22. Cary Grant*; 23. Dirk Bogarde; 24. Pablo Picasso.

GREAT LAKES (from page 49)

Lake Superior† / Lake Michigan / Lake Huron
Lake Erie / Lake Ontario‡

VOCAL RANGES (from page 52)

Soprano / Mezzo-soprano / Contralto (or Alto)
Tenor / Baritone / Bass

CURRENCIES (from page 55)

1. Russia or Belarus; 2. Japan; 3. India, Pakistan or Sri Lanka; 4. Thailand; 5. Israel; 6. Lesotho, South Africa or Swaziland; 7. Bolivia; 8. Poland; 9. Turkey, Malta or Cyprus; 10. Brazil; 11. Indonesia; 12. Iceland or Sweden; 13. Denmark or Norway; 14. China§; 15. Venezuela; 16. Guatemala; 17. North Korea or South Korea; 18. Albania; 19. Ecuador; 20. Latvia; 21. Morocco; 22. Costa Rica; 23. Peru; 24. Mongolia.

ROYAL RESIDENCES (from page 58)

Buckingham Palace, London .... Official
Windsor Castle .... Official
Palace of Holyroodhouse, Edinburgh .... Official
Hillsborough Castle, County Down, Northern Ireland .... Official
Sandringham House, Norfolk .... Private
Balmoral Castle, Scotland .... Private

---

* Archibald Leach was the name of the character played by John Cleese in *A Fish Called Wanda*.

† Lake Superior is the largest freshwater lake in the world (by surface area).

‡ Lake Ontario is at the lowest elevation of all the Great Lakes. Water travels to Lake Ontario via the Niagara Falls.

§ In spoken Chinese the yuan is pronounced 'kuai'. Chinese currency is often referred to as renminbi (RMB).

NOVELS BY JANE AUSTEN* (from page 61)

LINKED MISCELLANY V (from page 65)

1. The Old Bailey; 2. 'Rockin' All Over the World'; 3. Forty days; 4. 4 July;
5. David Sole; 6. Carrie Fisher; 7. Viking 1; 8. Portland Bill; 9. Trafalgar Square†;
10. *The Hebrides Overture.*

The link is British Shipping Zones‡.

AFRICAN COUNTRIES BEGINNING WITH 'M' (from page 68)

Madagascar / Malawi / Mali / Mauritania
Mauritius / Morocco / Mozambique

WONDERS OF THE ANCIENT WORLD (from page 70)

The Pyramids of Giza§
The Hanging Gardens of Babylon
The Temple of Artemis
The Mausoleum of Halicarnassus
The Colossus of Rhodes
The Pharos of Alexandria
The Statue of Zeus at Olympia

FIRST LINES OF POP SONGS II (from page 72)

1. 'Stairway to Heaven' (Led Zeppelin); 2. 'Crazy' (Gnarls Barkley); 3. 'Whiter
Shade of Pale' (Procol Harum); 4. 'The Joker' (Steve Miller Band); 5. 'Gangsta's
Paradise' (Coolio featuring LV); 6. 'Thriller' (Michael Jackson); 7. 'Is There
Something I Should Know?' (Duran Duran); 8. 'I Got You Babe' (Sonny and Cher);
9. 'Get the Party Started' (Pink); 10. 'Once in a Lifetime' (Talking Heads);
11. 'Honky Tonk Woman' (Rolling Stones); 12. 'Crazy in Love' (Beyonce);

---

* Dates of publications are supplied. *Northanger Abbey* and *Persuasion* were published
posthumously.

† The sculpture was exhibited on the empty 'Fourth Plinth'.

‡ Bailey, Rockall, Forties, Forth, Sole, Fisher, Viking, Portland, Trafalgar and
Hebrides.

§ The pyramids are the only one of the Seven Wonders that still exists today. The
Great Pyramid at Giza took twenty years to construct and was completed around
2600BC. The pyramid, which stands 137 metres tall, was the world's tallest structure
for nearly 4,000 years and was only superseded during the cathedral-building era of
medieval Europe.

13. 'Don't You Want Me' (Human League); 14. 'Comfortably Numb' (Pink Floyd); 15. 'Video Killed the Radio Star' (The Buggles); 16. 'Get It On' (T-Rex); 17. 'Stuck in the Middle With You' (Stealers Wheel); 18. 'Walk This Way' (Run DMC); 19. 'Groovejet (If This Ain't Love)' (Spiller); 20. 'Handbags and Gladrags' (Stereophonics); 21. 'Dead Ringer for Love' (Meatloaf); 22. 'I Should Be So Lucky' (Kylie Minogue); 23. 'Cry Me a River' (Justin Timberlake); 24. 'Big Mouth Strikes Again' (The Smiths).

WONDERS OF THE NATURAL WORLD (from page 76)

The Grand Canyon

Mount Everest

The Harbour of Rio de Janeiro

The Great Barrier Reef

Victoria Falls

Paricutin Volcano

The Northern Lights (*Aurora Borealis*)

CHART-TOPPING SINGLES BY KYLIE MINOGUE (from page 78; as at the time of publishing)

'I Should Be So Lucky' .... January 1988

'Especially For You'* .... December 1988

'Hand on Your Heart' .... May 1989

'Tears on My Pillow' .... January 1990

'Spinning Around' .... July 2000

'Can't Get You Out of My Head' .... September 2001

'Slow' .... November 2003

CHARACTERS IN LITERATURE II (from page 80)

1. *A Christmas Carol* (Charles Dickens); 2. *The Hitchhiker's Guide to the Galaxy* (Douglas Adams); 3. *Tess of the d'Urbervilles* (Thomas Hardy); 4. *Pygmalion* (George Bernard Shaw); 5. *Watership Down* (Richard Adams); 6. *Jane Eyre* (Charlotte Brontë); 7. *Emma* (Jane Austen); 8. *The Mystery of Edwin Drood* (Charles Dickens); 9. *To Kill a Mockingbird* (Harper Lee); 10. *Pride and Prejudice* (Jane Austen); 11. *Animal Farm* (George Orwell); 12. *A Room with a View* (E.M. Forster); 13. *Master and Commander* (Patrick O'Brian); 14. *Treasure Island* (Robert Louis Stevenson); 15. *Breakfast at Tiffany's* (Truman Capote); 16. *Gormenghast* novels (Mervyn Peake); 17. *Lolita* (Vladimir Nabokov); 18. *His Dark Materials* trilogy (Philip Pullman); 19. *David Copperfield* (Charles Dickens); 20. *War and Peace* (Leo Tolstoy); 21. *To Kill a Mockingbird* (Harper Lee); 22. *Tom Sawyer* and *Huckleberry Finn* (Mark Twain); 23. *Anna Karenina* (Leo Tolstoy); 24. *Jeeves and Wooster* books† (P.G. Wodehouse).

---

* With Jason Donovan.

† In *Right Ho, Jeeves*, Bertie offers his opinion that Gussie looks like a fish. Jeeves confirms that there is 'something of the piscine' about him.

IVY LEAGUE (from page 82)

Brown / Columbia / Cornell / Dartmouth
Harvard / Pennsylvania / Princeton / Yale

RESERVOIR DOGS (from page 85)

Mr White . . . . Harvey Keitel
Mr Orange . . . . Tim Roth
Mr Blonde . . . . Michael Madsen
Mr Pink . . . . Steve Buscemi
Mr Brown . . . . Quentin Tarantino
Mr Blue . . . . Edward Bunker
Joe Cabot . . . . Lawrence Tierney
'Nice Guy' Eddie Cabot . . . . Chris Penn

MISCELLANY XII (from page 88)

1. Nepotism; 2. 'A dish best served cold'; 3. The Taj Mahal; 4. The Pennine Way;
5. David Copperfield; 6. Six; 7. *Frasier*; 8. Atlantic Ocean; 9. Mount Everest;
10. St Paul's Cathedral; 11. A New York ticker tape parade; 12. Derbyshire;
13. The Millennium Stadium; 14. Sherlock Holmes; 15. Tungsten; 16. Bishop*;
17. Annie Nightingale; 18. Mikhail Gorbachev; 19. Albus Dumbledore; 20. The
War of American Independence; 21. Set both of the hourglass timers running.
When the two-minute hourglass has run out, start cooking the egg. When the five-
minute hourglass has run out, stop cooking the egg; 22. Haricot beans;
23. Elephant; 24. £45.

LOSING WORLD CUP FINALISTS (from page 95; as at the time of publishing)

Argentina 1930, 1990
Brazil 1950, 1998
Czechoslovakia 1934, 1962
France 2006
Germany / West Germany 1966, 1982, 1986, 2002
Hungary 1938, 1954
Italy 1970, 1994
Netherlands 1974, 1978
Sweden 1958

COUNTRIES WITH FOUR-LETTER NAMES (from page 97)

Chad / Cuba / Fiji / Iran / Iraq
Laos / Mali / Oman / Peru / Togo

POLITICAL QUOTATIONS (from page 100)

1. Margaret Thatcher; 2. Bill Clinton; 3. John F. Kennedy; 4. Martin Luther King;
5. Richard Nixon; 6. George H.W. Bush; 7. Harold Wilson; 8. Winston Churchill;

---

* A crosier is a bishop's crook.

9. Horatio Nelson*; 10. John F. Kennedy; 11. Julius Caesar†; 12. Karl Marx;
13. Abraham Lincoln; 14. Queen Elizabeth I; 15. Winston Churchill; 16. Abraham
Lincoln; 17. Harold Macmillan; 18. Henry II; 19. Neville Chamberlain; 20. Harry
S. Truman; 21. Henry Kissinger; 22. Mao Tse-tung; 23. Nikita Khrushchev;
24. Oliver Cromwell.

WEALTHIEST FOOTBALL CLUBS (from page 102; as at the time of publishing)

Real Madrid / Barcelona / Juventus
Manchester United / AC Milan
Chelsea / Inter Milan / Bayern Munich
Arsenal / Liverpool

MINERALS (from page 105)

Calcium / Chromium / Copper / Fluorine / Iodine / Iron
Magnesium / Phosphorus / Potassium / Sodium / Zinc

FORMS OF ADDRESS (from page 109)

1. Reverend; 2. Father; 3. Sir [first name]; 4. Your Honour; 5. Your Majesty;
6. Ma'am; 7. Your Royal Highness; 8. Sir; 9. Your Excellency; 10. Your Holiness;
11. Ma'am; 12. Your Grace; 13. My Lord or Your Lordship; 14. My Lord; 15. Sir;
16. Madam; 17. Your Grace; 18. Madam; 19. Your Grace; 20. Your Eminence;
21. My Lord; 22. My Lord; 23. My Lady or Your Ladyship; 24. Venerable Sir.

ORIGINAL MEMBERS OF THE FOOTBALL LEAGUE (from page 111)

Accrington / Aston Villa / Blackburn Rovers
Bolton Wanderers / Burnley / Derby County
Everton / Notts County / Preston North End / Stoke
West Bromwich Albion / Wolverhampton Wanderers

DICTATORS (from page 114)

1. Adolf Hitler; 2. Joseph Stalin; 3. Saddam Hussein; 4. Fidel Castro; 5. Robert
Mugabe; 6. Idi Amin; 7. Benito Mussolini; 8. Pol Pot; 9. Mao Tse-tung;
10. Ayatollah Khomeini; 11. Francisco Franco; 12. Slobodan Milosevic;

---

* Nelson's famous nine-word signal was hoisted from HMS *Victory*, flagship of the
British fleet, at 11.30 on the morning of 21 October 1805, as it sailed into action
against the combined fleets of France and Spain at the Battle of Trafalgar. Nelson's
intention had been to express his trust in his men but the word 'expects' was rather
easier to signal than the word 'confides' and was substituted by Nelson's signal
officer. The signal was therefore given a rather harder meaning (that it was
unacceptable for any man to do anything but his duty) than the vote of confidence
that Nelson had intended.

† 'Veni, vidi, vici.' Caesar said this after the Battle of Zela and the defeat of
Pharnaces II of Pontus.

13. Augusto Pinochet; 14. Manuel Noriega; 15. Kim Jong-il; 16. Nicolae Ceausescu*; 17. Ferdinand Marcos; 18. Josip Tito (Marshall Tito); 19. Haile Selassie; 20. Laurent Kabila; 21. Charles Taylor; 22. George Speight; 23. Hastings Banda†; 24. Sani Abacha‡.

EUROZONE (from page 116; as at the time of publishing)

Austria / Belgium / Cyprus / Finland / France / Germany / Greece / Ireland
Italy / Luxembourg / Malta / Netherlands / Portugal / Slovakia / Slovenia / Spain

COUNTRIES IN SOUTH AMERICA (from page 119)

Argentina / Bolivia / Brazil / Chile / Colombia
Ecuador / French Guiana / Guyana / Paraguay
Peru / Suriname / Uruguay / Venezuela

AMERICANISMS II (from page 122)

1. Candy; 2. Elevator; 3. Potato chips; 4. Gas; 5. Resumé; 6. Checkers; 7. Closet; 8. Drapes; 9. Faucet; 10. Freeway; 11. Line; 12. Sidewalk; 13. Subway; 14. Tuxedo; 15. Zucchini; 16. Jelly; 17. Tic-tac-toe; 18. Yam; 19. Teller; 20. Icebox; 21. Suspenders; 22. Stroller; 23. Parakeet; 24. Mortician.

HOST COURSES OF THE OPEN CHAMPIONSHIP (from page 125)

St Andrews§[R] / Muirfield[R] / Royal St George's[R]
Royal Liverpool¶[R] / Royal Troon[R] /Royal Lytham & St Annes[R]
Carnoustie[R] / Royal Birkdale[R] / Westin Turnberry Resort[R]
Prestwick / Musselburgh / Royal Cinque Ports
Prince's / Royal Portrush

[R] indicates course in current rotation

FILMS BY DAVID LEAN (from page 128)

In Which We Serve 1942
This Happy Breed 1944

---

* Ceausescu was the only communist leader to suffer a violent death as a result of the fall of the Soviet Union in 1989. He was executed, along with his wife Elena, by firing squad.

† Banda managed to accumulate $320m-worth of personal assets during his rule, equivalent to about one-fifth of his country's GDP.

‡ It is thought that Abacha, who died of a heart attack at the age of fifty-four, had siphoned $3bn of public funds into private bank accounts much of which ended up in the control of family members. In 1999, Abacha's eldest son Mohammad was arrested for fraud, money laundering, embezzlement and murder, but charges were dropped in exchange for the return of 80% of the family's assets. The Abacha family is still thought to be worth at least $100m.

§ The St Andrews Old Course is the oldest golf course in the world, founded c.1500.

¶ Often referred to as 'Hoylake'.

^{O} indicates Oscar for Best Director

LATIN PHRASES I (from page 131)

1. Ante meridiem (a.m.); 2. Anno Domini* (AD); 3. Post scriptum (PS); 4. Quod erat demonstrandum (QED); 5. Status quo; 6. Per annum; 7. Coitus interruptus; 8. Id est (i.e.); 9. Alma mater; 10. Prima facie; 11. Circa (*c.*); 12. Ad hoc; 13. Per pro (pp.); 14. Exempli gratia (e.g.); 15. Confer (cf.); 16. Annus mirabilis; 17. Magnum opus; 18. Quid pro quo; 19. Bona fide; 20. De facto; 21. Primus inter pares†; 22. Et alii (et al.); 23. In flagrante delicto; 24. Obiter dictum.

STORIES BY ROALD DAHL (from page 134)

---

* AD is an abbreviation of 'Anni Domini Nostri Jesu Christi' meaning 'The Years of Our Lord Jesus Christ'. The Latin for the epoch prior to this – 'Ante Christum Natum' ('Before the birth of Christ') has been dropped in favour of Before Christ (BC). The religiously neutral terms CE ('Common Era' or 'Christian Era') and BCE ('Before the Common Era) may alternatively be used for the periods after and before year 1 of the Gregorian calendar.

† Used to describe the leader of a republic, the phrase was employed as a piece of political spin by the first Roman emperors to give the impression they were not dictators (which they were).

POPULAR LANGUAGES* (from page 137)

Mandarin Chinese / English / Spanish / Hindi and Urdu / Arabic†
Portuguese / Bengali / Russian / Japanese / German
Wu Chinese / Javanese / Korean / Punjabi / Telugu‡
French / Marathi§ / Tamil / Italian / Yue Chinese¶

PSEUDONYMS II (from page 139)

1. Cher; 2. Engelbert Humperdinck; 3. Ernie Wise; 4. George Orwell; 5. Jennifer Aniston; 6. Lenin; 7. Muhammad Ali; 8. Ringo Starr; 9. Audrey Hepburn; 10. Cilla Black; 11. Demi Moore; 12. Elton John; 13. George Eliot; 14. Greta Garbo; 15. Prince; 16. Sophia Loren; 17. Twiggy; 18. Walter Matthau; 19. Bing Crosby; 20. Bruce Lee; 21. Calamity Jane; 22. Charlie Sheen; 23. Michael Caine; 24. Vera Lynn.

WEALTHY COUNTRIES (from page 141)

Luxembourg	$118,045
Qatar	$106,460
Norway	$102,525
Denmark	$67,387
Switzerland	$67,379
Ireland	$64,660
Iceland	$60,122
United Arab Emirates	$56,667
Sweden	$55,624

---

* Note that estimates for the number of language speakers are unreliable because (i) quality of data sources varies from country to country; (ii) treatment of dialects can be ambiguous (Hindu and Urdu, treated here as a single language, could be separated); (iii) treatment of mother tongue, first-language and second-language speakers is often ambiguous; (iv) figures changes rapidly as populations grow. The languages listed here are accepted by most sources as the twenty most widely spoken and are spoken by roughly three-quarters of the world's population.

† Arabic has twenty-seven different varieties.

‡ Spoken in the Andhra Pradesh area of India.

§ Spoken in the Maharashtra area of India.

¶ Cantonese.

Finland	$54,578
Netherlands	$54,445
Austria	$52,159
Australia	$50,150
Belgium	$49,430
France	$48,012
Canada	$47,073
United States	$47,025
Germany	$46,499
Kuwait	$46,397
United Kingdom	$45,681

Figures for per capita Gross Domestic Product from the IMF, 2008

ROLLING STONES HITS (from page 145; as at the time of publishing)

'Not Fade Away'	1964 (reaching number 3)
'It's All Over Now'	1964 (1)
'Little Red Rooster'	1964 (1)
'The Last Time'	1965 (1)
'(I Can't Get No) Satisfaction'	1965 (1)
'Get Off My Cloud'	1965 (1)
'Nineteenth Nervous Breakdown'	1966 (2)
'Paint It Black'	1966 (1)
'Have You Seen Your Mother Baby Standing in the Shadow'	1966 (5)
'Let's Spend the Night Together' / 'Ruby Tuesday'	1967 (3)
'We Love You' / 'Dandelion'	1967 (8)
'Jumping Jack Flash'	1968 (1)
'Honky Tonk Women'	1969 (1)
'Brown Sugar'	1971 (2)
'Tumbling Dice'	1972 (5)
'Angie'	1973 (5)
'It's Only Rock and Roll'	1974 (10)
'Fool to Cry'	1976 (6)
'Miss You' / 'Far Away Eyes'	1978 (3)
'Emotional Rescue'	1980 (9)
'Start Me Up'	1981 (7)

MISCELLANY XX (from page 148)

1. Iceland; 2. Diamonds; 3. They are palindromes; 4. Yuri Geller; 5. *The Times*; 6. The title character does not appear in the play; 7. 'Bohemian Rhapsody' and 'A Whiter Shade of Pale'; 8. Houston*; 9. Thirteen and three-quarters; 10. Freelance; 11. Wyoming; 12. Charles Bronson; 13. Aberdeen; 14. With vinegar and brown paper; 15. Directly beneath it; 16. Four boys, three girls; 17. Italy and Switzerland; 18. Charles II; 19. Leylandii; 20. Their

---

* 'Houston, Tranquillity Base here. The Eagle has landed.'

fans sing 'You'll Never Walk Alone'; 21. Cancer*; 22. Thirty-six; 23. Pulmonary artery; 24. Forty-five.

ENGLAND FOOTBALL CAPTAINS (from page 152; as at the time of publishing)

Billy Wright	90 appearances as captain
Bobby Moore	90
Bryan Robson	65
David Beckham	58
Alan Shearer	34
Kevin Keegan	31
Emlyn Hughes	23
Robert Crompton	22
Johnny Haynes	22
Eddie Hapgood	21
John Terry	20
David Platt	19
Gary Lineker	18
Norman Bailey	15
Gilbert Smith	15
Jimmy Armfield	15
Peter Shilton	15
Tony Adams	15
Vivian Woodward	14
George Hardwick	13
Roy Goodall	12
Ray Wilkins	10
Stuart Pearce	10

GREEK ALPHABET (from page 155)

α Alpha / β Beta / γ Gamma / δ Delta / ε Epsilon / ζ Zeta / η Eta / θ Theta ι Iota / κ Kappa / λ Lambda / μ Mu / ν Nu / ξ Xi / ο Omicron / π Pi† / ρ Rho σ Sigma / τ Tau / υ Upsilon / φ Phi / χ Chi / ψ Psi / ω Omega

---

* St Swithin's Day falls on 15 July. According to folklore: 'St Swithun's day if thou dost rain / For forty days it will remain / St Swithun's day if thou be fair / For forty days 'twill rain na mair.'

† The ratio of the circumference of a circle to its diameter is represented by Pi and is equal to 3.1415926535 8979323846 2643383279 5028841971 6939937510 5820974944 5923078164 0628620899 8628034825 3421170679 (to 100 decimal places). Mathemat-icians describe Pi as an irrational number, that is, a number that cannot be expressed as the ratio of any two integers. This was an irksome fact to the State of Indiana in 1897; so much so that legislation was drafted (based on the work of local mathematician Edward J. Goodwin) setting Pi alternative values of 3.2, 3.23 and 4. The bill passed its first reading, but, fortunately for Indiana, was held up at the second reading largely due to remarks made by a passing maths professor, C.A. Waldo, questioning the mental health of the bill's authors.

RECENT HISTORY III (from page 158)

1. 2004; 2. 2005; 3. 2002; 4. 1988; 5. 1992; 6. 1990; 7. 1977; 8. 1989; 9. 1940;
10. 1979; 11. 1980; 12. 1953; 13. 1981; 14. 1943; 15. 1983; 16. 1982; 17. 1912;
18. 1917; 19. 1929; 20. 1948; 21. 1946; 22. 1956; 23. 1922; 24. 1924.

COUNTRIES WITH FIVE-LETTER NAMES (from page 165)

Benin / Chile / China / Congo / Egypt / Gabon
Ghana / Haiti / India / Italy / Japan / Kenya
Korea* / Libya / Malta / Nauru / Nepal
Niger / Palau / Qatar / Samoa / Spain
Sudan / Syria / Tonga / Yemen

FORMULA ONE WORLD CHAMPIONS (from page 168; as at the time of publishing)

Michael Schumacher	1994, 1995, 2000, 2001, 2002, 2003, 2004
Juan Manuel Fangio	1951, 1954, 1955, 1956, 1957
Alain Prost	1985, 1986, 1989, 1993
Jack Brabham	1959, 1960, 1966
Jackie Stewart	1969, 1971, 1973
Niki Lauda	1975, 1977, 1984
Nelson Piquet	1981, 1983, 1987
Ayrton Senna†	1988, 1990, 1991
Alberto Ascari	1952, 1953
Graham Hill	1962, 1968
Jim Clark	1963, 1965
Emerson Fittipaldi	1972, 1974
Mika Hakkinen	1998, 1999
Fernando Alonso^C	2005, 2006
Giuseppe 'Nino' Farina	1950
Mike Hawthorn	1958
Phil Hill	1961
John Surtees	1964
Denny Hulme	1967
Jochen Rindt‡	1970
James Hunt	1976
Mario Andretti	1978
Jody Scheckter	1979

---

* Korea is actually divided into North Korea and South Korea. There could also be
an argument for the inclusion of East Timor and the Czech Republic in the list.
† Senna died on 1 May 1994 after a experiencing a mechanical failure while leading
the San Marino Grand Prix. Senna's Williams hit a concrete wall virtually head on at
136 mph after his steering failed at the exit of the Tamburello corner at Imola.
‡ Rindt won the title posthumously after suffering a fatal crash on the Parabolica at
Monza in the Italian Grand Prix.

Alan Jones	1980
Keke Rosberg	1982
Nigel Mansell	1992
Damon Hill	1996
Jacques Villeneuve	1997
Kimi Raikkonen[C]	2007
Lewis Hamilton[C]	2008

[C] indicates currently driving

CATCHPHRASES II (from page 172)

1. Oliver Hardy; 2. Vic Reeves; 3. Michelle of the Resistance (*'Allo 'Allo!*); 4. Fox Mulder (*The X-Files*); 5. Shaggy (*Scooby Doo*); 6. Jim Trott (*The Vicar of Dibley*); 7. Roy Walker (*Catchphrase*); 8. Frankie Howerd; 9. Joan Rivers; 10. Mike Reid (*Runaround*); 11. Harold Steptoe (*Steptoe and Son*); 12. Bluebottle (*The Goon Show*); 13. Alf Garnett (*Till Death Us Do Part*); 14. Papa Lazarou (*The League of Gentlemen*); 15. Jack Regan (*The Sweeney*); 16. Eric Morecambe*; 17. C.J. (*The Fall and Rise of Reginald Perrin*); 18. Arnold Rimmer (*Red Dwarf*); 19. Lorraine Chase; 20. Bender Bending Rodriguez (*Futurama*); 21. Arnold Jackson (*Diff'rent Strokes*); 22. Arthur Askey; 23. Julia Lang (*Listen with Mother*); 24. George Dixon (*Dixon of Dock Green*).

THAMES CROSSINGS (from page 175)

Queen Elizabeth II†	Road bridge
Tower	Road bridge
London‡	Road bridge
Cannon Street	Railway bridge
Southwark	Road bridge
Millennium	Footbridge
Blackfriars	Railway bridge
Blackfriars	Road bridge
Waterloo	Road bridge
Hungerford§	Railway bridge
Hungerford	Footbridge
Westminster	Road bridge
Lambeth	Road bridge

---

* Eric would then reply 'Rubbish!' through clenched teeth and give the appearance of it being spoken by a nearby inanimate object.

† Built to carry the clockwise carriageway of the M25; the Dartford tunnel carries the anti-clockwise carriageway.

‡ London Bridge has been rebuilt many times, most recently in 1973. The old bridge was purchased by Robert McCulloch for $2.4m and moved to Lake Havasu, Arizona, where it was opened in 1973. It has been claimed that McCulloch mistakenly thought he was purchasing the more spectacular Tower Bridge but he has always denied this.

§ Serving Charing Cross station.

Vauxhall	Road bridge
Grosvenor*	Railway bridge
Chelsea	Road bridge
Albert	Road bridge
Battersea	Road bridge
Battersea	Railway bridge
Wandsworth	Road bridge
Putney	Railway bridge
Putney	Road bridge
Hammersmith	Road bridge
Barnes	Railway and foot bridge
Chiswick	Road bridge
Kew	Railway bridge
Kew	Road bridge
Richmond Lock	Footbridge
Twickenham	Road bridge
Richmond	Railway bridge
Richmond	Road bridge
Teddington Lock†	Footbridge

OFFICER RANKS IN THE BRITISH MILITARY (from page 178)

Royal Navy	Royal Air Force	Army
Admiral of the Fleet	Marshal of the RAF	Field-Marshal
Admiral	Air Chief Marshal	General
Vice-Admiral	Air Marshal	Lt-General
Rear-Admiral	Air Vice Marshal	Major-General
Commodore	Air Commodore	Brigadier
Captain	Group Captain	Colonel
Commander	Wing Commander	Lt-Colonel
Lt-Commander	Squadron Leader	Major
Lieutenant	Flight Lieutenant	Captain
Sub-Lieutenant	Flying Officer	Lieutenant
Midshipman	Pilot Officer	2nd Lieutenant

LINKED MISCELLANY XIII (from page 182)

1. Brazil; 2. The Hunter; 3. WAGs (wives and girlfriends); 4. The Mission; 5. Jacqueline Kennedy; 6. *Casino Royale*; 7. Heat; 8. Cape Town; 9. A driver; 10. A bull market.
The link is Robert De Niro films‡.

---

* Serving Victoria station.

† Teddington Lock marks the boundary between the jurisdiction of the National Rivers Authority and the Port of London Authority. Beyond Teddington Lock to the sea, the Thames is tidal.

‡ *Brazil, The Deer Hunter, Wag the Dog, The Mission, Jackie Brown, Casino, Heat, Cape Fear, Taxi Driver* and *Raging Bull.*

ROYAL CONSORTS (from page 185)

Matilda of Flanders	married to William I
Matilda of Scotland	Henry I
Adeliza of Louvain	Henry I
Matilda of Boulogne	Stephen
Eleanor of Aquitaine	Henry II
Berengaria of Navarre	Richard I
Isabella of Angoulême	John
Eleanor of Provence	Henry III
Eleanor of Castile	Edward I
Margaret of France	Edward I
Isabella of France*	Edward II
Philippa of Hainault	Edward III
Anne of Bohemia	Richard II
Isabella of Valois	Richard II
Joanna of Navarre	Henry IV
Catherine of Valois	Henry V
Margaret of Anjou	Henry VI
Elizabeth Woodville	Edward IV
Anne Neville	Richard III
Elizabeth of York	Henry VII
Catherine of Aragon	Henry VIII
Anne Boleyn	Henry VIII
Jane Seymour	Henry VIII
Anne of Cleves	Henry VIII

* Isabella of France was nicknamed the 'She-Wolf of France'. Isabella became disenchanted with her husband, Edward II, who was in the habit of bestowing titles and favours on attractive young men in his court. While on a diplomatic mission to France, Isabella was seduced by Roger Mortimer, a charismatic character who had recently escaped from the Tower of London and was living in exile. The pair raised an army to take the Crown from Edward, and, such was the King's lack of popularity, faced very little opposition in doing so. Edward found himself with no allies and, forced to flee, was eventually captured on 16 November 1326 and made to suffer the humiliation of deposition and imprisonment in Berkeley Castle, while his teenage son was crowned Edward III. With the new king still a minor, Isabella had effectively claimed the control of the realm for herself, as she and Mortimer ruled the country as regents. The following year the pair arranged the murder of the former king while he was still a prisoner at Berkeley. (An account written thirty years later attests to the use of a red-hot iron in the grisly killing.) Isabella's fortunes changed for the worse in 1330, when her son, Edward III, turned eighteen and in a deliberate act to assert his independence had Mortimer sent to the Tower of London and executed without trial. Isabella was sent to Castle Rising in Norfolk where she was forced to remain for the rest of her life. She died in 1358. Her liaison with William Wallace, as depicted in the film *Braveheart*, is fictional.

AMERICAN PRESIDENTS (from page 188)

---

* Contemporary accounts tell us Caroline was fat, vulgar, promiscuous and in possession of a striking body odour. The Prince of Wales, the future King George IV, was a heavy drinker, a womaniser and generally considered to be a national disgrace. The match between George and Caroline had been arranged on the insistence of Parliament which had grown weary of scandal and the cost of supporting the Prince (by 1795 George had not only married secretly and illegally, he had run up gambling debts of over £500,000 – an astronomical sum for the time). The couple first met only three days before the wedding ceremony, and it seems that George spent the intervening period drinking brandy; he collapsed on their wedding night in a stupor. George refused to change his womanising ways and Caroline consoled herself with ever more brazen and scandalous behaviour. She took off on a tour of Europe during which she had an affair with an Italian manservant and had a habit of wearing see-through clothes, unbecoming of a woman of her figure let alone the future Queen of England. Sadly, in 1818, their daughter, Charlotte, died and George lost his heir. George pressed for a divorce and lobbied Parliament to grant it on the grounds of Caroline's adultery, determined that she should not become Queen. But public opinion favoured Caroline over the widely loathed Prince and the bill was defeated. In spite of this, George had her barred from his coronation in 1821. She died nineteen days later and was buried in Brunswick. On her coffin were inscribed the words 'Caroline the Injured Queen of England'.

John Quincy Adams ^{DR} 1825–9
Andrew Jackson ^{Dem} 1829–37
Martin Van Buren ^{Dem} 1837–41
William Henry Harrison ^{Wg} 1841
John Tyler ^{Wg} 1841–5
James K. Polk ^{Dem} 1845–9
Zachary Taylor ^{Wg} 1849–50
Millard Fillmore ^{Wg} 1850–3
Franklin Pierce ^{Dem} 1853–7
James Buchanan ^{Dem} 1857–61
Abraham Lincoln ^{Rep} 1861–5
Andrew Johnson ^{DNU Imp} 1865–9
Ulysses S. Grant ^{Rep} 1869–77
Rutherford B. Hayes ^{Rep} 1877–81
James A. Garfield ^{Rep} 1881
Chester A. Arthur ^{Rep} 1881–1885
Grover Cleveland ^{Dem} 1885–9
Benjamin Harrison ^{Rep} 1889–93
Grover Cleveland ^{Dem} 1893–7
William McKinley ^{Rep} 1897–1901
Theodore Roosevelt ^{Rep} 1901–9
William H. Taft ^{Rep} 1909–13
Woodrow Wilson ^{Dem} 1913–21
Warren G. Harding ^{Rep} 1921–3
Calvin Coolidge ^{Rep} 1923–9
Herbert C. Hoover ^{Rep} 1929–33
Franklin D. Roosevelt* ^{Dem} 1933–45
Harry S. Truman ^{Dem} 1945–53
Dwight D. Eisenhower ^{Rep} 1953–61
John F. Kennedy ^{Dem} 1961–3
Lyndon B. Johnson ^{Dem} 1963–9
Richard M. Nixon ^{Rep Res} 1969–74
Gerald Ford ^{Rep} 1974–7
Jimmy Carter ^{Dem} 1977–81
Ronald Reagan ^{Rep} 1981–9
George H.W. Bush ^{Rep} 1989–93
Bill Clinton ^{Dem Imp} 1993–2001
George W. Bush ^{Rep} 2001–2009
Barack Obama^{Dem} 2009–

Parties are indicated as: ^{Dem} Democrat; ^{Rep} Republican; ^{DR} Democrat-Republican; ^{DNU} Democrat/National Union; ^{Wg} Whig; ^{Imp} Impeached; ^{Res} Resigned

---

* Franklin Roosevelt was the only President to serve more than two terms in office – he was elected four times and died one year into his fourth term. The Twenty-second Amendment to the US Constitution restricting Presidents to two terms in office became law in 1951.

SINGERS AND BACKERS III (from page 190)

1. Adam; 2. KC; 3. Gloria Estefan; 4. Gladys Knight; 5. John Lennon; 6. Bob Marley; 7. Kool; 8. Huey Lewis; 9. Bruce Springsteen; 10. Kid Creole; 11. Freddie; 12. Nick Cave; 13. Buddy Holly; 14. Gary Numan; 15. Cliff Richard; 16. Frank Zappa; 17. Sheila E; 18. Smokey Robinson; 19. Duane Eddy; 20. Wyclef Jean; 21. Billy J. Kramer; 22. Brian Poole; 23. Georgie Fame; 24. Bobby Angelo.

OLYMPIC DISCIPLINES (from page 200; as at the time of publishing)

Alpine Skiing[Ski] / Archery / Artistic Gymnastics[Gym]

Athletics* / Badminton / Baseball / Basketball

Beach Volleyball[Vol] / Biathlon / BMX[Cyc] / Bobsleigh[Bob]

Boxing / Cross-country Skiing[Ski] / Curling

Diving[Aq] / Dressage[Eq] / Eventing[Eq] / Fencing

Figure Skating[Ska] / Flatwater[Can] / Football

Freestyle Skiing[Ski] / Freestyle Wrestling[W]

Greco-Roman Wrestling[W] / Handball / Hockey / Ice Hockey

Indoor Volleyball[Vol] / Judo / Luge / Modern Pentathlon

Mountain Bike[Cyc] / Nordic Combined[Ski] / Road Racing[Cyc]

Rowing / Rhythmic Gymnastics[Gym] / Sailing / Shooting

Short Track Speed Skating[Ska] / Showjumping[Eq]

Skeleton[Bob] / Ski Jumping[Ski] / Slalom[Can] / Snowboard[Ski]

Softball / Speed Skating[Ska] / Swimming[Aq]

Synchronised Swimming[Aq] / Table Tennis / Taekwondo

Tennis / Track[Cyc] / Trampoline[Gym]

Triathlon / Water Polo[Aq] / Weightlifting

Sports with multiple disciplines indicated as [Aq] Aquatics [Bob] Bobsleigh [Can] Canoeing [Cyc] Cycling [Eq] Equestrian [Gym] Gymnastics [Ska] Skating [Ski] Skiing [Vol] Volleyball [W] Wrestling

BRITISH OLYMPIANS II (from page 204)

1. Kelly Holmes; 2. Linford Christie; 3. Matthew Pinsent; 4. Jonathan Edwards; 5. Sally Gunnell; 6. Duncan Goodhew; 7. Steve Backley; 8. Robin Cousins; 9. Audley Harrison; 10. Christine Ohuruogu; 11. Colin Jackson; 12. John Curry; 13. Chris Boardman; 14. Kriss Akabusi; 15. Darren Campbell; 16. James Cracknell; 17. Mary Peters; 18. Mary Rand; 19. Greg and Jonathan Serle; 20. Ian Stark; 21. Shelley Rudman; 22. Chris Hoy; 23. Ben Ainslie; 24. Eric Liddell†.

---

* Athletics is the highest-profile sport at the Olympics. There are twenty-six track-and-field events.

† Together with Harold Abrahams he was the subject of the film *Chariots of Fire*.

FIRST LINES OF POPULAR NOVELS I (from page 3)

1. *The Hobbit* (J.R.R. Tolkien); 2. *The House at Pooh Corner* (A.A. Milne); 3. *Pride and Prejudice* (Jane Austen); 4. *A Tale of Two Cities* (Charles Dickens); 5. *The Lion, the Witch and the Wardrobe* (C.S. Lewis); 6. *The Wind in the Willows* (Kenneth Grahame); 7. *The Canterbury Tales* (Geoffrey Chaucer); 8. *Nineteen Eighty-four** (George Orwell); 9. *The Mill on the Floss* (George Eliot); 10. *Rebecca* (Daphne du Maurier); 11. *Wild Swans* (Jung Chang); 12. *Little Women* (Louisa May Alcott); 13. *Captain Corelli's Mandolin* (Louis de Bernières); 14. *Emma* (Jane Austen); 15. *Fever Pitch* (Nick Hornby); 16. *Wuthering Heights* (Emily Brontë); 17. *The Exorcist* (William Peter Blatty); 18. *The Time Machine* (H.G. Wells); 19. *Lord of the Flies* (William Golding); 20. *2001: A Space Odyssey* (Arthur C. Clarke); 21. *The Da Vinci Code* (Dan Brown); 22. *The Maltese Falcon* (Dashiell Hammett); 23. *Tess of the d'Urbervilles* (Thomas Hardy); 24. *White Teeth* (Zadie Smith)

MUSKETEERS† (from page 7)

Aramis / Athos / Porthos

SONS OF ADAM AND EVE (from page 9)

Cain‡ / Abel / Seth

FILMS AND THEIR STARS I (from page 5)

1. *Titanic*; 2. *Star Wars*; 3. *Dr No*; 4. *Some Like It Hot*; 5. *Psycho*; 6. *Butch Cassidy and the Sundance Kid*; 7. *As Good As It Gets*; 8. *An Officer and a Gentleman*; 9. *Breakfast at Tiffany's*; 10. *The Belles of St Trinian's*; 11. *Crash*; 12. *Planet of the Apes*; 13. *Shine*; 14. *Zulu*; 15. *Fargo*; 16. *Diner*; 17. *Guess Who's Coming to Dinner*; 18. *1492: Conquest of Paradise*; 19. *Field of Dreams*; 20. *Mars Attacks!*; 21. *Papillon*; 22. *Dr Strangelove*; 23. *The Last Temptation of Christ*; 24. *Who's Afraid of Virginia Woolf?*

GRAND SLAM TENNIS TOURNAMENTS (from page 14)

Australian Open / French Open / US Open / Wimbledon

CLASSICAL COLUMNS (from page 20)

Tuscan / Ionic / Doric / Corinthian

HOBBIES AND PROFESSIONS I (from page 22)

1. One skilled in folding paper; 2. A candle maker or vendor of nautical supplies; 3. A collector of stamps; 4. One who makes carts and wagons; 5. A beekeeper; 6. One who embroiders; 7. A worker on a drilling rig; 8. Wine expert; 9. A textile dealer; 10. One who makes bells or metal castings; 11. A butcher specialising in

---

* Originally titled *The Last Man in Europe*, the book introduced the phrases 'Big Brother', 'Room 101' and 'Thought Police'.

† D'Artagnan, the protagonist of the novel, is not one of the musketeers of the title.

‡ Cain killed Abel.

pork; 12. A dealer of stocks and shares; 13. One who works leather; 14. One who makes archery bows; 15. A freelance journalist; 16. A bell ringer; 17. One who makes barrels; 18. A butterfly and moth collector; 19. Tree surgeon; 20. A coin collector; 21. One who analyses minerals and ores; 22. A collector of cigarette cards; 23. A peddler of cheap books and pamphlets; 24. One who distributes charity.

ENGLISH QUARTER DAYS (from page 24)

Lady Day	25 March
Midsummer Day	24 June
Michaelmas Day	29 September
Christmas Day	25 December

GOONS (from page 26)

Michael Bentine* / Spike Milligan / Harry Secombe / Peter Sellers

SPORTS GOVERNING BODIES I (from page 30)

1. Marylebone Cricket Club; 2. Fédération Internationale de Football Association†; 3. Professional Golfers' Association; 4. World Boxing Organisation; 5. National Hockey League; 6. Test and County Cricket Board; 7. Fédération Internationale de l'Automobile; 8. International Association of Athletics Federations; 9. World Boxing Association; 10. Confederation of North, Central American and Caribbean Association Football; 11. British Amateur Gymnastics Association; 12. All England Lawn Tennis Club; 13. National Basketball Association; 14. International Ice Hockey Federation; 15. Fédération Internationale de Ski; 16. International Tennis Federation; 17. Fédération Internationale de Motocyclisme; 18. British Darts Organisation; 19. Fédération Internationale de Basketball Amateur; 20. International Table Tennis Federation; 21. World Professional Billiards and Snooker Association; 22 World Water Skiing Union; 23. Fédération Internationale de Gymnastique; 24. World Karate Federation.

FACES OF MOUNT RUSHMORE (from page 33)

George Washington / Thomas Jefferson
Abraham Lincoln / Theodore Roosevelt

THE YOUNG ONES (from page 35)

Mike	Christopher Ryan
Neil	Nigel Planer
Rick	Rik Mayall
Vyvyan	Adrian Edmondson
Jerzei Balowski	Alexei Sayle

---

* Bentine appeared in only the first series of *The Goon Show*.

HOLY PLACES (from page 38)

1. Christianity; 2. Catholicism; 3. Islam*; 4. Christianity; 5. Anglicanism;
6. Catholicism†; 7. Islam; 8. Mormonism (Church of Jesus Christ of Latter-Day
Saints); 9. Sikhism; 10. Judaism‡; 11. Buddhism or Shinto; 12. Judaism;
13. Islam§; 14. Hinduism; 15. Eastern Orthodox¶; 16. Buddhism**;
17. Hinduism; 18. Buddhism (Tibetan); 19. Christianity; 20. Eastern Orthodox;
21. Buddhism or Taoism; 22. Eastern Orthodox; 23. Jainism; 24. Buddhism††

NOVELS BY F. SCOTT FITZGERALD (from page 40)

This Side of Paradise (1920) / *The Beautiful and Damned* (1922)
The Great Gatsby (1925) / *Tender Is the Night* (1934)
The Last Tycoon (unfinished, 1941)

OLYMPIC RINGS (from page 42)

Blue / Yellow / Black / Green / Red

BATTLES I (from page 44)

1. Norman Conquest (1066); 2. English Civil War (1644); 3. Crimean War
(1854); 4. Second World War (1942); 5. First World War (1916); 6. American
Civil War (1863); 7. First World War (1916); 8. Second World War (1945);
9. American War of Independence (1775); 10. Greco-Persian Wars (480BC)‡‡;
11. Hundred Years' War (1428–9); 12. Vietnam War (1969); 13. American Civil
War (1862); 14. Second World War (1941–4); 15. American War of Independence
(1781); 16. Hundred Years' War (1415); 17. Texan–Mexican War (1836)§§;
18. Seven Years War (1759); 19. Wars of Alexander the Great¶¶ (333BC);

---

* Mecca is the birthplace of Muhammad and the direction Muslims must face to
pray five times a day.
† Where the Virgin Mary appeared to St Bernadette in a vision in 1858.
‡ Where Moses received the Ten Commandments from God.
§ Where Muhammad ascended into heaven in AD621.
¶ The Seat of the Ecumenical Patriarchate of Constantinople.
** Where the Buddha reached enlightenment.
†† Where the Buddha died.
‡‡ Salamis is a small island in the Saronic Gulf near Athens. The battle was fought
between Persian and Greek fleets numbering approximately 1,200 and 400 ships
respectively and was recorded by Herodotus. The Greek triremes were fitted with an
'embolon' – a bronze pole which was effective at ramming and causing damage to
opposing ships. The decisive factor in the Greek victory was probably the agility of
the smaller Greek fleet, fighting in a small and enclosed expanse of water against a
larger, less manoeuvrable Persian force.
§§ In which Colonel Travis, Jim Bowie, Davy Crockett and 180 other Texans were
killed by Mexican troops.
¶¶ In which Alexander defeated Darius III leading to the fall of the Persian Empire.
The battle altered the course of Asian and European history.

20. Seven Years' War (1757); 21. Hundred Years' War (1346); 22. Hundred Years' War (1356); 23. English Civil War (1642); 24. American War of Independence (1777).

THE A-TEAM (from page 47)

Col. John 'Hannibal' Smith .... George Peppard
Lt. Templeton 'Faceman' Peck .... Dirk Benedict
Sgt. Bosco 'B.A.' Baracus .... Mr T
Capt. H.M. 'Howling Mad' Murdock .... Dwight Schultz
Amy Amanda 'Triple A' Allen .... Melinda Culea

BRITISH WINNERS OF THE BALLON D'OR (from page 49)

Stanley Matthews (Blackpool) 1956
Denis Law (Manchester United) 1964
Bobby Charlton (Manchester United) 1966
George Best (Manchester United) 1968
Kevin Keegan (Hamburg) 1978, 1979
Michael Owen (Liverpool) 2001

MISCELLANY VII (from page 52)

1. Fifteen; 2. The ace of Spades; 3. Mr Humphries; 4. Refraction; 5. Debra Messing; 6. Eddie 'The Eagle' Edwards; 7. A piece of text that includes every letter in the alphabet*; 8. Epsom†; 9. Q; 10. HMY; 11. The Dam Busters; 12. 1888 (MDCCCLXXXVIII); 13. Ascot; 14. Palm reading; 15. The letters are in alphabetical order; 16. Loch Ness; 17. Ireland; 18. Mercury; 19. Either side of the Strait of Gibralta; 20. Venezuela (Venice); 21. Drew Barrymore (in *E.T. the Extra Terrestrial*); 22. The Siegfried Line; 23. Michelin (the Michelin Man); 24. Nine miles.

VILLAGE PEOPLE (from page 56)

Biker / Construction Worker / Cowboy
Indian / Motorcycle Cop / Soldier

MONTY PYTHON (from page 58)

John Cleese / Eric Idle / Graham Chapman
Michael Palin / Terry Gilliam / Terry Jones

---

* For example 'Cozy sphinx waves quart jug of bad milk', 'Brick quiz whangs jumpy veldt fox', 'Woven silk pyjamas exchanged for blue quartz', 'The quick brown fox jumps over the lazy dog'.
† The Derby is run at Epsom Downs; magnesium sulphate is otherwise known as Epsom salts.

FOREIGN WORDS AND PHRASES I (from page 62)

1. Déjà vu; 2. Kindergarten; 3. Zero; 4. Robot; 5. Mogul; 6. Intelligentsia; 7. Tariff;
8. Angst; 9. Almanac; 10. Dolce vita; 11. Bungalow; 12. Tycoon; 13. Guru;
14. Vis-à-vis; 15. Verboten; 16. Kowtow; 17. Bonanza; 18. Doppelgänger;
19. Aficionado; 20. Husting; 21. Kitsch; 22. Hazard; 23. Tundra; 24. Checkmate.

HARRY POTTER NOVELS (from page 65)

Harry Potter and the Philosopher's Stone	1997
Harry Potter and the Chamber of Secrets	1998
Harry Potter and the Prisoner of Azkaban	1999
Harry Potter and the Goblet of Fire	268
Harry Potter and the Order of the Phoenix	2003
Harry Potter and the Half-Blood Prince	2005
Harry Potter and the Deathly Hallows	2007

DWARFS (from page 68)

Bashful / Doc / Dopey / Grumpy / Happy / Sleepy / Sneezy

HOBBIES AND PROFESSIONS II (from page 70)

1. Person who shapes hedges; 2. Person who sells sewing-related articles; 3. Wine
merchant; 4. Person who sells stockings; 5. Coffee purveyor*; 6. Amateur radio
operator; 7. Person who sells cloths and fabrics; 8. Member of royal household
responsible for horses; 9. Person who makes or sells hats; 10. Mechanic;
11. Teacher; 12. Dealer in rare books; 13. Army officer below the rank of Captain;
14. Person who makes arrows; 15. Person who shoes horses; 16. Shorthand typist;
17. Horse handler; 18. Clock collector; 19. Fortune teller who uses cards;
20. Tightrope walker; 21. Matchbox collector; 22. Striptease artist; 23. Street seller
of fruit and vegetables; 24. Magician skilled in sleight of hand.

CATHOLIC CHURCH HIERARCHY (from page 73)

Pope / Cardinal / Archbishop / Bishop
Monsignor† / Priest / Deacon

---

* Coffee is thought to have been discovered in Ethiopia in AD950, from where it quickly
became popular throughout the Arab world (especially as alcohol is forbidden to
Muslims). European traders brought it back in the seventeenth century and London
coffee houses came into being, quickly establishing themselves as places to exchange
news, gossip and conduct business. The Arab monopoly on coffee was broken when the
Dutch smuggled coffee seedlings from the Arab port of Mocha to the East Indies. Thirty
years later, in 1723, coffee was introduced to the New World. Coffee (in terms of dollar
value) is now the second most important legally traded commodity after oil, and is
notable for being the primary export of many of the world's developing countries. Some
25 million farmers around the world are dependent on income from coffee.

† Monsignor is an honorary title that may be conferred upon a priest by the Pope at
the request of a bishop.

COUNTRIES IN CENTRAL AMERICA (from page 76)

Belize / Costa Rica / El Salvador / Guatemala
Honduras / Nicaragua / Panama

LINKED MISCELLANY VI (from page 78)

1. *The Man with the Golden Gun*; 2. Duke of York; 3. Charlotte Rampling;
4. Concorde; 5. *Goodbye Mr Chips*; 6. Piper Alpha; 7. Edward I; 8. *No Jacket Required*; 9. Jersey; 10. *M*A*S*H*.

The link is potatoes*.

TAXONOMY OF LIVING THINGS† (from page 80)

Kingdom
Phylum (animals) or Division (plants or fungi)
Class
Order
Family
Genus
Species

BRITISH FILM CLASSIFICATIONS (from page 82)

Uc .... suitable for all but especially children; DVD/video only
U .... suitable for all
PG .... parental guidance; some scenes unsuitable for children under 8
12A .... suitable for 12 and over; under 12s accompanied by an adult
12 .... suitable for those aged 12 and over; DVD/video only
15 .... suitable for those aged 15 and over
18 .... suitable for those aged 18 and over
R18 .... suitable for those aged 18 and over and only at licensed cinemas

---

* Golden Wonder (Golden Wonder are the best potatoes for frying, but are difficult to get hold of as high volumes are supplied to the crisp manufacturer of the same name), Duke of York, Charlotte, Concorde, chips, Maris Piper, King Edward, jacket, Jersey Royal, mashed.

† For example, Homo sapiens is classified as Kingdom: Animalia, Phylum: Chordata, Class: Mammalia, Order: Primates, Family: Hominidae, Genus: Homo, Species: Homo sapiens. Note that sub-classifications are used in order to help classify diverse organisms such as insects. This taxonomy is known as the Six-kingdom System with the top level consisting of Protista, Archaebacteria, Eubacteria, Fungi, Plantae, and Animalia. A recent taxonomy has added an eighth level, Domain, to the top of the hierarchy. The Three-domain System was introduced by Carl Woese, a microbiologist, in 1990 and re-drew taxonomy based on genetic relationships rather than physical characteristics. Under Woese's system the top level consists of the domains of Bacteria, Archaea and Eucarya, the last of which contains plants, animals and fungi.

QUOTATIONS FROM POPULAR FILMS I (from page 85)

1. *Star Wars*; 2. *The Silence of the Lambs*; 3. *Gladiator*; 4. *Back to the Future*; 5. *The Hunt for Red October*; 6. *Top Gun*; 7. *Some Like It Hot*; 8. *Forrest Gump*; 9. *The Wizard of Oz*; 10. *Shrek*; 11. *A Fish Called Wanda*; 12. *The Terminator*; 13. *The Italian Job*; 14. *Marathon Man*; 15. *The Great Escape*; 16. *Apollo 13*; 17. *Pirates of the Caribbean: The Curse of the Black Pearl*; 18. *Fight Club*; 19. *Toy Story*; 20. *My Big Fat Greek Wedding*; 21. *The Jerk*; 22. *My Fair Lady*; 23. *American Beauty*; 24. *Midnight Cowboy*.

COUNTRIES ENDING WITH '~LAND'* (from page 89)

Finland / Iceland / Ireland / Netherlands / New Zealand
Poland / Swaziland / Switzerland / Thailand

MOST OSCAR-NOMINATED ACTORS (from page 95; as at the time of publishing)

Jack Nicholson	12 nominations (3 wins)
Laurence Olivier	10 (1)
Spencer Tracy	9 (2)
Paul Newman	9 (1)
Marlon Brando	8 (2)
Jack Lemmon	8 (2)
Al Pacino	8 (1)
Peter O'Toole	8 (0)
Dustin Hoffman	7 (2)
Richard Burton	7 (0)

ARTISTS (from page 97)

1. Leonardo da Vinci; 2. Vincent Van Gogh; 3. John Constable; 4. Michelangelo; 5. Claude Monet; 6. Alessandro Botticelli; 7. Pablo Picasso; 8. Andy Warhol; 9. Edvard Munch†; 10. Salvador Dalí; 11. J.M.W. Turner; 12. Jan Vermeer; 13. Édouard Manet; 14. Pierre-Auguste Renoir; 15. Titian; 16. Roy Lichtenstein; 17. Henri Matisse; 18. Gustav Klimt; 19. Edgar Degas; 20. Jan van Eyck‡;

---

* Examples of non-sovereign countries with this name ending are England and Scotland (UK) and Greenland (Denmark).

† The painting was inspired by an experience that Munch described in his diary on 22 January 1892: 'I was walking along the road with two friends. The sun was setting. I felt a breath of melancholy. Suddenly the sky became blood-red. I stopped, and leant against the railing, deathly tired. I looked out across the flaming clouds that hung like blood and a sword over the blue-black fjord and town. My friends walked on but I stood there, trembling with fear. I sensed a great, infinite scream pass through nature.'

‡ The painting celebrates the marriage of Giovanni Arnolfini and Giovanna Cenami, a wealthy Italian couple who had settled in Bruges. It is renowned, not only for the skill with which van Eyck employed the very latest painting techniques (he was the leading exponent of painting with oils), but also for the symbolism with which the painting is packed. Fertility and childbirth are alluded to by the presence *cont'd over/*

21. Rembrandt; 22. Hans Holbein*; 23. Hieronymus Bosch; 24. Pieter Bruegel the Elder.

EVENTS IN THE DECATHLON (from page 101)

100m / Long jump / Shot put / High jump / 400m
110m hurdles / Discus / Pole vault / Javelin / 1,500m

ROYAL PARKS† (from page 103)

Bushy Park / Green Park / Greenwich Park
Hyde Park / Kensington Gardens / Regent's Park
Richmond Park / St James's Park / Brompton Cemetery
Grosvenor Square Gardens

MISCELLANY XIV (from page 105)

1. Light Emitting Diode; 2. A4; 3. Queen Victoria; 4. Worcestershire sauce‡;
5. Sumo wrestling; 6. Kaleidoscope; 7. Tamagotchi; 8. *Daily Express*; 9. Australia;
10. Richard III; 11. Ipswich Town and Norwich City; 12. Cleopatra's Needle;
13. Fingers; 14. Dylan Thomas; 15. It was non-speaking; 16. Three; 17. Progress
through technology; 18. Libya (green); 19. Peninsular and Oriental; 20. I/eye, you/
ewe; 21. The Isle of Wight; 22. Glenn Miller§; 23. Ford Prefect; 24. The palm.

---

cont'd   of the bed behind the couple and by Giovanna's dress and posture which
give the appearance that she is pregnant (she was not). Discarded shoes were a
symbol for religious ceremony, an indication that the painting was perhaps meant to
be a visual wedding certificate.

* Holbein was artist to the court of Henry VIII but fell out of favour with the King
over a portrait of Anne of Cleves. Henry had agreed to marry Anne (his fourth wife)
on the basis of Holbein's portrait which he had liked, but was rather disappointed
when he met Anne for the first time on their wedding day; he likened her to a 'fat
Flanders mare'.

† Brompton Cemetery and Grosvenor Square Gardens are not designated Royal
Parks, but are managed by the Royal Parks. The Royal Parks also manage the
gardens of 10, 11 and 12 Downing Street.

‡ Worcestershire sauce originated as an Indian recipe which was brought to Britain
by Lord Marcus Sandys returning from his post as Governor of Bengal. Sandys
approached the Worcester chemists John Lea and William Perrins to make him a
batch from the recipe. Unfortunately the resulting brew was too spicy to be palatable
(according to Sandys it tasted 'filthy') and was hastily sealed and consigned to their
cellar. Some months later, the two chemists tasted the sauce again and to their
surprise discovered that it had matured and was really quite tasty. They purchased
the recipe from Lord Sandys and Lea & Perrins Worcestershire Sauce was launched
in 1838.

§ 'Chattanooga Choo Choo' in 1941.

GREEK GODS (from page 110)

Zeus / Hera / Poseidon / Ares / Hermes / Hephaestus
Aphrodite / Athena / Apollo / Artemis / Demeter / Hades

MISCELLANY XV (from page 111)

1. Texas; 2. Acting; 3. Beaches used by the D-Day landings; 4. High Street;
5. The CIA; 6. *Gone With the Wind*; 7. Brown; 8. Copenhagen was the Duke of
Wellington's horse; 9. Tea; 10. Elton John; 11. *Private Eye*; 12. Jet fighters (MiG);
13. Black; 14. Asthma and isthmus; 15. Cooking pot; 16. The Mekon;
17. Glasgow; 18. One (the ship floats on the tide); 19. Ridley Scott; 20. S;
21. The orchid; 22. George Bernard Shaw*; 23. Black and white†; 24. Fill the
three-gallon jug and pour this into the five-gallon jug. Fill the three-gallon jug again
and pour into the five-gallon jug, leaving one gallon of water remaining in the three-
gallon jug. Empty the five-gallon jug and then pour the one gallon of water from the
three-gallon jug into the five-gallon jug. Finally, fill the three-gallon jug and empty
this into the five-gallon jug, giving four gallons.

CHART-TOPPING SINGLES BY MADONNA (from page 115; as at the time of
publishing)

'Into the Groove' .... July 1985
'Papa Don't Preach' .... June 1986
'True Blue' .... October 1986
'La Isla Bonita' .... April 1987
'Who's That Girl' .... July 1987
'Like a Prayer' .... March 1989
'Vogue' .... April 1990
'Frozen' .... March 1998
'American Pie' .... March 2000
'Music' .... September 2000
'Hung Up' .... November 2005
'Sorry' .... March 2006
'4 Minutes' (feat. Justin Timberlake & Timbaland) .... March 2008

COUNTRIES WITH NAMES CONTAINING ADJECTIVES (from page 117)

Central African Republic / Dominican Republic / East Timor
Equatorial Guinea / New Zealand / North Korea
Papua New Guinea / South Africa / South Korea
United Arab Emirates / United Kingdom
United States of America / Western Sahara

---

* Shaw was awarded the Nobel Prize in Literature in 1925, and the Oscar for
Writing Adapted Screenplay in 1938 for the same work, *Pygmalion*.
† The colour sequence is used by the different traps in a greyhound race. Trap one
is red, trap two, blue, etc. The next in the sequence is black and white, the colours
of the dog running from trap six.

IMPERIAL UNITS (from page 120)

1. Foot; 2. Yard; 3. Pound; 4. Inch; 5. Pint; 6. Stone; 7. Mile; 8. Gallon;
9. Ton; 10. Fluid ounce; 11. Acre; 12. Furlong; 13. Ounce; 14. Hand;
15. Fathom; 16. Hundredweight; 17. League; 18. Chain; 19. Quart; 20. Gill;
21. Nautical mile; 22. Hide; 23. Cubit; 24. Bushel.

BRITISH NOBILITY (from page 122)

King / Queen / Prince / Princess
Marquess / Marchioness / Duke / Duchess
Earl / Countess / Viscount / Viscountess
Baron / Baroness

ENGLAND FOOTBALL MANAGERS (from page 125; as at the time of publishing)

Walter Winterbottom	1946*–62
Alf Ramsey	1963–74
Joe Mercer[C]	1974
Don Revie	1974–7
Ron Greenwood	1977–82
Bobby Robson	1982–90
Graham Taylor	1990–3
Terry Venables	1994–6
Glenn Hoddle	1996–9
Howard Wilkinson[C]	1999, 2000
Kevin Keegan	1999–2000
Peter Taylor[C]	2000
Sven-Göran Eriksson	2001–6
Steve McClaren	2006–2008
Fabio Capello	2008–present

[C] indicates Caretaker-manager

METRIC UNITS (from page 128)

1. Temperature; 2. Sound intensity; 3. Electric current; 4. Energy; 5. Absolute
temperature; 6. Frequency; 7. Power; 8. Pressure; 9. Resistance; 10. Force;
11. Potential difference; 12. Luminous intensity; 13. Electric charge; 14. Amount of
substance; 15. Angle within a plane; 16. Radioactivity; 17. Luminance; 18. Angle
within a solid; 19. Magnetic flux density; 20. Electrical capacitance; 21. Radiation
exposure; 22. Inductance; 23. Magnetic flux; 24. Electrical conductance.

NOVELS BY THOMAS HARDY (from page 132)

Desperate Remedies	1871
Under the Greenwood Tree	1872
A Pair of Blue Eyes	1873

---

* During Winterbottom's tenure the team was selected by the FA International
Selection Committee, a practice which continued until the appointment of Alf
Ramsey in 1963.

^SS indicates Short Stories

CHART-TOPPING SINGLES BY ELVIS PRESLEY (from page 134; as at the time of publishing)

* Hardy became disillusioned with literature after the negative reaction he received from the publication of *Jude the Obscure* (and earlier from *Tess of the d'Urbervilles*) which had outraged Victorian morality. From 1897 he wrote only poetry.

† Re-release reached number one in January 2005.

‡ Re-release became the thousandth number one in the history of the UK charts in January 2005.

§ Re-release reached number one in February 2005.

¶ Elvis vs. JXL.

FIRST LINES OF POP SONGS IV (from page 137)

1. 'The House of the Rising Sun' (The Animals); 2. 'Get Up (I Feel Like Being) A Sex Machine' (James Brown); 3. 'Baby One More Time' (Britney Spears); 4. 'Candle in the Wind' (Elton John); 5. 'Relight My Fire' (Take That vs. Lulu); 6. 'Hotel California' (The Eagles); 7. 'Millennium' (Robbie Williams); 8. 'Hey Ya!' (OutKast); 9. 'Hard to Handle' (Otis Redding); 10. 'Born to Be Wild' (Steppenwolf); 11. 'Sledgehammer'* (Peter Gabriel); 12. 'The Boys of Summer (Don Henley); 13. 'Every Little Thing She Does Is Magic' (The Police); 14. 'Firestarter' (The Prodigy); 15. 'Thank You' (Dido) or 'Stan' (Eminem); 16. 'Make Me Smile' (Steve Harley and Cockney Rebel); 17. 'Love of the Common People' (Paul Young); 18. 'Mickey'† (Toni Basil); 19. 'Pretty Vacant' (The Sex Pistols); 20. 'Where the Streets Have No Name' (U2); 21. 'I Am the Resurrection' (The Stone Roses); 22. 'Hung Up' (Madonna); 23. 'Times They Are a-Changin'' (Bob Dylan); 24. 'Lust for Life'‡ (Iggy Pop).

FREQUENTLY OCCURRING WORDS (from page 140)

the / of / and / to / a / in / is / that / was / it
for / on / with / he / be / I / by / as / at / you

FOOTBALL TEAM NAME ENDINGS (from page 144; as at the time of publishing)

Albion / Alexandra / Argyle / Athletic / City / County
Dons / Forest / Hotspur / North End / Orient / Palace§ / Rangers
& Redbridge / Rovers / Stanley / Town / United / Vale
Villa / Wanderers / Wednesday¶

INNOVATIONS II (from page 146)

1. Television; 2. Airship; 3. Helicopter; 4. Jumbo jet**; 5. Pasteurisation; 6. Wheel; 7. Penicillin; 8. Revolver; 9. Mechanical lift; 10. Centigrade thermometer; 11. Motor car (petrol engine); 12. Aqualung; 13. World Wide

---

* The innovative claymation video for 'Sledgehammer' revived Gabriel's career and remains the most aired video on MTV.

† 'Mickey' became a hit in the US and worldwide after first entering the charts in the UK. Toni Basil's real name is Antonia Basilotta.

‡ The song, whose lyrics celebrate giving up alcohol, was the theme to *Trainspotting*, a film about heroin addiction.

§ Technically 'Palace' is part of the name of the team's location.

¶ Sheffield Wednesday were so called because Sheffield factory workers were permitted by their employers to play football each Wednesday afternoon.

** The Boeing 747 was developed after intense lobbying of Boeing by Pan Am who wanted a jet airliner twice the size of the popular Boeing 707. Unsure of the passenger market for such a large aircraft, the company hedged their bets and designed the 747 so that it could be adapted into a freighter. The cockpit was raised to the top of the aircraft so that a payload door could be added to the nose cone, creating the recognisable bulge. The production schedule for *cont'd over/*

Web (HTML); 14. Computer (difference engine); 15. Phonograph* (or gramophone); 16. Vaccination; 17. Food processor; 18. Catseye (reflective road marker); 19. Photographic film; 20. Paper; 21. Bicycle; 22. Submarine; 23. Washing machine; 24. Spreadsheet†.

TAROT CARDS (from page 149)

0 Fool / I Magician / II High Priestess / III Empress / IV Emperor
V Hierophant / VI Lovers / VII Chariot / VIII Justice / IX Hermit
X Wheel of Fortune / XI Fortitude / XII Hanged Man / XIII Death
XIV Temperance / XV Devil / XVI Tower / XVII Star / XVIII Moon
XIX Sun / XX Judgement / XXI World

LANGUAGES OF THE EUROPEAN UNION (from page 152; as at the time of publishing)

Bulgarian / Czech / Danish / Dutch / English / Estonian / Finnish
French / German / Greek / Hungarian / Italian / Irish / Latvian
Lithuanian / Maltese / Polish / Portuguese / Romanian / Slovak
Slovenian / Spanish / Swedish

UNTIMELY DEATHS (from page 155)

1. Elvis Presley; 2. Sid Vicious; 3. John Lennon; 4. Marilyn Monroe; 5. Glenn Miller; 6. Michael Hutchence; 7. Grace Kelly; 8. James Dean; 9. Vincent Van Gogh‡; 10. Jimi Hendrix; 11. Kurt Cobain; 12. Tupac Shakur; 13. Marc Bolan; 14. Tony Hancock; 15. Marvin Gaye; 16. Kirsty MacColl; 17. Sylvia Plath; 18. Gianni Versace§; 19. Sonny Bono; 20. Notorious BIG¶; 21. Virginia Woolf; 22. Dodi Fayed; 23. Steve Irwin; 24. Janis Joplin.

POPULOUS COUNTRIES (from page 163; as at the time of publishing)

China 1,322
India 1,130

---

cont'd   the new aircraft was so ambitious that the engineers who worked on it became known as 'The Incredibles'. Having almost bankrupted the company, the 747 was a massive success and led to Boeing virtually monopolising the passenger aircraft market for the next thirty years.

* Edison famously recorded the nursery rhyme 'Mary Had a Little Lamb' on his new invention. Edison became known as 'The Wizard of Menlo Park' and was one of the most prolific inventors in history, eventually holding 1,097 US patents in his name.

† They created VisiCalc, the first spreadsheet software.

‡ Van Gogh died two days after shooting himself. His last words were: 'The sadness will last for ever.'

§ Versace was murdered by Andrew Cunanan who killed four other people during a three-month killing spree in 1997 before committing suicide aboard a Miami yacht.

¶ The deaths of Notorious BIG and Tupac Shakur may possibly be linked although nobody has ever been convicted of either crime.

United States	301
Indonesia	235
Brazil	190
Pakistan	169
Bangladesh	150
Russia	141
Nigeria	135
Japan	127
Mexico	109
Philippines	91
Vietnam	85
Germany	82
Egypt	80
Ethiopia	77
Turkey	71
Iran	65
Thailand	65
Congo, Dem. Rep.	65
France	61
United Kingdom	61
Italy	58
South Korea	49
Myanmar (Burma)	47

Figures represent millions of people and are approximate

TRACK-AND-FIELD-EVENTS (from page 165)

100m / 200m / 400m / 800m / 1,500m / 5,000m / 10,000m
Marathon / 100m hurdles [W] / 110m hurdles [M] / 400m hurdles
Steeplechase [M] / High jump / Long jump / Pole vault
Triple jump / Shot / Discus / Hammer / Javelin
Decathlon [M] / Heptathlon [W] / 20km walk
50km walk [M] / 4x100m relay / 4x400m relay
[M] indicates male-only events [W] indicates female-only events

MISCELLANY XXII (from page 169)

1. Crimean War; 2. Northumberland; 3. Ronnie Wood; 4. 'You do not talk about Fight Club'; 5. Seven; 6. *A Clockwork Orange*; 7. Cindy; 8. The Khyber Pass; 9. They feature Ghosts; 10. Charles Yeager; 11. Pole vault; 12. Order of the Bath; 13. The Panama*

---

* The Panama Canal Authority decides the tolls for each use of the canal based on vessel type, size and its cargo, although smaller vessels are charged based on length only. The toll of $249,165 levied for the container ship *Maersk Dellys* in May 2006 is at the time of writing the highest toll ever levied for using the Panama Canal. Richard Halliburton swam the canal in 1928 and was charged a toll of 36 cents.

Canal; 14. Nine days; 15. Maine; 16. *Star Trek**; 17. Brian Hanrahan†; 18. Baroque; 19. The Sargasso Sea; 20. Twelve; 21. Angostura bitters; 22. Carbon dioxide and water; 23. The Ministry of Truth; 24. A few seconds after twelve o'clock‡.

CARRY ON FILMS (from page 173)

---

* Captain Kirk (William Shatner) and Lieutenant Uhura (Nichelle Nichols) shared a kiss in the 1968 episode 'Plato's Stepchildren', albeit under the influence of a controlling alien mind.

† Hanrahan's reports from the Falklands Conflict had military restrictions placed on them to avoid revealing operational details; he used this phrase to report that all of the aircraft had returned safely without revealing how many there were.

‡ Martin hears the last chime of twelve o'clock as he arrives home.

§ 20th Century Fox started legal proceedings against Peter Rogers alleging that the *Carry On Cleo* film poster plagiarised the poster for *Cleopatra*. Rogers won the case and greatly benefited from the publicity. The film had actually made use of the lavish sets and costumes left over in Pinewood from the Burton and Taylor production. It was made on a shoestring as a result.

GLADIATORS (from page 176)

Ace / Amazon / Cobra / Diesel / Falcon / Flame
Fox / Gold / Hawk / Hunter / Jet / Khan
Laser / Lightning / Nightshade / Panther
Phoenix / Raider / Rebel / Rhino / Rio
Rocket / Saracen / Scorpio / Shadow / Siren
Trojan / Vogue / Vulcan / Warrior / Wolf / Zodiac

FIRST LINES OF POP SONGS V (from page 179)

1. 'Wuthering Heights' (Kate Bush); 2. 'Hit Me With Your Rhythm Stick' (Ian Dury and the Blockheads); 3. 'Bohemian Like You' (Dandy Warhols); 4. 'Lola' (The Kinks); 5. 'Torn' (Natalie Imbruglia); 6. 'Tainted Love' (Soft Cell); 7. 'Don't Stop Moving' (S Club 7); 8. 'Common People' (Pulp); 9. 'Addicted to Love' (Robert Palmer); 10. 'Like a Virgin' (Madonna); 11. 'Yellow' (Coldplay); 12. 'Heart of Glass' (Blondie); 13. 'Take Me Out' (Franz Ferdinand); 14. 'Always the Sun' (The Stranglers); 15. 'The Real Slim Shady' (Eminem); 16. 'Mulder and Scully' (Catatonia); 17. 'Aquarius (Let the Sun Shine In)' (Fifth Dimension); 18. 'Faith' (George Michael); 19. 'Mamma Mia' (Abba); 20. 'That Don't Impress Me Much' (Shania Twain); 21. 'I Want to Hold Your Hand' (The Beatles); 22. 'Just a Little' (Liberty X); 23. 'Israelites' (Desmond Dekker and the Aces); 24. 'Fat Bottomed Girls' (Queen).

MICHAEL JACKSON HITS (from page 182; as at the time of publishing)

'Got To Be There'	....	1972 (reaching no. 5)
'Rockin' Robin'	....	1972 (3)
'Ain't No Sunshine'	....	1972 (8)
'Ben'	....	1972 (7)
'Don't Stop Till You Get Enough'	....	1979 (3)
'Off the Wall'	....	1979 (7)
'Rock with You'	....	1980 (7)
'She's Out of My Life'	....	1980 (3)
'One Day in Your Life'	....	1981 (1)
'The Girl Is Mine'	....	1982 (8)
'Billie Jean'	....	1983 (1)
'Beat It'	....	1983 (3)
'Wanna Be Startin' Something'	....	1983 (8)
'Thriller'	....	1983 (10)
'Farewell My Summer Love'	....	1984 (7)
'I Just Can't Stop Loving You'	....	1987 (1)
'Bad'	....	1987 (3)
'The Way You Make Me Feel'	....	1987 (3)

FA CUP WINNERS (from page 185)

Arsenal / Aston Villa / Barnsley / Blackburn Olympic
Blackburn Rovers / Blackpool / Bolton Wanderers
Bradford City / Burnley / Bury / Cardiff City / Charlton Athletic
Chelsea / Clapham Rovers / Coventry City / Derby County
Everton / Huddersfield Town / Ipswich Town / Leeds United
Liverpool / Manchester City / Manchester United
Newcastle United / Nottingham Forest / Notts County
Old Carthusians / Old Etonians / Oxford University
Portsmouth* / Preston North End / Royal Engineers
Sheffield United / Sheffield Wednesday / Southampton
Sunderland / The Wanderers† / Tottenham Hotspur
West Bromwich Albion / West Ham United / Wimbledon
Wolverhampton Wanderers

LATIN PHRASES II (from page 188)

1. Post meridiem (p.m.); 2. Et cetera (etc.); 3. Post mortem; 4. Persona non grata;
5. Vice versa; 6. Per capita; 7. Modus operandi (MO); 8. Nota bene (NB); 9. Alter
ego; 10. Compos mentis; 11. Ceteris paribus; 12. Versus (vs.); 13. Pro tempore (p.t.);

---

* Portsmouth have retained the cup for the longest period of any team. Winning in
1939, the cup was not contested during the years of the Second World War.
† The Wanderers, a team formed by ex-public school and university players, were
the first winners of the FA Cup, beating the Royal Engineers 1–0.

14. Curriculum vitae (c.v.); 15. In loco parentis; 16. Habeas corpus*; 17. Mea culpa;
18. Sub poena; 19. A priori; 20. Non sequitur (non seq.); 21. Deus ex machina†;
22. Ipso facto; 23. Infra dignitatem (infra dig.); 24. Inter alia.

RED TRIANGULAR ROAD SIGNS (from page 191)

Distance to 'STOP' or 'GIVE WAY' line ahead‡

Crossroads

Junction on bend ahead

T-junction

Staggered junction

Sharp deviation of route to left (or right if chevrons reversed)

Double bend first to left (symbol may be reversed)

Bend to right (or left if symbol reversed)

Roundabout

Uneven road

Dual carriageway ends

Road narrows on right (left if symbol reversed)

Road narrows on both sides

Two-way traffic crosses one-way road

Two-way traffic straight ahead

Traffic signals

Slippery road

Steep hill downwards

Steep hill upwards

School crossing patrol ahead

Frail (or blind or disabled) pedestrians likely to cross road ahead

Pedestrians in road ahead

Pedestrian crossing

Traffic queues likely ahead

Cycle route ahead

Side winds

---

* The Habeas Corpus Act was introduced by Charles II in 1679 to prevent false arrest or false imprisonment; it demands that a prisoner be brought before a judge and that evidence be presented justifying why he or she has been detained. Prior to this, prisoners could be held indefinitely without charge.

† The phrase is commonly used in the television and film industry to describe a resolution of a plot in a way that is external to the plot line and therefore not a logical consequence of it. It originates in early Greek dramas where a stage hand would often lower a character representing a god on to the stage to settle a hopeless situation. Deus ex machina resolutions of plots are generally unsatisfying as they appear artificial or contrived.

‡ An upside-down empty red triangle with a plate below indicating 'STOP' or 'GIVE WAY' along with its distance from the sign.

Humpback bridge
Worded warning sign*
Risk of ice
Level crossing with barrier or gate ahead
Level crossing without barrier or gate ahead
Trams crossing ahead
Cattle
Wild animals
Wild horses or ponies
Accompanied horses or ponies
Quayside or river bank
Opening or swing bridge ahead
Low-flying aircraft or sudden aircraft noise
Falling or fallen rocks
Available headroom†
Overhead electric cable‡
Tunnel ahead
Road humps§
Other danger¶
Soft verges
Risk of grounding
Loose chippings
Road works

POPULAR PUB NAMES** (from page 196)

The Anchor / The Angel / The Beehive / The Bell / The Black Bull
The Black Horse / The Bull / The Castle / The Chequers
The Coach and Horses / The Cricketers / The Cross Keys††
The Crown / The Foresters' Arms / The Fox / The Fox and Hounds
The George / The George and Dragon / The Globe
The Golden Lion‡‡ / The Green Man / The Greyhound
The Hare and Hounds / The King's Arms / The King's Head
The Lamb§§ / The Masons' Arms / The Nag's Head

---

* A red triangle containing a word to describing the warning, for example, 'Ford'.
† The width of available headroom will also be indicated.
‡ Safe height is indicated on a plate below.
§ Distance the humps extend is indicated on a plate below.
¶ A red triangle containing an exclamation mark and a plate below describing the warning, for example, 'Hidden dip'.
** Note the list does not include pubs that are part of commercial chains.
†† The symbol of St Peter, the gatekeeper of heaven.
‡‡ The heraldic symbol of Henry I.
§§ Symbolic of Jesus Christ (from John 1: 29 'Behold the Lamb of God, which taketh away the sins of the world') and the Knights Templar.

The New Inn / The Plough* / The Prince of Wales
The Queen's Head / The Railway / The Red Lion†
The Rising Sun‡ / The Rose and Crown
The Royal Oak§ / The Ship / The Star / The Sun / The Swan
The Three Horseshoes¶ / The Travellers' Rest / The Victoria
The Wagon and Horses / The Wheatsheaf / The White Hart**
The White Horse / The White Lion†† / The White Swan

LINKED MISCELLANY XIV (from page 200)

1. Michelle Pfeiffer; 2. Raccoon; 3. Norwegian; 4. Pepper; 5. Eleanor of
Aquitaine‡‡; 6. Madonna; 7. USSR; 8. Sixty-four; 9. *Diamonds Are Forever*;
10. 'The Walrus and the Carpenter'.

The link is songs by the Beatles§§.

---

* As well as the agricultural symbolism, the constellation was the symbol of the
Virgin Mary, also seen in pubs named the Seven Stars.
† The heraldic symbol of John of Gaunt and also of Scotland; James I used this to
popularise the united reign of Britain.
‡ The heraldic symbol of Edward III.
§ Associated with Charles II, who hid in an oak tree to escape capture during the
English Civil War.
¶ Pub names with 'three' in them denote one of the London Livery Companies
(Trade Guilds).
** The heraldic symbol of Richard II.
†† The heraldic symbol of Edward IV.
‡‡ Eleanor of Aquitaine was one of the most powerful women of the Middle Ages.
In 1137, as the sole heir to vast territories that extended from the Loire to the
Pyrenees, fifteen-year-old Eleanor was the most eligible princess in Europe. Her
first marriage to King Louis VII of France ended after his disastrous military
campaign in the Second Crusade, after which she divorced him and took back all
her lands. At the age of thirty, Eleanor embarked on her second marriage, this
time to an upwardly mobile prince, Henry Plantagenet, eleven years her junior and
a year later, in 1154, King Henry II of England. The pair had a tempestuous
relationship caused as much by Eleanor's involvement in the politics of the realm
as by Henry's much publicised infidelities. In 1173 she led her sons in a rebellion
against Henry, which caused the King to have her imprisoned for the last years of
his reign. When Henry died, in 1189, Eleanor enjoyed a rise in her fortunes and
lived to see two of her sons ascend to the English throne. She survived into her
eighties.
§§ 'Michelle'; 'Rocky Raccoon'; 'Norwegian Wood (This Bird Has Flown)'; 'Sgt.
Pepper's Lonely Hearts Club Band'; 'Eleanor Rigby'; 'Lady Madonna'; 'Back in the
USSR'; 'When I'm Sixty-Four'; 'Lucy in the Sky with Diamonds'; 'I Am the
Walrus'.

SEAS* (from page 205)

Adriatic Sea / Aegean Sea / Alboran Sea / Amundsen Sea
Andaman Sea / Arabian Sea / Arafura Sea / Aral Sea / Aru Sea
Balearic Sea / Bali Sea / Baltic Sea / Banda Sea / Barents Sea
Beaufort Sea / Bellingshausen Sea / Bering Sea / Bismarck Sea
Black Sea / Bo Hai Sea / Canarias Sea / Caribbean Sea
Caspian Sea / Celebes Sea / Celtic Sea / Ceram Sea / Chukchi Sea
Coral Sea / East China Sea / East Siberian Sea / Flores Sea
Greenland Sea / Halmahera Sea / Hebridian Sea / Iceland Sea
Inland Sea of Japan / Ionian Sea / Irish Sea / Java Sea / Kara Sea
Labrador Sea / Laccadive Sea / Laptev Sea / Ligurian Sea
Lincoln Sea / Mediterranean Sea / Mindanao Sea / Molucca Sea
Natuna Sea / North Greenland Sea / North Sea / Norwegian Sea
Philippine Sea / Red Sea / Ross Sea / Savu Sea / Scotia Sea
Sea of Azov / Sea of Japan / Sea of Marmara / Sea of Okhotsk
Solomon Sea / South China Sea / Sulawesi Sea / Sulu Sea
Tasman Sea / Timor Sea / Tyrrhenian Sea / Weddell Sea
White Sea / Yellow Sea

LAST LINES OF POPULAR FILMS II (from page 207)

1. *Alien*; 2. *Gone With the Wind*; 3. *The Godfather*; 4. *Four Weddings and a Funeral*; 5. *Apollo 13*; 6. *Erin Brockovich*; 7. *Who Framed Roger Rabbit*; 8. *Goodfellas*; 9. *Lord of the Rings: The Fellowship of the Ring*; 10. *Blade Runner*; 11. *A Fish Called Wanda*; 12. *It's a Wonderful Life*; 13. *Raging Bull*; 14. *My Fair Lady*; 15. *Footloose*; 16. *Rebecca*; 17. *Gandhi*; 18. *White Christmas*; 19. *Love Story*; 20. *Some Like It Hot*; 21. *The Prime of Miss Jean Brodie*; 22. *The Big Lebowski*; 23. *Die Hard*; 24. *Memento*.

---

* Note that the IHO does not currently recognise the Sargasso Sea, the Dead Sea or the Sea of Galilee.

GAMES

'Whoever undertakes to set himself up as
a judge of Truth and Knowledge is
shipwrecked by the laughter of the gods.'

Albert Einstein

NOTES ON THE GAMES

1.   Settle any disputes or tied games by posing a quiz question from elsewhere in the book.

2.   To avoid time-wasting, players may wish to agree a time limit for responses.

3.   Certain games will be better suited to certain types or sizes of quiz.

4.   Some games are better suited to individual play (for example *Round Robin, Bluff and Subterfuge* and *Nominate*) and some for team play (for example *Auction* and *Contract*).

5.   Adjudicators may wish to read out any footnotes accompanying the questions for clarity or to assist the players.

6.   If selecting a list, shorter lists are found towards the beginning of the Quizzes section and longer lists towards the end of it. If selecting a list for an elimination game, choose a list that has at least as many items as the number of players.

7.   All *Linked Miscellanies* contain ten questions; otherwise all other quizzes (those which are composed of questions rather than a list) have twenty-four questions. In the main, the questions will get harder as you go through.

8.   If the end of a list in an elimination game is reached with more than one player or team remaining in the game, the player or team to name the last item is declared the winner. A winner in an elimination game is otherwise the last player or team remaining. The winner does not need to provide any further response after the penultimate player or team has been eliminated.

9.   Readers are encouraged to devise their own games.

ROUND ROBIN The players elect an adjudicator and divide themselves either into teams or individual players. The adjudicator selects a quiz that is to their personal liking and poses it to the players (or teams of players). Moving clockwise from the adjudicator, players or teams respond alternately either to name a single item from the chosen list or respond to a single question (depending on the type of quiz that has been chosen). If a player or team responds incorrectly or is unable to respond, that player or team is eliminated. The game is won when only one player or team remains. For longer lists, the adjudicator may allow players to commence the game with three 'lives'.

DON'T MISS THE TARGET Players divide themselves into two teams: an inquisitive team and an answering team. The inquisitive team select a quiz and present it to the others, stating the associated target number. The answering team, depending on the type of quiz that has been chosen, either attempt to name as many items or respond to as many questions as they can with the objective of achieving the target number. If they fail to achieve this, the game is won by the inquisitive team; if they succeed, the teams exchange roles and another quiz is selected. The game is won as soon as a team fails to hit the target. For quizzes that contain lists, the answering team may have as many attempts to answer as there are items of the list but no more.

AUCTION The players elect an adjudicator and divide themselves either into teams or individual players. The adjudicator selects a quiz of their liking and reads the title and description out to the players (or teams of players) as well as the associated target number. Moving clockwise from the adjudicator, teams lodge bids according to either the number of items they expect to be able to name or the number of questions they expect to be able to answer (depending on the type of quiz that has been chosen). Each bid must be greater than the previous bid; if a team or player is unable to bid they drop out of the bidding and the bid passes clockwise to the next team or player. The bidding concludes when only one team or player remains. This team or player must then attempt to honour their bid by naming their predicted number of items or answering their predicted number of questions. If the bid is achieved this team or player is awarded five points. If the bid is not achieved the remaining teams or players are awarded two points. Play continues with another selected quiz. The game is won when a team or player reaches ten points. In constructing their bids, players should use the target numbers as a guide. Adjudicators may opt to give players a few minutes in consideration of their bids.

CONTRACT The game is played in the same way as *Auction* except that instead of a bidding round, the competing players or teams submit unseen written bids to the adjudicator. When all of the bids have been received, the adjudicator announces the results. The team or player with the winning bid then attempts to honour their bid and play continues in the same way as in auction.

BLUFF AND SUBTERFUGE The game is played in the same way as *Round Robin* except that the adjudicator does not respond to any of the answers. Players supply responses in the normal way and at any time one of the remaining players may challenge this response. The adjudicator will then declare the correct answer and therefore the success of the challenge. If a challenge is successful, that is, the original response was wrong, the player making this response is eliminated (or loses a life). If the challenge is unsuccessful, that is, the original response was correct, the challenger is eliminated (or loses a life).

NOMINATE This game is played in the same way as *Round Robin* except that instead of passing clockwise, after providing a successful response the successful player nominates a player to provide the next response. If the nominated player offers a correct response, they in turn nominate the next player to respond. If the nominated player cannot offer a correct response they are eliminated (or lose a life) and play passes clockwise to the next player.

INCREMENTAL This game is played in the same way as *Don't Miss the Target* except that the game is played only with those quizzes containing lists. The game also always begins with a list containing three items and is incremented on each successive round.

So, if in the first question the target number (out of three) is reached, the two teams swap roles and a list is selected containing four items. Play continues with the number of items in the list incremented by one each time until a team fails to hit the target.

QUIZ This game is played with the quizzes containing multiple questions. The players elect an adjudicator and divide themselves into teams. The adjudicator selects four quizzes from the book and announces the titles to the teams (for example *Miscellany, Linked Miscellany, Films and Their Stars* and *First Lines of Pop Songs*). Starting with the first of the four, the adjudicator poses the questions to the teams, who write down their answers. After the teams have had some thinking time, the answers are marked and scores recorded. This is repeated for the three further rounds. The team with the highest score at the end is declared the winner.

ROUND ROBIN ROUND ROBIN This game is played in the same way as *Round Robin* except that at the outset it is agreed to play the same number of games as there are players. Play commences as normal but at the end of the first game, the players are awarded points in the reverse order of how they were eliminated (for example with four players the winner gets four points, the first player eliminated gets one point; the adjudicator receives no points for that game). The role of adjudicator then passes clockwise from the player who was previously the adjudicator and a new game commences. The player with the most points on completion of the agreed cycle of games is the winner.

SPOT THE LINK The players elect an adjudicator and divide themselves either into teams or individual players. The adjudicator selects a *Linked Miscellany* and reads out each question in turn, pausing after each. The players write down the answers. The game is won by the first player to shout out the correct link.

SPLOSH Players agree on a forfeit to be carried out by the loser of each round. A player is elected to adjudicate for the first round and selects a list from the book which has at least as many items as there are players. The adjudicator then writes down one of the items from the list but keeps this out of the view of the other players. Players take turns, starting to the left of the adjudicator, to name items from the list. When a player names the item the adjudicator has written down, or is unable to respond in a timely fashion, that player is declared the loser and must pay the forfeit*. Further rounds are played with the role of adjudicator passing clockwise until each player has had a turn as the adjudicator.

---

* A suggested forfeit is for the adjudicator to decant an eggcup full of water over the unwitting loser. For added drama, keep the eggcup in view of the players for the duration of the round. The author can not accept responsibility for any damage to personal effects, property or personal pride incurred in the course of this game.